Advances in the Economics
of Aging

A National Bureau
of Economic Research
Project Report

Advances in the Economics of Aging

Edited by   David A. Wise

The University of Chicago Press

Chicago and London

DAVID A. WISE is the John F. Stambaugh Professor of Political Economy at the John F. Kennedy School of Government, Harvard University, and director for Health and Retirement Programs at the National Bureau of Economic Research.

The University of Chicago Press, Chicago 60637
The University of Chicago Press, Ltd., London
© 1996 by the National Bureau of Economic Research
All rights reserved. Published 1996
Printed in the United States of America
05 04 03 02 01 00 99 98 97 96   1 2 3 4 5
ISBN: 0-226-90302-8 (cloth)

Library of Congress Cataloging-in-Publication Data

Advances in the economics of aging / edited by David A. Wise
        p.   cm.—(National Bureau of Economic Research project report)
    Includes bibliographical references and index.
    1. Aged—United States—Economic conditions—Congresses.
    2. Old age—Economic aspects—United States—Congresses.   3. Retirement—Economic aspects—United States—Congresses.   I. Wise, David A.   II. Series.
    HQ1064.U5A6318   1996
    305.26—dc20   95-53331
                                                                      CIP

⊗ The paper used in this publication meets the minimum requirements of the American National Standard for Information Sciences—Permanence of Paper for Printed Library Materials, ANSI Z39.48-1984.

Contents

Preface

This volume consists of papers presented at a conference held at Carefree, Arizona, in May 1993. It is part of the National Bureau of Economic Research's ongoing Project on the Economics of Aging. Most of the work reported here was sponsored by the U.S. Department of Health and Human Services, through National Institute on Aging grant numbers P01-AG05842, R37-AG08146, and T32-AG00186.

Any opinions expressed in this volume are those of the respective authors and do not necessarily reflect the views of the National Bureau of Economic Research or the sponsoring organization.

Introduction

David A. Wise

This is the fifth in a series of volumes dealing with the economics of aging. The prior volumes, also published by the University of Chicago Press, are *The Economics of Aging* (1989), *Issues in the Economics of Aging* (1990), *Topics in the Economics of Aging* (1992), and *Studies in the Economics of Aging* (1994). The papers in this volume deal with labor market behavior, health care, housing and living arrangements, and saving and wealth.

Labor Market Behavior

In "The Effect of Labor Market Rigidities on the Labor Force Behavior of Older Workers," Michael Hurd explores compensation arrangements and other employment practices that constrain workers to a particular number of hours per day, days per week, or weeks per year. Labor market rigidities include the inability to change hours, days, or weeks in an existing job; impediments to taking a different job with a more desirable combination of hours, days, and weeks; and situations that require a disproportionate sacrifice in compensation, job satisfaction, mental or physical requirements, or location in order to obtain a more desirable work schedule. The paper surveys the evidence on labor market rigidities, particularly as they affect older workers.

Hurd concludes that most workers of all ages face rigidities, and that these rigidities tend to arise from fixed employment costs and the requirements of team production. For example, part-time work will tend to have lower money wages than full-time work, because a greater fraction of the work time will be necessary to cover the fixed costs of employment. Similarly, the efficiencies

David A. Wise is the John F. Stambaugh Professor of Political Economy at the John F. Kennedy School of Government, Harvard University, and director for Health and Retirement Programs at the National Bureau of Economic Research.

associated with team production will tend to concentrate work hours and penalize those who want to work irregular hours or work part-time. These rigidities imply that an older worker cannot easily reduce hours (or phase into retirement) in a career job.

However, there are additional impediments to older workers who want to change jobs. Because it takes time to acquire job-specific skills, and because older workers can be expected to stay in a new job for fewer years than a younger worker, employers are likely to be more reluctant to invest in new job training for older workers. In general, this means that older workers who move to jobs with fewer work hours must accept positions with fewer job-specific skills, high turnover rates, and lower compensation.

Labor market rigidities for older workers also result from the structure of retirement policies. For example, the financial structure of Social Security and pension plans tends to inhibit retirement (or job mobility) at some ages, and induce retirement (or job mobility) at other ages. Pension plans may also discourage part-time work by basing pension benefits on final salary rates. The Social Security earnings test may discourage work beyond the earnings limit. Employer-provided health insurance may reduce job mobility, particularly among workers with preexisting conditions. While the effects of these policy-related rigidities are difficult to quantify, Hurd suggests that they are probably less important than the labor market rigidities that result from fixed employment costs and team production.

Because the cost of changing jobs late in the work life tends to be high, efforts to facilitate phased retirement or other flexible work conditions may be more effective within the context of a career job. Hurd cautions, however, that any changes must be advantageous both to employers and employees, so that older workers will not be viewed as liabilities to their employer. Indeed, determining whether more flexible arrangements can work effectively within the constraints of team production and fixed employment costs is far from easy.

Robin Lumsdaine, James Stock, and David Wise previously wrote a series of papers on the incentive effects of employer-provided pension plans, emphasizing that plan provisions typically provide substantial incentives to retire early. If employees do not retire before 65, a large fraction retire at age 65 exactly. In this volume, Lumsdaine, Stock, and Wise consider why retirement rates are so high at 65.

Age 65 is no longer the typical retirement age. Most employees now retire before 65, and those who are covered by defined-benefit pension plans often retire well before 65. Nonetheless, a large fraction of persons who are still working at 64 retire at 65. For example, at one of the Fortune 500 firms that are studied in this paper (Firm 3), 48% of men working at 64 retire at 65. In contrast, only 21% of men who work through age 63 retire at 64. Women at this firm show a similar increase in retirement rates, from 18% at age 64 to 41% at age 65. Similar jumps in retirement rates at age 65 are found at other individual firms and more generally in nationwide measures of labor force participation. In each of the six data sets discussed in this paper, the highest retirement rate occurs at age 65.

In earlier papers, Lumsdaine, Stock, and Wise attributed the mismatch between predicted and actual rates to an "age-65 retirement effect," having in mind the influence of custom or accepted practice. This paper considers other commonly proposed explanations for the underprediction of age-65 retirement. It is difficult to directly demonstrate the influence of custom and the like. Thus the spirit of the paper is to rule out other explanations and thus, by implication, leave the age-65 retirement effect as the remaining possibility. The results suggest that such an effect is the only plausible explanation that cannot be rejected. In particular, the authors conclude that the availability of Medicare at 65 does not explain the age-65 retirement jump.

The unexplained age-65 spike is important because it limits our ability to predict the effect of potential policy changes, like the planned increase in the Social Security normal retirement age from age 65 to age 67. Would there then be a spike at 67, or would it remain at 65?

Lumsdaine, Stock, and Wise seek to quantify the age-65 retirement puzzle and to explore potential explanations for it. These include in particular the potential gap in health insurance coverage between retirement and the Medicare eligibility age. They also consider whether family status affects age-65 retirement. And they explore the possibility that previous results were importantly affected by small samples of older workers. Because so many employees retire early, the number still employed at 65 is typically small.

None of these possibilities explains the age-65 spike, lending indirect support to the "age-65 retirement effect" explanation. To support the plausibility of an age-65 effect, the authors also consider the possibility that for some employees the utility cost to electing to retire at this "customary" retirement age is small. They conclude that the economic cost is indeed small for some, although for most employees it is quite large. Thus, for most employees, choosing to retire at age 65 would impose noticeable economic cost.

John Ausink and David Wise consider the military pension, compensation, and retirement of U.S. Air Force pilots. Ausink and Wise emphasize that econometric models of job exit are of interest for at least two reasons. There has been a significant decline in the civilian labor force participation of older Americans for the past twenty years (Wise 1985). During the same period, private pension coverage has increased markedly, and Social Security benefits have risen. The study of relationships between the two trends is of interest to economists attempting to explain the incentives that pension plans may provide in encouraging workers to change jobs or stop working, and is also important to firms who may want to affect employee retirement behavior by changing the provisions of their pension plans.

In the military, there is a slightly different perspective. The armed forces must maintain adequate numbers of trained and experienced personnel without the realistic possibility of lateral job entry to replace losses. A shortage of experienced military pilots cannot be eliminated by hiring pilots from another military, for example. The absence of this remedy for the loss of personnel means that shortfalls in any cohort are difficult to correct, and the potential incentive effects of changes in compensation must be considered before they are made.

In this paper, Ausink and Wise use the option value model of retirement behavior developed by Stock and Wise to examine the effects of compensation on the decision of Air Force pilots to leave the military. The authors conclude that the option value model captures Air Force pilot departure behavior much better than the annualized cost of leaving model that has been used by the military, and substantially better than a more complex stochastic dynamic programming specification. The superiority of the option value model to the dynamic programming formulation raises the possibility that individual decision making may not always be best described with a model that is intended to approximate "correct" economic financial calculations. This is consistent with the results of previous work by Lumsdaine, Stock, and Wise (1992).

Predictions of the effects of changes in compensation using the option value model indicate that individuals at early stages in their careers are more sensitive to losses of future benefits than indicated by previous models. The effects of temporary annual bonuses, such as Aviator Continuation Pay, are small, and bonus amounts must be extremely large to induce departure rates that come close to Air Force objectives.

Ausink and Wise emphasize that the extraordinary changes in the world's political and military climate since the summer of 1991 have already led to adjustments in the defense structure of the United States, and the number of Air Force personnel is declining. To encourage people to leave the military, the Air Force has instituted two incentive programs since 1992. The authors point out that both programs were introduced with little econometric modeling of their potential effects and that fewer officers than expected applied to either program. As the Air Force and other services struggle to reduce in size, other separation incentives will be proposed and studied. The authors conclude that the procedures studied in this paper may be useful in predicting the effects of such programs.

Jonathan Gruber and Brigitte Madrian consider health insurance and early retirement. The dramatic decline in the labor force participation of older men in the past several decades has prompted many studies of retirement behavior. In particular, a great deal of attention has been given to the incentive effects of Social Security provisions and, more recently, to the effects of employer-provided pension plans. A potentially important factor that has not received much attention is the availability of health insurance for retirees. Gruber and Madrian point out that the increased availability of health insurance for older Americans, especially retirees, has come in several forms. First among them is the introduction in the mid-1960s of Medicare, a federal program that provides near-universal health insurance coverage for those over age 65. A second source of health insurance that has grown in importance, particularly for those under age 65, is employer-provided postretirement health insurance. While only 30% of men who retired in the early 1960s received health insurance from their former employers, this fraction increased to almost half for those retiring in the 1980s (Madrian 1993).

This paper looks at the effect on retirement of a third source of health insurance for early retirees, namely, continuation coverage benefits. During the late 1970s and early 1980s, many states mandated that employers allow employees who leave their jobs to continue purchasing their group health insurance for a specified number of months. These continuation benefits were then extended to all workers in 1986 as part of the federal Consolidated Omnibus Budget Reconciliation Act (COBRA). Although this coverage is available to all workers regardless of age, it should be particularly attractive to older workers who face a relatively high price for health insurance in the private market and who are more likely to be subject to the preexisting-conditions exclusions that are characteristic of such policies.

Madrian and Gruber estimate the effect of health insurance on retirement by examining the effect of state and federal continuation coverage mandates on retirement behavior. They conclude that continuation coverage mandates have had a sizable effect on retirement. Contrary to their expectations, however, they conclude that the effects are not necessarily the strongest at older ages.

Health Care

In "Medicare Reimbursement and Hospital Cost Growth," Mark McClellan poses four questions. Why did Medicare's prospective payment system (PPS) lead to a decline in hospital admissions? Why is the average intensity per discharge increasing? Why do real per capita hospital costs keep increasing? And why aren't the diagnosis-related groups (DRGs) that serve as a basis for Medicare reimbursement of hospitals more related to diagnoses?

McClellan's study suggests that the PPS led to several unanticipated consequences. Under PPS, Medicare reimburses hospitals a fixed amount per patient, based on the patient's DRG. While many DRGs are indeed defined by diagnosis, McClellan makes the important observation that some DRGs are actually reimbursements for specific procedures (rather than just the diagnoses associated with those procedures). The results of the study indicate that hospitals are performing a lot more of the intensive treatments that are explicitly reimbursed (as DRGs), while intensity and admissions have remained constant or fallen for most diseases that are reimbursed by diagnosis alone.

McClellan begins by setting forth in some detail a formal model of hospital production, emphasizing the critical roles of four parties: fully insured patients, physicians, hospitals, and regulators who set the price schedule for hospitals. He then compares the predictions of the model with empirical evidence, emphasizing that the four questions posed above are not so puzzling when understood in the context of the model that he sets out.

Among other conclusions, McClellan emphasizes that hospitals have responded quite dramatically to PPS, to the point that intensive surgical treatments dominate hospital care for the elderly. He concludes that all growth in the case-mix index of Medicare admissions since PPS implementation appears attributable to increasing use over time of the particular intensive technologies that are reimbursed separately under PPS. While these trends may be attributable to exogenous technological change, the model of hospital incentives for investing in intensive technologies for the treatment of health problems suggests they are not. He also concludes that feasible reforms in the structure of PPS reimbursement would be likely to mitigate these trends, at least for some health problems.

Housing and Living Arrangements

In "Living Arrangements: Health and Wealth Effects," Axel Börsch-Supan, Daniel McFadden, and Reinhold Schnabel report several methodological developments in modeling living arrangement decisions. Estimating models with multiple-outcome situations (such as living arrangements) has been a topic of econometric investigation for some time, and these authors have been instrumental in finding solutions. The methodological developments in this paper are applied to the question of how health status and wealth affect living arrangement decisions, using panel data from the Longitudinal Study on Aging. Among the contributions of the paper are the econometric indicators of health status that are used in the analysis.

The authors emphasize that the choice of a living arrangement—in an independent household, in a shared living arrangement with adult children or others, or in an institution—has many implications for the well-being of an elderly person. First, there are important relationships between one's living arrangement and the level of care and assistance received by the elderly. For example, living with other family members eases situations of illness, while living alone makes coping with illnesses more difficult. Second, living arrangement decisions interact importantly with government assistance programs, such as food stamps, supplemental Social Security, and Medicaid, as well as social support services such as district nursing or meals-on-wheels. Eligibility for public assistance both affects and is affected by living arrangement decisions. And third, because a large portion of the wealth of most older people is invested in housing, and because different housing arrangements have different out-of-pocket costs, there are important interactions between financial status and living arrangement decisions. Selling a home, for example, may dramatically increase the liquid wealth of the elderly.

The analysis in this paper accounts for many of these relationships. The authors conclude that, while wealth is an important economic variable in the choice of living arrangements, income is of little relevance once wealth is included. As expected, health is one of the main predictors of living arrangement choices. Health is well captured in the analysis by two factors: one associated with independent activities and strongly related to age, and the other associated with more basic and person-specific capabilities. Living together with others, mainly children, is positively affected by financial and housing wealth. Moving to an institution is negatively affected by homeownership.

Saving and Wealth

Leslie Papke, Mitchell Petersen, and James Poterba ask, "Do 401(k) plans replace other employer-provided pensions?" The authors point out that, although a growing body of evidence suggests that 401(k) contributors do not offset their contributions by reducing their accumulation of other financial assets, this does not necessarily mean that 401(k) contributions represent net additions to private saving. They could be offset by reduced contributions to other pension plans. Based on a survey of firms with 401(k) plans in 1987, Papke, Petersen, and Poterba investigate the degree of substitution between 401(k) plans and other employer-provided retirement saving arrangements.

They conclude that 401(k) plans do not appear to have displaced previous defined-benefit plans. None of the firms in their data reported substituting the 401(k) plan for a defined-benefit plan. They did find, however, that several firms reported replacing previous thrift or profit-sharing plans with a 401(k) plan. The authors also explored the link between 401(k) participation rates and corporate matching rates. They found that a 50% matching rate increased employee participation by only 10%. Thus they conclude that other factors must explain the high overall participation rate in 401(k) plans.

Jonathan Skinner observes that recent fluctuations in housing prices have led to concern that the windfall gains enjoyed by many of those currently retired could be matched in the future by windfall losses when the baby-boom generation retires. In his paper "Is Housing Wealth a Sideshow?" Skinner considers the extent to which housing price fluctuations play an important role in the economic security of retirees. In particular, he asks whether housing wealth is an important determinant of the consumption and saving of the elderly or whether it is just a "sideshow."

Skinner pursues his analysis by considering the degree to which the data are consistent with three economic models of behavior: the standard life-cycle model, a life-cycle model that includes a bequest motive, and a precautionary saving model. Skinner finds that an increase in housing wealth is associated with a small reduction in other saving, but that the elderly do not generally use their housing equity to finance consumption after retirement. He reconciles these two empiric irregularities by suggesting that housing wealth is a precautionary buffer against unanticipated financial needs. In this sense, the paper adds to the evidence for a precautionary view of saving and weighs against the standard life-cycle view.

Stylized Models and Simulations

The intent of the papers in this part is to consider stylized models of behavior among the elderly, and how the behavior of hypothetical individuals in the models would be predicted to change by varying some of the model parameters. The papers are not empirical in that they do not confront the stylized models with empirical evidence. Rather, they suggest factors that may be important to include in behavioral models, and how those factors appear to influence behavior in hypothetical simulations.

Jonathan Feinstein develops a stylized dynamic model in "Elderly Health, Housing, and Mobility." The goal of the paper is to elucidate the potentially complex relationship between health and housing decisions, and the role of mobility costs and other economic factors in this relationship. Rather than presenting empirical evidence on health and housing decisions, the conclusions of the paper are based on hypothetical simulations that characterize the model's implications. Feinstein gives particular emphasis to the importance of "transitional" housing, such as retirement communities, life care, and shared living arrangements.

David Weil's paper, "Intergenerational Transfers, Aging, and Uncertainty," presents the findings of another thought experiment. Weil considers the degree to which anticipated bequests may reduce the saving of potential recipients. Using a stylized overlapping-generations model, Weil characterizes the particular influence of uncertainty about the age of the donor's death and about the size of the future bequest. Based on his simulations, Weil concludes that uncertainty delays the reduction in individual saving that might otherwise take place by potential recipients of bequests, and delays the reduction in aggregate saving that may result from population aging.

References

Lumsdaine, Robin L., James H. Stock, and David A. Wise. 1992. Three Models of Retirement: Computational Complexity versus Predictive Validity. In *Topics in the Economics of Aging,* ed. David A. Wise, 19–57. Chicago: University of Chicago Press.

Madrian, Brigitte C. 1993. Post-Retirement Health Insurance and the Decision to Retire. Massachusetts Institute of Technology, Cambridge, MA. Mimeo.

Wise, David A., ed. 1985. *Pensions, Labor, and Individual Choice.* Chicago: University of Chicago Press.

I Labor Market Behavior

1   The Effect of Labor Market Rigidities on the Labor Force Behavior of Older Workers

Michael D. Hurd

1.1   Introduction and Summary

Over their work life, most workers will desire to change jobs occasionally and to vary their amount of work. Impediments to these changes could reduce lifetime productivity by preventing the worker from moving to the most productive job, and they could reduce welfare by causing a worker to work too much or too little. Older workers approaching retirement, in particular, often desire job mobility because a job that was chosen for its characteristics during most of the working life may not be well suited to workers later in life. Furthermore, older workers often want to reduce hours of work to make a gradual transition into retirement. They face not only the same impediments to changes in job and hours as younger workers, but additional impediments due to the structure of pension plans, the provisions of the Social Security system, and their need for health care insurance.

Some rigidities are part of normal business practice, arising from production technologies. For example, team production requires that most workers be present in the workplace at the same time. Other rigidities may be holdovers from a time when most of the working population was young and wanted full-time, year-round jobs, when most retired late in life and life expectancy was short so that the length of retirement was short. Still other rigidities may be due to public policy, for example, the Social Security laws; while some may

Michael D. Hurd is professor of economics at State University of New York, Stony Brook, and a research associate of the National Bureau of Economic Research.

The author appreciates and acknowledges the support of the Commonwealth Fund's Americans over 55 at Work Program. The views expressed are the author's and do not necessarily reflect those of the Commonwealth Fund. The author thanks Randy Becker for excellent research assistance, Alan Gustman, Olivia Mitchell, and Joseph Quinn for their comments and suggestions, and Michael Barth for conceiving the project.

serve legitimate social goals, others may not because the laws have not been changed to keep up with changing circumstances.

The objective of this paper is to examine some evidence about rigidities in the labor market, and particularly how rigidities affect the labor market experience of older workers by causing impediments to change. It discusses some of the causes of the rigidities, and points in the direction of how the situation for older workers might be improved. It is, however, beyond the scope of the paper to offer remedies: the labor market is exceptionally complicated, and experience has shown that uninformed interference in the labor market can be counterproductive.

1.1.1   Labor Market Rigidities

Labor market rigidities are employment practices and work-related financial arrangements that constrain or influence the volume of work with respect to hours per day, days per week, or weeks per year. Rigidities include the inability to change hours, days, or weeks on a given job, and impediments to changing to a job that offers the desired combination of hours, days, and weeks. Rigidities also include situations in which the volume of work can be varied, but the change requires a disproportionate sacrifice in compensation, job satisfaction, mental or physical requirements, or location.

Different jobs may offer different mixes of compensation (as between, say, pension accumulation and money income), but this would not necessarily be a rigidity as long as total compensation is the same. Total compensation may change with age if the change reflects changes in productivity, and, again, this would not be a rigidity.

Understanding rigidities is important from the point of view of the individual because of the costs associated with rigidities. From a theoretical point of view, people will want to stop working when they have accumulated enough resources to finance the rest of their lifetime consumption. But withdrawal from the labor force will be gradual. Both leisure and consumption are valued (produce utility), and as tastes shift with age toward leisure, the desired amount of work will slowly fall. Furthermore, an individual operates in an uncertain environment with respect to health status, life expectancy, rates of return on investments, inflation, and so forth: because the uncertainty is resolved gradually, change will be gradual.

In a simplified situation where the wage rate is fixed and there are no rigidities, a fall in the desire to work will produce a fall in the volume of work (for simplicity, hours of work). If hours cannot be varied, the optimal constrained choice will be to work more than is desired for several years, and then not to work at all. The constrained choice entails a loss of welfare, both in the years surrounding retirement and in later years because the level of economic resources is not optimal.

These welfare effects are based on the simple choice between labor and leisure, but many older workers have other important reasons for wanting part-time work. For example, many have very old parents whose need for attention and care is not compatible with a full-time job. The constrained choices are not to work at all, which may not be economically feasible, or to work full-time and allow public support systems to care for the parents.

The aggregate effects on individuals affect society. Early retirement influences the national saving rate because on average the retired dissave whereas workers save. Ceteris paribus, early retirement is associated with lower resources during the retirement years, so that the poverty rates of the elderly will be higher, affecting needs-based programs for the elderly. To the extent that early retirement means that aggregate earnings fall, the tax base is reduced by early retirement.

1.1.2 Summary of Findings

Most workers of all ages face rigidities that arise from fixed employment costs and the requirements of team production. Fixed employment costs must be covered by a substantial number of hours of work. Therefore, part-time work will tend to have low money wages because a greater fraction of the work time will have to cover fixed employment costs. Team production tends to concentrate work hours and penalizes those who want to work irregular hours or work part-time. These rigidities imply that an older worker cannot easily reduce hours on the career job, so a job change is required.

Older workers have additional impediments to job change arising from normal business practice. If they change jobs to reduce hours, they lose their job-specific skills. Because they will be expected to stay on a new job for fewer years than a younger worker, an employer will be reluctant to invest in job training. A new job with fewer hours will have to be a job that requires few job-specific skills and that is compatible with high turnover. A better-educated, higher-skilled, older worker will be competing for a new job with a young, less-educated, lower-skilled worker. These factors make it highly likely that the new job will be low paying.

Older workers face impediments that are partly the effect of policy toward retirement. Social Security has incentives that influence work choices, but the incentives will gradually decline over the next decade because of changes in the Social Security law. The Social Security earnings test seems to affect work decisions, but it has little obvious social benefit. Defined pension plans can reduce job mobility. The requirements of an older worker for health care insurance may prevent job change, particularly if a worker has a preexisting condition. There is only scattered evidence of labor market discrimination against older workers. The effects of these impediments are difficult to quantify, but they probably are considerably less important than the effects due to fixed costs and team production.

Because the costs of job change late in the work life are so high, the main effort to reduce labor market rigidities should be toward changes in employment conditions on the career job. This would involve training and job restructuring to allow hours flexibility. However, any changes must be advantageous both to employers and employees: otherwise, older workers will be viewed as a liability, and employers will be reluctant to hire them. Determining whether these kinds of changes can be accommodated within the requirements of team production and the constraints of fixed costs is far from easy.

1.2   Evidence about Labor Market Rigidities

The objective of this section is to examine the pattern of labor market activity before retirement and the hours of work of younger workers to see what evidence they give about labor market rigidities. The idea is that, given the wage rate, if hours of work can be freely chosen, we would expect to find considerable variation in hours of work of an individual as he or she ages, and considerable dispersion in hours across individuals.

1.2.1   Retirement Behavior

As workers age, tastes for work gradually change, making work less desirable. Declining tastes might be caused by gradual changes that make work more unpleasant or by changes in health status that make work increasingly burdensome. Within any time period this would change the desired ratio of work time to leisure time. An individual, anticipating this change, would plan a lifetime in which work effort in a time period would gradually decline with age, eventually falling to complete leisure, or retirement. This can be represented by a gradual shift in the labor supply function of the worker. If the wage rate facing the individual is fixed so that hours of work may be freely chosen, the change in tastes causes work hours to decline gradually. A gradual decline in productivity with age simply accelerates the rate of change: if the fall in productivity leads to a fall in the wage rate, hours of work will fall continuously as long as hours can be freely chosen.

I have made no distinction between hours per day, days per week, weeks per month, or months per year: a worker would probably want to reduce along all dimensions but probably at different rates. Because little research has been done to understand all these dimensions, I will speak of hours of work with the understanding that the changes could be along all dimensions.

Labor force participation by age in cross-section data does decline slowly in accordance with this description. Figure 1.1 shows average labor force participation rates of men and women by single years of age as measured in the Current Population Survey (CPS). The rates are the average of 1988 and 1989. Although the figure is consistent with a gradual decline in work effort of all individuals, leading to different individuals withdrawing completely at different ages, it is also consistent with each individual withdrawing suddenly at different ages without any intervening fall in hours.

Table 1.1 shows how full-time work among the employed changes with age in cross-section data. It shows falling full-time employment, which is consis-

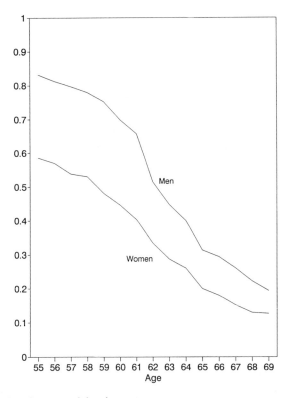

Fig. 1.1   Labor force participation rates
Source: Author's calculations from 1988 and 1989 Current Population Survey participation rates by single years of age.

Table 1.1   **Percentage of the Employed Who Are Full-Time Workers**

Age	1968	1974	1980	1987
55–59	82.4	82.1	81.5	80.5
60–62	80.9	79.2	76.3	74.4
63–65	74.3	71.6	68.9	66.9
66–70	57.0	51.5	40.8	44.5
71+	43.2	39.5	36.0	34.9
All	75.5	74.2	71.7	70.6

Source: Sum and Fogg (1990), based on the Current Population Survey.

tent with the idea of gradual withdrawal from the labor force: for example, in 1987, 80.5% of 55–59-year-old workers worked full-time, yet just 34.9% of workers 71 or older worked full-time. The table also shows a time trend over all ages to less full-time work. The trend is particularly strong among older workers. Yet, because the entries are percentages of workers, the trend cannot

Table 1.2   **Percentage of Persons Not Working or Working Fifty-one or Fifty-two Weeks, 1986**

Age	55–59	60–62	63–65	66–70	71+
Percentage	84.0	83.9	86.6	89.4	96.0

Source: Sum and Fogg (1990), based on Current Population Survey.

be used to verify a gradual withdrawal from the labor force: complete withdrawal of full-time workers and a more gradual withdrawal of part-time workers would produce the same age pattern of full-time work.

Table 1.2 shows that at any time the great majority of the older population works either full-time or not at all. Thus, only a fraction of the age-55-or-over population works part-time, and the fraction falls with age. The implication is that, as the labor force participation rate decreases, most workers move from full-time employment to not working at all.

Although it is not directly relevant for this argument, I note that over time the percentage of the 55-or-over population working part-time has fallen from 14.1% in 1967 to 10.8% in 1986 (Sum and Fogg 1990), probably owing to the overall decline in participation.

Any employment or participation rates that are based on cross-section data will not show the change in labor force status as an individual ages, which is what we need to understand labor market rigidities. Such change requires panel data. Using the 1969–79 Retirement History Survey (RHS), a panel data set of two-year periodicity, Rust (1990) estimated that, at a minimum, 75% of men age 58–64 in 1969 moved directly from full-time work to completely retired with no intervening part-time work. The exact percentage depends on the method of classifying work as to full-time or part-time. For example, if the classification is based on annual hours of work, just 22% of employed men changed from full-time employment to part-time employment during the ten years of the survey. By the end of the survey the youngest men were 68, and the great majority had retired, so it is unlikely that the termination of the survey caused many transitions from full-time to part-time employment not to be recorded. If the analysis is based on weekly hours, just 8% of employed men had a transition to part-time employment. Rust concludes that, although there are some transitions from full-time to part-time work, the great majority of men retire without any intervening transition.

Similar results are found by others: Based on the RHS, Quinn, Burkhauser, and Myers (1990) estimated that, among men who leave their full-time career jobs, 73% leave the labor force completely, 15% move to part-time employment, and 12% go on to further full-time employment. A rough estimate would be that about 83% eventually leave full-time employment for complete retirement.[1] Berkovec and Stern (1991) estimate that in the National Longitudinal

---

1. The calculation assumes that the fraction moving from any full-time job to part-time is .15, which is the fraction that move from a full-time career job to a part-time job.

Table 1.3   **Distribution of Workers by Hours of Work before Retirement (%)**

Hours Worked One Year prior to Retirement	Age			
	<62	62–64	65–67	68+
1–34	14.8	15.3	17.6	57.6
35–40	58.7	62.1	54.1	28.3
41+	26.5	22.6	28.3	14.1

Source: Jondrow, Brechling, and Marcus (1987), based on 1978 Panel Study of Income Dynamics.

Survey of Older Men (NLS) 67% changed directly from full-time work to completely retired. Based on quarterly labor force status in the RHS, Blau (1994) found that just 12.6% of men initially observed to be working full-time changed to part-time work at some during the ten years of the panel. Again, because the youngest was 68 by the end of the survey, it is unlikely that the termination of the survey left many transitions unrecorded.

Table 1.3 has the distribution of hours worked during the year prior to retirement in the Panel Study of Income Dynamics (PSID).[2] It shows that, at ages below 68, a large fraction of those who retired during the year were working full-time the preceding year; that is, the year before retirement was generally not a year of reduced hours.[3] It also shows that at older ages some people do retire from part-time jobs, as would be expected from table 1.1, but the total number is small because most retire completely before the age of 68.

I take these results to be good evidence that a large fraction of men leave the labor force completely with no intervening period of part-time work. However, these kinds of findings and this interpretation are not accepted by everyone. Ruhm (1989, 1990a, 1990b) used the RHS to conclude that most older workers have bridge jobs at some point before retirement, and that "fewer than two-fifths of household heads retire directly from career jobs" (Ruhm 1990a, 482). He defines a bridge job as any job held after the career job, which he defines to be the longest job ever held. In my view, however, many bridge jobs as defined by Ruhm are different from jobs taken to accomplish gradual retirement: for example, 24% of the bridge jobs in Ruhm's data were generated by workers leaving their career jobs before the age of 50. Almost all of these bridge jobs were held for more than ten years. This kind of job turnover is part of the normal job mobility of the working life, not of the movement toward retirement. A more reasonable definition of a bridge job would be a job taken at an age approaching retirement and held for a few years before retirement. For example, define a bridge job to be a new job taken at age 55 or over following a change from a career job, and held for one to four years before retirement. According to this definition just 14.4% of all workers in the RHS had bridge

2. Retirement here is self-assessed, not based on observed behavior. It includes both men and women.

3. The pattern is similar two years before retirement: the great majority were working full-time.

jobs.[4] This is similar to the fraction who partially retire in Blau (1994) and in Rust (1990).

Gustman and Steinmeier (1984), using the same data as Rust, find that about one-third of men partially retire at some time. The explanation of the difference seems to be in the definitions. The authors I have discussed based their conclusions on observed behavior: hours worked or weeks worked. Gustman and Steinmeier take retirement and partial retirement from a self-assessed question.[5] People who say they are retired are often, in fact, working for pay and even working full-time. In that rigidities in the labor market refer to hours worked and wages received, I believe we should base our conclusions on behavior, not self-assessed evaluations, which are subject to differing interpretations.

Although the argument at the beginning of this section suggests that the prevalence of complete retirement from full-time work is due to aspects of the labor market that discourage part-time work, not to workers' tastes, the argument will be more convincing if in jobs that have flexibility the change to retirement is more gradual. It is reasonable to suppose that the self-employed can more easily determine their hours of work, and, indeed, in the RHS hours of work by the self-employed have more dispersion: among white married males, 24% of the self-employed worked less than two thousand hours per year compared with 11% of wage and salary workers (Quinn 1980). Therefore, with increasing age the self-employed should stay in the labor force longer, and wage and salary workers should switch to self-employment so that they can stay in the labor force at reduced hours. Both effects will cause the fraction of the workforce that is self-employed to increase with age.

Table 1.4 gives the percentage self-employed at each age. The rising prevalence of self-employment is consistent with the view that workers would like to reduce hours gradually and that most of the abrupt withdrawal is due to labor market characteristics, not to workers' tastes for sudden retirement. However, cross-section data cannot show the relative importance of some workers switching from wage or salary jobs to self-employment and of the self-employed retiring later.

In panel data we find that both are important factors. In the RHS about 5% of wage and salary workers changed from wage and salary work to self-employment each year (Fuchs 1982). Most were from occupations similar to self-employed occupations: almost no blue-collar workers switched. Furthermore, the self-employed work to greater ages, further increasing the fraction of workers who were self-employed.[6]

Additional evidence that labor market characteristics are substantially responsible for the abrupt withdrawal from work of most workers is that the self-

4. My calculation based on table 2 in Ruhm 1990a.
5. "Do you consider yourself to be retired or partially retired?"
6. Quinn (1980) in the RHS and Iams (1987) in the New Beneficiary Survey found similar patterns.

Table 1.4   **Percentage of Workers Self-Employed by Age, 1990**

	55–59	60–64	65+
Men	13.7	15.8	24.0
Women	8.0	9.1	13.3
All	11.2	12.9	19.2

Source: Employment and Earnings, January 1991, based on the Current Population Survey.

Table 1.5   **Transitions from Career Jobs (%)**

	Wage and Salary Workers		Self-Employed Men
	Women	Men	Self-Employed Men
All			
Part-time on career job	10	5	25
Part-time on new job	10	10	13
Full-time on new job	7	12	13
Out of labor force	74	73	49
Total	100	100	100
Age 65 or over			
Part-time on career job	7	8	44
Part-time on new job	19	12	16
Full-time on new job	0	5	0
Out of labor force	74	74	41
Total	100	100	100

Source: Quinn, Burkhauser, and Myers (1990), based on Retirement History Survey.
Note: Distribution of self-employed women not reported.

employed change from full-time work to part-time work more often than wage and salary workers do. Table 1.5 shows transitions of full-time workers from career jobs.[7] Men and women who work for a wage or salary had quite similar patterns: they mainly left the labor force; just a small percentage moved to part-time on the same job. The transitions among the self-employed were very different: only 49% left the labor force completely; 25% reduced hours on the career job. At age 65 or over the differences are even greater: 44% of the self-employed men became part-time workers on their career job, compared with 7–8% of wage and salary workers. If workers desire hours flexibility as they age and self-employment offers hours flexibility, this is to be expected.

The conclusion is that retirement behavior provides convincing evidence of labor market rigidities: the great majority retire from full-time work with no intervening part-time work. This is not compatible with slowly changing tastes for work when hours can be freely chosen.

7. Career jobs are thirty-five hours or more per week on a job held for more than ten years. The sample is limited to those who could be followed for four or more years in the panel (Quinn, Burkhauser, and Myers 1990).

1.2.2   Work Patterns and Job Flexibility at All Ages

Almost all male workers and many female workers work full-time: 94% of men and 79% of women aged 25–44 worked full-time in 1990.[8] Full-time work tends to be full-year work: in the 1969 RHS 36% of men said they worked two thousand hours, almost all the rest worked more than two thousand hours, except for 19% who did not work at all. Economic theory and common sense say that it is not credible that almost all workers would freely choose similar hours per week and per year: variation in assets, wage rates, family circumstances, and tastes will cause variation in desired hours and, hence, in observed hours.

An indicator of rigidities in the labor market is that flextime, the ability to choose the start and stop time of the workday, is rare: in the 1985 CPS just 12.3% of workers said they were on flextime (Mellor 1986). Even this fraction is probably an overstatement of the amount of flexibility, because in the questionnaire the ability to vary hours by as little as thirty minutes was classified as flextime. Flextime varies by industry and occupation: in blue-collar jobs only 6.5% had flextime. Furthermore, the amount of flexibility was limited even among those with flextime because nearly all jobs required attendance at the place of employment during core times.

Further evidence of inflexibility comes from surveys in which workers are asked directly if they can vary hours of work. In the PSID 56% of those responding to the question said they could not reduce hours of work (Gustman and Steinmeier 1985). In an early release of the Health and Retirement Survey (HRS), only 14% of wage workers aged 55–61 said they were free both to increase and to decrease hours.

Productivity

The discussion has been about flexibility in the choice of hours of work, but wage flexibility is an important aspect of a flexible labor market. If the productivity of a worker or group of workers falls, yet employers are not free to reduce wages, employment practices will develop leading to job separation rather than income reduction. There is little direct evidence on wage flexibility at the individual level in response to individual productivity changes because there is little direct evidence on changes in productivity at the individual level: this would require panel data with measures of productivity. There is some evidence about average changes in productivity with age in cross-section.

The general finding is that on average productivity falls, but only marginally as workers age through their 50s and early 60s. The evidence is of three kinds: surveys of managers, opinions of experts, and studies of physical productivity. A typical survey result is reported in Rhine 1984: In a survey of 363 senior human resources administrators (mostly vice presidents), just 13% agreed with the statement that the performance of workers peaks at a young age. When

---

8. *Employment and Earnings,* January 1991, based on the CPS. Full-time is thirty-five or more hours per week.

asked about occupations where this happened, 60% of the 13% said the declines were in occupations that required physical exertion. This seems to be common: where there is a decline, it is when physical exertion is required.

Paul (1983a) reports on three studies of the physical output of workers. Each of them shows little if any fall in output with age. McNaught and Barth (1992) analyzed data on physical output of reservation operators for Days Inn of America: they found only small differences in the productivity of older and younger workers. Jablonski, Kunze, and Rosenblum (1990) report on a number of studies of physical output, conducted by the Bureau of Labor Statistics. Examples of typical findings are that the average output of 55–64-year-old males in the footwear industry was 93% of the output of 35–44-year-olds. Among mail sorters output is basically flat until age 60 or over, when it is 96% of the output of average output. Among clerical workers only those aged 25 or less have productivity that is much below average: productivity does not fall with age. Jablonski, Kunze, and Rosenblum conclude that in these studies of physical output there is evidence for a modest decline in productivity with age. However, they make the important point that, even if average productivity declines with age, the variation within age groups in productivity is much greater than the variation across age groups: that is, the productivity of many older workers will be greater than the productivity of many younger workers.

Of course, physical productivity cannot be measured in most jobs, but statements by management confirm the findings about physical productivity. Paul (1983a) reports that, when supervisors rate the performance of workers compared with the requirements of the job, older workers do as well on average as younger workers.

The general finding is well summarized as follows: "Because chronological age is not related to maintenance of performance, older employees are not more costly to firms because of declining productivity. This is not to suggest, however, that certain older (as well as younger) individuals do not experience declining performance. This can and does occur and is very costly to organizations" (U.S. Senate 1984, 63).

A final example of productivity variation by age comes from what practically amounts to a controlled experiment. In the United Kingdom a new do-it-yourself store, one of a chain of stores, was staffed entirely by workers aged 50 or over (Hogarth and Barth 1991). By a number of human resource measures such as labor turnover and absenteeism, it was the most successful store in a control group of similar stores owned by the same chain. By other measures such as sales per employee and wage costs, it was about average. The management of the chain found the experiment a success and staffed other stores only with older workers.

Interpreting this example requires some caution because the workers were undoubtedly not average in the 50-or-over population: only the healthy and active wanted to work. That is, it is likely that the experiment compared productivity of an above-average group of older workers with an average group of younger workers. This difficulty is also found in the productivity studies discussed above: in cross-section data the composition of the labor force cannot be kept constant as age increases because the least productive (least healthy) will leave the sample of workers. This is alleviated but not eliminated in panel data: we observe the same individuals as they age, so we may be able to conclude correctly that the productivity of the individuals who remain in the labor force does not fall. But, if workers whose productivity begins to fall leave the labor force, we may conclude, possibly incorrectly, that the productivity of the cohort does not fall with age.

Wage Rates

The variation of wage rates with age has been the subject of controversy because of the difficulties of measurement. In cross-section wage rates will not be a good measure of the wage path of an individual, particularly at older ages, because of changes in the composition of the workforce. For example, as unhealthy workers who have lower wage rates leave the labor force, the average wage of those remaining will tend to increase with age. Similarly, early retirement of the highly paid will tend to reduce the average wage of those remaining. But even in the absence of such changes in composition, the averages can, at best, describe wage rates that include any job changes that may happen with age. Among the elderly particularly, wages fall with a job change because the change is typically from a full-time job to a part-time, less well paid job. Thus the average wage path in cross-section cannot be matched to the productivity path of a worker who stays on the same job. These composition and job-change problems are reduced in panel data where we can follow the wage path of individuals and control for job change.

Gustman and Steinmeier (1985) in the RHS investigated the effects of composition and job-change effects. They found that conventional estimates that do not control for those effects "may overstate the decline with experience in wages for those working full time by as much as 60 per cent" (264). Jablonski, Kunze, and Rosenblum (1990) make adjustments for composition effects and find slowly declining real wage rates. The conclusion is that wage rates probably decline somewhat for those who remain on the main job, but the decline is modest. However, because the cost to the employer of fringe benefits rises with age, total compensation may well continue to increase with age.[9] Again, because we only observe those who stay on the job, we cannot say with confidence that the wages and compensation of those who left would have been roughly constant had they stayed.

This somewhat limited evidence suggests that, among workers who remain on their main job, productivity and total compensation change with age at about the same rate. Even so, the productivity of some individuals surely changes markedly with age because of changes in health status, failure to up-

---

9. I have seen no studies that make corrections for composition and job change in studying the relationship between age and total compensation.

grade skills, and attitudinal changes. What was a good match between the worker and the firm at a younger age becomes a worse match at older ages. This change could be accommodated if wages could be reduced at the individual level in line with the productivity change. There is, of course, a vast literature on wage rigidity, which I will not review here. It is sufficient to say that the wages of all workers are not easily reduced even during periods of falling demand: layoffs are the more usual response. It is probably even more difficult to reduce the wage of an individual worker.

If a firm is not able to reduce wages, it will adopt policies that will encourage separation, even though they are suboptimal compared to a wage reduction. A simple but effective policy will be not to allow reductions in hours worked: for example, someone whose productivity has fallen because of health changes or who finds the job particularly distasteful will have had a "taste" change toward not working. Given the all-or-nothing choice between working full-time or not working at all, such a person may choose not to work. A healthy or satisfied worker will not have had a change in "tastes" and will remain on the job. Therefore, given that individual wages cannot be reduced, hours rigidity will be an effective tool for inducing those workers to leave that the firm would like to leave.

A conclusion that is consistent with the evidence is that most jobs are full-time jobs, and although there is some variation by occupation and industry, the jobs have little flexibility. Workers choose jobs early in their careers according to what will be important to them during their work lives: the type of work, wages, benefits, promotion possibilities, and so forth. It may be that different jobs have different hours of work, but it is rare that hours may be varied once a job has been chosen. With the approach of retirement some workers will want to reduce hours because the hours that were optimal earlier in the work life are not optimal later in life. But, because of wage and hours rigidities on their own jobs, they cannot reduce hours without changing jobs or retiring completely.

This conclusion is supported by survey evidence. In a survey of 1,030 men aged 55–64 and 969 women aged 50–59, 93% of the working men and 80% of the working women worked full-time.[10] However, a substantial fraction of the full-time workers said they would like to work part-time: 18% of the men and 33% of the women. Although the workers were not asked why they could not reduce their hours, I imagine that, just as in other surveys, their employers would not allow them to.

1.3   Explanations or Causes of Job Rigidities

This section has two main goals. The first is to give evidence about the causes of the rigidities in the employment of workers of all ages and to find

---

10. Quinn and Burkhauser 1990, based on a survey conducted by Louis Harris and Associates.

how these affect older workers. The second is to give evidence about additional factors that primarily affect older workers.

1.3.1   Factors Affecting All Workers

Many job rigidities are normal to the workplace and affect workers of all ages. They may be caused by the economic necessity to use the capital stock fully or to be able to service customers during usual business hours. An important cause of rigidities from the point of view of this paper comes from the theory of team production.

Team Production

The theory of team production says that the productivity of a particular worker is increased (up to a point) when additional human factors of production are present. Other workers, other firms, and customers are, broadly speaking, additional factors of production. Clearly the extent and importance of team production varies across occupations and industries: all stations of an assembly line must be covered if production is to proceed; a barber shop must be open when customers want to come; yet a novelist probably requires no other human inputs most of the time. This implies that those who work in jobs requiring team production and who work during peak labor periods will, ceteris paribus, have higher wages than those who work during off-peak times (Henderson 1981). Such a relationship will vary across occupations and industries because of the varying intensities of team production. Wilson (1988) found that wages of professionals, skilled and semiskilled workers, and production workers were the most sensitive to start time. Wages of clerical or sales workers were less sensitive. This accords with expectations about the requirements for interaction among workers in these occupations.

If wages are higher for workers who follow similar schedules, we would expect considerable bunching of work hours. Indeed, full-time workers have similar schedules: in the 1985 CPS, 50.9% of full-time workers worked one of the four schedules: 8–5, 8–4, 7–4, or 9–5 (Mellor 1986). There is even more bunching in start and stop times: 78.8% of full-time workers began work at either 7 A.M., 8 A.M., or 9 A.M.; 69.5% stopped at either 4 P.M., 5 P.M., or 6 P.M. The amount of bunching was by necessity much less for part-time workers.

When a job requires team production, flexibility in work hours becomes difficult, and this applies whether a worker permanently works different hours from the other workers, or when a worker is on flextime. By case study, Swart (1978) investigated the drawbacks of flextime and found that many are associated with the requirements of team production. For example, a common management complaint about flextime was that communication between departments was weakened. Nollen and Martin (1978) found that complaints about and problems of flextime were associated with communication and scheduling, aspects of team production.

Despite the obvious advantages of reduced congestion and travel time and the accommodation of taste variation and preferences, only a small fraction of workers are on flextime, 12.8% in 1977 (Ronen 1984) and 12.3% in 1985 (Mellor 1986). The percentage by occupation of those working flextime varies from 19.9% in sales occupations, where many employees can work alone, to 4.0% among machine operators, assemblers, and inspectors, where the job requires the presence of others. This variation supports the view that team production is an important aspect of the workplace in many occupations and industries.

If team production affects the availability of flextime, it will also affect the availability and pay of part-time work. Suppose that a substantial fraction of workers (not even necessarily a majority) want to work full-time during "normal hours." If in most occupations and industries individual production is higher when other workers are present, jobs during normal working hours will have higher productivity and tend to pay more than off-hour jobs, drawing additional workers to those hours. Eventually a good deal of employment will be concentrated in normal hours. Anyone wanting to work outside of those hours, whether part-time or full-time, will have lower productivity and lower pay. The firm will discourage anyone from working part-time during normal working hours because that worker's absence during part of the normal working day will affect the productivity of the full-time workers.

We do not, of course, observe everyone working the same hours. Several factors prevent the concentration of hours from being complete. Some workers have such strong tastes for unconventional hours that they are willing to work off hours even if their wages are less. Some services such as bus service and entertainment must be produced during off hours. The firm will desire to use its capital stock during off hours: when the capital-labor ratio is high and team production is important, a firm will want to have several complete teams of workers to use the capital stock continuously. Apparently not enough workers want to work off hours that a complete team can be assembled at the normal wage: overtime pay has to be paid. The fact that the overtime bonus is typically 50% shows the strength of team production: the productivity of the marginal worker must be high indeed to justify such a large bonus.

Fixed Costs of Employment

The costs to a firm of employing a worker can, in principle, be divided into fixed costs and variable costs. Table 1.6 has estimates of such a division.[11] They are, of course, an average because the allocation will vary from firm to firm. In particular, some firms have few training costs and offer no health benefits; then, fixed costs would be negligible. Probably the most controversial entry is

---

11. The table does not include the costs of any capital the firm furnishes to the worker.

Table 1.6   **Distribution of Employment Costs**

Cost Item	Percentage of Cost
Fixed costs	
Training	13.5
Hiring	1.0
Health insurance	5.1
Total	19.6
Variable costs	
Wages and salary	53.6
Pension	4.5
Time off with pay	11.5
FICA tax	5.4
Unemployment insurance contributions	1.0
Workman's compensation	1.2
Total	77.2
Other, not classified	3.2
Total costs	100.0

Source: Jondrow, Brechling, and Marcus, 1987.

the attribution of health insurance to fixed costs. Apparently, however, companies that offer health insurance to part-time workers typically pay the same amount for the insurance as they do for a full-time worker (Paul 1983b); that is, health insurance is not prorated by work effort as are pension benefits, paid time off, and so forth.[12] In this case it is a fixed cost.

The figures are calculated for 1981. Since then, according to Health Care Financing Administration estimates, the real cost per person of health care has grown by about 38%.[13] This would put health insurance costs at about 7% of total employment costs and total fixed costs at about 21.5% of employment costs.

Fixed costs vary with age. In particular, recruitment, hiring, and training costs must be amortized over expected years of employment: because newly hired older workers probably have a shorter work life with the new employer than newly hired younger workers, the implicit cost per year of employment will be larger.[14] Health insurance costs increase with age. Paul (1984) reports from a survey of employers that employees aged 55–59 have the highest health

12. If work hours fall below one thousand per year, under the Employee Retirement Income and Security Act the firm is not obligated to offer the benefit at all. In some cases, therefore, health insurance is not truly a fixed cost.

13. My calculations based on the scenario of moderate growth of health care costs (Advisory Council 1991).

14. Firms may react to the shorter work life by giving less training to older workers. Although I have seen no studies confirming this, the net result may be that training costs are roughly invariant with age. However, the fixed costs of recruitment and hiring would still be greater per year of employment among older newly hired workers.

Table 1.7   **Percentage of Workers Participating in Health Care Plans**

Age	20–49	50–59	60–64	65–69
Participation	61	68	79	78

Source: Repko (1987), based on data from J. C. Penney.

Table 1.8   **Relative Cost of Medical Insurance**

Age	All Employees	Single Male
≤45	1.00	1.00
45–49	1.25	1.87
50–54	1.41	2.79
55–59	1.56	2.84
60–64	2.00	4.51
65–69	2.81	—

Source: U.S. Senate (1984).

care costs, followed by those 65 or over, then those 60–64, followed by younger groups.[15]

This is partly caused by increasing participation in health care plans with age, as shown in Table 1.7. Furthermore, given participation in a plan, older workers file claims more frequently than younger workers; therefore, health care costs increase with age. Whether this is seen as an age-related employment cost by the employer depends on the method of financing health care insurance. Firms that self-insure would bear fully the cost difference by age. If a firm buys insurance for its employees, its premium will depend on whether it is experience rated or community rated. If experience rated, the cost of premiums depend on the historical health care costs incurred by the firm's employees. Therefore, a firm that employs a disproportionate number of older workers should expect higher health care insurance premiums. If community rated, the firm's premiums depend on the average health care costs of covered employees in some large local pool of employees. Then firms would have no differential cost for medical insurance premiums as the result of employing older workers.

Table 1.8 has estimated relative costs of providing medical insurance to employees by age to all employees and to single males. The costs are calculated from health maintenance organization (HMO) claims data on families covered by group contracts, so there is surely a question about the generality of the results. Nonetheless, there certainly is general agreement that health benefit costs increase with the age of the employee.

The Special Committee on Aging (U.S. Senate 1984) estimated that average costs of health care were about 5% of pay. The report of the committee noted that, "[w]hile medical benefits may be worth about 5 percent of pay overall,

---

15. Costs increase with age for both single employees and employees with dependents.

for lower paid older workers this percentage could be 20 to 30 percent of pay. This is particularly true if the employer offers medical benefits to employees who work on reduced schedules. Some employers offer medical coverage to employees who work 20, 25, or 30 hours per week. Older persons are one of the groups who prefer such schedules" (46). If a firm truly does spend 4.51 times as much in health care costs for a 60–64-year-old single male as a younger single male (table 1.8), the large percentages of pay for health care costs in the quotation are comprehensible. In this case the fixed costs associated with hiring an older male would be a large fraction of total costs.

Individuals also have fixed costs of working. The only estimate of an individual's fixed cost of which I am aware is an econometric estimate based on observed hours of work of women. The basic idea is that fixed costs to the individual could explain why almost no women work just a few hours per year. Because many women either work a substantial number of hours or not at all, the estimate of fixed costs is large: 28% of average yearly earnings (Cogan 1981). These costs would come from the requirement for extra private transportation, work-related clothing, meals at work, and day care.[16] Casual observation suggests that, because of day care, 28% may not be unreasonable. It seems high for men: in the 1986 Consumer Expenditure Survey average expenditures on items that could be counted as fixed employment costs of men are food away from home, 6.1%; private transportation, 19.3%; and apparel and services, 5.6%. These items total 31%, but, of course, not all of these expenditures are work-related and fixed. In the example that follows I will use an estimate of 10%.

The effect of fixed costs on the ability of an employer to pay a generous wage to a part-time employee is rather sharp. Consider as an example someone who works two thousand hours per year at $10 per hour. In line with table 1.6, suppose that the nonwage costs of employment equal the wage costs and that the firm breaks even on the worker. Then the earnings of the worker would be $20,000 and the product would be $40,000. Of this, I assume that fixed costs are 25% (adding in 3.5% for fixed capital costs to the 21.5% derived from table 1.6), variable nonwage costs are 25% of which 18% are compensation in the form of pension benefits and paid time off and 7% are in the form of Federal Insurance Contributions Act (FICA) taxes, unemployment insurance, and other, which are not compensation to the worker. If hours are reduced to one thousand, total product would be worth $20,000. Table 1.9 shows how that product would be allocated.

Fixed costs remain at $10,000, the variable costs are now $5,000, leaving wages of $5,000. Thus, hours fell by 50%, but earnings fell by 75% and the wage fell by 50%. The fall in total compensation, including variable nonmonetary compensation, would not be quite as great, but it would also be substantial.

The percentage change in earnings divided by the percentage change in

16. Of course, some of these costs could have both fixed and variable components.

Table 1.9   Example of Allocation of Employment Costs

Type of Cost	Percentage at Full-Time	Full-Time ($)	Half-Time ($)
Wages	50	20,000	5,000
Fixed costs	25	10,000	10,000
Variable (compensation)	18	7,200	3,600
Variable (not compensation)	7	2,800	1,400
Total	100	40,000	20,000

Source: Author's calculations, based on table 1.6.

hours is an elasticity, and with no fixed costs it would be 1.0. Here the estimate is 1.5. Although this may seem like a large elasticity, it is similar to estimates based on the observed relationship between hours and earnings. For example, Jondrow, Brechling, and Marcus (1987) estimated the elasticity to be 1.53; Owen (1976) and Rosen (1976) both estimated an elasticity of 1.4; and Clark, Gohmann, and Sumner (1982) estimated it to be 1.6.

The interpretation of my example is that a reduction in hours would require the wage rate of an individual to fall in order for the firm to break even. It is difficult to estimate this relationship from observations of individuals because individuals rarely reduce hours at the same firm. Gustman and Steinmeier (1985) reported that, in the RHS when individuals changed from full-time to partially retired at the same firm, their wage rate fell by 10% on average; but "partially retired" is self-assessed and Gustman and Steinmeier do not report the change in hours worked, so this result cannot be compared with the others I have cited. Regardless of the exact comparison, however, it seems clear that, in many occupations and industries, fixed costs are an important component of total employment costs, and, in order that a firm can cover fixed costs, money wage rates must be lower for part-time work than for full-time work. Therefore, earnings will decline at a faster rate than hours, and at some point it will not be worthwhile to work.

If the worker also has fixed costs associated with working, that point will probably be reached at a fairly high number of hours. Suppose in my example that the worker has fixed costs of working of 10% of full-time income, or $2,000. Then, pretax discretionary income (after subtracting the fixed costs of working) would be $18,000 at full-time hours. Pretax discretionary income at half-time hours would be just $3,000, so the worker would be earning $3.00 per hour in discretionary income. This is a low wage, indeed, to compensate for the disutility of working.

This example and the estimates from the literature of the importance of fixed costs imply that most workers will work enough hours to cover both the fixed costs of the firm and of the worker, yet still leave adequate money earnings for the worker. Part-time work will be associated with low pay, and there will be a minimum number of hours of work. The relationship between hours and the wage rate will vary across occupations and industries because of the variation in fixed costs; similarly the minimum number of hours will vary across occupations and industries. This is what we observe both across occupations and industries and across individuals: occupations and industries in which there is considerable part-time work have lower average wage rates, and individuals who work part-time have lower average wage rates.[17]

1.3.2   Factors Particularly Affecting Older Workers

This section discusses other factors that particularly affect older workers, and how normal work practices affect the labor market activity of older workers. The discussion considers the effects on reducing hours on the main job, the effects on changing jobs to reduce hours, and the effects on complete retirement.

Social Security

The earnings test under Social Security reduces the Social Security benefits of a retired worker between the ages of 62 and 65 by $1 for every $2 earned, beginning at the exempt amount of $7,680 in 1993.[18] Thus, a worker with a wage of $10 per hour could work no more than 768 hours per year without facing a Social Security benefit reduction. From the discussion of fixed costs and team production of the last section, this level of work effort would not sustain a wage rate of $10 unless the worker had a job with little fixed costs, including fixed-cost fringe benefits.

The earnings test interacts with the Social Security provision of reduced benefits for early retirement: an eligible worker may draw Social Security benefits beginning at age 62, but the benefit is permanently reduced by $5/9\%$ for each month in which benefits are drawn before the age of 65. The reduction factor, about 7% per year, was meant to be actuarially fair, and at a real interest rate of 3% it is approximately fair. Therefore, a worker contemplating drawing benefits at age 62 should realize that the total value of the expected stream of benefits is approximately independent of retiring at 62 or working an additional month because the eventual increase in the stream of benefits will compensate for the lost benefits from delaying retirement for a month. What the worker may not realize, however, is that any monthly benefits lost under the earnings test are treated in the same way, except benefits are not increased until age 65, when they are recalculated to take into account lost benefits due to the earnings test. For example, a worker who retired at 62 and then at age 63 took a part-time job resulting in the loss of three months' benefits would have monthly benefits increased permanently by $3 \times (5 \div 9)\%$ beginning at age 65. Therefore, before age 65 the earnings test is not really a tax: it is forced saving. According to lifetime utility-maximizing models in which individuals can

---

17. I realize that the empirical observations may not hold constant individual characteristics that affect productivity and, therefore, do not correspond to the theory as completely as I would like.
18. Over age 65 the reduction is $1 to $3, beginning at the exempt amount of $10,560.

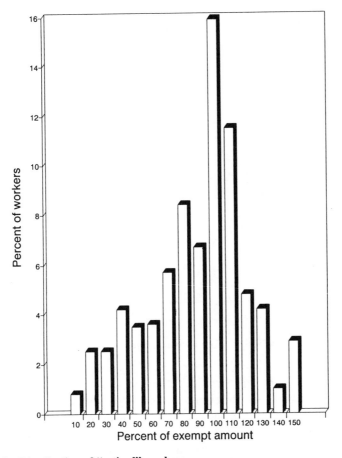

Fig. 1.2   Distribution of "retired" workers
Source: Burtless and Moffitt (1985), based on the Retirement History Survey.

freely borrow and lend, the earnings test should have no effect on the choice of how much to work.

The empirical fact, however, is that the earnings test seems to have important effects. Burtless and Moffitt (1985) calculated from the RHS the distribution of annual hours of work where the points in the distribution are percentages of the exempt amount. This calculation can show the importance of the earnings test because, if it is an important determinant in the choice of hours, we would expect to see many workers choosing hours at or just beneath the exempt amount. Figure 1.2 shows the distribution of hours in the RHS of "retired" workers aged 62 or over who are still working.[19] The figure shows a remarkable

19. Someone is defined to be retired if he or she has a sudden and discontinuous drop in hours of work (Burtless and Moffitt 1985).

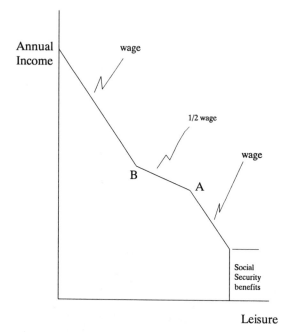

Fig. 1.3   Effect of earnings test on annual income

bunching of workers near the exempt amount: 16% have hours in the range of 91% to 100% of the exempt amount; 12% have hours in the range of 101% to 110%. Given that the data have observation error and that it is probably difficult for a worker to reach exactly the exempt amount, the figure shows that workers respond to the earnings test in a way not predicted by the utility-maximizing models. The models hold that lifetime wealth is the important determinant of behavior, whereas the figure suggests that annual (or monthly) income is also important.

The difference is illustrated in Figure 1.3, which shows the relationship between annual work and annual income. If a worker could not borrow or lend, this would be the annual budget constraint. Point A is the exempt amount of annual hours, which corresponds to the 100% point in figure 1.2. Between points A and B benefits are reduced by $1 for each $2 of earnings, effectively reducing income from working by 50%. At B (the breakeven point) benefits have been reduced to zero, so earnings increase at the wage rate. With this budget constraint, utility maximization will lead to bunching of hours at zero and at A. We should also observe hours spread from zero to A, and far above B. This is almost exactly what we find: we already know that most have zero hours; Burtless and Moffitt found that 22% of the working retired had hours more than 150% of the exempt amount and 65% had hours between zero and

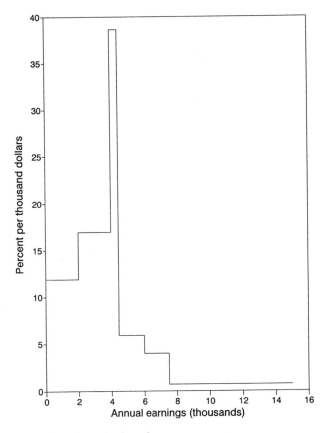

Fig. 1.4   Distribution of retired workers
Source: Author's calculations from Iams (1987), based on the New Beneficiary Survey.

110% of the exempt amount. Just 13% had hours between 110% and 150% of
the exempt amount.

I know of no other study that gives such detailed distributions of hours. Iams
(1987) gives the distribution of workers aged 64 or less by earnings level in
the New Beneficiary Survey (NBS).[20] In this sample, the workers have already
drawn some Social Security benefits, so they are aware of the test. Figure 1.4
shows the density of workers who have already left their longest employer, so
they are in transition jobs. The figure shows a very sharp peak near the exempt
amount ($4,440). This is a somewhat more convincing case than in Burtless
and Moffitt: some of the Burtless and Moffitt sample is 65 or over, and at those
ages the earnings test is really a tax, whereas in Iams all are younger than 65.

I conclude that in both the RHS and the NBS, many working recipients of

---

20. These would be men who had "retired" in the sense that they had begun to receive Social
Security benefits, but they either were still working or had gone back to work.

Social Security retirement benefits have hours of work that place them near the exempt amount. This is good evidence that workers believe that the earnings test has at least some characteristics of a tax.

One explanation for the tax nature of the earnings test is that most workers do not know that benefits forgone through the earnings test will be regained at age 65. Some mild support for this point of view comes from Quinn, Burkhauser, and Myers (1990). They study the bunching of hours near the exempt amount as the age of the worker varies. The relative amount of bunching of those 65 or over is about the same as of those 62–64, even though the earnings test is a true tax at 65 or over but not below 65. Furthermore, I believe this explanation is likely because I have spoken to economists who do research in the economics of aging, and many of them were unaware of the automatic benefit recalculation. Another explanation is that we have an inadequate understanding of how workers react to a complicated program that has a feature that acts partly like a tax and partly like a savings mechanism. My conclusion is that we really do not know what causes the clustering around the exempt amount.

The earnings test seems to discourage work. Besides its obvious effects on the lifetime income of the worker, it seems to affect the employment opportunities of older workers. Paul (1987, 172) reports on a survey of twenty-five managers who administered work programs in their organizations.

> The Social Security retirement earnings test was identified by eight of the managers as the greatest disincentive to work for Social Security beneficiaries. The managers administering retiree labor pools expressed frustration in the fact that once retirees who are receiving Social Security earn $6,000 (the 1982 maximum earnings limitation[21]) they usually cease working, or they will limit their work hours, upon re-employment, so as not to exceed the $6,000 limit. This common work pattern of many retirees not only *restricts management's use of this type of employee,* but is also symptomatic of the financial disincentive associated with prolonged employment during retirement.

I put the emphasis in this quotation to point out that the earnings test may well discourage the development of programs for part-time work: management will often need to ask workers with particular skills to work more than the exempt amount, and if workers consistently refuse, it may not be worth the cost of maintaining such programs.

Pension Plans

Apparently defined-benefit pension plans have substantial effects on the work choices of employees. Most of the research has been directed to their

---

21. The discussion is about workers aged 65 or over. For them the exempt amount is higher than for workers aged 62–64.

most obvious effect, the effect on retirement, which I will discuss later in this paper, but they also have an influence on hours of work before retirement.

Although there are thousands of defined-benefit pension plans, many have formulas for rates of accrual of pension benefits of the form $b = k \times e \times y$, in which b is the benefit, k is a constant factor, e is some measure of earnings near the end of work life such as the final year's earnings or an average of the final two years' earnings, and y is years of service. In that b is the annual benefit for the retired lifetime, a reduction in earnings near retirement will have a large effect on lifetime wealth. For example, if e is just the final year's earnings, a decrease in earnings of 10% will reduce pension benefits by 10%, which translates into a lifetime wealth loss of about 150% of annual earnings.[22] That is, the financial loss of reducing hours in the year before retirement can easily be greater than an entire year's earnings. Therefore, a worker will not want to reduce hours if pension benefits depend on current earnings.

A common way to avoid this problem is to have the worker "retire," fixing the benefit, and then be rehired as a consultant or outside employee who has no benefits, and particularly no accrual of pension. In some cases, however, the consultant can work only a limited number of hours without losing pension benefits: under the Employee Retirement Income and Security Act (ERISA) retirees who are reemployed for more than forty hours per month can have their pension benefits suspended. Although some managers mentioned this as a barrier to hiring retirees on a part-time basis, it was viewed to be a minor factor compared with the Social Security earnings test (Paul 1987).

An aspect that could be quite important under some circumstances has to do with inflation risk. While a worker is employed under a defined-benefit plan, pension benefits are on average protected against inflation risk because prices and money wages change at about the same rates. Thus, if there is general inflation during the last five years of work life, money wages should increase by the same amount, keeping the real value of the pension at the point of retirement about the same. Typically, however, pensions once taken are not protected against inflation, so that a worker who retires early and is then rehired at fewer hours will not have inflation protection for the pension.[23] This method of reducing hours on the main job exposes a worker to considerable inflation risk compared with staying on the main job longer and then retiring completely.

ERISA and Health Insurance

I have already discussed how firms that are experience rated or that self-insure will have to spend more on the health insurance of older workers, mak-

22. Discounting will convert a real lifetime income flow of $1 at age 65 into a wealth equivalent of about $15.

23. During the high-inflation decade of the 1970s, firms often made ad hoc adjustments in pensions for inflation (Allen, Clark, and Sumner 1986).

ing the fixed costs of older workers greater. This will, of course, restrict the lower bound on hours that will be financially acceptable both to the firm and the employee. The fixed cost of health insurance can be eliminated, however, if annual hours are not allowed to reach one thousand; then, under ERISA, the firm need not pay health insurance or other benefits available to all workers. Apparently this is often a management strategy: in a survey of six programs that form pools of labor from retirees, Paul (1987) found that they all restricted the number of hours to less than one thousand. The general attitude of the managers who were surveyed was that "if the 1000-hour rule were eliminated, their organizations would permit part-time personnel, particularly retirees, to work more hours" (172). It is difficult to know how much of this is simply self-serving, but because of the costs involved, I believe it should be taken seriously. A further reason is that these surveys were made during the early 1980s, when health care costs were substantially lower than today, and when the projections of health care costs were not nearly so pessimistic as they are today.

Under the thousand-hour rule the firm would like to keep hours below one thousand hours so that medical insurance could be eliminated. The worker might want to work more than one thousand hours, both because the drop from two thousand to one thousand hours is too abrupt and because he or she requires medical insurance. The outcome of these incompatible desires will depend on the alternatives of each side. The main option of the older worker is to retire. The firm can hire young workers who may not care about health insurance and who want to work less than one thousand hours. Then the firm can retain the health insurance benefit for its full-time workers while eliminating it for its part-time workers.

1.3.3   Impediments to a Job Change at Older Ages

This section discusses the factors that may impede a job change to reduce hours.

Special Job Skills

Over time an employee acquires skills and knowledge about the firm that increase productivity at that firm. Such skills and knowledge are called specific human capital because they are specific to the firm. Skills and knowledge that would increase productivity should the worker change to another firm are called general human capital. When a firm hires a worker who is expected to remain for many years, it will be in the firm's interest to invest in the specific human capital of the worker; this kind of investment is thought to be an important cause of rising productivity paths early in a worker's career. Obviously some skills cannot be defined as either specific or general: the definition will depend on the alternative employment. For example, most of the skills of a General Motors employee will transfer to Ford, but few of them will transfer to a Wall Street law firm. The general point is nonetheless valid: over time workers become more valuable to a particular firm than to any other firm, so that, at least potentially, the firm can pay the worker more than any other firm could.

Some productivity-increasing activities are not specific human capital in an obvious way, but they still have the characteristics of specific human capital. For example, the search for a good match between a firm and a worker may involve several rounds of hiring and quitting or firing. This is a costly activity, but both the worker and the firm are willing to bear the cost if the payback period is sufficiently long. Once a good match has been found, the costs of the search that led to the match should be considered part of specific human capital. This particular example is germane to understanding why the turnover rates of young and older workers cannot easily be compared. Young workers have higher turnover rates because of the search for a good match: if a good match is found, however, the payback period is much longer. Therefore, both the firm and the worker are willing to bear the greater turnover costs of younger workers.

Often unions negotiate job pay or title by seniority rather than by productivity. From the point of view of the worker this looks like specific human capital because the seniority has no value at another firm. From the point of view of the firm it is the way of determining the shape of the lifetime wage trajectory, but to the extent that pay late in the career is not connected to productivity, the firm will have an incentive to get rid of highly paid older workers. It is surely no accident that, as will be discussed later, defined-benefit pensions are most often found in unionized firms, and that the pensions have provisions that encourage retirement.

As this discussion suggests, older workers who change employers, whether the change is to full-time or part-time employment, can expect a fall in productivity because of the loss of specific human capital. Furthermore, because of a short payback period on the new job, extensive job search to find the best match is not warranted, so the starting wage will be lower than the highest that could be found in the market. The new employee cannot expect rapid wage growth because, again, the short payback period will cause the new employer not to want to invest in specific human capital.

If an older worker had maintained or increased his or her general human capital, a job change would not occasion a large fall in productivity. However, most older workers probably have little general human capital: during the many years since schooling the initial stock of general human capital would have depreciated; there is little financial incentive for investment in general human capital on the part of the firm because the employee can simply leave, taking the investment to another firm.

If an older worker wants to reduce hours but cannot on the main job because of fixed costs or team production, it is unlikely that other firms in the same industry will offer a similar job, but at reduced hours, because of its own fixed costs and requirements of team production. Therefore, the older worker will have to change occupations or industries. This seems to be common. In the NLS 59% of the job changes following retirement from the main job were to a different occupation and 52% were to a different industry (Parnes and Nestel 1981). In the RHS just 12% of the changes from career jobs by men aged 60 or over were to the same occupation and industry (Ruhm 1990a). In the CPS job changes at older ages tend to concentrate workers in just a few industries (Hutchens 1988).

These figures show a remarkable amount of mobility across occupations and industries. Practically by definition these will be easy entry jobs that require few specific skills, a rather low level of general skills, and minimal search costs because of the short payback period. They cannot have large fixed costs or the wage rate would be unacceptably low, given the reduced hours. Furthermore, because the older worker loses the specific human capital acquired during the work life with a particular firm, he or she must compete in a labor market with a pool of rather unskilled labor, which may have low opportunity costs of its time. For example, students need jobs with approximately the same characteristics as a job the older worker would switch to; and students are willing to work for rather low wages. Therefore, forces of supply and demand will tend to keep the wage rate low. We would expect, then, that jobs taken after retirement from the main job for the purpose of reducing hours, will have low wage rates.

This is a universal finding: In the RHS wage rates of men fell 30% on average at job change (Gustman and Steinmeier 1985). In the NLS the median wage change was -39%, and 71% of those changing jobs had a wage loss (Parnes and Nestel 1981). Average wage rates fell by 18%, according to a survey of eighteen hundred retirees from three large corporations (Morse, Dutka, and Gray 1983). In the NBS the wage rates of men who continued to work after initial receipt of Social Security benefits fell by about 50% (Iams 1987).

Table 1.10 has some details of the change in wage rates at a job change. Of those who reduced hours on their career job, 36% had a wage gain of more than $2.50 (1984 dollars), and just 24% had a wage loss of more than $2.50. It appears, therefore, that if someone can reduce hours on the career job, the wage rate can be expected to remain about the same. Almost half of those who changed to a new full-time job had roughly constant wage rates, but the percentage having a wage loss (42%) is much greater than the percentage having a wage gain. The table makes clear that changing to part-time on a new job causes the largest decline in wages. This is, of course, consistent with an explanation based on the loss of specific job skills and fixed costs.

Fringe Benefits

Fringe benefits are a barrier to job change at older ages. Partly this is because the new jobs often do not offer fringe benefits, so the fall in total com-

Table 1.10   **Wage Change of Men on Leaving Full-Time Lifetime Jobs**
              (% distribution)

	Type of Transition		
Wage Change	To Part-Time on Same Job	To Full-Time on New Job	To Part-Time on New Job
>$2.50	36	12	11
−$2.50 to $2.50	42	46	21
<−$2.50	24	42	68
Total	100	100	100
Number of observations	57	151	134

Source: Quinn, Burkhauser, and Myers (1990), based on Retirement History Survey.

pensation is greater than what is indicated from the wage rate changes. This would be true for someone of any age changing into those jobs.

Changes in fringe benefits at a change in job have not been studied nearly as much as changes in wages; in particular, I have not seen any data from the PSID, the RHS, or the NLS on how benefits changed. However, at older ages the incidence of fringe benefits surely falls at job change because many job changes are into the service sector, which has a much lower incidence of fringe benefits than the manufacturing sector. Some evidence comes from Morse, Dutka, and Gray (1983), who report that just 29% of the retirees who continued to work in their survey had fringe benefits on their new jobs.

Fringe benefits are a barrier to job change at older ages, however, partly because of the particular requirements of older workers for some kinds of fringe benefits. Health insurance is especially important for older workers, so its loss entails a large loss in compensation on average. But preexisting conditions may well mean that, even if the new job offers medical insurance, the new worker may not be allowed the benefit. This means that the equivalent monetary loss of moving to a new job and losing medical insurance is much greater than the average cost of medical insurance: were someone with a preexisting condition to purchase medical insurance privately, the cost would depend on the condition, increasing the fair market price.

It is difficult to know the extent and importance of the reduction in job mobility due to preexisting conditions. Surveys of the population show a large incidence: 30% of the respondents to a CBS–*New York Times* poll answered yes to the question "Have you or anyone else in your household ever decided to stay in a job you wanted to leave mainly because you didn't want to lose health coverage?" (*New York Times,* 6 September 1991). Madrian (1994) used the 1987 National Medical Expenditure Survey to study job mobility of married men. She estimated that the "job-lock" aspects of not having medical insurance reduced job mobility from 16% per year to 12%. Based on the 1973 Quality of Employment Survey, Mitchell (1983) estimated that men would have to be compensated $1,800 (out of mean earnings of $9,000) to move from a firm with health insurance to one without health insurance. This is much more than the cost of simply purchasing health insurance, which indicates that preexisting conditions are important.

Defined-benefit plans have many provisions that can affect job mobility, but some have only minor effects. In particular, vesting in a new plan is not particularly important to younger workers because of the long period before retirement benefits are paid: private defined-benefit plans are not indexed between the time of separation from the firm and the receipt of benefits, so that inflation as well as discounting makes the present value from vesting small. Among workers nearing retirement, vesting is more important. For example, five years of service could give a pension of 5–10% of salary, which has a wealth equivalent of about a year's earnings.

The effect on the mobility of worker with many years of service will depend on the nature of the pension plan and on the wage path of the worker. Consider again the simplified plan $b = k \times e \times y$, in which b is the benefit, k is a constant factor taken in this example to be 0.02, e is the final year's earnings, and y is years of service. If e increases linearly with years of service, as would be the case when the same raise is given each year, then b increases in the square of y. Then, the gain in benefits from an additional year of service is linear in y, and the value of an additional year of service is very much greater at the end of a long work life than at the beginning. This should, of course, reduce mobility toward the end of work life.[24]

Even if someone has reached the maximum number of years' service for pension accrual so that no additional pension is earned with additional service, early retirement from the firm to change jobs will cause a loss of real pension wealth: defined-benefit plans are not formally inflation-protected following separation from the firm, so the pension will lose value at the rate of inflation. Furthermore, because the rate of inflation can change unexpectedly, the pension is exposed to inflation risk: a rate of pension loss that is judged acceptable at retirement could increase in an unexpected way.

Defined-benefit pensions can change in an important way the financial incentives to remain with an employer. We would expect that, depending on the nature of the plan and the characteristics of the employee, they would have strong effects of mobility. Apparently, as I will discuss in the next section, they do.

1.3.4   Factors Influencing Complete Retirement

Pension Plans

Defined-benefit plans have widely differing patterns of accrual and of benefit adjustments for the age of retirement. I will speak of typical plans, but it should be kept in mind that the plans are very heterogeneous.

---

24. I will discuss below the research findings on how accrual rates affect job mobility.

At some combinations of years of service and age, defined-benefit plans strongly discourage mobility. For example, a plan may effectively offer Social Security benefits at age 60 to someone who stays with the firm until 60 and then retires. This would be done by augmenting until age 62 the worker's pension benefits by the amount of Social Security the worker will get at 62. Thus, a 59-year-old worker could earn two years of Social Security benefits by working one year, in addition to salary and any increment in pension. Such a worker would be discouraged from complete retirement or from reducing hours by changing employers. This example is one of many aspects of defined-benefit plans that change the compensation of working another year on the main job.

The adjustment for delaying retirement past the normal retirement age is often not actuarially fair in a defined-benefit plan. Although eliminating accrual on the basis of age is not longer allowed under the Age Discrimination in Employment Act (1986), it can be capped for reaching maximum years of service. In combination with the actuarial adjustment, the financial reward for another year of work can be substantially below money earnings. Kotlikoff and Wise (1987) give an example based on a firm's actual defined-benefit plan in which the wage of a 61-year-old worker is effectively reduced by 14%. In other examples, the reduction can be considerably greater.

The influence of the particular features of the plans on worker mobility rates is well documented (Burkhauser 1979; Stock and Wise 1990a, 1990b; Kotlikoff and Wise 1989; Lumsdaine, Stock, and Wise 1994). In these studies and others, workers respond strongly to the incentives built into the plans: at some ages, the incentive to remain at the firm is strong and we observe little mobility; at other ages the incentives to leave are strong, and we observe considerable separation. For example, in a firm studied by Kotlikoff and Wise, someone leaving the firm at age 55 could get substantially higher pensions benefits than someone leaving at age 54. The difference depends on the circumstances of the worker: Kotlikoff and Wise give a case of someone with earnings of $42,000 whose pension wealth is increased by $30,000 by staying from age 54 to 55. Accordingly the rate of separation of those with twenty-one or more years of service is 2% at age 54 and 11% at age 55.

Defined-contribution plans do not have such strong incentives as defined-benefit plans. They do, of course, have a wealth effect because they represent forced saving that the worker might not have done otherwise; if this happens, the worker will arrive at retirement age with more economic resources than otherwise. By itself, this is not an impediment to the choice of work effort: provided a worker can finance consumption from other assets, the level of consumption can be chosen independently from income in a particular year. However, even defined-contribution pensions may influence the age of retirement through a so-called liquidity effect. Imagine a defined-contribution plan that puts a large fraction of a worker's compensation in the plan, so much that the worker does not want to save anything in addition for retirement. As the worker approaches retirement, he or she may have accumulated so much in the plan that consumption will be higher in retirement than before retirement, which would cause the worker to want to borrow against the future retirement benefits to finance greater consumption before retirement. If there are capital market imperfections or if the benefits cannot be used as collateral, the borrowing will not happen and consumption before retirement is liquidity constrained: the worker has the assets (future benefit payments) but cannot use them to achieve the desired consumption path. Then, the level of the benefit payment will influence the choice of retirement age: the worker will tend to retire earlier than if consumption could be chosen independently from retirement. That is, the person's income stream is conditioned by work status, and capital market imperfections cannot be used to allow consumption to be chosen independently from the income stream. Thus, consumption and work status must be chosen jointly, causing the choice of retirement age to depend on the defined-contribution plan.[25]

As far as I know, the effects of defined-contribution plans on retirement age through the liquidity constraint have not been empirically studied. However, Social Security can, in principle, have a similar effect, and there is some empirical evidence that it does have. I will look at this evidence in connection with my discussion of Social Security.

Defined-contribution plans can affect retirement in at least two other ways. The continuing accrual of benefits under a defined-contribution plan may be capped for years of service, which changes the reward from working. Inflation affects the assets in a defined-contribution plan differently from the assets in a defined-benefit plan. Before retirement a defined-benefit plan subjects a worker to little inflation risk; the effect of inflation on a defined-contribution plan will depend on how the worker's assets are invested, so no generalization can be made. After retirement the effects will be the same if both types of pension plans lead to a nominal annuity.

Overall we observe that workers covered by pensions have fewer job changes at younger ages and higher retirement rates at greater ages. At younger ages mobility is reduced primarily because of the incentives from the plans and because the jobs associated with pension plans seem to be better jobs. For example, in the 1984 Survey of Income and Program Participation, the rate of job change by 30–50-year-old males was 20% among those without pensions and 6% among those with pensions (Gustman and Steinmeier 1993). Yet there was little difference in mobility according to whether the plan was a defined-benefit plan or a defined-contribution plan. Because defined-contribution plans are completely portable, offering no impediments to job change, this result suggests that the reduced mobility is caused by other factors associated with jobs that have pensions. In particular, jobs with pensions seem to be better

---

25. The same reasoning applies if the defined-contribution plan can be cashed out rather than taken as an annuity.

jobs: they pay more even after accounting for observable worker characteristics. Furthermore, workers who leave jobs that have pensions have lower earnings on their new jobs, whereas workers who leave jobs that do not have pensions have higher earnings (Gustman and Steinmeier 1993).

Early retirement has long been associated with pensions because of the historical dominance of defined-benefit plans with their incentives for retirement. However, defined-contribution plans have grown at a much greater rate, so that by 1987 only about 68% of active participants in a pension plan had a defined-benefit plan (Turner and Beller 1992). The pension coverage rate was 42% of the workforce in 1988, so that only about one-third of workers were covered under a defined-benefit plan. Of course, benefit levels in many of these plans are not great enough to influence behavior in a substantial way.[26] Therefore, defined-benefit plans may explain the retirement behavior of some, but only of a minority. And their influence is diminishing.

Social Security

Social Security affects retirement in a number of ways. Historically, incremental Social Security taxes caused benefits to increase at such a high rate that, taken by itself, the accrual of benefits encouraged later retirement (Blinder, Gordon, and Wise 1983). In effect the reward from an additional year of work was substantially greater than the wage rate. Because of the indexing of wages and maturing of the system, that is no longer the case for most workers: in fact, Social Security contributions will be a true tax for a worker with many years of contributions and steady earnings because any additional contributions will not increase the benefit. However, a worker with a small number of years of contributions could accrue higher benefits from additional Social Security contributions, but I imagine the overall effect of the accrual of benefits is rather small.

As I discussed earlier, the reduction in benefits for early retirement is approximately actuarially fair. The system should not affect retirement before the age of 65 through any "price" effects,[27] although it has a wealth effect through forced saving in the manner I discussed in connection with defined contribution plans. After age 65 the delayed retirement credit increases benefits for each month by which retirement is delayed or for each month in which benefits are lost due to the earnings test. Until 1986 the delayed retirement credit was 3% per year, far lower than what is actuarially fair. This undoubtedly encour-

26. In 1988 just 17% of households aged 65–74 received more than 20% of their income from private pensions (Grad 1990). Thus, even among the recently retired, pension income is a rather minor source for most households.

27. By price effects I mean the change in the present value of benefits when the age of retirement changes. Between the ages of 62 and 65, this change is roughly zero. The system could still affect the retirement of someone with a number of years of zero or low Social Security contributions because additional work would increase average monthly earnings.

aged the very high rates of retirement at age 65: for example, in the RHS 24% of men working on their sixty-fifth birthday had retired within three months of their birthdays (Blau 1994).

Beginning in 1990 the delayed retirement credit began to rise; in 1993 it was 4% per year, and by the year 2009 it will be 8% per year, which will be approximately actuarially fair. Therefore, by 2009 the system should, in principle, have no price effects either through the reduction for early retirement or through the delayed retirement credit once a worker has reached 62.

Despite the apparent fairness of the reduction for early retirement, we observe high rates of retirement at age 62. What is the explanation? A liquidity constraint is one possible explanation. As discussed in connection with defined-contribution pensions, an income stream such as Social Security benefits that is contingent on work status can affect retirement when a worker cannot borrow against the future income stream (Crawford and Lilien 1981). The effect will be to reduce retirement in the ages just before eligibility for benefits and increase retirement at the age of first benefit. Hurd and Boskin (1984) found in the RHS that workers with a high ratio of Social Security benefits to private assets had less retirement at age 61 and more retirement at age 62 than workers with a lower ratio. This is mild evidence for a liquidity constraint. Burtless and Moffitt (1986) and Kahn (1988) also find evidence for a liquidity constraint. As far as the Social Security tax is concerned, the system has effects similar to the income tax because earnings are taxed, whereas the Social Security benefits of most beneficiaries are not taxed. I know of no empirically based estimates of these effects.

Over the past fifty years, the Social Security system has provided enough retirement income so that people could retire earlier and earlier. Today the labor force participation rate of men is about 45% at age 63. The structure of the program causes retirement to be concentrated at certain ages. Figure 1.5 has the retirement hazard rates of men and women. The retirement hazard rate is the probability of retirement at each age, given participation at the preceding age.[28] For example, the hazard rate of men at age 62 is about 0.22, indicating that, of those men who reach 62 and are still working, 22% leave the labor force while 62. Particularly for men, the graph has spikes at 62 and 65, which are, of course, important ages in the Social Security system. Retirement rates appear to be slightly depressed at 64, probably because people are waiting until 65 to retire, and at 66, probably because of the large number that retired at 65. Retirement of women is less highly concentrated at 62 and 65 because husbands and wives tend to coordinate their retirement dates: because of the age difference between husbands and wives (about three years on average),

---

28. The hazards in the figure were calculated from the assumption that participation is steady over time: the retention rate at age t is just the labor force participation rate at age t divided by the participation rate at age $t - 1$, and the hazard rate is just one minus the retention rate. Although the hazard rate in the figure is calculated from cross-section CPS data, its shape is similar to what would be found in panel data (Hurd 1990b).

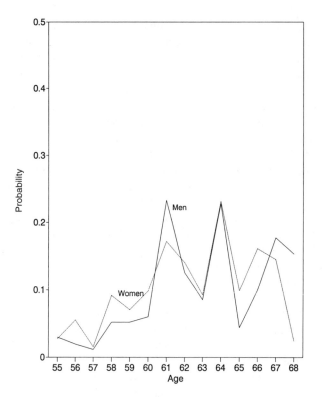

Fig. 1.5   Retirement hazard rates
Source: Author's calculations from 1988 and 1989 Current Population Survey participation rates by single years of age.

more women retire before the age of 62 (Hurd 1990a). If the spikes were smoothed out, the retirement hazards would have an upward trend, which is consistent with the view that gradually changing tastes as the population ages increase the probability of retirement gradually.

In my view the spikes in the retirement hazards are good evidence of the effects of Social Security system on retirement. First, in microdata where we can control for details of any pension plan, retirement spikes at age 62 and 65 are still found (Burkhauser 1979; Stock and Wise 1990a, 1990b). Second, in data from other countries where the important ages for retirement under the public pension system are different from the ages in the United States, we find spikes at those ages. For example, in Germany public pension income is about 95% of total retirement income. Special ages for retirement under the pension system are 60, 63, and 65, and the retirement hazard rate peaks at those ages. The third reason for thinking that Social Security has an important effect on retirement is that there is no other alternative explanation for the fall in participation over time of older workers: most retirees depend on Social Security for most of their income, so it is hard to imagine that they would have retired as early had their Social Security benefits been considerably smaller.

Despite the obvious links between retirement and Social Security, econometric models of retirement based on lifetime utility maximization typically find that variations in Social Security have only small effects on retirement (Burtless and Moffitt 1984, 1985; Fields and Mitchell 1984; Gustman and Steinmeier 1986). Although it is hard to show because of how complicated the models are, I believe the difference primarily comes from observation errors: we do not observe accurately in the data the variables that influence decisions.[29] Due to observation error we see apparent change in explanatory variables, but with no change in behavior, and so we conclude that workers are not responsive to financial incentives, whether they are incentives in the Social Security system or simply the wealth effect of the Social Security program. However, in situations where we have good data on the incentives facing workers, we find that they respond strongly to incentives: for example, in the research on defined-benefit pensions where we have detailed information of the firm's plan, we find strong responses.

Health Care Insurance

Although employer-provided medical insurance may not have been an important determinant of retirement fifteen or twenty years ago, I believe that, because of the rapid growth in the per capita cost of medical care, it must be today. It affects retirement in two broad ways. First, medical insurance provided by an employer is a valuable benefit simply because it is expensive; that is, it is an important component of total compensation. Second, it provides employees access to the firm's risk pool.

A firm's risk pool (its employees) is selected for reasons other than health status, so that the pool should have average health characteristics. This would not be the case if the employees as individuals had to purchase medical insurance privately because fellow purchasers (the risk pool) are self-selected and tend to be at higher than average risk for medical expenses. Therefore, privately purchased health insurance is more expensive than group insurance obtained through an employer. At older ages many workers have medical conditions (preexisting conditions), and should they want to purchase medical insurance they will join the risk pool of everyone with preexisting conditions. Because the risk of high expenses is great for that pool, medical insurance will be more expensive than if the risk pool contains everyone.[30]

This illustrates the difference between ex ante and ex post risk. A group can agree to share future medical expenditures, knowing ex ante that some

---

29. We probably do not observe the structure of the Social Security with much error; I have in mind other aspects of the budget set.

30. Of course, some individuals with preexisting conditions are almost uninsurable.

individuals in the group (but not which ones) will eventually require high medical expenditures. Ex post, after some information is available about which individuals are more likely to require high medical expenditures, the group divides into subgroups along the new risk lines. The individuals in the high-risk group can expect to share higher medical costs than they anticipated ex ante. Under the usual assumption that individuals are risk averse, it is in the interest of everyone ex ante not to allow the formation of ex post risk groups. This, however, is exactly what happens when someone leaves a firm's risk pool with a preexisting condition: he or she moves from an ex ante risk pool to an ex post risk pool and will face higher medical insurance costs in the new pool.

It can be worth a considerable amount to an individual to remain in the ex ante risk pool. This is particularly true if the writers of privately purchased medical insurance have the right to cancel a policy when new health information is revealed. Then, the privately purchased insurance no longer has the aspects of true insurance.

It has been difficult to study quantitatively the effects of medical insurance on retirement because it is hard to control for other influences on retirement. It is even more difficult to control for unobserved heterogeneity arising from variation in risk aversion across individuals and from prior conditions, both of which make the response to the availability of medical insurance differ across individuals.[31] We do see considerable retirement at age 65, which may be partially due to the availability of Medicare at 65: someone with medical insurance on the job but without employer-provided medical insurance to its retirees would probably delay retirement from age 64 to 65 when Medicare is available. Lumsdaine, Stock, and Wise (1994) speculate on such an effect: their model accounts for the financial incentives in pension plans and Social Security, yet it cannot explain the excessive retirement at age 65. The only remaining explanation seems to be the availability of Medicare at age 65. This is an important topic for future research.

Age Discrimination

I have been discussing rigidities caused by legitimate employment practices and financial incentives. A very different kind of rigidity comes from age discrimination. Several examples of past employment practices suggest that age discrimination was widespread at one time, and although age discrimination is now illegal, employers may still desire to discriminate on the basis of age. In the 1970s mandatory retirement was quite common. For example, in the RHS 44% of white males in wage and salary jobs aged 58–61 faced mandatory retirement (Gustman and Steinmeier 1984). Defined-benefit pension plans

---

31. Gustman and Steinmeier (1993) find small effects of health insurance on retirement. In their simulations health insurance is simply a component of compensation, but this does not get at the issues of risk pooling, risk aversion, and prior conditions discussed earlier.

were often structured to encourage retirement at specific ages. In an example from Kotlikoff and Wise (1989) pension accrual after age 65 was negative $18,000, amounting to a reduction in the wage of 21%.

As these examples show, at one time many employers did not want to retain older workers whether full-time or part-time. The extent to which employers today have those views is not known, partly because age discrimination is illegal, so employers are reluctant to admit to age discrimination. It is difficult to believe, however, that the conditions that led some employers to want to discriminate in the past have changed sufficiently so that today no employers want to discriminate.

Generally the cause of an employer's wanting to terminate an employee is that as fully measured the product of the worker is less than the compensation paid to the worker. The widespread use of mandatory retirement and defined-benefit plans to regulate the separation of older workers has led to the conclusion that older workers as a group are overpaid, and has produced a vast literature on why a worker's product can differ from compensation.[32] The literature is mostly theoretical and centers on implicit contracts, the notion that the firm and its workers agree (implicitly) on an employment contract that covers a long period of employment. In this framework it can be in the best interest of both the firm and the worker for the firm to pay less than a worker's product in the early years of employment and more in the late years. But at the age when the worker has been fully paid back (total product during the work life equals total compensation), either employment must be terminated or the contract renegotiated. If termination is chosen, the outcome can look like age discrimination.

The empirical support for implicit contracts as an explanation for apparent age discrimination is rather marginal (Straka 1992). As I discussed above, empirical studies show slowly falling real wage rates on the lifetime job at older ages, but possibly slowly rising total compensation. The productivity studies show approximately constant productivity. However, their generality should be questioned: they are limited to just a few occupations, they do not control for sample selection, and there is general agreement that at least in some jobs (physically demanding jobs) productivity falls with age. We do know that wages fall substantially with job change at older ages, which is consistent with the implicit contract theory, but as I have already discussed there are other more straightforward explanations.

An alternative explanation for apparent age discrimination is based on changes in productivity at the individual level. Older workers tend to have supervisory positions where it is both difficult to monitor their productivity and where a fall in productivity can be very costly to a firm. If a few supervisors have large declines in productivity but they cannot be identified, it may be cost effective for a firm to ask all workers over a certain age to retire even though

32. See Straka (1992) for a review of the arguments and empirical findings.

the productivity of most has not fallen. Regardless of the theoretical explanation, in the past many firms apparently desired to terminate the employment of older workers at some fixed age and used employment practices such as mandatory retirement before they were made illegal. Today when employment practices cannot be based on age alone, a firm could respond to an overpaid older workforce by reducing wages. However, for reasons centered on worker morale, this seems to be difficult and apparently does not happen sufficiently to eliminate overpayment. The firm could continually train its workforce to maintain or increase productivity, but because of a shortened payback period, this becomes infeasible at older ages.

A firm may engage in (illegal) employment practices that are not related to pay and are difficult to observe, such as unfair treatment of older workers in promotions or job assignment. The objective of the firm would be to induce workers to retire at ages similar to the former mandatory retirement age. Needless to say, evidence about the use of such practices is sketchy at best.

According to surveys, the opinion of managers about older workers is generally positive. In a 1982 survey of executives of 363 companies, older workers were seen to be better than younger workers along a number of dimensions (Rhine 1984). They have lower turnover rates, they are more conscientious, and they have better judgment. They were judged, however, to be less flexible than younger workers by a majority of the executives, which suggests they may be at a disadvantage in a rapidly changing work environment. In a 1991 survey of 406 senior human resource managers, older workers were rated better than younger workers in six categories and worse in three (Johnson and Linden 1992). Older workers were generally viewed favorably, and certainly at a minimum as no worse than younger workers.[33] These survey responses give no reason to think that managers would use employment practices to discriminate systematically against older workers.

In a widely cited study by Rosen and Jerdee (1977), however, managers said that they viewed older workers favorably, yet when given specific situations the managers made hypothetical decisions that were unfavorable to older workers. The survey was made at a time when many kinds of age discrimination were not illegal, so it is certainly possible that the managers felt more free to reveal age discrimination than in later surveys. Of course, we have no knowledge of whether these kinds of survey answers carry over into actual business decisions.

Rather small fractions of older workers say they have been subject to age discrimination: only 6% of workers aged 40 or over in a 1985 survey (Secretary of Labor 1989). In the new HRS, 83% of wage and salary workers aged 51–65 disagreed with the statement "In decisions about promotion, my employer gives younger people preference over older people." Eighty-one percent dis-

---

33. See McNaught and Henderson (1990) and Barth, McNaught, and Rizzi (1993) for additional survey findings of a similar nature and a discussion of the literature.

agreed with "My co-workers make older workers feel that they ought to retire before age 65."[34] There was little evidence of a differential response by the age of the worker.

There is some evidence that the inability of older workers to reduce hours is not really the problem: the main problem is that many employers do not want to retain older workers either full-time or part-time. This causes the transition from full-time work to complete retirement that we observe so often. The extent of age discrimination is not known because we have no direct observations. However, management and worker surveys give the impression of only a modest amount. I conclude that for most older workers it is, indeed, the inability to reduce hours without substantial pay loss that causes the transition to complete retirement from full-time work.

1.4   Conclusions

Many rigidities facing the elderly are normal to the workplace and are faced by workers of all ages. Rigidities in the choice of hours seem to be caused in part by fixed costs and the requirements of team production. These lead to regular and long hours for the great majority of workers. Anyone who wants to work shorter hours or odd hours typically will have a lower wage rate because productivity is lower. Therefore, we should expect that if older workers want to retire gradually by decreasing hours of work as they age, their wage rates will fall.

Some occupations and industries, however, seem to have much higher fixed costs and less flexibility than others, and therefore they have little part-time employment. Lifetime workers in those occupations and industries who want to reduce hours will have to change jobs. The loss of specific human capital and the costs of job change will reduce further the financial payoff from work, so many find a change is not financially acceptable and choose to retire instead.

The implications of this analysis are observed in data, which I have interpreted as support for the theory. However, the empirical findings all incorporate sample selection: we observe wages and hours only of those who remain employed. In particular, we do not observe what the wage rates would have been of those who retired. For example, suppose some workers retired because their job opportunities were even worse than those who changed jobs and remained in the labor force; then we would substantially underestimate the difficulties of reducing hours by changing jobs. That this is plausible can be inferred from the difficulties that involuntarily unemployed older workers have in finding a new job: many leave the labor force following a spell of unemployment. This example illustrates a general and serious problem in understanding the labor market behavior of older workers: we have no individual-level data from which we can construct the range of options each worker faces.

---

34. Author's calculations from the HRS.

Older workers face some rigidities that are the result of policy. The delayed retirement credit under Social Security is not actuarially fair; however, it is gradually being increased so that in a few years it should not provide any incentives to retire. The reduction for early retirement is approximately actuarially fair, so, to the extent that workers maximize utility over an extended time horizon, the reduction should not have any incentive effects.

The earnings test seems to have an effect on behavior, but we do not really know why it does. Because of the automatic benefit recalculation, it does not affect the present value of the Social Security benefits of someone aged 62–64, so our models say it should have no effect; naturally, then, the models cannot explain the observed behavior. For this reason we do not know the magnitude of the effect: that is, how many workers would change their labor market behavior were the earnings test to be eliminated. From the point of view of public policy the earnings test is an anachronism: because the earnings test is approximately actuarially fair, the financial impact on government of a suspension of benefits for earnings is approximately zero.[35] I can see no public policy reason for the earnings test.

The obvious effect of the earnings test on behavior points out an area of professional ignorance: many people seem to trade present consumption for future consumption in a way that is different from how they trade present income for future income. That is, people will save at some rate of interest through financial institutions (trade present for future consumption), yet they will not make the same trade in income streams. The Social Security earnings test is a good example. Workers can forgo income at age 62 (the income lost due to the earnings test) for higher income at age 65, and the rate of exchange is about the same as the rate of interest adjusted for mortality. Consumption need not be affected if the person has assets, because spending assets can make the consumption paths from the two income streams the same. Therefore, if people would work without the earnings test, they should work with the earnings test, yet apparently a considerable number do not. This is an area for research that would be of interest to advance our knowledge of human behavior both in the abstract and for policy purposes. It is particularly relevant because of the growth in defined-contribution pension plans: they may affect retirement in a way similar to the earnings test.

Defined-benefit pension plans have important incentives for some, but we do not know the importance in the population because of data limitations. That is, we cannot find the quantitative effects in the population of pensions on retirement by extending our solid empirical results, which are based on individual firm pension plans. Furthermore, because our panel data sets have not

---

35. Because the delayed retirement credit is less than actuarially fair after age 65, eliminating the earnings test would cost the Social Security system money. The amount is probably small, however: my rough estimate based on the work patterns of 65–69-year-olds reported in Leonesio (1990) is that the loss is about 5% of the benefits of the group when the delayed retirement credit is 4%. The revenue loss will gradually disappear as the credit becomes fair by the year 2009.

had detailed information on both pensions and Social Security earnings, we know little about how defined-benefit pensions interact with Social Security to affect retirement decisions. I expect that with the availability of the HRS over the next decade we will learn a great deal more about the effects in the population.

The rigidities induced by employer-provided health insurance are, I believe, large, but I have seen no research to support this view. Older research typically finds effects on costs of employment that, while large in percentage terms, are small in absolute terms (Zedlewski 1991). Consequently, the employment effects of changes such as making employer-provided health insurance the primary payer for workers aged 65–69 (Tax Equity and Fiscal Responsibility Act) are small (Anderson, Kennell, and Sheils 1987). This kind of research is probably outdated because of the sharply rising costs and the accompanying increased awareness of health care costs. Similarly, eligibility for Medicare surely has much greater effects on retirement decisions than a decade ago: at one time someone would retire before age 65 and self-insure or purchase health care insurance until age 65. Because of the costs and risk this is becoming infeasible.

Defined-benefit pension plans are not portable, but I believe it is unreasonable to make them portable as they are now structured. Consider the risk faced by the first employer. A former employee who has a sharply rising wage path with another firm will end up with a large pension. Because of the heavy backloading of many plans this will not be expected by the first firm, yet the first firm will have to pay a fraction of the pension.[36] Furthermore, the first employer has no control over the earnings path of the former employee, which introduces an element of unfairness.

Indexing defined-benefit plans until the age of retirement would certainly reduce rigidities by removing inflation risk. This could be accomplished rather easily if the government issued indexed bonds. Then the employer could diversify the inflation risk by purchasing indexed bonds whose return matched the firm's flow of future real pension benefits.

I have discussed many factors that prevent labor market flexibility, but little evidence on their quantitative importance. This is because the complexity of the labor market and data limitations have restricted solid quantitative research that can be confidently used to infer quantitative effects. Nonetheless, I believe that many of the factors probably have substantial effects on a minority of workers and, therefore, could be changed to increase flexibility, yet in the aggregate they have rather small overall effects on hours reduction, which has been the main focus of this paper. I would put in this category the Social Secu-

36. Furthermore, if the first employer has to pay only what was accrued until the time of separation, the plan no longer has real portability: the employee with a long earnings history becomes a costly new hire, which will interfere with the normal process of job mobility.

rity earnings test and pension plans. I would also include health care insurance, but with much less confidence because our knowledge of its effects on job mobility is scanty.

I believe that the important factors restricting the ability of most workers to reduce hours are, first, fixed employment costs and production requirements that encourage or require full-time work and, second, the costs of changing jobs late in the work life. While the costs and productivity losses associated with job change might be reduced, they are probably unavoidable. This leads to the conclusion that the best opportunity for hours reduction by older workers is with the career employer, not with a job change. There is an extensive literature on how the workplace could be made more hospitable for older workers. It mentions factors such as continuous training, job redefinition, and so forth. I have no knowledge of the practicality of implementing these proposals.

It should be apparent, however, that regardless of any workplace changes there are some genuine difficulties associated with hours reduction on the main job. A prominent difficulty is the provision for medical insurance. Older workers need medical insurance, yet it is a large fixed cost for employers. A possible solution is to make the benefit a variable cost to the employer: that is, the employer would pay a fraction of the cost, which would depend on hours of work. The great advantage of this arrangement is that the worker could stay with the firm, remaining part of the risk pool; people would not be penalized for preexisting conditions, so risk sharing would be ex ante. The disadvantage comes from the fact that total costs of medical coverage remain the same, just the division changes. Medical insurance costs would become variable costs (varying with hours of work) for both employer and employee, whereas in the main they have been fixed costs to both. Fixed costs give an incentive to the firm to increase hours and an incentive to the worker to reduce hours. These incentives would be eliminated, but unless the wage rate rose to compensate, the worker would face increased costs. There are, of course, tax advantages to having employer-provided medical insurance, but this could be handled with legislation about the tax treatment of the part paid by the employee. Similar considerations apply to converting other fixed costs to variable costs.

As evidenced by the lack of flextime in the United States, team production and the attendant requirement for full-time work appear to be major impediments to a gradual reduction in hours on the career job. But the U.S. experience is not universal: in Germany and Switzerland from 30 to 40% of the workforce is on flextime (Swart 1978; Ronen 1981). As many as 30% of production workers in Germany may be on flextime (Young 1982). Could these practices be transferred to the United States? There are differences in supervisors' and workers' attitudes toward work that seem to make flextime more successful in Germany (Young 1982). At the same time, there are many similarities between German and American firms, so there seem to be no absolute barriers to increased flextime in the United States. If flextime can be accommodated in the

Table 1.11   Weekly Hours and Probabilities of Working Past 62 or 65 among Those Who Cannot Reduce Hours

	Percentage	Weekly Hours	Probability of Working Full-Time after Age 62	Probability of Working Full-Time after Age 65
Yes (would like to)	15	42.9	0.36	0.15
		(0.5)	(.02)	(.02)
No (would not like to)	85	41.2	0.48	0.23
		(0.1)	(.01)	(.01)

Source: Author's calculations, based on Health and Retirement Survey.

Note: Sample is 1,292 full-time wage workers. Standard errors are in parentheses.

United States, part-time work can be accommodated, provided fixed costs can be controlled.

There are few solid empirical findings that directly link rigidities to retirement beyond the suggestive data I discussed at the beginning of this paper. However, some new findings based on the HRS indicate that rigidities may have an important effect in inducing retirement. Wage workers aged 51–61 were asked if they could reduce hours on their present job. Those who said they could not reduce were asked further if they would like to reduce hours even if their earnings were reduced in the same proportion. All wage workers were also asked the probability they would be working full-time after age 62 and after age 65. Table 1.11 gives the distribution of responses, weekly hours, and the probabilities of working after 62 or 65 among those who cannot reduce hours.

Those who would like to reduce hours, but are not allowed to on their present job, expect a labor force participation rate at age 62 that is about 75% of the participation rate of those who do not want to reduce hours, and at age 65 a rate that is about two-thirds. The differences are statistically significant.

The difference can be put in perspective as follows: In 1989 the participation rate at age 65 was 25%. Under the assumption that this rate will not change over time, the results in the table imply that those who desire to reduce hours will have a participation rate of about 16%, or a difference in participation rates of 9%. This is a larger difference than the estimated effects on retirement of rather large changes in the Social Security system. For example, according to the econometric model of Gustman and Steinmeier (1985), increasing the delayed retirement credit from 3% to 8% (the 1983 law change) would increase participation at age 65 by about 4%.

In this sample the fraction that wants to reduce hours is small (15%), but I would expect it to increase with age. If these results hold up when we observe actual retirement in the panel of HRS, they will provide convincing evidence on the effects of rigidities on retirement behavior.

References

Advisory Council on Social Security. 1991. *Income Security and Health Care: Economic Implications, 1991–2020.* Washington, DC: Government Printing Office.

Allen, Steven, Robert H. Clark, and Daniel Sumner. 1986. Postretirement Adjustments of Pension Benefits. *Journal of Human Resources* 21 (1): 118–37.

Anderson, Joseph, David Kennell, and John Sheils. 1987. Health Plan Costs, Medicare, and Employment of Older Workers. In *The Problem Isn't Age,* ed. Steven H. Sandell, 206–17. New York: Praeger.

Barth, Michael C., William McNaught, and Philip Rizzi. 1993. Corporations and the Aging Workforce. In *Building a Competitive Workforce: Investing in Human Capital for Corporate Success,* ed. Philip Mirvis. New York: John Wiley and Sons.

Berkovec, James, and Steven Stern. 1991. Job Exit Behavior of Older Men. *Econometrica* 59 (1): 189–210.

Blau, David. 1994. Labor Force Dynamics of Older Men. *Econometrica* 62 (1): 117–56.

Blinder, Alan S., Roger H. Gordon, and Donald E. Wise. 1983. Social Security, Bequests, and the Life Cycle Theory of Saving: Cross-Sectional Tests. In *The Determinants of National Saving and Wealth,* ed. Franco Modigliani and Richard Heming, 89–122. New York: St. Martin's Press.

Burkhauser, Richard V. 1979. The Pension Acceptance Decision of Older Workers. *Journal of Human Resources* 14 (1): 63–75.

Burtless, Gary, and Robert A. Moffitt. 1984. The Effect of Social Security Benefits on the Labor Supply of the Aged. In *Retirement and Economic Behavior,* ed. Henry J. Aaron and Gary Burtless, 135–71. Washington, DC: Brookings Institution.

———. 1985. The Joint Choice of Retirement Age and Postretirement Hours of Work. *Journal of Labor Economics* 3 (2): 209–36.

———. 1986. Social Security, Earnings Tests, and Age at Retirement. *Public Finance* 14 (1): 3–27.

Clark, Robert L., Stephan F. Gohmann, and Daniel A. Sumner. 1982. Wages and Hours of Work of Elderly Men. Department of Economics and Business, University of North Carolina State. Typescript.

Cogan, John. 1981. Fixed Costs and Labor Supply. *Econometrica* 49 (4): 945–63.

Crawford, Vincent, and David Lilien. 1981. Social Security and the Retirement Decision. *Quarterly Journal of Economics* 96 (August): 509–29.

Fields, Gary S., and Olivia S. Mitchell. 1984. *Retirement, Pensions, and Social Security.* Cambridge: MIT Press.

Fuchs, Victor R. 1982. Self-Employment and Labor Force Participation of Older Males. *Journal of Human Resources* 17 (3): 339–57.

Grad, Susan. 1990. *Income of the Population 55 or Older, 1988.* Washington, DC: U.S. Department of Health and Human Services, Social Security Administration.

Gustman, Alan L., and Thomas L. Steinmeier. 1984. Partial Retirement and the Analysis of Retirement Behavior. *Industrial and Labor Relations Review* 37 (3): 403–15.

———. 1985. The Effect of Partial Retirement on the Wage Profiles of Older Workers. *Industrial Relations* 24 (2): 257–65.

———. 1986. A Structural Retirement Model. *Econometrica* 54 (3): 555–84.

———. 1993. Pension Portability and Labor Mobility: Evidence from the Survey of Income and Program Participation. *Journal of Public Economics* 50: 299–325.

Henderson, J. Vernon. 1981. The Economics of Staggered Hours. *Journal of Urban Economics* 9: 349–64.

Hogarth, Terence, and Michael C. Barth. 1991. Costs and Benefits of Hiring Older Workers: A Case Study of B&Q. *International Journal of Manpower* 12 (8): 5–17.

Hurd, Michael D. 1990a. The Joint Retirement Decision of Husbands and Wives. In

Issues in the Economics of Aging, ed. David A. Wise, 231–54. Chicago: University of Chicago Press.

———. 1990b. Research on the Elderly: Economic Status, Retirement, and Consumption and Saving. *Journal of Economic Literature* 28 (June): 565–637.

Hurd, Michael D., and Michael J. Boskin. 1984. The Effect of Social Security on Retirement in the Early 1970s. *Quarterly Journal of Economics* 99 (November): 767–90.

Hutchens, Robert M. 1988. Do Job Opportunities Decline with Age? *Industrial and Labor Relations Review* 42 (1): 89–99.

Iams, Howard. 1987. Jobs of Persons Working after Receiving Retired-Worker Benefits. *Social Security Bulletin* 50 (11): 4–18.

Jablonski, Mary, Kent Kunze, and Larry Rosenblum. 1990. Productivity, Age, and Labor Composition Changes in the U.S. Work Force. In *The Aging of the American Work Force,* ed. Irving Bluestone, Rhonda Montgomery, and John D. Owen. Detroit: Wayne State University Press.

Johnson, Arlene, and Fabian Linden. 1992. Availability of a Quality Work Force. Conference Board, New York. Pamphlet.

Jondrow, Jim, Frank Brechling, and Alan Marcus. 1987. Older Workers in the Market for Part-Time Employment. In *The Problem Isn't Age,* ed. Steven H. Sandell, 84–99. New York: Praeger.

Kahn, James. 1988. Social Security, Liquidity, and Early Retirement. *Journal of Public Economics* 35: 97–117.

Kotlikoff, Laurence J., and David A. Wise. 1987. The Incentive Effects of Private Pension Plans. In *Issues in Pension Economics,* ed. Zvi Bodie, John B. Shoven, and David A. Wise, 283–336. Chicago: University of Chicago Press.

———. 1989. Employee Retirement and a Firm's Pension Plan. In *The Economics of Aging,* ed. David A. Wise, 279–330. Chicago: University of Chicago Press.

Leonesio, Michael. 1990. Effects of the Social Security Earnings Test on the Labor-Market Activity of Older Americans: A Review of the Evidence. *Social Security Bulletin* 53 (5): 2–21.

Lumsdaine, Robin L., James H. Stock, and David A. Wise. 1994. Pension Plan Provisions and Retirement: Men and Women, Medicare, and Models. In *Studies in the Economics of Aging,* ed. David A. Wise, 183–212. Chicago: University of Chicago Press.

McNaught, William, and Michael C. Barth. 1992. Are Older Workers "Good Buys"? A Case Study of Days Inns of America. *Sloan Management Review* 33 (3): 53–63.

McNaught, William, and Peter Henderson. 1990. Working with Business to Improve Employment Opportunities for Older Americans: A Literature Review. Commonwealth Fund Americans over 55 at Work Program, Background Paper no. 2. New York.

Madrian, Brigitte. 1994. Employment-Based Health Insurance and Job Mobility: Is There Evidence of Job-Lock? *Quarterly Journal of Economics* 109(1): 27–54.

Mellor, Earl F. 1986. Shift Work and Flexitime: How Prevalent Are They? *Monthly Labor Review* 109 (November): 14–21.

Mitchell, Olivia S. 1983. Fringe Benefits and the Cost of Changing Jobs. *Industrial and Labor Relations Review* 37 (1): 70–78.

Morse, Dean, Anna B. Dutka, and Susan Gray. 1983. *Life after Early Retirement: The Experience of Lower-Level Workers.* Totowa, NJ: Rowman and Allanheld.

Nollen, Stanley, and Virginia H. Martin. 1978. *Alternative Work Schedules: Part 1: Flexitime.* New York: AMACOM.

Owen, John D. 1976. Workweeks and Leisure: Analysis of Trends, 1948–1975. *Monthly Labor Review* 99 (8): 3–8.

Parnes, Herbert S., and Gilbert Nestel. 1981. The Retirement Experience. In *Work and Retirement,* ed. Herbert S. Parnes, 155–97. Cambridge: MIT Press.

Paul, Carolyn. 1983a. Company Productivity and Worker Age. Andrus Gerontology Center, University of Southern California. Typescript.

———. 1983b. Employee Benefit Costs for Workers at Older Ages: Implications for Management. Andrus Gerontology Center, University of Southern California. Typescript.

———. 1984. *Age and Health Care Costs: A Technical Report.* Washington, DC: U.S. Department of Health and Human Services.

———. 1987. Work Alternatives for Older Americans: A Management Perspective. In *The Problem Isn't Age,* ed. Steven H. Sandell, 165–76. New York: Praeger.

Quinn, Joseph. 1980. Labor Force Participation Patterns of Older Self-Employed Workers. *Social Security Bulletin* 43 (4): 17–28.

Quinn, Joseph, and Richard Burkhauser. 1990. Retirement Preferences and Plans of Older American Workers. Commonwealth Fund Americans over 55 at Work Program, Background Paper no. 4. New York.

Quinn, Joseph, Richard Burkhauser, and Daniel Myers. 1990. *Passing the Torch: The Influence of Economic Incentives on Work and Retirement.* Kalamazoo, MI: Upjohn Institute.

Repko, David V. 1987. *Government Mandating of Employee Benefits.* Washington, DC: Employee Benefit Research Institution.

Rhine, Shirley. 1984. *Managing Older Workers: Company Policies and Attitudes.* New York: Conference Board.

Ronen, Simcha. 1981. *Flexible Working Hours: An Innovation in the Quality of Work Life.* New York: McGraw-Hill.

———. 1984. *Alternative Work Schedules.* Homewood, IL: Dow Jones–Irwin.

Rosen, Benson, and Thomas Jerdee. 1977. Too Old or Not Too Old. *Harvard Business Review* 55: 97–106.

Rosen, Harvey S. 1976. Taxes in a Labor-Supply Model with Joint Wage-Hours Determination. *Econometrica* 44 (3): 485–507.

Ruhm, Christopher. 1989. Why Older Americans Stop Working. *Gerontologist* 29 (3): 294–99.

———. 1990a. Bridge Jobs and Partial Retirement. *Journal of Labor Economics* 8 (4): 482–501.

———. 1990b. Career Jobs, Bridge Employment, and Retirement. In *Bridges to Retirement,* ed. Peter B. Doeringer, 92–107. Ithaca: ILR Press.

Rust, John P. 1990. Behavior of Male Workers at the End of the Life Cycle: An Empirical Analysis of States and Controls. In *Issues in the Economics of Aging,* ed. David A. Wise, 317–78. Chicago: University of Chicago Press.

Secretary of Labor. 1989. Labor Market Problems of Older Workers. Washington, DC: U.S. Department of Labor.

Stock, James H., and David A. Wise. 1990a. The Pension Inducement to Retire: An Option Value Analysis. In *Issues in the Economics of Aging,* ed. David A. Wise, 205–24. Chicago: University of Chicago Press.

———. 1990b. Pensions, the Option Value of Work, and Retirement. *Econometrica* 58 (5): 1151–80.

Straka, John W. 1992. *The Demand for Older Workers: The Neglected Side of a Labor Market.* Washington, DC: Office of Research and Statistics, Social Security Administration.

Sum, Andrew, and W. Neal Fogg. 1990. Profile of the Labor Market for Older Workers. In *Bridges to Retirement,* ed. Peter B. Doeringer, 33–63. Ithaca: ILR Press.

Swart, J. Carroll. 1978. *A Flexible Approach to Working Hours.* New York: AMACOM.

Turner, John A., and Daniel J. Beller. 1992. *Trends in Pensions, 1992.* Washington, DC: Government Printing Office.

U.S. Senate. Special Committee on Aging. 1984. *The Costs of Employing Older Workers.* Washington, DC: Government Printing Office.

Wilson, Paul. 1988. Wage Variation Resulting from Staggered Work Hours. *Journal of Urban Economics* 24: 9–26.

Young, William McEwan. 1982. Flexitime for Production Workers in Britain and Germany. In *New Work Schedules in Practice: Managing Time in a Changing Society,* ed. Stanley D. Nollen, 33–53. New York: Van Nostrand Reinhold.

Zedlewski, Sheila. 1991. *Expanding the Employer-Provided Health Insurance System: Effects on Workers and Their Employers.* Washington, DC: Urban Institute.

Comment   Angus S. Deaton

It is a pleasure to read this paper; it is a thoughtful and interesting essay that addresses a range of issues about older workers in the labor market. As Hurd emphasizes, it does not attempt to make policy recommendations. The aim is rather to survey the literature and to identify a research agenda for the future, something that is especially appropriate as we look forward to the data from the new Health and Retirement Survey.

Like all good papers in economics, this one is about supply and demand. It looks at various aspects of labor market behavior of older workers, trying to identify features that are due to supply, features that are due to demand, and features that come from workers being forced off their supply curves, or at least that interfere with the smooth equation of supply and demand. As is often the case, identification can be controversial, and while it is sometimes easy to agree with Hurd's identification of what is going on, his discussion is a good deal more convincing on some points than on others. This is nowhere more so than when we are discussing rationing, or quantity restrictions. Literature from a decade or so ago, associated particularly with papers by Orley Ashenfelter and John Ham, tried to detect cases where workers were forced off their labor supply curves, and forced to accept wage and hours combinations where, given a free choice, they would have either increased or decreased hours at their current wage. While that literature is technically quite sophisticated, working out all the consequences of quantity rationing, it was perhaps not ultimately persuasive. Partly, the economics profession likes to believe in markets, and is resistant to interpretations in which markets do not work properly, but it was also the case that models of rationing, while offering good explanations of the spillover effects from one market to another, did not by themselves offer a

Angus S. Deaton is the William Church Osborn Professor of Public Affairs and professor of economics and international affairs at Princeton University and a research associate of the National Bureau of Economic Research.

better explanation of hours than that offered by the standard model of labor supply. While it is true that many—perhaps even most—workers report that they work fifty forty-hour weeks each year, there is still a great deal of variation in weeks and hours, variation that is difficult to explain unless a large fraction of workers are free to choose how much they work. There are presumably also a lot of workers who want to work fifty forty-hour weeks, so that it was (and is) far from clear that the labor supply story is beaten out by one in which employers determine hours, and workers take what they can get. As always, it is remarkably difficult to identify a demand-side phenomenon that could not be a supply-side phenomenon, and vice versa. This paper suffers from at least some of these problems of the earlier literature.

Before I turn to specific areas of agreement and disagreement, I should like to make two general points about the interpretation of the evidence. First, when we look at how wage patterns, participation rates, and hours vary with age, especially among older workers, it is important to make sure that cohort effects are properly controlled for. At several points in the paper, evidence is cited—for example, on the mild decline in wages among older workers—that is clearly cross-section evidence, where we have no way of knowing whether the decline comes from a real decline in wages with age, or whether what we are seeing is that older workers have lower lifetime wage profiles. The second point is that wage profiles should not be too readily associated with life-cycle variations in productivity. We know from the various theories of wage contracts that firms may tailor income profiles so as to match workers' desired consumption profiles, or there may be incentive reasons to have systematic differences between wages and productivity. Even in academia, where, contrary to what happens in most industries, there is a genuine negative return to years of service, common experience suggests that older workers—senior tenured professors—are paid a great deal more than their marginal product, while junior workers—junior assistant professors—are paid a great deal less. One can think of many reasons for this, and it might not even be true, but it is certainly hard to rule out the possibility that wages and productivity follow different lifetime profiles.

Suppose, however, that we accept the evidence. To what extent can we accept Hurd's interpretation of it, that older workers face a number of rigidities that importantly constrain their choice of jobs? Let me start with some parts of the story that I find less than convincing. The first is the assumption that what workers would like as they grow older is to reduce their hours gradually, so that when we see people switching from full-time to no-time, we are seeing something that comes from the demand side. While this story is certainly possible, I can also think of lots of reasons, particularly health-related, why a major change in hours could come from the supply side. Many people like to work as long as they can, continuing the work and living habits of a lifetime until some event, usually a health-related event, leaves them either unable or unwilling to continue as before. In this situation, we would observe immediate withdrawals from the labor force that have nothing to do with the demand for workers.

The second story that I am less than convinced by is the teamwork explanation. While it is true that it is hard to run an assembly line without all the workers in place, the workers don't have to be the same workers all the time, and substitution of one person for another can allow as much flextime as people want. One example is supermarket checkouts, which have to be manned when the store is open, but where workers are close to perfect substitutes and where part-time and flextime is common. In cases where there is more human capital, and job-specific human capital, people are likely to be less easily substitutable for one another, and it would be interesting to inquire as to whether retirement patterns can be linked to relevant observable characteristics of the job. Even in those cases where teamwork is important, it is hard to be sure that the phenomenon is only on the demand side. Many people like to spend their leisure time with their spouse, or to play team sports, or to go to the theater, and all these activities are timed to make it easy for people who work standard hours.

It is much easier to agree with Hurd's analysis of the role played by fixed costs, and with the difficulties that they present for those who do not wish to work full-time. Indeed, I have come to think that work-related costs are important for a number of issues in the economics of aging. In recent work on the Family Expenditure Survey in Britain, Richard Blundell and his coworkers have shown that much of the sharp drop in consumption at the time of retirement is associated with the elimination of work-related costs. In the United States, the Consumer Expenditure Survey data on the consumption patterns of one- and two-earner families also suggest that a large share of consumption is associated with these costs, in clothing, in transportation, and in meals away from home.

My final point is in the nature of a quibble, but it ties in with an issue that arises in a number of the papers in this volume. In examining the effects of the Social Security benefits test, Hurd finds that people do not behave as they ought to, given that the benefits test is essentially forced saving. He points out that, since the test does not change the net present value of lifetime earnings, life-cycle theory predicts there should be no change in behavior. But of course, this is only life-cycle theory for agents with quadratic, certainty-equivalence preferences. When there is uncertainty, and when there are precautionary motives in saving, money today is worth more than an actuarially fair amount tomorrow, which is in the direction of the results that are reported. Of course, one may also suspect that there is something else going on, perhaps behavioral considerations, or more simply, as Hurd himself suggests, that people do not understand how the test works.

2   Why Are Retirement Rates So High at Age 65?

Robin L. Lumsdaine, James H. Stock, and David A. Wise

Age 65 is no longer the typical retirement age. Most employees now retire before 65, and those who are covered by defined-benefit pension plans often retire well before 65. Nonetheless, a large fraction of persons who are still working at 64 retire at 65. For example, at one of the large Fortune 500 firms that are studied in this paper (Firm 3), 48% of men working at 64 retire at 65. In contrast, only 21% of men who work through age 63 retire at 64. Women at this firm show a similar increase in retirement rates, from 18% at age 64 to 41% at age 65. Similar jumps in retirement rates at age 65 are found at other individual firms and more generally in nationwide measures of labor force participation. In each of the six data sets discussed in this paper, the highest retirement rate occurs at age 65.

In a series of earlier papers, Stock and Wise (1990a, 1990b) and Lumsdaine, Stock, and Wise (1990, 1991, 1992, 1994) developed "option value" and stochastic dynamic programming models of retirement. These models have been estimated on several firm data sets. A striking feature of the estimates is the extent to which they track actual retirement patterns that often exhibit sharp jumps in retirement rates at specific ages. Indeed, the models predict very well the retirement rates under special unanticipated "window" plans designed to encourage early retirement. Although in general these models fit most spikes in the data surprisingly well, in particular at ages 55, 60, and 62, they invariably

Robin L. Lumsdaine is assistant professor of economics at Princeton University and a faculty research fellow of the National Bureau of Economic Research. James H. Stock is professor of political economy at the John F. Kennedy School of Government, Harvard University, and a research associate of the National Bureau of Economic Research. David A. Wise is the John F. Stambaugh Professor of Political Economy at the John F. Kennedy School of Government, Harvard University, and the director for Health and Retirement Programs at the National Bureau of Economic Research.

Financial support was provided by the National Institute on Aging. The authors are grateful to Brigitte Madrian for providing some of the data.

underpredict the age-65 retirement rates of persons who do not retire before that age. In earlier papers we attributed the mismatch between predicted and actual rates to an "age-65 retirement effect," having in mind the influence of custom or accepted practice. This paper considers other commonly proposed explanations for the underprediction of age-65 retirement. It is difficult to directly demonstrate the influence of custom and the like. The spirit of the paper is to rule out other explanations and thus, by implication, to leave the age-65 retirement effect as the remaining possibility. The results suggest that such an effect is the only plausible explanation that cannot be rejected. In particular we conclude that the availability of Medicare at 65 does not explain the age-65 retirement jump.

The age-65 spike is in large part unexplained by our economic models of retirement, and to our knowledge is rarely explained by other models that do not force, by age-specific variables or by other means, a "fit" to the age-65 rate. Exceptions include Gustman and Steinmeier (1986, 1994) and Phelan and Rust (1993), as discussed below. There are a number of economic reasons why individuals might choose to retire at age 65. Social Security treats age 65 as the normal retirement age, and after age 65 the rate of increase in benefits is less than actuarially fair. Kotlikoff and Smith (1983) estimate that 90% of firm pension plans also treat 65 as the normal retirement age, and under many defined-benefit plans there is a strong implicit financial penalty to working past the normal retirement age, as shown by Kotlikoff and Wise (1988), for example. However, measured in terms of expected lifetime benefits, the economic incentive to retire at 65, instead of 64 or 66, for example, is not large enough to explain the age-65 rate. In particular, although our economic models of retirement—which incorporate the financial incentives implicit in the detailed provisions of firm pension plans and Social Security provisions—predict high retirement rates at age 65, these predicted rates typically fall far short of the actual age-65 rates.

In addition, Medicare eligibility begins at age 65. Thus a person not covered by employer-provided retiree health insurance has an incentive to remain in the firm until age 65 to avoid a lapse in medical insurance coverage.

The unexplained age-65 spike is important because it limits our ability to predict the effect of potential policy changes, like the planned increase in the Social Security normal retirement age from age 65 to age 67. Would there then be a spike at 67, or would it remain at 65?

We seek to quantify the age-65 retirement puzzle and to explore potential explanations for it. These include in particular the potential gap in health insurance coverage between retirement and the Medicare eligibility age. We also consider whether family status affects age-65 retirement. And we explore the possibility that our previous results were importantly affected by small samples of older workers. Because so many employees retire early, the number still employed at 65 is typically small.

None of these possibilities explains the age-65 spike, lending indirect support to the "age-65 retirement effect" explanation. To support the plausibility of an age-65 effect, we also consider the possibility that for some employees the utility cost to electing to retire at this "customary" retirement age is small. We conclude that the economic cost is indeed small for some, although for most employees it is quite large. For most employees, choosing to retire at age 65 would impose noticeable economic cost. However, for some it might not be very costly to retire at the "customary" age of 65. To the extent that this is true, the customary effect might not persist in the face of new financial disincentives for age-65 retirement.

2.1   Age-65 Retirement Rates

We review additional evidence in the literature on age-65 retirement effects. In addition, we document the spike in retirement rates at age 65 in six separate data sources, three reflecting the experience of individual firms and three based on nationally representative surveys. As emphasized above, however, it is not solely the jump in retirement rates at 65 that motivates this paper, but rather that the jump is not explained by financial considerations incorporated in formal models.

2.1.1   Previous Literature

Many previous studies have found evidence of an age-65 retirement spike. However, few have successfully fit this spike without explicitly incorporating age or age dummies as explanatory variables. Gustman and Steinmeier (1986) were successful in fitting both the age-62 and age-65 retirement spikes in data from the Retirement History Survey (RHS). However, they modeled the trade-off between labor and leisure as a smoothly increasing function of age and, importantly, did not have detailed firm pension data; thus the Social Security normal and early retirement ages were allowed to play important roles in determining the profile of retirement benefits.

Also using the RHS, Phelan and Rust (1991) calculated a frequency distribution of retirement ages. They considered six different definitions of retirement, including the year that a person first worked less than full-time, the age of first receipt of Old Age, Survivors, and Disability Insurance (OASDI), and a self-reported retirement date. Although the retirement frequency distributions differ for the different definitions, all exhibit a spike at age 65. A spike in the frequency distribution of retirement at 65, while not the same as a spike in the departure rate at that age, implies a spike in the age-65 hazard rate as well. In a subsequent study (1993) Phelan and Rust consider retirement rates of individuals with and without employer-related health insurance and find that the age-65 spike is more pronounced for individuals with health insurance.

Blau (1994) too uses the RHS in his study of labor force dynamics. Using quarterly data, he finds that a substantial fraction of individuals retire in the first quarter after their 65th birthday. He provides simulations of the sensitivity

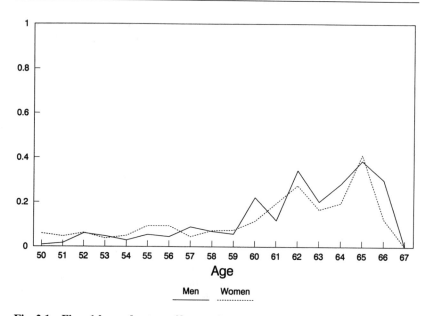

Fig. 2.1   Firm 1 hazard rates: office workers

of the age-65 retirement spike to an individual's level of Social Security benefit. Geweke, Zarkin, and Slonim (1993) also document evidence of a large
spike in the probability of application for Social Security benefits in the first
quarter after an individual's 65th birthday.

2.1.2   Firm-Specific Data Sets

The first three data sets are from employment records of three firms, here
referred to as Firm 1, Firm 2, and Firm 3. For each firm we have data on past
wages, years of service, and the details of the firm's pension plan. Depending
on the firm, we also have information on occupation and some additional individual attributes. Departure rates for selected groups of employees in each of
these firms are plotted in figures 2.1, 2.2, and 2.3, respectively. Although the
details of each firm's pension plan differ, their overall characteristics are similar. The early retirement age is 55 and the normal retirement age 65 in each of
the firms. The departure rates have generally similar shapes.

Firm 1 departure rates pertain to office workers and are shown by gender.
There were 1,354 men and 2,497 women aged 50 and over in 1981.[1] Firm 3
departure rates pertain to all firm employees and are also shown by gender,
with 10,221 men and 2,889 women aged 50 and over in 1982.[2] Only 718 obser-

---

1. Departure rates for salesmen in Firm 1 were analyzed by Stock and Wise (1990a, 1990b). In
this firm the date of retirement is inferred from the year in which the employee ceased to receive
a paycheck from the firm.
2. In this firm, retirement is determined by the retirement date recorded in the data set.

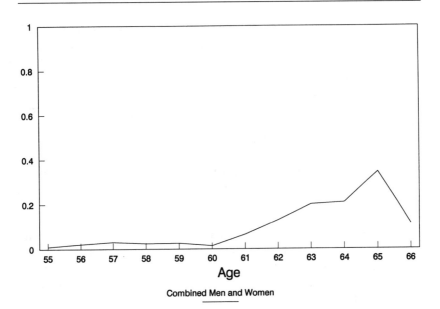

Fig. 2.2   Firm 2 hazard rates

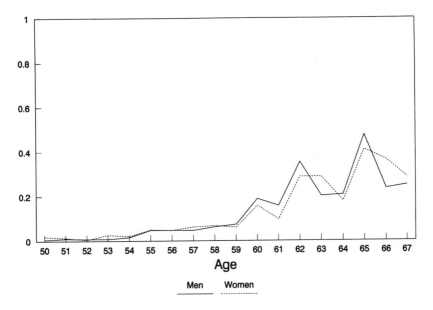

Fig. 2.3   Firm 3 hazard rates

vations of men and women 55 and over in 1979 are available for Firm 2, and the departure rates are shown for men and women combined. All three firms are large Fortune 500 companies with defined-benefit pension plans.[3]

Departure rates in Firms 1 and 3 show spikes at 65.[4] For example, at Firm 1 the retirement rate for 64-year-old men is 28%, while for 65-year-old men it is 39%. For women at Firm 1, the retirement rates at ages 64 and 65 are respectively 20% and 41%. The pattern is similar in Firm 3: the age-64 retirement rate is 21% for men and 18% for women, and rises to 48% for men and 41% for women at age 65.[5] The evidence for Firm 2 is less pronounced, although there is a noticeable spike at 65 and the general pattern of departure rates in Firm 2 is similar to the pattern in Firms 1 and 3.

2.1.3   Cross-Firm Data Sets

The high age-65 retirement rates could be typical in large firms with defined-benefit plans but not representative of the broader population of firms and workers. Evidence from three additional surveys with data on workers from many different firms, however, reveals a similar pattern in the broader population.[6] The first survey is the 1987 National Medical Expenditure Survey (NMES), a survey of approximately fourteen thousand households. The NMES respondents were asked their date of retirement. The departure rates reported here are for respondents who were at least 70 years old and retired.

The second and third data sets have been constructed from different waves (quarterly interviews) of the Survey of Income and Program Participation (SIPP): the 1984 wave with the "Education and Work History" supplemental questions (SIPP-EWH) and the 1984, 1985, and 1986 waves with the "Characteristics of Job from Which Retired" supplemental questions (SIPP-CJR). The retirement definition used in the SIPP-CJR is the date at which an individual left the firm that was providing pension benefits. In the SIPP-EWH, the retirement date is the last date worked. Hazard rates, like those based on the NMES

3. These data have been collected as part of the National Bureau of Economic Research project on the economics of aging. The data for each firm and its pension plan have been discussed in detail elsewhere, and we will not repeat the discussion here. For a discussion of the data for Firm 1 and its pension plan, see Stock and Wise (1990b). The Firm 2 data and its pension plan are discussed in Lumsdaine, Mutschler, and Wise (1992). The Firm 3 data and its pension plan are discussed in Lumsdaine, Stock, and Wise (1994).

4. For Firm 1 there are also noticeable spikes at 62 and 60, corresponding respectively to the Social Security early retirement age and to special provisions of the pension plan.

5. The data for Firms 2 and 3 have exact dates of retirement and birth, while the data for Firm 1 contain only the year of retirement and birth. This introduces some measurement error into the Firm 1 hazard rates, which is not present in the Firms 2 and 3 hazard rates. For Firm 1 the ages are computed to be the age of the individual on January 1; thus some retirements that in fact occur at age 65 (retirements by workers who began the year at 64 and retired that year but after their 65th birthday) are miscounted as age-64 retirements.

6. We are grateful to Brigitte Madrian for graciously providing us with these data, specifically the number of retirees by age for each of the three data sets, broken down by whether or not they have employer-provided retiree health insurance.

data, were computed for respondents who were at least 70 years old and retired. For additional discussion of the data sets and definitions of retirement
dates, see Madrian (1993).

Hazard rates for men based on the three national data sets, as well as the
three firm data sets, are reported in table 2.1. Age-65 (and age-64) retirement
rates based on the national data are very similar to the rates in the individual
firms, with the national age-65 rates ranging from 44 to 52%. Thus the age-65
retirement spike seen in the firm data is common nationwide.

Although an age-65 spike is revealed in each of the data sets, there are important differences at other ages. There are more early retirements in the individual firms than in the national data sets. For example, the age-60 retirement
rate in Firm 3 is 19% for men, while it is less than 8% in each of the national
data sets. This age-60 spike in Firm 3 corresponds to pension plan provisions
that encourage retirement at age 60. More generally, the defined-benefit pension plan provisions in each of the firms provide substantial incentives to leave
the firm by age 65, and usually before that. Such incentives are not common
to all of the respondents in the national data sets. Indeed, only about one-half
of workers are covered by employer-provided pension plans and only about
two-thirds of these are covered by defined-benefit pension plans, with provisions that are likely to be similar to those in the three firms. The proportion of
older workers covered is higher, however.

Another explanation is that the firm data measure separation from the firm,
and some of those who leave the firm could remain in the labor force, especially those who leave the firm at younger ages. Thus, notwithstanding the

Table 2.1   **Retirement Rates for Men from Six Data Sets**

Age	Firm 1	Firm 2	Firm 3	NMES	SIPP-EWH	SIPP-CJR
55	0.054	0.000	0.048	0.022	0.026	0.016
56	0.045	0.016	0.048	0.018	0.019	0.027
57	0.089	0.017	0.047	0.025	0.019	0.019
58	0.069	0.019	0.062	0.033	0.029	0.038
59	0.057	0.023	0.073	0.048	0.035	0.054
60	0.222	0.027	0.188	0.063	0.064	0.075
61	0.119	0.069	0.157	0.110	0.107	0.095
62	0.344	0.000	0.354	0.174	0.150	0.170
63	0.203	0.174	0.201	0.160	0.146	0.188
64	0.283	0.357	0.207	0.350	0.274	0.353
65	0.386	0.357	0.476	0.441	0.456	0.518
66	0.300	0.200	0.235	0.324	0.306	0.391
67	0.000	0.667	0.250	0.424	0.378	0.404
68	0.000	1.000	0.100	0.569	0.528	0.523
N	1,354	436	10,221	1,064	979	1,190

Notes: Entries are empirical hazard rates. The data sets are discussed in the text.

firm pension provision incentives for early retirement, early departure from the worker's primary job can be consistent with later departures from the labor force, the concept measured in the NMES and SIPP-CJR data.

Because a large fraction of workers at the three firms retire before age 65, the age-65 retirement rate is based on a relatively small number of workers. In earlier work (Stock and Wise 1990b; Lumsdaine, Stock, and Wise 1992, 1994), we emphasized that, although the retirement models fit departure rates very well in general, they typically underpredict age-65 departure rates. However, because early retirement is less common nationally than in the firms we have studied, the national data sets contain a rather large sample of persons who work until age 65. And a substantial fraction of those who do, retire at 65. For example, according to the SIPP-EWH data, of those retiring between ages 55 and 69, 18% retire at age 65.

2.2   Descriptive Evidence on Early Retirement

We consider several hypotheses that have been suggested to explain the large age-65 retirement rates. First, we consider the possibility that the age-65 jump is driven by health insurance, the availability of Medicare at age 65. Second, using data on 65-year-olds from Firm 3, we estimate simple models of retirement linking the retirement decision to various economic and demographic attributes, such as marital status.

2.2.1   Health Insurance and Medicare Eligibility

Medicare coverage is available at age 65. The extent to which it provides an incentive to remain employed until 65 depends on the nature of health coverage before age 65. For employees not covered by firm health insurance, medical insurance does not affect the retirement decision beyond the need for income to meet health care costs. Most large firms, however, provide health insurance for current employees and typically also provide retiree health insurance. Coverage usually can be extended to the families of employees and retirees. For these workers, Medicare availability provides no additional incentive to postpone retirement until age 65. But many workers are in a third situation: they are covered by employer medical insurance while employed but not after retirement. They may retain the option to continue coverage through the firm group health plan but must pay the full cost of the premium. Employees in this group will have an incentive to postpone retirement until age 65, when they become eligible for Medicare. This is a possible reason for the large age-65 retirement rate.

Some evidence investigating this view has been noted recently. In chapter 4 in this volume, Gruber and Madrian estimate that the effect of continuation coverage laws is an increase in retirement rates at all ages, not just at the age of Medicare eligibility. In a more structural analysis, Phelan and Rust (1993) incorporate risk aversion and find significant differences in the retirement patterns of individuals who have health insurance versus those who do not. However, Gustman and Steinmeier (1994) estimate that, although most of the effect of health insurance on the retirement decision is via retiree health insurance (as opposed to insurance while working), this effect is quantitatively small.

In addition, we offer two types of indirect evidence that may cast doubt on this explanation. The first is based on the data from Firm 3, the firm for which we have the most detailed information about postretirement medical coverage. Retirees from the firm continue to be covered under the firm's group medical plan at no additional cost. Even beyond age 65, the plan reimburses costs not covered by Medicare. Thus lapse of coverage before Medicare eligibility would not have been a consideration in retirement from this firm. Nonetheless, as discussed in the previous section, for both men and women at Firm 3 the departure rates are highest at age 65 and more than double the age-64 departure rate.

The second type of indirect evidence is drawn from the three national data sets. Madrian (1993) has performed a careful analysis of the effect of firm-provided retiree health insurance on retirement, and we draw on her evidence here. Table 2.2 provides NMES and SIPP retirement rates for employees with and without firm-provided retiree health insurance. The striking feature of the data is the qualitative and quantitative similarity of the hazard rates for those with and without firm-provided employee health insurance. Indeed, the NMES and SIPP-EWH age-65 hazard rates are less for those without than with retiree

Table 2.2   **Retirement Rates for Men: NMES and SIPP Data Sets, with and without Firm-Provided Retiree Health Insurance**

	NMES			SIPP-EWH			SIPP-CJR		
Age	Without	With	Difference	Without	With	Difference	Without	With	Difference
55	.023	.019	.004	.024	.028	−.004	.024	.010	.014*
56	.015	.022	−.006	.022	.013	.009	.023	.030	−.008
57	.023	.030	−.007	.022	.013	.009	.009	.027	−.018**
58	.030	.038	−.008	.031	.026	.005	.030	.045	−.015
59	.048	.048	.000	.032	.040	−.008	.029	.072	−.044***
60	.058	.069	−.012	.061	.070	−.009	.071	.078	−.007
61	.104	.119	−.015	.111	.098	.013	.088	.100	−.011
62	.155	.203	−.048*	.140	.172	−.032	.153	.184	−.030
63	.143	.187	−.044	.155	.126	.029	.178	.197	−.019
64	.305	.424	−.119***	.258	.306	−.048	.355	.350	.005
65	.430	.464	−.034	.444	.483	−.039	.563	.480	.082
66	.294	.390	−.096	.326	.258	.068	.397	.387	.010
67	.427	.417	.010	.381	.370	.012	.409	.400	.009
N	624	440		657	322		493	697	

Notes: Entries are empirical hazard rates, computed as discussed in the text. The difference between hazard rates for employees without and with retiree health insurances is significant at the following level: * = 10%; ** = 5%; *** = 1%.

health insurance, although the differences are not statistically significant. For the SIPP-CJR, the age-65 hazard is higher for those without than with insurance, but the difference is not statistically significant. The age-65 national data hazard rates are also comparable to the rate in Firm 3, which provides postretirement health insurance. At other ages the differences between the national data hazard rates for persons with and without retiree health insurance are typically statistically insignificant. These comparisons suggest that Medicare eligibility is not an important determinant of age-65 retirement. More formal models of the retirement decision based on these national data sets have been estimated by Madrian (1993).

2.2.2   Other Determinants of Retirement at Age 65

We consider next age-65 retirement among Firm 3 employees, for whom Medicare eligibility is not plausibly an important consideration. Because we have historical payroll and demographic data for a large number of Firm 3 employees, along with complete details of retirement benefits offered by the firm, the Firm 3 data provide an opportunity to examine non-Medicare economic and noneconomic determinants of age-65 retirement. The analysis in this section is based on a sample of 203 employees who turned 65 in 1981 and were employed at Firm 3 on their 65th birthday. Of these 203 employees, 40 were women and 163 were men. The combined age-65 retirement rate for these employees was 58.1%.

The departure rates at age 65 for several subgroups of these employees are summarized in table 2.3. Only a few of the differences are statistically and substantively significant. Age-65 married men are significantly more likely to retire than single men. Employees with less than 10 years of service at the firm are less likely to retire, although there are only small differences between the retirement rates for those with 10–19, 20–29, and 30+ years of service. Those with low earnings, and therefore typically with lower pension benefits and lower lifetime wealth, are somewhat less likely to retire at 65 than those with a high income, although this difference is not significant at the 5% level. Age-65 retirement rates do not vary with the job classification.

To determine whether these factors are related to age-65 retirement, after controlling for economic variables, we estimated a series of probit retirement specifications using this sample of 65-year-olds. In addition to the variables identifying the table 2.3 subgroups, the specifications include several economic variables: predicted annual age-65 income, the expected present value of Social Security payments, the expected present value of pension payments, the change in expected Social Security wealth resulting from working an additional year (that is, retiring at age 66 rather than age 65—Social Security accrual), and the change in expected pension wealth resulting from postponing retirement until age 66 (pension accrual).

An additional economic variable is the "option value" of remaining employed an additional year, calculated using the Stock-Wise (1990b) option

Table 2.3   **Age-65 Retirement Rates for Different Categories of Worker
(data set: 65-year-olds at Firm 3)**

Category	N	Rate	Category	N	Rate	Difference[a]
All	203	.581				
		(.035)				
Women	40	.475	Men	163	.607	−.132*
		(.079)			(.308)	(.088)
Married	142	.641	Single	61	.443	.198**
		(.040)			(.064)	(.075)
Married men	132	.659	Single men	31	.387	.272**
		(.041)			(.087)	(.096)
Married women	10	.400	Single women	30	.500	−.100
		(.155)			(.091)	(.180)
Income ≤ median	101	.535	Income ≥ median	102	.634	−.099*
		(.050)			(.048)	(.069)
<10 yrs. service	41	.463				
		(.078)				
10–20 yrs. service	50	.620				
		(.069)				
20–30 yrs. service	32	.594				
		(.087)				
>30 yrs. service	80	.613				
		(.054)				
Service job	101	.554				
		(.049)				
Technical job	50	.580				
		(.070)				

Notes: Entries are the fraction of 65-year-olds in the indicated group who retire at age 65. Standard errors are in parentheses. Differences are significantly different from zero at the following level: * = 10%; ** = 1%.

[a]Entries in the "difference" column are the difference between retirement rates for the group in the first and second category columns in that row.

value model. It is computed as the difference between the lifetime expected present value of income and retirement benefits were the individual to retire at the optimal age (which could be later than 65), and the present value of income and retirement benefits under age-65 retirement. For this calculation the optimal age of retirement is taken to be the age that maximizes the current expected value of lifetime earnings. Thus this option value is a measure of the monetary opportunity cost of retiring at age 65 rather than later. Of course, for some employees the opportunity cost is zero, that is, age-65 retirement maximizes lifetime wealth.

All of the present values—the option value, Social Security accrual, and pension accrual—were computed using forecasts of future earnings based on the past employee earnings and the firm's historical age-income profile.[7] Pres-

7. The earnings forecasting equation for employees at Firm 3 is discussed in detail in Lumsdaine, Stock, and Wise (1994).

ent values assume a discount factor of 0.90 and incorporate mortality rates calculated from life tables.

Parameter estimates are presented in table 2.4. In each specification, married male employees have a significantly higher tendency than single men to retire at age 65. Consistent with the results in table 2.3, married women are slightly less likely than single women to retire at 65, although the difference is not

Table 2.4   **Probit Models of Age-65 Retirement (data set: 65-year-olds at Firm 3)**

Variable			Model		
	(1)	(2)	(3)	(4)	(5)
Constant	0.018	−0.343	−1.585	−1.341	−0.644
	(0.195)	(0.386)	(1.006)	(0.927)	(0.512)
Female		0.334	0.117	0.309	0.322
		(0.337)	(0.363)	(0.343)	(0.339)
Married women		−0.261	−0.095	−0.110	−0.161
		(0.464)	(0.471)	(0.472)	(0.475)
Married men		0.691***	0.664**	0.670**	0.675**
		(0.258)	(0.262)	(0.261)	(0.263)
Service job		−0.061	0.286	0.304	0.061
		(0.249)	(0.344)	(0.350)	(0.303)
Technical job		−0.070	0.119	0.157	−0.021
		(0.286)	(0.342)	(0.350)	(0.299)
Option value	1.068	0.569	−1.199	−0.658	0.726
	(1.016)	(1.036)	(1.876)	(1.812)	(1.135)
Social Security present value			3.243		
			(2.596)		
Pension present value			0.623		
			(0.410)		
Social Security accrual				−16.134	
				(15.387)	
Pension accrual				−5.130	
				(3.042)	
10–19 years					0.221
					(0.282)
20–29 years					0.316
					(0.318)
30+ years service					0.269
					(0.302)
−ln likelihood	−137.26	−132.55	−129.56	−129.78	−131.97
Likelihood-ratio test					
Versus model 1		9.42*			
Versus model 2			5.98*	5.54*	1.16

Notes: The sample consists of 203 workers in Firm 3 who were employed by the firm when they turned 65 and who retired either at age 65 or after; the dependent variable is one if retirement is at age 65 and zero otherwise. All monetary values are in $100,000 (1980 dollars). Standard errors are in parentheses. Significant at the following level: * = 10%; ** = 5%; *** = 1%.

statistically significant. Gender, job category, and even job tenure are only weakly related to this retirement decision, both unconditionally and after controlling for the economic variables. Conditional on not retiring before age 65, although the overall age-65 retirement rate is very high, none of the economic variables is a statistically significant determinant of age-65 retirement. In contrast, these variables predict retirement at other ages. Indeed, calculations that underlie these variables play the central role in the structural option value and stochastic dynamic programming retirement models that predict very successfully retirement over all ages. This analysis provides no economic or demographic explanations for age-65 retirement decisions. The only conclusion is that married men are more likely than unmarried men to retire at 65, given that they have worked until then.

2.3   Evidence from a Structural Retirement Model

As explained above, the motivation for this series of analysis is the general failure of structural models of retirement to account for the high age-65 retirement rate, without including age-specific dummy variables or other model specifications that assure a close match to retirement rates at specific ages. We document this failure and explore alternative specifications that might, in a mechanical sense, permit the models to fit the age-65 retirement rate. We first estimate a "base" stochastic dynamic programming model of retirement, which we take as representative of the new generation of retirement models. We then modify this model to incorporate noneconomic reasons for retiring at age 65.

2.3.1   The Stochastic Dynamic Programming Model

The stochastic dynamic programming model used here is described in detail in Lumsdaine, Stock, and Wise (1992). It incorporates aspects of the models of Berkovec and Stern (1991) and Daula and Moffitt (1991). The model is summarized briefly here. It is a simplified version of a fuller stochastic dynamic programming model in which retirement is treated as an absorbing state and annual consumption is set equal to annual income. Rust (1989) discusses the computational complexity in a more general approach.

In this model, if the worker is employed and earns income Y_t in year t, then the systematic component of utility in that year is

$$(1) \qquad\qquad U_w(Y_t) = Y_w^\gamma.$$

A retired person receives monetary retirement benefits B_t and the systematic component of utility in year t is

$$(2) \qquad\qquad U_R(B_t) = [kB_t(r)]^\gamma,$$

where the retirement benefits $B_t(r)$ depend on the year r in which the worker retired. The factor k represents a multiplicative increase of utility obtained from receiving payments B_t without having at the same time to work.

The stochastic dynamic programming model predicts retirement by comparing the expected value of retiring today to the expected value of working another year and thereby retaining the option to retire later. The decision is based on the recursive representation of the value function, W_t,

$$(3) \quad W_t = \max\left\{ E_t[U_W(Y_t) + \varepsilon_{1t} + \beta W_{t+1}], E_t \sum_{\tau=t}^{S} \beta^{\tau-t}[U_R(B_\tau(t)) + \varepsilon_{2\tau}] \right\}$$

with

$$W_{t+1} = \max\left\{ E_{t+1}[U_W(Y_{t+1}) + \varepsilon_{1t+1} + \beta W_{t+2}], \right.$$
$$\left. E_{t+1} \sum_{\tau=t+1}^{S} \beta^{\tau-t-1}[U_R(B_\tau(t+1)) + \varepsilon_{2\tau}] \right\},$$

where β is the discount factor and S is the maximum length of life (taken to be age 95). Discounting incorporates mortality rates.

The errors ε_{1t} and ε_{2t} in (3) represent random shocks to utilities associated with income when working and when retired, respectively. The specification estimated here assumes that the errors, ε_{1t} and ε_{2t}, are independent normally distributed. Details of the estimation method are presented in Lumsdaine, Stock, and Wise (1992).

2.3.2   Data and Results

Our previous retirement model estimates, based on firm data, have used samples in which older employees were underrepresented relative to those in their 50s and early 60s. This is a consequence of high departure rates at younger ages, leaving few employees still employed at age 65; a random sample includes few older employees. Thus a possible explanation of the mismatch between actual and predicted age-65 retirement rates is the disproportionate weight given to the younger of the older employees. To address this possibility, the sample used here includes approximately equal numbers of employees at all ages, with a total of 1,007 women and 1,727 men between age 50 and 69. The balanced sample is made possible by the large number of employees in Firm 3.

The estimated parameters for the stochastic dynamic programming model are presented in table 2.5 for women and in table 2.6 for men. The discount factor β was set to 0.9 in models 1–3; it was estimated in model 4. The parameter values for the base model 1 in each table indicate little curvature in the utility function; the hypothesis that $\gamma = 1$ cannot be rejected at the 10% level for either the men or the women. The parameter k is approximately three for both men and women. Interpreted literally, these results imply that utility is approximately linear in income, with $1 received while retired worth approximately $3 of income while working.

Actual and predicted departure rates for this sample are compared in figure 2.4 for women and in figure 2.5 for men. The top panel in these figures shows

Table 2.5   **Parameter Estimates for Dynamic Programming Model**
                   (data set: Firm 3, women, $N = 1,007$)

	Model			
Parameter	(1)	(2)	(3)	(4)
γ	1.177	1.087	1.057	1.190
	(0.219)	(0.203)	(0.213)	(0.239)
k	2.974	2.973	2.932	8.628
	(0.238)	(0.093)	(0.249)	(0.991)
k_{age65}		2.457	1.075	2.100
		(0.850)	(0.502)	(1.139)
$k_{married\&65}$			−0.947	−0.965
			(1.851)	(0.053)
β	0.9[a]	0.9[a]	0.9[a]	0.969
				(0.022)
σ	0.159	0.160	0.163	0.097
	(0.020)	(0.017)	(0.021)	(0.028)
Summary statistics				
−ln likelihood	303.59	299.43	299.07	297.08
Likelihood-ratio test versus				
model 1		8.32**	9.04*	13.02**

Notes: Estimation is by maximum likelihood. All monetary values are in $100,000 (1980 dollars). Significant at the following level: * = 5%; ** = 1%.
[a]Parameter values imposed.

Table 2.6   **Parameter Estimates for Dynamic Programming Model**
                   (data set: Firm 3, men, $N = 1,727$)

	Model			
Parameter	(1)	(2)	(3)	(4)
γ	1.019	1.009	1.009[a]	1.009
	(0.113)	(0.105)		(0.007)
k	3.591	3.576	3.576	3.577
	(0.176)	(0.171)	(0.154)	(0.013)
k_{age65}		−0.574	−0.294	−0.574
		(0.700)	(0.402)	(0.004)
$k_{married\&65}$			−0.250	−0.400
			(0.383)	(0.005)
β	0.9[a]	0.9[a]	0.9[a]	0.903
				(0.004)
σ	0.158	0.158	0.158[a]	0.157
	(0.015)	(0.014)		(0.011)
Summary statistics				
−ln likelihood	588.53	587.75	587.84	587.83
Likelihood-ratio test versus				
model 1		1.56	1.38	1.40

Notes: Estimation is by maximum likelihood. All monetary values are in $100,000 (1980 dollars).
[a]Parameter values imposed.

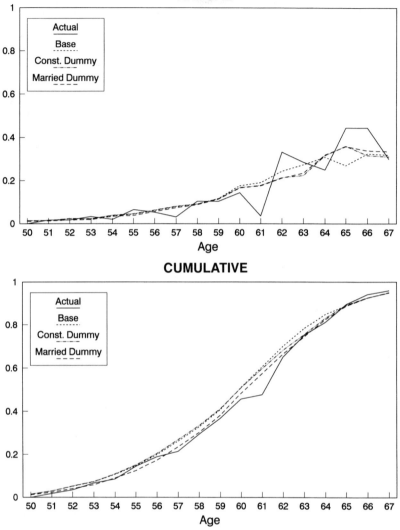

Fig. 2.4   Departure rates: women

annual departure rates, the lower panel cumulative departure. The base model 1 fits the general trends in the hazard rates reasonably well. However, at age 65 in particular, but also at age 62, the models underestimate the high retirement rates. For example, the hazard rate at age 65 predicted by the base model is 27% for women and 34% for men; the actual hazard rates are 44% for women and 61% for men.

The underprediction of age-65 retirement is typical of the results from our

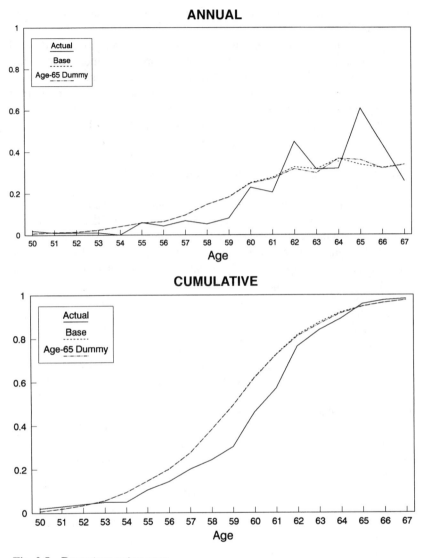

Fig. 2.5   Departure rates: men

prior analyses based on this and other firm data. The predicted departure rates are often 40 to 60% of the actual rates. For example, Lumsdaine, Stock, and Wise (1992) considered two variants of the stochastic dynamic programming model estimated in this paper (one with normal errors, as here, and one with logistic errors) and the Stock-Wise (1990b) "option value" model. All the models underpredicted age-65 retirement rates by amounts comparable to those found here. Thus the use of a random sample with relatively few older employees is not the explanation for the mismatch between actual and predicted age-65 departure rates.

To investigate age-65 retirement in more detail, we examined an additional parameterization that allows employees to behave as though they receive additional utility—in addition to financial inducements at that age—from retirement at 65. Because the analysis of section 2.2 suggests that age-65 retirement varies with marital status, we included a dummy variable for marital status as well. We parameterize k in equation 2 as a function of age and marital status,

$$(4) \qquad k = k_0 + \exp\{k_{65}D_{65} + k_{married\&65}D_{married}D_{65}\},$$

where D_{65} and $D_{married}$ are one if the individual is 65 and married, respectively, and zero otherwise.

Results using the parameterization (4) for women are given in models 2–4 of table 2.5. The coefficient on the age-65 dummy is individually statistically significant, and the coefficients on the two dummies when estimated together are jointly significant. When the marital status dummy is included, its estimated coefficient is approximately equal to the coefficient on the age-65 dummy, and opposite in sign, so the predicted probability of retirement at age 65 is higher only for single women. This accords with the evidence from table 2.3, showing that single women aged 65 have somewhat higher retirement rates than married women.

The predicted model 2 and 3 departure rates for women are also plotted in figure 2.4. At younger ages, the age-65 utility "bonus" has little effect on the predicted rates. However, the bonus results in somewhat lower retirement rates just before age 65 (from 60 to 64) and higher rates at 65. Still, this parameterization (4) "explains" only half of the age-65 mismatch.

The results for men are given in the final three columns of table 2.6, and the hazard rates based on model 2 are plotted in figure 2.5. Unlike the results for women, none of the coefficients on the dummy variables are significant, even though the retirement rates reported in table 2.3 are significantly higher for married than for single age-65 men. We interpret this to mean that differential rates for age-65 men result from different earnings histories—and thus pension and Social Security wealth. The departure rates based on model 2 for men are very similar to those of the base model, consistent with the small numerical value of the coefficient on the age-65 dummy variable.

In summary, for neither men nor women does the base model explain the age-65 retirement spike. For single women the equation (4) parameterization appears to explain some of the difference between actual and predicted age-65 departure rates. For men this parameterization explains essentially none of the mismatch.

2.3.3 The Opportunity Cost of an Age-65 Rule of Thumb

The optimization model of the previous section is a mathematically tractable framework for approximating retirement decisions. Indeed, the model typically predicts retirement rates rather accurately. Age 65 is the exception. One explanation for the "unexplained" retirement at 65 is that the cost of choosing that age, relative to 64 or 66 for example, is small, so that there is no overriding reason to deviate from the age that some may consider "normal." In particular this may be true for employees who choose not to retire substantially before age 65. In this sense age 65 could serve as a customary focal date for retirement, which might be sustained if the opportunity cost of retiring at that focal age is small.

We explore in this section the cost of choosing to retire at 65. That is, we evaluate the opportunity cost of adopting a "retire-at-65" rule of thumb. From an economic perspective, whether such a rule of thumb is plausible depends on the opportunity cost of following the rule. To illustrate the possible magnitudes involved, we measure this opportunity cost by the lifetime utility forgone by choosing to retire at 65 rather than at some other age. For a given individual the expected lifetime utility of retiring at age r is

$$(5) \qquad V_t(r) = \sum_{s=t}^{r-1} \beta^{s-t} U_W(Y_s) + \sum_{s=r}^{S} \beta^{s-t} U_R(B_s(r)).$$

The individual does not live beyond age S. In particular the lifetime utility obtained by adopting the age-65 rule of thumb is $V_t(t_{65})$. We compute the maximum lifetime utility as it is computed in the Stock-Wise (1990b) option value model, $V_t(r^*)$, where r^* is the value of r ($r = t, \ldots, t_{74}$) that maximizes $V_t(r)$.

The measure of opportunity cost tabulated here is the fraction of lifetime utility forgone, f_t, by adopting the age-65 rule of thumb relative to choosing to retire at r^*, that is,

$$(6) \qquad f_t = \frac{V_t(r^*) - V_t(t_{65})}{V_t(t_{65})}$$

Because γ is insignificantly different from 1, for the computation of the distribution of equation (6) we set $\gamma = 1$. This would make the units of lifetime utility current dollars, except that dollars received while retired are weighted by the leisure parameter k. The estimates of the leisure parameters from model 1 in tables 2.5 and 2.6 for women and men, respectively, are used in the calculations.

Selected percentiles of the estimated distributions of lifetime utility forgone as a result of the age-65 rule of thumb for employees between the ages of 55 and 64 are shown in table 2.7 for employees in our balanced sample. For some employees the retirement date that maximizes the expected value of lifetime utility is 65, so for them $f_t = 0$. These are the employees with the highest predicted age-65 retirement rates. If expected lifetime utility is maximized by retiring at other than age 65, then f_t is positive. The table shows that for at least half the employees the cost of electing to retire at 65 rather than the optimal age is substantial, exceeding 20%. For example, the typical 60-year-old man would gain 23% by electing to retire at the optimal age rather than age 65;

Table 2.7   **Distribution of Fractional Utility Losses from Adopting an Age-65 Rule of Thumb**

	Percentile		
Age	10%	25%	50%
A. Men			
55	.007	.043	.123
56	.007	.051	.143
57	.009	.055	.157
58	.009	.060	.172
59	.012	.074	.209
60	.013	.081	.232
61	.019	.108	.277
62	.016	.098	.282
63	.009	.086	.297
64	.009	.063	.200
B. Women			
55	.018	.074	.158
56	.011	.074	.172
57	.007	.073	.188
58	.017	.096	.228
59	.014	.110	.268
60	.022	.131	.303
61	.016	.118	.342
62	.016	.131	.373
63	.025	.150	.400
64	.020	.102	.313

Notes: Entries are the percentiles of the distribution of $[V_i(r^*) - V_i(t_{65})]/V_i(t_{65})$ by age, as defined in the text. For women, the lifetime utilities were computed using $\gamma = 1$, $k = 2.974$, and $\beta = 0.9$; for men, $\gamma = 1$, $k = 3.591$, and $\beta = 0.9$.

the typical woman would gain 30%. Nonetheless, the gain for a minority of employees is small, 1 or 2% at the tenth percentile. Thus these calculations are inconsistent with the possibility that the typical employee would lose little by electing to retire at 65.

The reasoning of Akerlof and Yellen (1985) seems not to help in this instance. They point out that apparently large deviations from optimality when measured in terms of decision variables are consistent with nearly rational behavior, when the individual's objective function is rather flat in a region around the optimum. For most employees the opportunity cost of following an age-65 rule of thumb is large, and for them it would be expensive to retire at a customary but suboptimal date. However, for a minority of employees it seems not to be costly to shift retirement from an optimal date to age 65. These shifts by a relatively small fraction of workers to the customary retirement age could in principle be sufficient to explain the age-65 spike, because the absolute number of retirees at age 65 is small even though the retirement rate is large. An implication of this explanation, and in particular of the large opportunity costs for most workers, is that shifts in Social Security or pension plan provisions that made age-65 retirement less advantageous could overcome an age-65 customary retirement effect.

These computations are based only on future labor income and pension and Social Security benefits; they omit other sources of wealth like home equity and personal financial assets. Postretirement utilities should be augmented in accordance with the amount of personal wealth that the worker does not plan to bequeath. For example, the specification in equation (2) could in principle include the annuity value of personal financial assets. We do not have individual asset data for Firm 3 employees. However, incorporating other wealth into V_t would tend to decrease the proportional lifetime utility losses in table 2.7.

2.4   Conclusions

The high age-65 retirement rate for the small proportion of employees who work until that age is not explained by Medicare eligibility, based on comparison of the retirement rates of employees with and without employee-provided retiree health insurance. This conclusion is supported by the high age-65 retirement rates of Firm 3 employees, who have generous retiree health insurance. Still the age-65 retirement rate for Firm 3 employees is twice as high as the age-64 rate. Nor is the high age-65 rate explained by demographic attributes of employees. Nor is it explained by the use of data sets with small proportions of persons who are still employed at age 65.

Disproportionate age-65 retirement might be explained by an age-65 rule of thumb, which could be rationalized economically if the cost of such a rule were small. But our calculations suggest that the opportunity cost would typically be very large, even for employees who worked until 64.

Thus we are left with the hypothesis with which we started. We are inclined to attribute the unexplained high age-65 departure rates to an "age-65 retirement effect," that is, to the influence of custom or accepted practice.

References

Akerlof, George A., and Janet L. Yellen. 1985. Can Small Deviations from Rationality Make Significant Differences to Economic Equilibria? *American Economic Review* 75: 708–20.

Berkovec, J., and S. Stern. 1991. Job Exit Behavior of Older Men. *Econometrica* 59 (1): 189–210.

Blau, David M. 1994. Labor Force Dynamics of Older Men. *Econometrica* 62 (1): 117–56.

Daula, Thomas V., and Robert A. Moffitt. 1991. Estimating a Dynamic Programming Model of Army Reenlistment Behavior. In *Military Compensation and Personnel Retention: Models and Evidence,* ed. C. L. Gilroy, D. K. Horne, and D. Alton Smith.

Alexandria, VA: U.S. Army Research Institute for the Behavioral and Social Sciences.

Geweke, John, Gary A. Zarkin, and Robert B. Slonim. 1993. The Social Security Acceptance Decision. Department of Economics, University of Minnesota. Manuscript.

Gustman, Alan, and Thomas L. Steinmeier. 1986. A Structural Retirement Model. *Econometrica* 54 (3): 555–84.

———. 1994. Employer-Provided Health Insurance and Retirement Behavior. *Industrial and Labor Relations Review* 48: 86–102.

Kotlikoff, Laurence J., and Daniel E. Smith. 1983. *Pensions in the American Economy.* Chicago: University of Chicago Press.

Kotlikoff, Laurence J., and David A. Wise. 1988. Pension Backloading, Wage Taxes, and Work Disincentives. In *Tax Policy and the Economy,* vol. 2, ed. L. Summers, 161–96. Cambridge: MIT Press.

Lumsdaine, Robin L., Phyllis Mutschler, and David A. Wise. 1992. Pension Provisions, Anticipated Windows, and Retirement. Department of Economics, Princeton University. Manuscript.

Lumsdaine, Robin L., James H. Stock, and David A. Wise. 1990. Efficient Windows and Labor Force Reduction. *Journal of Public Economics* 43: 131–59.

———. 1991. Windows and Retirement. *Annales d'Économie et de Statistique* 20/21: 219–42.

———. 1992. Three Models of Retirement: Computational Complexity versus Predictive Validity. In *Topics in the Economics of Aging,* ed. David A. Wise, 19–57. Chicago: University of Chicago Press.

———. 1994. Pension Plan Provisions and Retirement: Men and Women, Medicare, and Models. In *Studies in the Economics of Aging,* ed. David A. Wise, 183–220. Chicago: University of Chicago Press.

Madrian, Brigitte C. 1993. Post-Retirement Health Insurance and the Decision to Retire. Working paper, Department of Economics, Massachusetts Institute of Technology.

Phelan, Christopher, and John P. Rust. 1991. U.S. Social Security Policy: A Dynamic Analysis of Incentives and Self-Selection. Department of Economics, University of Wisconsin. Manuscript.

———. 1993. How Social Security and Medicare Affect Retirement Behavior in a World of Incomplete Markets. Department of Economics, University of Wisconsin. Manuscript.

Rust, John P. 1989. A Dynamic Programming Model of Retirement Behavior. In *The Economics of Aging,* ed. David A. Wise, 359–98. Chicago: University of Chicago Press.

Stock, James H., and David A. Wise. 1990a. The Pension Inducement to Retire: An Option Value Analysis. In *Issues in the Economics of Aging,* ed. David A. Wise, 205–24. Chicago: University of Chicago Press.

———. 1990b. Pensions, the Option Value of Work, and Retirement. *Econometrica* 58 (5): 1151–80.

3 The Military Pension, Compensation, and Retirement of U.S. Air Force Pilots

John Ausink and David A. Wise

Econometric models of job exit are of interest for at least two reasons. There has been a significant decline in the civilian labor force participation of older Americans for the past twenty years (Wise 1985). During the same period, private pension coverage has increased markedly, and Social Security benefits have risen. The study of relationships between the two trends is of interest to economists attempting to explain the incentives that pension plans may provide in encouraging workers to change jobs or stop working, and is also important to firms who may want to affect employee retirement behavior by changing the provisions of their pension plans.

In the military, there is a slightly different perspective. The armed forces must maintain adequate numbers of trained and experienced personnel without the realistic possibility of lateral job entry to replace losses. A shortage of experienced military pilots cannot be eliminated by hiring pilots from another military, for example. The absence of this remedy for the loss of personnel means that shortfalls in any cohort are difficult to correct, and the potential incentive effects of changes in compensation must be considered before they are made.

Both the civilian trend and the military problem are sufficient to have encouraged extensive research. The military, through research at the RAND Corporation, the Center for Naval Analyses, and the Pentagon, has been refining models of military retirement since 1975. Indeed, Baldwin (Baldwin and

John Ausink is a lieutenant colonel in the U.S. Air Force and associate professor of mathematics at the U.S. Air Force Academy. David A. Wise is the John F. Stambaugh Professor of Political Economy at the John F. Kennedy School of Government, Harvard University, and director for Health and Retirement Programs at the National Bureau of Economic Research.

This paper is based on Ausink's Ph.D. dissertation, "The Effect of Changes in Compensation on a Pilot's Decision to Leave the Air Force," Harvard University, May 1991. Funding was provided by the National Institute on Aging. Any opinions expressed herein are those of the authors and not necessarily those of the U.S. Air Force, Harvard University, or the National Bureau of Economic Research.

83

Daula 1985) states that the economics of military manpower emerged as a branch of defense economics with the end of the draft.

In this paper, we use the option value model of retirement behavior developed by Stock and Wise (1990) to examine the effects of changes in compensation on the decision of Air Force pilots to leave the military. Section 3.1 provides background information. We start with a brief discussion of the problem of pilot retention in the Air Force and the compensation changes that have been suggested to solve it. Because a large part of career military compensation is in the form of pension benefits, we discuss the value of these benefits. In section 3.2, after a description of the data used in this study, we describe the option value model and highlight how it differs from other models that have been used to study this topic. Section 3.3 presents graphical displays of the predictive accuracy of the option value model and compares these to the accuracy of competing models. Of particular interest is that the option value model, which can be viewed as a simplified dynamic programming specification, predicts complicated military retirement patterns much better than the dynamic programming formulation to which it is compared. The effects on the distribution of the pilot population (by years of service) of selected changes in compensation are discussed in section 3.3.2.

3.1   Background

3.1.1   Pilot Compensation

Military pilots have received extra pay ever since the Army Appropriation Act of 2 March 1913, which provided an increase of 35% in pay and allowances for Army officers flying heavier-than-air craft. According to Bartholomew (1982, 93), the pay was strictly to compensate pilots for the extremely hazardous duty they were undertaking. The Career Compensation Act of 1949 initiated a change in philosophy for the special pay, saying "the incentive to engage and remain in hazardous occupations provided a more realistic and practical basis for determining the rates of special pay than the theory of recompense for shorter career expectancy. The recompense or replacement concept, although promoted for many years as the sole argument for hazard pay, was found wanting for several reasons" (Bartholomew 1982, 94). In other words, instead of trying to make their shorter lives happier because of higher pay, the government should pay pilots enough to make them prefer employment in the military to employment in civilian positions. The incentive pay structure adopted by the Career Compensation Act provided extra pay that depended only on the rank of the member who was flying.

By 1955, the services were having difficulty recruiting pilots and retaining younger pilots who had completed their service obligation, and the incentive pay system was changed so that flight pay depended not only on grade, but on years of service.

Another change in philosophy occurred in 1974, when Congress decided that flight pay should be more than compensation for actual flying duties. Instead, because of the large investment made by the military in the training of its pilots, it was felt that extra pay should be structured so that a pilot has the incentive to remain in the service for a full career. The Aviation Career Incentive Pay (ACIP) Act was an effort to do this.

As the 1980s drew to a close, it became apparent that ACIP was no longer sufficient to retain enough pilots to meet projected defense needs. According to the 17 January 1989 Report of the Secretary of Defense, the armed forces were losing one experienced fighter pilot per day in 1988, and this represented a cost of more than $2.5 million to the government (Department of Defense 1988, 103). The DoD annual report for 1989 echoes the concern that high pilot losses jeopardized combat readiness of the armed forces (Department of Defense 1989a, 125). Assuming the low 1989 retention rates continued from 1991 to 1994, the Air Force predicted that "shortfalls" of pilots in the groups with one to fourteen years of service would rise from 895 in fiscal year 1989 to over 2,100 in 1994 (Department of Defense 1988, 6-24).

The major reason for the loss of pilots is increased hiring by commercial airlines. A surge of pilot hiring in the 1960s, which translated into a large retirement rate of commercial pilots in the 1990s, has led to another surge of hiring. According to the Department of Defense, 37% of the commercial jet pilot force (approximately forty-three thousand) will need to be replaced in the 1990s (Department of Defense 1988, 2-5). Despite turmoil in the airline industry because of the Persian Gulf crisis in 1990, many major airlines continued the aggressive hiring practices that contributed to the fact that, for the third year in a row, Air Force pilot losses exceeded production by more than eight hundred.

The desire of military pilots to leave the service to fly for commercial airlines is understandable when potential earnings are considered. For example, a married Air Force pilot with eight years of service in 1989 would be earning slightly more than $45,000 annually, and could look forward to making over $61,000 per year (using 1989 pay tables) by the time he or she reached twenty years of service. If this same pilot left the Air Force after eight years of service and landed a job with a major airline, annual salary could be well over $100,000 after ten years. (These figures are based on table 2-4 of Department of Defense 1988.)

According to the *Department of Defense Aviator Retention Study,* "When faced with the choice between an 'average' private sector job and a military flying career, the military career competes favorably with its challenging jobs, security, job satisfaction, and opportunities for travel, advanced education, and service to country. The evidence is overwhelming, however, that lucrative airline pilot careers, when readily available, are preferred and account for the majority of military pilot separations" (Department of Defense 1988, 2-8).

With continuing Navy pilot shortages and increasing losses of Air Force pilots, Congress authorized a new bonus program in 1988 called Aviator Continuation Pay (ACP). In the Air Force, this program provides bonuses that depend on the pilot's years of service and require that the pilot agree to serve for a total of fourteen years in order to receive the money. For example, a pilot with six years of service can receive an annual bonus of $12,000 by agreeing to remain in the service until completing fourteen years of service; the bonus will not be received without incurring the obligation. The size of the bonus decreases with seniority, until a pilot who has completed twelve years of service will be offered $6,500 per year to remain through fourteen years of service (Bowman 1990). In 1989, the cost of this program from fiscal year 1990 through fiscal year 1994 was anticipated to be approximately $94 million.

While the added compensation from ACP and ACIP is substantial, the advantage of remaining in the military long enough to earn retirement benefits (benefits that are available to pilots and nonpilots alike) must also be considered. Compared to most civilian pension plans, the military pension is simple to calculate and extremely generous, although it does have the disadvantage, from the military member's point of view, of having cliff vesting (with a vengeance): pension benefits are not available until a person serves for twenty years; anyone who leaves the military before twenty years of service receives no pension benefits.

3.1.2   The Military Pension

The structure of the military pension system has remained relatively unchanged since 1916, when an act of Congress (Public Law 64-241, *U.S. Statutes at Large* 39 [1916]: 579) established the formula that retired pay would equal 2.5% of monthly pay per year of service up to a maximum of 75% at thirty years of service (Bartholomew 1982, 235). Most changes since then have dealt with the nature of cost of living adjustments (COLAs) that are part of the pension, what type of pay is used for the calculation of the benefit, and when retirement is authorized. Probably the most complicated aspect of the pension now is the fact that, depending on when individuals entered the service, they may be covered by one of three different plans. Table 3.1 describes the differences among them, and which military members are affected by them. Using 1988 pay tables, a typical lieutenant colonel retiring after twenty years of service would have an annual pension of approximately $22,152 under the first plan, $21,000 under the second, and $17,000 under the third. The DoD estimates that the present values of the pension benefits at the time of retirement would be $595,000, $553,000, and $445,000, respectively.

3.2   The Data and Models

3.2.1   The Sample

The Air Force maintains the Longitudinal Cohort File, a file of information on Air Force personnel that is updated in October every year and includes data

Table 3.1   **Characteristics of Current Retirement System**

Date of Entry	Calculation of Benefit	Cost of Living Adjustment
Before 8 Sept. 1980	After 20 years of service, 50% of final basic pay. Benefit increases 2.5% for each additional year served, up to 75%.	Annual COLA to match inflation.
Between 8 Sept. 1980 and 1 Aug. 1986	After 20 years of service, 50% of the average basic pay of the highest 3 earnings years. Benefit increases 2.5% for each additional year served, up to 75%.	Annual COLA to match inflation.
After 1 Aug. 1986	After 20 years of service, 40% of the average basic pay of the highest 3 earnings years. Benefit increases 3.5% for each additional year served, up to 75%.	Annual COLA 1% below consumer price index (CPI) until age 62. At age 62, pension is recalculated to be what it would have been if entry was before 8 Sept. 1980. After age 62, annual COLA is again 1% below CPI.

Source: Information is from Air Force Regulation 35-7, chap. 7.

from 1974 to 1991. From this file, the Air Force Military Personnel Center (AFMPC) produced a random sample of five thousand male pilots who in 1987 had completed between six and twenty-seven years of commissioned service. Individuals who had served as enlisted personnel before being commissioned as officers were excluded from the sample, because historically, departure patterns for those with prior service have been different from those of officers without prior service.

Officers in the file are recorded as being present or not present in the Air Force when the file is updated annually. We have no record of actual employment after leaving the Air Force, but we assume that departures are voluntary and that the decision to leave is made based on a comparison of future compensation from the military to potential compensation from a civilian airline position. The file lists the Air Force Command to which the pilot belongs, and the model parameter estimates in this paper are based on the 1,803 officers who were in the Strategic Air Command (SAC) or Military Airlift Command (MAC). Pilots in these two commands had fairly similar departure rates from 1987 to 1989, and the "heavy" aircraft flown in these commands require skills similar to those needed in civilian airline positions. For the purposes of calculating income, the first full year of civilian pay or pension receipt was considered to be the year after an individual was recorded as not present. For example, a pilot present in 1987 but absent in 1988 receives the first full year of civilian pay (and pension benefits, if entitled to them) in 1989.

3.2.2 The Option Value Model

Following Stock and Wise (1990), in any given year s, an Air Force pilot may expect to earn Y_s dollars in the Air Force and, if he or she leaves the military, a salary C_s in a new civilian job plus any retirement benefits B_s that have been earned as a result of military service. If we say that the individual indirectly derives utility $U_M(s)$ from military income in year s and utility $U_C(s)$ from civilian employment plus military pension benefits, we can develop an expression for the utility of working until different times in the future. Suppose that no one lives beyond year T, that individuals discount future earnings by a factor β, and that r is the first year in which civilian earnings and/or retirement benefits are received. For an individual in year t considering being out of the Air Force in year r, the value of that decision is

$$(1) \qquad V_t(r) = \sum_{s=t}^{r-1} \beta^{s-t} U_M(s) + \sum_{s=r}^{T} \beta^{s-t} U_C(s),$$

that is, the discounted sum of the utility of working in the Air Force from now until year $r - 1$ plus the discounted sum of the utility of working elsewhere and receiving pension benefits (if any) from year r until death.

Similarly, the value of leaving the Air Force now, in year t, is

$$(2) \qquad V_t(t) = \sum_{s=t}^{T} \beta^{s-t} U_C(s).$$

The expected gain in utility from delaying departure until year r is given by

$$(3) \qquad G_t(r) = E_t V_t(r) - E_t V_t(t).$$

It will be to the person's advantage to delay the decision to leave the military until year r if the expected gain in utility is greater than zero. We will assume that an individual will leave the Air Force if, when considering all future departure dates, the maximum gain possible is less than or equal to zero, that is, if $G_t(r^*) \leq 0$, where r^* is the potential departure year with the maximum gain.

Assume that an individual's utility has a constant relative risk aversion form.

$$(4) \qquad U_M(s) = Y_s^\gamma + \omega_s \quad \text{and} \quad U_C(s) = (C_s(r) + k B_s(r))^\gamma + \xi_s$$

The potential civilian income $C_s(r)$ may, and the retirement benefits $B_s(r)$ will, depend on the year r that the individual is first in a civilian position, and so they are shown as functions of the departure year. Additionally, the coefficient k is introduced to account for the possibility that a person may value military pension earnings differently than earnings that require labor. The error terms are meant to capture unobserved determinants of departure. For example, they could reflect individual preferences for work versus leisure. They could also account for differing tastes for military life, variable tax filing status that will change the effect of nontaxable portions of military income, differing assessments of potential for military advancement, and variable unobserved wealth. For a given individual in the military, there should be considerable persistence in these random effects over time, and so the error terms are assumed to follow a first-order Markov process.

$$(5) \qquad \omega_s = \rho \omega_{s-1} + \varepsilon_{\omega s} \qquad E_{s-1}(\varepsilon_{\omega s}) = 0$$

$$\xi_s = \rho\xi_{s-1} + \varepsilon_{\xi s} \qquad E_{s-1}(\varepsilon_{\xi s}) = 0$$

At time t, the individual knows both ω and ξ, but not the values that evolve over time. With these specifications, the expected gain from postponing departure until year r can be written

$$G_t(r) = \sum_{s=t}^{r-1}\beta^{s-t}E_t(Y_s^\gamma + \omega_s) + \sum_{s=r}^{T}\beta^{s-t}E_t[(C_s(r) + kB_s(r))^\gamma + \xi_s]$$

(6)
$$- \sum_{s=t}^{T}\beta^{s-t}E_t[(C_s(t) + kB_s(t))^\gamma + \xi_s]$$

$$= g_t(r) + \phi_t(r).$$

The function ϕ contains the random effects, and the function g contains the rest. We must also take into account the likelihood that an individual will survive to receive the earnings anticipated. If we let $\pi(s \mid t)$ represent the probability that a person will be alive in year s given he or she is alive in year t, and assume this probability is independent of the individual error effects, the functions $g_t(r)$ and $\phi_t(r)$ become

(7) $\quad g_t(r) = \sum_{s=t}^{r-1}\beta^{s-t}\pi(s \mid t)E_t(Y_s^\gamma) + \sum_{s=r}^{T}\beta^{s-t}\pi(s \mid t)E_t[(C_s(r) + kB_s(r))^\gamma]$

$$- \sum_{s=t}^{T}\beta^{s-t}\pi(s \mid t)E_t[(C_s(t) + kB_s(t))^\gamma]$$

and

$$\phi_t(r) = \sum_{s=t}^{r-1}\beta^{s-t}\pi(s \mid t)E_t(\omega_s - \xi_s).$$

Under the Markov assumption for the individual specific errors, the expectation at time t can be written $E_t(\omega_s) = \rho^{s-t}\omega_t$ and $E_t(\xi_s) = \rho^{s-t}\xi_t$, and so the function ϕ takes the form

(8) $$\phi_t(r) = \sum_{s=t}^{r-1}\beta^{s-t}\pi(s \mid t)\rho^{s-t}(\omega_t - \xi_t) = K_t(r)v_t,$$

where

$$K_t(r) = \sum_{s=t}^{r-1}\beta^{s-t}\pi(s \mid t)\rho^{s-t} \quad \text{and} \quad v_t = \omega_t - \xi_t.$$

The term $K_t(r)$ cumulates the deflators that yield the present value in year t of the future expected values of the random components of utility. The further r is in the future, the larger is $K_t(r)$. That is, the more distant the potential retirement age, the greater the uncertainty about it, yielding a heteroskedastic disturbance term. Finally, then, the expected gain in year t from postponing departure from the Air Force until year r is

(9) $$G_t(r) = g_t(r) + K_t(r)v_t.$$

If we let R be a random variable representing the year of departure, the probability that an individual will be gone in year t is given by

$$Pr[R = t] = Pr[G_t(r) \leq 0]$$

(10)
$$= Pr[g_t(r) + K_t(r)v_t \leq 0]$$

$$= Pr\left[\frac{g_t(r)}{K_t(r)}\right] \leq -v_t, \qquad \forall\ r \in [t + 1, \ldots, T]$$

$$= Pr\left[\frac{g_t(r^*)}{K_t(r^*)}\right] \leq -v_t,$$

where r^* is the future year that gives the largest value for the gain from remaining in the Air Force.[1]

3.2.3 Other Models

An alternative model has been used by the military for some time to study retirement behavior, and we compare the predictive validity of that model with the option value model discussed above. It is also of interest to consider how the option value model compares with a more complex stochastic dynamic programming model. Lumsdaine, Stock, and Wise (1992) have done this for civilian employees. The cumulating evidence from their work suggests that the more economically accurate stochastic dynamic programming model does no better than the simpler option value model at approximating the actual decisions of employees. The military pension structure offers a particularly good test of the predictive validity of these models, and we present such comparisons in this paper. We describe a popular DoD model and a dynamic programming model.

The Annualized Cost of Leaving Model

The annualized cost of leaving (ACOL) model was developed by John T. Warner (1979) and was the analytical basis for the *Fifth Quadrennial Review of Military Compensation*'s study of changes in the military pension system (Department of Defense 1984). It is used frequently enough by the Air Force Personnel Analysis Center to have been incorporated in an interactive computer program called the Compensation Model for determining the effects of various changes in compensation policies (Norris 1987). The *Department of Defense Aviator Retention Study* (1988) and the Congressional Budget Office (1989) also relied on the model, either directly or indirectly, to predict the effects of the 1989 pilot bonus program.

---

1. The analysis presented in this paper is based on retirement decisions in a single year. Stock and Wise (1990) describe an extension of the model to accommodate repeated observation for the same person over time. Estimates based on more than one consecutive year are presented in Ausink (1991), and the results are virtually the same as those presented here.

The description here is intended to bring out the relationship between the ACOL and the option value models. Assume that individuals are risk neutral ($\gamma = 1$), that military compensation and pension benefits are valued the same (the k in the option value model is one), and that individuals have unobserved random taste Γ for military employment. In year s, the utilities associated with Air Force work and with civilian employment are then

$$(11) \qquad U_M(s) = Y_s + \Gamma \quad \text{and} \quad U_C(s) = C_s(r) + B_s(r).$$

In year t, the expected value of beginning civilian employment in year r is

$$(12) \quad V_t(r) = \sum_{s=t}^{r-1} \beta^{s-t} \pi(s \mid t)(Y_s + \Gamma) + \sum_{s=r}^{T} \beta^{s-t} \pi(s \mid t)(C_s(r) + B_s(r)),$$

and the value of leaving the Air Force for a new job now is

$$(13) \qquad V_t(t) = \sum_{s=t}^{T} \beta^{s-t} \pi(s \mid t)(C_s(t) + B_s(t)).$$

In year t, the cost of leaving instead of remaining until year r, $COL_t(r)$, is the benefit forgone by making the decision to leave in year t,

$$COL_t(r) = V_t(r) - V_t(t)$$

$$(14) \qquad = \sum_{s=t}^{r-1} \beta^{s-t} \pi(s \mid t)Y_s + \sum_{s=r}^{T} \beta^{s-t} \pi(s \mid t)(C_s(r) + B_s(r))$$

$$+ \Gamma \sum_{s=t}^{r-1} \beta^{s-t} \pi(s \mid t).$$

This description has the same form as equation 9, $G_t(r) = g_t(r) + K_t(r)v_t$, in the option value model, with the random taste term replacing the Markov error structure.

A person retires if, when considering all future departure dates, the maximum of

$$(15) \qquad ACOL_t(r) = \left[\sum_{s=t}^{r-1} \beta^{s-t} \pi(s \mid t)\right]^{-1}\left[\sum_{s=t}^{r-1} \beta^{s-t} \pi(s \mid t)Y_s\right.$$

$$\left. + \sum_{s=t}^{r-1} \beta^{s-t} \pi(s \mid t)(C_s(r) + B_s(r))\right] + \Gamma$$

is less than zero,[2] or if $ACOL_t(r^*) = g_t(r^*)/K_t(r^*) + \Gamma < 0$, using the option value definitions (equation 10).

In practice, the model is estimated using the logit formulation

$$(16) \qquad y = \alpha_0 + \alpha_1 ACOL^* + \varepsilon$$

with $ACOL^*$ calculated based on an assumed discount rate.[3]

---

2. This term is also equal to the annualized cost of leaving, which gives rise to the model name.
3. This is similar to a probit specification used in Lumsdaine, Stock, and Wise (1992), comparing the predictive validity of more and less complex models.

A Stochastic Dynamic Programming Specification

We use the stochastic dynamic programming specification used by Lumsdaine, Stock, and Wise (1992), which is a variant of the model proposed by Daula and Moffitt (1989) to study Army enlisted behavior, which is in turn a variant of the Gotz and McCall (1984) dynamic programming model of retention behavior for Air Force officers. When estimating retirement in one period, the Gotz-McCall model is the same as the Daula-Moffitt model.

The main conceptual difference between the option value model and the dynamic programming approach is that in the option value model an individual compares the utility of leaving the military now with the maximum value of expected future utilities. In the dynamic programming models, the decision is based on the expected value of the maximum of current versus future options. An example will help clarify the difference.

For Air Force officers, retirement is mandatory (with few exceptions) after thirty years of service. After the twenty-ninth year of service, the separation decision is thus based on comparing the utility of leaving with the utility of serving one more year and retiring after thirty years of service. At this point, the decision rule for the option value model and the dynamic retention model are the same: the option value model decision maker compares the expected value of retiring with the expected value of working one more year and then retiring, and makes the choice with the maximum value. The dynamic decision maker does the same thing, and we will call the value of this decision W_{29}.

After twenty-eight years of service, the decision rules are different. The option value decision maker compares the expected values of separating after twenty-eight, twenty-nine, and thirty years of service, and makes the decision based on the maximum of these. The dynamic programming rule has the decision maker comparing the value of leaving after twenty-eight years of service with the value of serving one more year and then making decision W_{29}. Since in year twenty-eight the actual circumstances of the twenty-ninth year are not known, the decision is based on the expected value of W_{29}, which is the maximum of two random variables. For any year $t < 28$, an individual can in theory calculate recursively the value of remaining in the service and receiving W_{t+1} from future "correct" decisions.

Again, analogous to the option value specification, assume that an individual's utility from Air Force employment in year s is

(17) $$U_M(s) = Y_s^\gamma + \Gamma + \varepsilon_{1s},$$

and utility from leaving for a new job is

(18) $$U_C(s) = [C_s(r) + kB_s(r)]^\gamma + \varepsilon_{2s}.$$

The term Γ is a random additive taste for military employment, and is assumed to be distributed as $N(0, \lambda^2)$. If $\lambda = 0$, as we will assume in this paper, there is no random taste factor. The disturbance terms are random perturbations to the utilities in a given year of service, and are assumed to be known to the individual at time t. Unlike the option value errors, these are assumed to be independent over time. The estimation procedure is described in the appendix.

3.3   Results

3.3.1   Parameter Estimates and Comparisons

Table 3.2 shows the utility function parameters obtained for the three models of retirement behavior. An easy way to compare the results of the three models is to graph the actual and predicted voluntary loss rates for the pilot population under consideration.[4]

Figure 3.1a shows the actual and option value predicted 1988 voluntary loss rates of pilots in the sample. Figure 3.1b shows the implied cumulative voluntary loss rates. Both panels include a 95% confidence interval around the actual rates.

The option value model predictions fall outside the 95% confidence interval only at seven, eight, nine, and twenty-three years of service. The model underestimates the departure rates at seven and eight years of service; pilots in these years are just completing their initial service obligations for pilot training, and many may be leaving because they realize that military flying is not to their liking. A difference in the characteristics of the pilot population still within a year or two of completion of the initial service obligation and the population that remains after the initial obligation would help explain the inability of the model to pick up the large initial departures.

Promotion to the rank of major occurs sometime after the eleven-year point in an officer's career. Those who accept promotion are obligated to remain in the service for two more years; those who refuse promotion will leave, and those who do not receive the promotion may decide to leave rather than try for promotion at a later date. The jump in actual departures at the twelve-year point seems to be a result of those who are leaving after not accepting (or not receiving) the promotion to major. The model may not pick up this increase because the decision made here involves nonpecuniary factors such as lack of desire to be committed beyond twelve years of service.

It is striking that the model captures rather well the wide jumps in departure rates between twenty and twenty-eight years of service.

By way of comparison, figures 3.2 and 3.3 show the predicted voluntary loss rates using the dynamic programming and ACOL models. Although the dynamic programming formulation matches the data about as well as the op-

---

4. The voluntary loss rate in year t is the percentage of pilots without any service obligation in year t who are not present in year $t + 1$.

Table 3.2   **Parameter Estimate Summary**

Parameter	Option Value Model		Dynamic Programming Model		ACOL
	(1)	(2)	(1)	(2)	
γ	1[a]	1.82	1[a]	1.81	
k	3.32	3.28	1.59	1.44	
	(.032)	(.020)	(.238)	(.184)	
ρ	1[a]	1[a]	—	—	
β	.948	.896	.852	.852	
	(.005)	(.006)	(.012)	(.012)	
σ[b]	.893	.754	.413	1.39	
	(.012)	(.028)	(.031)	(.351)	
α_0					.669
					(.075)
α_1					5.01
					(.007)
Summary statistics					
$-$log likelihood	505.9	496.4	509.3	501.1	529.9
χ^{2c}	50.9	29.3	72.3	52.7	70.0

Notes: Estimation is by maximum likelihood. Numbers in parentheses are asymptotic standard errors. Monetary values are in $100,000 (1986 dollars).

[a]Parameter fixed.

[b]Note that σ for option value model and dynamic programming model are not comparable.

[c]For the above table, the χ^2 goodness-of-fit statistic is calculated as

$$\chi^2 = \sum_{j=7}^{j=28} n_j \frac{(r_{aj} - r_{pj})^2}{r_{pj}},$$

where r_{aj} is the actual departure rate for those with j years of service, r_{pj} is the predicted departure rate for those with j years of service, and n_j is the number of individuals who have completed j years of service.

tion value for persons with less than twenty years of service, it underpredicts the large increase in departures at twenty years, and is much less successful at following retirement patterns after twenty years of service. The ACOL model substantially overpredicts loss rates in the early years of service, does not pick up the large increase in departures after twenty years of service, and does not follow at all the pattern of changes in departure rates after twenty years of service.

We have two "out-of-sample" tests of the predictive power of the models investigated here. The first uses the parameters for the MAC and SAC pilots to predict the loss rates for Tactical Airlift Command (TAC) pilots in the initial sample; the second uses the 1988 parameters to predict 1989 SAC and MAC loss rates after the introduction of ACP.

Figure 3.4a compares the actual voluntary loss rates of TAC pilots in 1988 with the predicted rates using the option value and dynamic programming

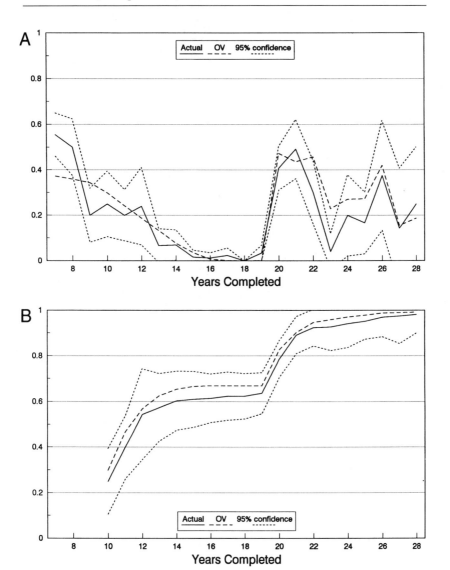

Fig. 3.1   Actual and predicted 1988 voluntary loss rates, option value model

models. Figure 3.4b compares the predictions of the option value and ACOL models. As with the in-sample comparisons, the option value and dynamic programming models yield very similar predictions before twenty years of service, but after twenty years of service the option value model follows the actual departure pattern much better than does the dynamic programming model. The ACOL model predictions are much worse than the other two.

Figures 3.5 and 3.6 compare the predicted 1989 departure rates using 1988

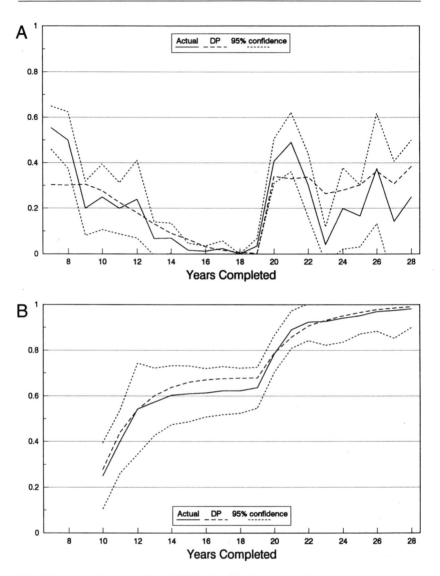

Fig. 3.2   Actual and predicted 1988 voluntary loss rates, dynamic programming model

parameter estimates. The top graph in each figure shows the option value model predictions (both with and without the introduction of the bonus). Again, the option value and dynamic programming models are very similar until the twenty-year point, after which the option value predictions are much closer to the actual departure rates. The ACOL predictions are the farthest from the actual rates. In addition, the ACOL model predicts a much larger reduction

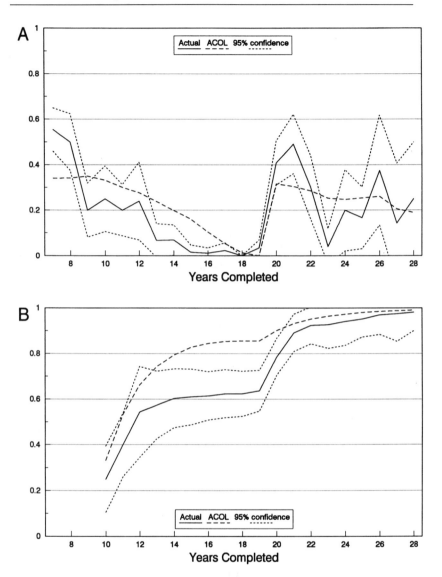

Fig. 3.3   Actual and predicted 1988 voluntary loss rates, ACOL model

in departure rates as a result of the bonus payments than does either the option value or the dynamic programming model.[5]

5. The introduction of ACP did not produce the desired reduction in pilot losses. The Air Force view is that those who accepted the bonus were planning to remain in the service anyway. However, the bonus is not viewed as a failure. Those who accept the bonus incur a service commitment, and so Air Force personnel planners know which pilots will not be able to leave the military in future years.

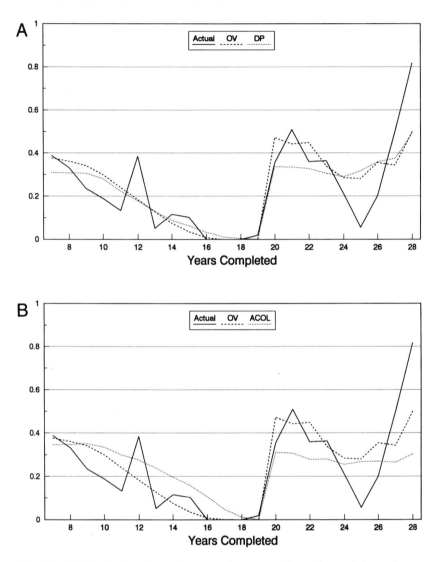

Fig. 3.4   **TAC voluntary loss rate comparisons: *a*, option value and dynamic programming models; *b*, option value and ACOL models**

The importance of the improved predictive capability of the option value model from a policy perspective is apparent in figure 3.7. The figure compares the potential effects of the 1986 change in the military pension predicted by the option value model to those predicted by the ACOL model.[6] Numbers be-

6. This was done by assuming that the relative changes in departure patterns caused by the pension change in the sample are representative of the changes that would be observed in the

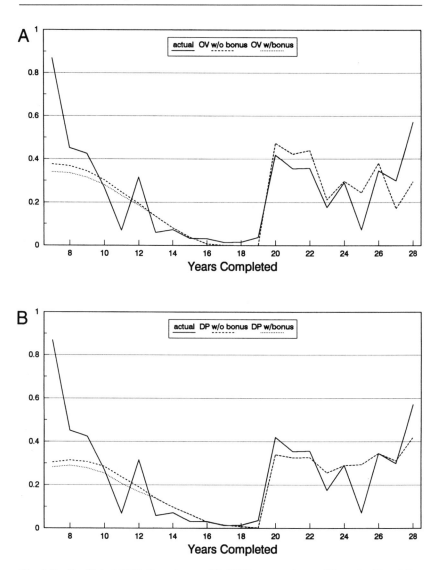

Fig. 3.5   Predicted 1989 departures with 1988 parameters, with and without the pilot bonus: *a*, option value model; *b*, dynamic programming model

low the zero reference line mean that pilots will leave because of the change; numbers above it mean that more will stay. For example, at twelve years of service, the option value model predicts that almost one hundred pilots will

entire pilot population. The simulation assumes that pilots present in 1987 are suddenly faced with the prospect of being subject to the new pension plan.

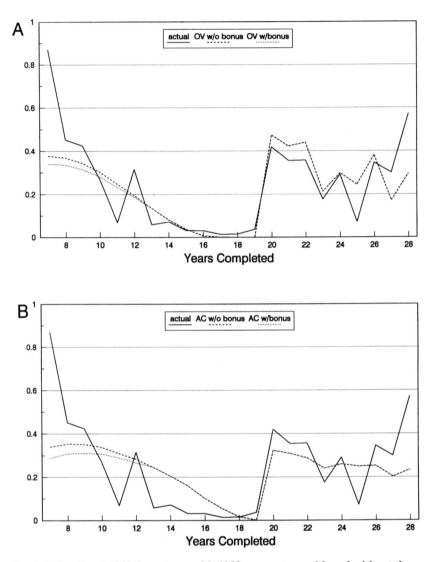

Fig. 3.6   Predicted 1989 departures with 1988 parameters, with and without the pilot bonus: *a*, option value model; *b*, ACOL model

leave because of the new pension plan, while the ACOL model predicts that only ten will leave. What is most important here is that the changes in pension benefits may affect officers at an earlier stage in their career than previously expected. The ACOL model shows very little effect until after twelve years of service; the option value model shows large effects as early as seven years of service. Using 1987 pilot populations, the option value model shows the Air Force losing 714 pilots in the seven-to-nineteen-years-of-service cohorts under

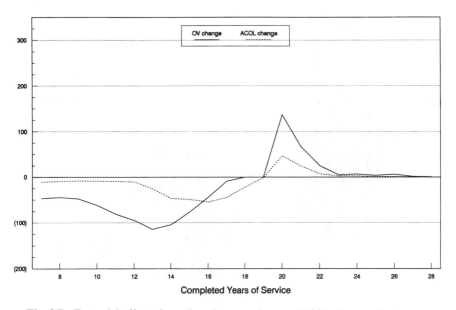

Fig. 3.7   Potential effect of pension change, using total 1987 pilot population

the new system, while the ACOL model shows a loss of only 229. The possibility of the pension change having larger effects on younger military members was raised by Argüden (1987), using the Gotz-McCall dynamic programming model with the Air Force enlisted population.

3.3.2   Potential Changes in Pilot Distribution

Using factors such as the expected number of aircraft available in future years and the number of crews required to fill them, the DoD and the Air Force develop an "objective force" as part of the five-year defense plan to show the desired distribution of pilots by years of service. Decisions concerning changes in the management of the pilot force are made with the objective force structure in mind.

Figure 3.8 shows the 1994 objective force (taken from the *Department of Defense Aviator Retention Study*), the actual distribution of pilots by years of service in 1990, and the distribution of pilots if the departure rates of 1990 continued for the next four years. The figure assumes that sixteen hundred pilots complete pilot training each year. Compared to the objective force, current pilot levels are low in all years except five, six, seven, and the years after fifteen. With the 1990 departure rates, the shortages will increase in all years from six through nineteen, and, of course, this is the problem that the pilot bonus was meant to solve.

We noted in section 3.3.1 that the implementation of ACP did not have the desired effect on pilot retention rates. We have attempted to devise a bonus

Number of Pilots

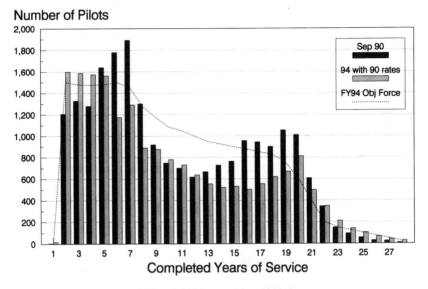

Fig. 3.8   Population in 1990 and 1994, assuming 1990 departure rates

that would induce the departure rates necessary to maintain the 1994 objective force.

We do this by noting the percentage decrease in 1990 departure rates necessary to reach the 1994 steady-state rates and determining the bonus necessary to achieve this decrease of departure rates in the 1988 sample of MAC and SAC pilots.[7]

The result of this exercise is shown in figure 3.9. The best fit using a new bonus amount requires that current bonuses be increased sixfold—that is, for a pilot who has completed six years of service, the annual bonus for the next eight years needs to be $72,000 instead of $12,000! The population changes over the five-year period from 1990 to 1994 lead to the distribution in the figure. The pilot shortages from seven years of service to twelve years of service are largely reduced (overcome more than we want in nine, ten, and eleven), but shortages continue from thirteen years on. This would obviously be an extremely expensive program.

If we assume that the pension plan change that affects military members who entered the service after August 1986 were suddenly applicable to pilots present in 1990, the long-term effects of the decrease in pension compensation result in the distribution of figure 3.10. Pilot shortages increase from eight years of service through nineteen years of service, then surpluses exist through twenty-seven years of service.

7. We assume that the new bonuses are a constant multiple k of the current bonuses available. The k that produces the best fit (in a least squares sense) to the desired departure rates gives us the new bonuses.

Number of Pilots

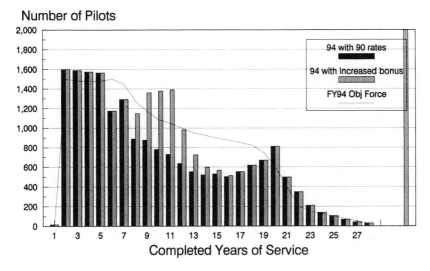

Fig. 3.9   Population in 1990 and 1994: 1990 departures versus increased bonus.
Base total = 18, 911; new total = 21,552.

Number of Pilots

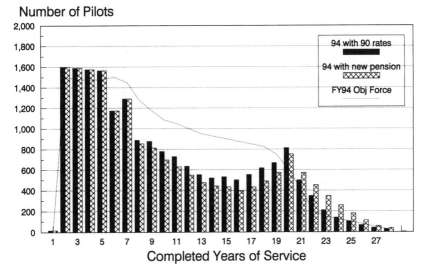

**Fig. 3.10   Population in 1990 and 1994: 1990 departures versus new
pension rates**

3.4   Conclusions

The option value model captures Air Force pilot departure behavior much better than the ACOL model that has been used by the military, and substantially better than a more complex stochastic dynamic programming specification. The superiority of the option value model to the dynamic programming formulation raises the possibility that individual decision making may not always be best modeled with a model that is intended to approximate "correct" economic financial calculations. This is consistent with the results of Lumsdaine, Stock, and Wise (1992).

Predictions of the effects of changes in compensation using the option value model indicate that individuals at early stages in their careers are more sensitive to losses of future benefits than indicated by previous models. The effects of temporary annual bonuses such as ACP are small—and bonus amounts must be extremely large to induce departure rates that come close to achieving the 1994 objective force.

The extraordinary changes in the world's political and military climate since the summer of 1991 will lead to adjustments in the defense structure of the United States. Already, decreases in the defense budget have led to a drop in the planned number of Air Force tactical fighter wings and a 25% decrease in the number of cockpits available for pilots. Entries into undergraduate pilot training will be reduced by 270 pilots per year starting in 1992, and the total number of pilots in the Air Force is expected to be down from over 21,000 in 1990 to 16,500 in 1997.[8]

Overall Air Force strength is projected to decrease markedly in the next few years—from 545,000 personnel in 1990 to approximately 415,000 by 1995. To encourage people to leave the service, the Air Force instituted two incentive programs in 1992. The first, called the Voluntary Separation Incentive (VSI), provides an annual payment to an individual (payment based on base pay and number of years of service) that will last for twice the number of years the individual has been in the service. For example, a major with sixteen years of service could leave the Air Force and receive an annual payment of $17,466 for thirty-two years (a present value of $236,343, according to the Air Force).

The second, called the Special Separation Benefit (SSB), is a lump-sum payment that is 15% of an individual's base pay multiplied by the number of years served. The major mentioned above would receive a one time SSB payment of $104,795.

Both programs were introduced with little econometric modeling of their potential effects, and fewer officers than expected applied to accept either program.

As the Air Force and the other services struggle to reduce in size, other

---

8. These figures for pilot reductions were reported in the 15 July 1991 *Air Force Times*.

separation incentives will be proposed and studied. The procedure discussed here may be useful in predicting their effects.

3.5   Postscript: VSI/SSB Results

The present value of the SSB is significantly less than the present value of the VSI. Nonetheless, initial applications to leave the Air Force under either program showed a large preference for the lump-sum payment. By June 1992, of the 4,870 officers who accepted one of the programs, a small majority chose the annuity (2,366 accepted the lump sum); of 24,807 enlisted personnel who accepted one of the programs, the vast majority—22,140—chose the lump-sum payment.

Acceptance rates varied with age and rank. All enlisted ranks preferred the lump-sum payment. On the officer side, first lieutenants preferred the VSI to the SSB by a slight margin (51.7% to 48.3%), captains preferred the SSB by a slight margin (51% to 49%), and majors preferred the VSI 68.6% to 31.4%.[9] In an exit survey conducted by the AFMPC, reasons given for selecting the lump sum over the annuity included "quick money" and "investment." Reasons for preferring the annuity included "greater value" and "long-term income." On a more sour note, 95 of 900 written comments received in the survey addressed lack of trust in the government to follow through on the annuity payments as a reason to accept the lump sum instead.[10]

The unexpected pattern of benefit acceptance raises questions about how individuals treat lump-sum payments as opposed to annuities. It is no surprise that the option value model shows that the pilot population should prefer the VSI program to the SSB because of the former's higher present value; however, one experiment with the option value model showed an interesting result.

In figure 3.11, the "Base, few hires" line shows hazard rates predicted by the option value model if the probability of being hired by an airline gradually decreases as an individual gets older and neither VSI nor SSB is offered. The VSI6 line in the figure (which we could call the predictions for the "pessimistic" pilots) shows the predicted hazard rates for pilots who believe that airline hiring will decline and would treat VSI as a retirement benefit; that is, the benefit is multiplied by the k parameter in the model.

On the other hand, if we assume that the probability of being hired by an airline after leaving the Air Force remains certain and also assume that an SSB lump-sum payment is treated as ordinary income (that is, it is not multiplied by the k parameter in the model), the predicted hazard rates are as shown by the SSB8 line (the "optimistic" pilots).

---

9. These figures come from information provided by Major Jerry Ludke, of the AFMPC/DPYO at Randolph Air Force Base.

10. The survey was conducted by the Analysis Division, Directorate of Personnel Operations, AFMPC, Randolph Air Force Base, Texas.

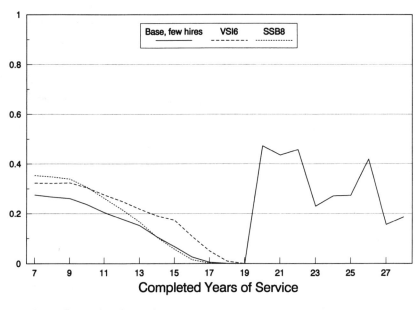

Fig. 3.11   Postscript simulations

The lines cross at about ten years of service. A very loose interpretation of this result could be that before ten years of service pilots are optimistic about getting an airline position and prefer the SSB income; after ten years of service pilots are less optimistic about an airline job and treat the VSI as an early pension.

In actuality, the pilot population did prefer the SSB to the VSI before about ten years of service, and the VSI afterward. However, the population involved is very small (482 pilots were eligible for either program, only 370 applied, and 313 of these were in the eleven-to-sixteen-year cohorts), and it is premature to read too much into the result of this experiment. Nonetheless, it is intriguing that the model hints at what should be obvious: individuals consider a variety of issues besides the present value of a benefit when making a decision about leaving employment.

Appendix
Stochastic Dynamic-Programming Model

In year t, the individual makes the decision to stay or leave based on the value function W_t given by

$$(A1) \qquad W_t = \max\left[E_t(Y_t^\gamma + \Gamma + \varepsilon_{1t} + \beta W_{t+1}),\right.$$

$$E_t(\sum_{s=t}^{T} \beta^{s-t}(C_s(t) + kB_s(t))^\gamma + \varepsilon_{2t})\Big],$$

where β is the discount factor and T is the time of death. The first expected value in the brackets is that of remaining in the service one more year and then making the best decision in year $t + 1$; the second term is the expected value of leaving now.

Since the disturbances are independently and identically distributed, $E_t\varepsilon_{i,t+s} = 0$ for $s > 0$. With this fact, and again taking into account the probability of surviving to year s given a person is alive in year t, we can write

(A2) $$W_t = \max[W_{1t}^* + \varepsilon_{1t}, W_{2t}^* + \varepsilon_{2t}],$$

where

(A3) $$W_{1t}^* = Y_t^\gamma + \Gamma + \beta\pi(t + 1 \mid t)E_tW_{t+1}$$

and

(A4) $$W_{2t}^* = \sum_{s=t}^{T} \beta^{s-t}\pi(s \mid t)(C_s(t) + kB_s(t))^\gamma.$$

An individual will decide to leave the military if

(A5) $$W_{1t}^* + \varepsilon_{1t} < W_{2t}^* + \varepsilon_{2t},$$

and so the probability of leaving in year t is

(A6) $$Pr[W_{1t}^* + \varepsilon_{1t} < W_{2t}^* + \varepsilon_{2t}] = Pr[\varepsilon_{1t} - \varepsilon_{2t} < W_{2t}^* - W_{1t}^*].$$

If we assume that the ε_{it} are independent draws from a normal distribution with zero mean and variance σ^2, the variance of $(\varepsilon_{1t} - \varepsilon_{2t})$ is $2\sigma^2$, and we can write equation A6 as

(A7) $$Pr[R = t] = Pr\left[\frac{(\varepsilon_{1t} - \varepsilon_{2t})}{\sqrt{2}\sigma} < \frac{(W_{2t}^* - W_{1t}^*)}{\sqrt{2}\sigma}\right] = \Phi(a_t),$$

where Φ is the cumulative normal distribution function and $a_t = (W_{2t}^* - W_{1t}^*)/\sqrt{2}\sigma$.

To find this probability, we need to get an expression for the recursive part of the function W_t, that is, $E_{t-1}W_t$. This can be shown to be

(A8) $$E_{t-1}\left(\frac{W_t}{\sigma}\right) = \frac{W_{1t}^*}{\sigma}(1 - \Phi(a_t)) + \frac{W_{2t}^*}{\sigma}\Phi(a_t) + \sqrt{2}\phi(a_t),$$

where ϕ is the standard normal density function.

In equation A8, $\Phi(a_t)$ represents the probability that the individual leaves the military and receives utility W_{2t}^*, and $(1 - \Phi(a_t))$ represents the probability that the decision is made to remain and receive utility W_{1t}^*. The remaining term comes from the expectation of the disturbances. In sum, we use equation A8 to recursively calculate the values of W^*_{1t} and W^*_{2t}, and then use equation A7 to calculate the probability of retirement.[11]

The error structures of the option value and dynamic programming approaches are similar, but arise from different assumptions. In both cases, future errors are normally distributed with nonzero covariance. This is the result of the Markov assumption for the generation of the errors in the option value model, but comes from a "components of variance structure, with an individual specific effect" (Lumsdaine, Stock and Wise 1992, 14) in the dynamic programming model.

References

Argüden, Yilmaz R. 1987. *Unintended Effects of the New Military Retirement System.* RAND Note N-2604-AF. Santa Monica, CA: RAND Corporation.

Ausink, John A. 1991. The Effect of Changes in Compensation on a Pilot's Decision to Leave the Air Force. Ph.D. dissertation, Harvard University.

Baldwin, Robert H., and Thomas V. Daula. 1985. Modeling the Retention Behavior of First Term Military Personnel: Methodological Issues and a Proposed Specification. *Research in Labor Economics* 7: 339–63.

Bartholomew, Herbert A. 1982. *Military Compensation Background Papers: Compensation Elements and Related Manpower Cost Items, Their Purposes, and Legislative Backgrounds.* 2d ed. Washington, DC: Department of Defense, Office of the Secretary of Defense.

Bowman, Charlie T. 1990. Aviator Continuation Pay Memorandum. HQ AFMPC/DPMATM, Randolph Air Force Base, TX, 3 October.

Congressional Budget Office. 1989. *Alternative Compensation Plans for Improving Retention of Air Force Pilots: A Special Study.* Washington, DC: Government Printing Office.

Daula, Thomas V., and Robert A. Moffitt. 1989. A Dynamic Model of Enlisted Retention Behavior in the Army. April. Manuscript.

Department of Defense. 1984. *Fifth Quadrennial Review of Military Compensation.* 6 vols. Washington, DC: Government Printing Office.

———. 1988. *Department of Defense Aviator Retention Study, 1988.* Washington, DC: Government Printing Office.

———. 1989a. *Department of Defense Annual Report, 1989.* Washington, DC: Government Printing Office.

———. 1989b. *Report of the Secretary of Defense.* Washington, DC: Government Printing Office.

Gotz, Glenn A., and John J. McCall. 1984. *A Dynamic Retention Model for Air Force Officers.* RAND Corporation Report R-3028-AF. Santa Monica, CA: RAND Corporation.

Lumsdaine, Robin L., James H. Stock, and David A. Wise. 1992. Three Models of Retirement: Computational Complexity versus Predictive Validity. In *Topics in the*

---

11. When no taste factor is used, this is all that is needed in the estimation. When the taste factor is allowed, it is also necessary to integrate over the taste distribution. This integration substantially increases the computation time for the dynamic programming model.

Economics of Aging, ed. David A. Wise, 19–57. Chicago: University of Chicago Press.

Norris, James M. 1987. *The DPAC Compensation Model: An Introductory Handbook.* Maxwell Air Force Base, AL: Air Command and Staff College.

Stock, James H., and David A. Wise. 1990. Pensions, the Option Value of Work, and Retirement. *Econometrica* 58 (5): 1151–80.

Warner, John T. 1979. *Alternative Military Retirement Systems: Their Effects on Enlisted Retention.* Alexandria, VA: Center for Naval Analyses.

Wise, David A., ed. 1985. *Pensions, Labor, and Individual Choice.* Chicago: University of Chicago Press.

Comment on Chapters 2 and 3   Robert J. Willis

The two papers that I am to discuss represent significant new applications of theories of optimal retirement, including dynamic programming models and the option value model developed by Stock and Wise (1990), to real world problems. The application by Ausink and Wise (AW) to decisions by pilots to leave the Air Force appears to be a nearly unqualified success, while the paper by Lumsdaine, Stock, and Wise (LSW) attempts, without success, to eliminate a small but interesting blemish on their otherwise excellent track record in predicting retirement behavior using forward-looking optimal models.

Since it is difficult to quarrel with success, I will postpone that task and turn first to a discussion of the LSW paper, which attempts to explain the spike in the retirement hazard at age 65. The paper's title describes its focus on an interesting empirical puzzle that was noted but remained unexplained in Lumsdaine, Stock, and Wise (1992), a previous paper in this conference series. As a discussant, it is heartening to note that at least one idea from comments on their paper concerning the effect of continuation of employer health benefits after retirement (Schieber 1992) received serious attention in this year's paper. But it is both surprising and chastening to discover that this good suggestion has no merit: the current LSW paper shows that the presence or absence of such benefits has absolutely no effect on retirement decisions at any age. I was also surprised that marital status had so little effect and that retirement patterns for men and women are so similar.

After finding that other possible explanations, at best, go only partway toward explaining the age-65 spike, the tentative explanation advanced by the authors is that retirement at age 65 is a norm that remains normative because, according to their calculations, adherence to the norm has a low opportunity cost (for most people) relative to the optimal age calculated from a dynamic program. Given that the continual reoptimization needed to calculate optimal

Robert J. Willis is professor of economics at the University of Michigan.

retirement is difficult and, perhaps, anxiety-inducing, the authors argue that adoption of a simple rule of thumb to retire at age 65 is understandable.

Before discussing my reactions to the theoretical issues embedded in this explanation, I first wish to express a little skepticism about the claim that the spike in the retirement hazard at age 65 represents a norm, at least in the sense that the term "norm" can be equated with the term "normal age of retirement." First, to complement the figures presented in the paper that plot the retirement hazards for data from three firms, in figure 3C.1 I plot the hazards for males from the three national samples that are reported in the final three columns of table 2.2 in LSW. These hazards are nearly identical to one another and are similar in shape to the empirical hazard functions for individual firms, which are displayed in figures 2.1–2.3 of LSW. In particular, they each show a spike at age 65. However, the spike at age 65 is followed by quite elevated hazards at ages after 65, possibly suggesting that it is retirement at age 65 or over that is normative.[1]

I also used the data in table 2.2 to calculate cumulative hazard functions for all six samples, which are plotted in figure 3C.2. The functions from the NMES data and from the two SIPP samples lie between the plot for Firm 2, which shows a pattern of relatively delayed retirement, and the plots for Firms 1 and 3, in which retirement is relatively accelerated. I note in passing that it is slightly misleading for LSW to emphasize the similarities in the shapes of the hazard functions in the three firms without pointing out how different Firm 2 is in the pattern of cumulative retirement. Focusing on the national samples, we see that about 50% of retirements occur before age 65, with 20% occurring before age 62 and 30% between ages 62 and 64. Moreover, almost one-third of the retirements occurring at age 65 or later take place after age 65. Put simply, my skepticism about viewing retirement at age 65 as a norm is based on evidence that only a small minority of retirements take place at age 65.

To be persuasive, I believe that the empirical argument presented in the paper in favor of viewing the choice of retirement at age 65 as a rule of thumb needs to be generalized to consider the opportunity cost of an arbitrary decision to retire at any given age before or after age 65 relative to the benefits of choosing an "optimal age." Apart from windows and special early retirement features, I would guess that the data for another age such as 64 or 66 would look much like the data presented in table 2.7. If so, the argument for regarding the peak at age 65 as a norm does not seem compelling. A rule of thumb that selected another age would be just as attractive. The argument that age 65 is special seems to appeal to an idea of what was typical behavior two or three decades ago but which is now quite atypical.

---

1. A possible caveat, however, is that the hazard rates at older ages may be biased upward because the samples are restricted to persons of at least age 70 who declared themselves to be retired at the time of interview. Unless the samples are concentrated at the lower end of this age limit, this bias seems unlikely to be very large.

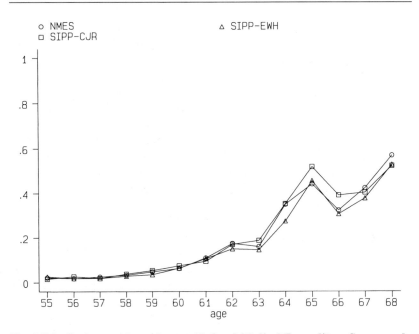

Fig. 3C.1   Retirement hazard rates, National Medical Expenditure Survey and Survey of Income and Program Participation

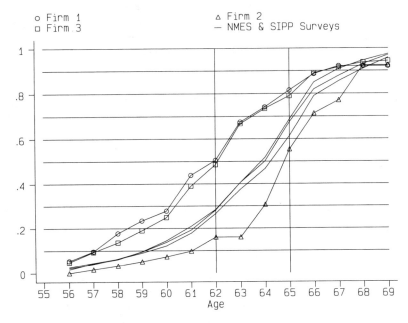

Fig. 3C.2   Cumulative proportion retired

Even if it is not a fully satisfactory way of explaining the age-65 peak, the rule-of-thumb argument may still be useful. As I understand it, LSW argue that those components of an individual's retirement resources that are outside the control of a firm's personnel policies (e.g., Social Security wealth, defined-contribution pensions, personal assets) do not provide strong incentives to retire at a particular age. Given this lack of incentive, workers may enjoy the luxury of choosing an age to retire with certainty and without complex calculation, thereby improving their capacity to make unmodeled decisions, such as the purchase of a retirement home in Sun City. On the other hand, if firms attempt to manipulate pension provisions in an attempt to keep or get rid of workers of a given age, we may infer from the predictive success of the option value and dynamic programming models that workers are capable of rational decision making of at least moderate complexity. To the extent that the opportunity costs of varying the age of employment are small, at least in the vicinity of age 65, it may be possible for employers to generate considerable alterations in behavior at quite modest cost. I hope that this possibility is kept from my employer, which has responded to the elimination of mandatory retirement for professors as of 1 January 1994 with a plan to pay a bonus of twice their academic salary to professors who agree to retire at age 65. Unfortunately, choices made by my senior colleagues may reveal the secret before I am eligible to collect my windfall.

Let me now turn to the AW paper on Air Force pilots. This is a wonderful application of the option value/dynamic programming methodology to a very important problem that acquired vastly greater importance with the end of the Cold War. The predictive success of these models is extremely impressive, and the demonstration of their superiority over the DoD's existing ACOL model is persuasive, although I would like to see some added discussion of what features of the option value and dynamic programming (OV/DP) models are responsible for this superiority. I suspect that the success of these models will lead to the replacement of the ACOL model with OV/DP models to design and evaluate military manpower policies for dealing with the dynamics of downsizing the military. Pictures such as those in figure 3.9 of the paper are, therefore, of more than academic interest.

My only serious reservation about the paper, and about the application of these models to policy, concerns the use of data on civilian opportunities. After pointing out that military pilots almost always leave to become pilots in civilian airlines, the paper is completely silent about what assumptions are made about employment conditions in the civilian sector. The reader should be told more about the data and/or assumptions about the civilian sector that underlie the estimates presented in the paper. More important, it seems likely that the current negative trends in the market for civilian airline pilots may have a very substantial effect on decisions by pilots to leave the Air Force and that predictions of rates of departure based on the booming market for pilots during the 1980s may be far off the mark in designing policies for the 1990s. It would be useful to add some discussion and, if possible, develop some quantitative measures of the sensitivity of model predictions to variations in civilian labor market conditions. Given the high cost of training pilots and the correspondingly high value of making good decisions about manpower decisions in this area, I would think that the Air Force might consider investing in the acquisition of some postretirement data on its pilots, at least by using their Social Security earnings histories.

My final comments concern issues of interpretation of these forward-looking models of retirement behavior and suggestions for directions for further research. Ostensibly, estimates of these models tell us about behavioral parameters that measure the value of leisure, the degree of risk aversion, and the rate of time discount. These parameters are of very general interest and importance in explaining many decisions in addition to retirement, such as consumption and savings, insurance purchases, housing choices, and so forth. Moreover, the values of these parameters have crucial implications for evaluating both the positive and normative aspects of policy toward the elderly.

My question is how seriously (or literally) we should take estimates of these parameters? For example, should I take estimates of $\gamma = 1.8$ for Air Force pilots as confirmation of my prior beliefs about this risk-loving bunch whom I should expect to see patronizing Las Vegas in large numbers? Should I take estimates of $\gamma = 1.0$ among the retirees of Firm 3 as evidence that they are risk neutral? Or, alternatively, should I regard this as evidence that these employees do not suffer diminishing marginal utility from concentrations of income in a given period because they are able to smooth their incomes through transactions in financial markets? What should I make of large differences in extra value of pension dollars to pilots, depending on whether their decisions are modeled with the option value or dynamic programming framework? Do men in Firm 3 value their leisure more than do women? A much more cautious view is that k, β, and γ are to be regarded as no more than parameters that provide enough flexibility of functional form to enable the model to fit the data. Stock and Wise (1990) discussed such questions in their initial presentation of the option value model and tended, at that time, to come down toward the cautious end of the interpretational spectrum. Now that they and their collaborators have had more experience in estimating these models with different data sets and in both dynamic programming and option value specifications, I would like to see them revisit these questions of whether the variations in incentives provided by pension programs provide natural experiments that can reveal underlying general behavioral parameters.

In a similar vein, I would like to see the authors discuss the potential of applying these models to general data sets such as the new Health and Retirement Survey that contain data on individuals who face a wide variety of pension plans, including no plans at all. Although I do not know this literature well, it appears that much of the excellent track record of the forward-looking models has been earned by predicting behavior of individuals who are all employees of a given firm. This is certainly true of both papers under discussion today, albeit the Air Force is a very large firm. When applied to one firm at a time, the models can be very useful management tools. For most questions of broad policy, however, one would like to have estimates of the impact on the retirement behavior of broad population groups. I know from the record of previous conferences in this series that the ambitious efforts of John Rust to apply dynamic programming methods to the RHS data have been frustrated by computational difficulties. What I am wondering is whether the simpler and more approximate, but computationally feasible, methods pioneered by the authors of these two papers can make a useful contribution when applied to broader populations.

References

Lumsdaine, R. L., J. H. Stock, and D. A. Wise. 1992. Three Models of Retirement: Computational Complexity versus Predictive Validity. In *Topics in the Economics of Aging,* ed. David A. Wise, 19–57. Chicago: University of Chicago Press.

Schieber, Sylvester J. 1992. Comment on Three Models of Retirement, by R. L. Lumsdaine, J. H. Stock, and D. A. Wise. In *Topics in the Economics of Aging,* ed. David A. Wise. Chicago: University of Chicago Press.

Stock, James H., and David A. Wise. 1990. Pensions, the Option Value of Work, and Retirement. *Econometrica* 58 (5): 1151–80.

4   Health Insurance and Early Retirement: Evidence from the Availability of Continuation Coverage

Jonathan Gruber and Brigitte C. Madrian

The dramatic postwar decline in the labor force participation of older men in the United States has motivated a sizable body of literature on retirement behavior. Three factors, in particular, have been studied extensively: the growth of the Social Security program (see, for example, Burtless 1986; Burtless and Moffitt 1984; Diamond and Hausman 1984; Hausman and Wise 1985; Sueyoshi 1989), the increased availability and generosity of private pensions (Stock and Wise 1990a, 1990b), and the expansion of federal disability insurance (Bound and Waidmann 1992). One potentially important factor that until recently has not received much attention is the availability of health insurance for retirees. This oversight is especially surprising given the rather consistent evidence that health status is an important determinant in the retirement decision (Bazzoli 1985; Diamond and Hausman 1984). If health status matters in the decision about when to retire, it seems quite natural that health insurance should matter as well.

The increased availability of health insurance for older Americans, especially retirees, has come in several forms. First among them is the introduction in the mid-1960s of Medicare, a federal program that provides near-universal health insurance coverage for those over age 65. A second source of health insurance that has grown in importance, particularly for those under age 65 who are not yet eligible for Medicare, is employer-provided postretirement health insurance. While only 30% of men who retired in the early 1960s re-

Jonathan Gruber is associate professor of economics at the Massachusetts Institute of Technology and a faculty research fellow of the National Bureau of Economic Research. Brigitte C. Madrian is assistant professor of economics at the University of Chicago and a faculty research fellow of the National Bureau of Economic Research.

The authors wish to thank David Cutler, James Poterba, Andrew Samwick, Richard Zeckhauser, and seminar participants at Harvard, MIT, and the NBER for their comments, and Aaron Yelowitz for his help in assembling the SIPP data. They also acknowledge financial support from the James Phillips Fund, the Harry and Lynde Bradley Foundation, and the National Institute on Aging.

ceived health insurance from their former employers, this fraction increased to almost half for those retiring in the 1980s (Madrian 1994).

This paper looks at the effect on retirement of a third source of health insurance for early retirees, namely continuation coverage benefits. During the late 1970s and early 1980s many states mandated that employers allow employees who leave their jobs to continue purchasing their group health insurance for a specified number of months. These continuation benefits were extended to all workers in 1986 as part of the federal Consolidated Omnibus Budget Reconciliation Act (COBRA) legislation. Although this coverage is available to all workers regardless of age, it should be particularly attractive to older workers who face a relatively high price for health insurance in the private market and who are more likely to be subject to the preexisting-conditions exclusions that are characteristic of such policies.

To identify the effect of continuation benefits on retirement, we exploit the fact that these benefits were mandated at different times by different states (and finally the federal government) and that the generosity of the mandates varied across states as well. Using data from the Current Population Survey (CPS), we find a strong correlation between the availability of continuation benefits and the likelihood that individuals are retired. Our key finding is that, among men aged 55–64, one year of continuation benefits increases the probability of being retired by 1 percentage point; this is 5.4% of the baseline probability of being retired for this group. Furthermore, we find that, although the estimated percentage-point effects are strongest near the age of Medicare eligibility, as a fraction of baseline retirement probabilities they actually decline with age. Although this latter result is somewhat counterintuitive, it is consistent with other work that examines the effect of continuation coverage on flows into retirement (Gruber and Madrian 1995). We also find that continuation coverage mandates significantly increase the likelihood that early retirees are covered by employer-provided health insurance after retirement. This effect is much larger than the implied effect on retirement, suggesting that much of the increase in coverage is occurring among those individuals who would have retired even in the absence of such benefits.

The organization of the paper is as follows. Section 4.1 provides some motivation for why health insurance should matter in the early retirement decision. Section 4.2 outlines the state and federal continuation coverage laws, which we use to identify the effect of health insurance on retirement. This is followed in section 4.3 by a model that formalizes the effect of health insurance on retirement. The data and regression framework are presented in section 4.4, and the results follow in section 4.5 along with a comparison with our findings from dynamic models of retirement behavior. Section 4.6 considers the impact of continuation coverage mandates on insurance coverage. The paper concludes in section 4.7 with a discussion of the methodological and policy implications of our results.

4.1 Health Insurance and Retirement: Should It Matter?

The high and variable level of medical expenditures for persons aged 55–64, without the guarantee of public coverage through Medicare for those over age 65, means that the availability of health insurance coverage could be a key factor in determining the timing of retirement. Until recently, however, there has been little study of the effect of retiree health insurance coverage on retirement patterns. Two recent papers have attempted to model the role of health insurance in the retirement decision. Lumsdaine, Stock, and Wise (1994) incorporate the value of Medicare into an option value model of retirement and find no effect of Medicare eligibility on the retirement hazard. Their result is not surprising, however, as they estimate their model on a sample of workers from the same firm, all of whom have employer-provided postretirement health insurance that is much more generous than Medicare. Gustman and Steinmeier (1994) use information from the Retirement History Survey, a longitudinal survey from the 1970s, to ascertain whether individuals have employer-provided retiree health insurance, and data from the 1977 National Medical Care Expenditure Survey, to impute the value of that insurance based on individual characteristics. They also find very small effects of retiree health insurance on retirement decisions.

The results of these two studies are at odds with both intuition and with what individuals report about the importance of health insurance in the retirement decision. In a recent Gallup poll, 63% of working Americans reported that they "would delay retirement until becoming eligible for Medicare [age 65] if their employers were not going to provide health coverage" despite the fact that 50% "said they would prefer to retire early—by age 62" (Employee Benefits Research Institute 1990). The apparent contradiction between the importance of health insurance as stated by individuals and that estimated by these two previous studies provides a further motivation for our research.

4.1.1 Health Status of Older Individuals

That individuals should cite health insurance as an important consideration in the retirement decision is not surprising, as older persons are fairly likely to need expensive medical care. Tables 4.1–4.4 compare the health status of individuals by age along a number of dimensions. The simplest measure, self-reported health status, is shown in table 4.1. The fraction of individuals who report being in fair or poor health increases markedly from ages 45–54 (19.7%) to ages 55–64 (31.3%). While recent research has suggested that self-reported health status may be a poor indicator of the actual severity of an individual's clinical conditions (Bazzoli 1985), it may be the most accurate measure of an individual's valuation of health insurance coverage. Thus, these figures suggest that insurance valuation will rise dramatically with age.

Furthermore, as table 4.2 shows, health status as measured by doctor-

Table 4.1   **Self-Reported Health Status by Age (%)**

	Health Status			
Age	Excellent	Good	Fair	Poor
25–34	36.4	53.1	9.5	1.1
35–44	32.0	54.6	11.9	1.5
45–54	27.8	52.5	15.6	4.1
55–64	18.0	50.7	24.9	6.4
65+	9.3	43.1	36.1	11.4

Source: Authors' calculations using data from the 1987 National Medical Expenditure Survey.
Note: The numbers in the table give the fraction of individuals who report having the given health status.

Table 4.2   **Incidence of Health Problems by Age (%)**

	Age				
Condition	25–34	35–44	45–54	55–64	65+
Stroke	0.4	0.8	1.6	3.6	7.4
Cancer	1.6	2.4	4.7	9.7	13.3
Heart attack	0.3	1.1	3.8	7.7	13.3
Gallbladder disease	1.6	3.6	7.3	9.4	14.6
High blood pressure	10.1	18.2	29.1	41.9	49.8
Arteriosclerosis	0.2	0.6	2.8	6.1	16.3
Rheumatism	0.8	1.6	5.2	8.2	16.4
Emphysema	0.4	1.0	2.6	5.2	8.0
Arthritis	5.1	11.6	24.9	41.2	54.9
Diabetes	1.7	3.0	5.7	9.8	14.7
Heart disease	0.8	2.2	6.1	11.9	22.2
Any of the above	18.2	31.7	51.8	72.3	84.2

Source: Authors' calculations using data from the 1987 National Medical Expenditure Survey.
Note: The numbers in the table give the fraction of individuals who report ever having had the listed medical condition.

diagnosed health problems deteriorates with age as well. The incidence of many of the health problems listed (stroke, cancer, heart attack, arteriosclerosis, emphysema, and heart disease) more than doubles between 45–54 and ages 55–64. Furthermore, almost three-quarters of those aged 55–64 have been diagnosed with at least one of the eleven conditions listed. Not surprisingly, relative to those aged 45–54, individuals 55–64 are more likely to be admitted to the hospital over the course of a year and spend more time there once admitted (table 4.3).

The most direct evidence that health insurance should be valued relatively highly by older workers, however, is that the actual medical expenses incurred by those aged 55–64 are much higher than those of younger individuals (table 4.4). In every category not only do expenditures rise with age, but the variance

Table 4.3   **Annual Medical Care Utilization by Age**

	Age				
	25–34	35–44	45–54	55–64	65+
Fraction admitted to hospital (%)	9.2	6.8	8.7	11.0	20.1
Number of admissions (if ever admitted)	1.17	1.24	1.39	1.5	1.5
Nights in hospital (if ever admitted)	5.5	6.8	9.3	11.8	13.8
Fraction with prescribed medicines (%)	52.9	55.6	61.1	71.1	81.9
Number of prescribed medicines (if any prescribed medicines)	5.2	6.6	11.5	14.7	18.5
Fraction who visited a doctor (%)	64.1	67.1	71.1	77.9	85.8
Number of doctor visits (if visited a doctor)	4.6	4.6	5.5	6.0	7.4

Source: Authors' calculations using data from the 1987 National Medical Expenditure Survey.

Table 4.4   **Average Annual Medical Expenditures by Age (1990 dollars)**

	Age					
	25–34	35–44	45–54	55–64	65–74	75+
Average expenditures						
Hospital/inpatient	794	744	894	1,526	2,142	3,700
	(3,763)	(3,186)	(3,648)	(6,211)	(6,567)	(10,811)
Physician/outpatient	334	330	391	473	543	560
	(716)	(653)	(890)	(1,176)	(1,582)	(916)
Prescription medication	477	65	111	163	195	221
	(98)	(154)	(208)	(299)	(271)	(276)
Total	1,176	1,135	1,395	2,144	2,877	4,481
	(4,025)	(3,537)	(4,001)	(6,532)	(7,070)	(11,045)
Average expenditure if expenditure > 0						
Hospital/inpatient	2,103	2,350	2,289	3,945	4,747	(7,482)
	(5,900)	(5,323)	(5,557)	(9,502)	(9,151)	(14,218)
Physician/outpatient	467	458	543	592	668	(662)
	(807)	(731)	(1,002)	(1,287)	(1,732)	(959)
Prescription medication	80	111	178	230	258	(269)
	(117)	(189)	(243)	(332)	(284)	(282)
Total	1,454	1,428	1,699	2,461	3,270	(4,820)
	(4,431)	(3,913)	(4,357)	(6,944)	(7,450)	(11,383)

Source: Authors' calculations using data from the 1980 National Medical Care Utilization and Expenditure Survey (inflated to 1990 dollars using the Medical Care Component of the consumer price index).

Note: Standard deviation of expenditures is in parentheses.

increases as well. In 1990 dollars, total medical expenditures of those 55–64 averaged $2,144. This represents 5.4% of average total family income for this age group, 6.9% of average total family income for retired individuals, and 30% of the average pension income of early retirees.[1] A one-standard-deviation increase in expenditures for a 55–64-year-old would represent an additional 16.5% of family income. Total *family* medical expenditures would naturally constitute a much higher fraction of income. Thus, it is easy to see why older individuals should be concerned about their health insurance coverage after retirement.

4.1.2   Health Insurance Coverage and Costs

Given the costs of health care for older workers, it should not be surprising that older individuals are no more likely to be uninsured than their younger counterparts, as is shown in table 4.5. The sources of health insurance coverage, however, differ with age. Even though employment-based health insurance is the predominant source of coverage regardless of age, older individuals are less likely than younger persons to have employment-based health insurance and much more likely to be covered by a nongroup (individual) or other group policy. This suggests that individuals who retire early but who do not have access to employer-provided health insurance turn to the individual market for insurance.

The bottom two panels of table 4.5 break down the sources of health insurance coverage by employment status. There are three major differences between the sources of health insurance coverage for those who are and are not employed. First, one-fifth of nonworking older persons are insured through Medicare or Medicaid, while only 1% of the older employed receive coverage from one of these two sources. Second, older nonworking individuals are 40% less likely to be uninsured than their younger counterparts. Third, relative to the young, the older nonworking are six times more likely to be covered by employer-provided health insurance in their own name.

These last two differences are explained in large part by the availability of employer-provided postretirement health insurance. Forty-five percent of individuals work in firms that provide retiree health insurance benefits.[2] The older nonworking, who are more likely to be retired than the young nonworking, are therefore more likely to be covered by employer-provided retiree health insurance.

There are, nevertheless, a substantial number of older individuals who are not covered by either employer or government-provided health insurance. It is these individuals who find themselves in the market for individual health insurance and who we would therefore expect to benefit from the availability of

1. Expenditures as a fraction of income are calculated using income data from the March 1990 CPS.
2. See Madrian (1994) for background on the structure and availability of postretirement health insurance.

Table 4.5   **Insurance Coverage by Age and Employment Status (%)**

	Employment-Based		Other Group	Nongroup	CHAMPUS/ CHAMPVA	Medicare/ Medicaid	Uninsured
	Any	Own Name					
All individuals							
25–54	71.6	51.1	1.2	5.9	5.7	5.6	15.4
55–64	64.5	44.8	4.1	14.5	7.7	10.4	12.0
Employed							
25–54	78.5	62.7	1.1	5.8	4.9	1.2	13.5
55–64	76.3	63.1	4.0	12.6	6.8	0.8	10.1
Not employed							
25–54	44.2	4.2	1.3	6.2	8.8	23.4	23.0
55–64	51.6	24.7	4.3	16.6	9.2	20.9	14.1

Source: Authors' calculations using data from the 1987 National Medical Expenditure Survey.

continuation coverage. The reason is simple—insurance in the individual market is typically quite expensive.

Employers have significant cost advantages in providing health insurance. By pooling the risks of many individuals, they are able to lower administrative expenses and reduce adverse selection. These two factors alone are estimated to reduce the cost of providing insurance in large (ten thousand or more employees) firms relative to small (one to four employees) firms by 40% (Congressional Research Service 1988). For older individuals the cost differential between employer-provided and individual health insurance is exacerbated because policies in the individual market are typically age-rated, while within the firm younger workers subsidize the health insurance costs of their older coworkers. The Congressional Research Service (1988) reports that the cost to employers of providing insurance coverage for 55–64-year-old males is three times that of providing coverage to males under 40; for females, the ratio is two to one.[3]

In Massachusetts the average cost of family health insurance coverage per employee in 1989 was $3,882.[4] When inflated by the medical care component of the consumer price index, this is equivalent to $5,047 in 1993 dollars. In contrast, a New England commercial insurance company is offering a family policy for a 58-year-old male with a one-year preexisting-conditions exclusion at a price of $8,640. This represents 26% of the average family income of retired individuals aged 55–64 in Massachusetts. Individual policies may also be medically underwritten so that sick individuals may face substantially higher prices or may not be able to purchase a policy at all.

3. Of course, to the extent employer costs can be shifted to the wages of employees in an age-specific fashion, older individuals will bear these higher costs. See the discussion in section 4.3.
4. Authors' calculation using unpublished data from the Health Insurance Association of America.

The coverage available in the private market not only is expensive, but also is typically less generous than employer-provided health insurance. Table 4.6 compares the health insurance benefits of individuals covered under group and nongroup policies in 1977. In every category, those covered under nongroup policies receive more limited benefits. Relative to those with nongroup coverage, those with group policies are more than twice as likely to receive major medical coverage or coverage for physician office visits and prescription drugs, and more than 50% more likely to receive ambulance, mental health, and outpatient diagnostic service coverage. Furthermore, nongroup policies generally feature both higher deductibles and higher copayments. Thus, relative to the individual market, group coverage offers individuals higher-quality insurance coverage at a significantly lower price.

4.2   Continuation Coverage Laws

For those individuals whose employers do not offer retiree health insurance, an alternative to purchasing health insurance in the individual market is provided by various state and federal continuation coverage laws. These laws mandate that employers sponsoring group health insurance plans offer terminating employees and their families the right to continue their health insurance coverage through the employer's plan for a specified period of time. The laws gener-

Table 4.6   **Group and Nongroup Health Insurance Benefits, 1977 (%)**

	Fraction of Individuals with Specified Benefit	
	Group Plans	Nongroup Plans
Primary benefits		
Major medical coverage	86.9	39.1
Hospital room and board	98.4	91.4
Surgery	97.6	91.6
Physician office visit	87.9	40.4
Other benefits		
Ambulance	89.0	54.0
Outpatient diagnostic services	95.9	66.0
Prescribed medicines	87.3	30.3
Mental health	92.2	66.0
Generosity of benefits (conditional on having benefit)		
Major medical deductible < $100	94.3	61.6
Full semiprivate room charge	77.8	38.2
80–100% of usual common and reasonable surgical charge	70.6	60.0
80–100% of usual common and reasonable physician charge	91.8	81.3

Source: Farley (1986), tables 45–58.

ally apply to all separations (except those due to an employee's gross misconduct), although in some states benefits are restricted to those who leave their jobs involuntarily.[5] They often also provide benefits to divorced or widowed spouses and their families. The first such law was implemented by Minnesota in 1974. More than twenty states passed similar laws over the next decade before the federal government, as part of the 1985 COBRA, mandated such coverage at the national level. Continuation coverage is now commonly referred to as COBRA coverage, a nomenclature we will also use.

The various state statutes are summarized in table 4.7.[6] The length of coverage is generally quite short, from three to six months, although nine states mandate coverage of nine months or more. Although most state laws stipulate that an employee must have been covered by an employer's insurance for three to six months before being eligible for continuation coverage, this requirement is not likely to be binding on older workers, most of whom have been with their current employer for many years.[7] The state laws also apply only to firms that actually purchase insurance through an insurance company; self-insured firms, under the 1974 Employee Retirement Income and Security Act (ERISA), are not subject to these (or any other) state mandates.[8]

Although similar in spirit, the state and federal laws differ in a number of important ways. First, the length of coverage mandated under the federal law, eighteen months, equals or exceeds that mandated by all but one state (as of January 1987, Connecticut law provides for up to twenty months of coverage).[9] Second, there is no minimal length of time for which an employee must be covered under an employer's plan before being eligible for continuation benefits. Third, the federal law applies to self-insured firms, who are exempt from the state laws, as well as to those who purchase their coverage from insurers. The federal law, however, does not apply to small firms employing less than twenty workers. Finally, employees of religious organizations and the federal government were exempt from COBRA, although federal employees have subsequently been included (beginning in 1990). When the specific details of the

---

5. Because retirement is a voluntary separation, we treat those states whose laws apply only to involuntarily terminated employees as states without laws.

6. Details on state laws are from Hewitt (1985) and Thompson Publishing Group (1992) and have been cross-checked against the actual state statutes. Table 4.7 lists only those states with laws that apply to employees who terminate their employment voluntarily.

7. Almost 95% of retirees have job tenure of at least ten years by the time they retire (Madrian 1994).

8. In a related paper we incorporate a correction factor that accounts for the exclusion of some firms from the effects of these laws (Gruber and Madrian 1995). This has little effect on the significance of the estimates of the effect of continuation coverage on retirement, although the magnitude increases two- to threefold.

9. Eighteen months is the maximum length of coverage available following the voluntary or involuntary termination of employment. COBRA also provides up to thirty-six months of coverage for family members who would otherwise lose their insurance coverage through events such as an employee's death, divorce from the employee, or the employee's eligibility for Medicare.

Table 4.7   State Continuation Coverage Laws

State	Effective Date	Months of Coverage	State	Effective Date	Months of Coverage
Arkansas	7/20/79	4	New York	1/1/86	6
California	1/1/85	3	North Carolina	1/1/82	3
Colorado	7/1/86	3	North Dakota	7/1/83	10
Connecticut	10/1/75	10	Oklahoma	1/1/76	1
	1/1/87	20	Oregon	1/1/82	6
Georgia	7/1/86	3	Rhode Island	1/1/88	18
Illinois	1/1/84	6	South Carolina	1/1/79	2
	8/23/85	9		1/1/90	6
Iowa	7/1/87	9	South Dakota	7/1/84	3
Kansas	1/1/78	6		3/3/88	18
Kentucky	7/15/80	9	Tennessee	1/1/81	3
Minnesota	8/1/74	6	Texas	1/1/81	6
	3/19/83	12	Utah	7/1/86	2
	6/1/87	18	Vermont	5/14/86	6
Missouri	9/28/85	9	Virginia	4/17/86	3
Nevada	1/1/88	18	Wisconsin	5/14/80	18
New Hampshire	8/22/81	10			
New Mexico	7/1/83	6			

Sources: Hewitt (1985); Thompson Publishing Group (1992); state statutes.

state and federal statutes are at odds, firm provision of continuation benefits is governed by the law that provides for more generous coverage.

The effective dates of the state laws are listed in table 4.7. The federal coverage mandated under COBRA was phased in. Beginning in July 1986, firms had to offer continuation benefits at the start of their next plan year. For workers provided health insurance under union contracts, such benefits did not have to be offered until the next contract negotiation after January 1987.

Both the state and federal laws stipulate that the employee must pay the full cost of the coverage. At the federal level, this is defined specifically as 102% of the average employer cost of providing coverage. The coverage must be identical to that provided to similarly situated active employees, including the option to continue enrollment in supplemental insurance plans (such as for vision or dental care) if these are available. Although 102% of the employer's cost is typically much more than individuals pay as active employees, it is, as already noted, substantially less than the cost of buying equivalent coverage in the private market, especially for older workers.

Because continuation coverage is a relatively new phenomenon (at least at the national level), information on the extent of continuation coverage is somewhat scarce. Zedlewski (1993) estimates that, in 1988, 5.2% of retired workers aged 55–64 were covered by COBRA health insurance. This figure must be interpreted relative to the number of individuals who could be expected to take up such coverage. The 52% of individuals aged 55–64 with retiree health insurance are not likely to be covered, and the 21% of individuals who were not insured through their former employer are not eligible. Similarly, those who have been retired for more than eighteen months have exceeded their potential eligibility. Tabulations from the 1987 National Medical Expenditure Survey indicate that one-third of retired individuals aged 55–64 have been retired for less than eighteen months. If we take the group who could potentially be affected by COBRA to be one-third of retired individuals between ages 55 and 64 who worked in firms that provided health insurance but did not provide retiree health insurance, we would expect at most 9% of early retirees to be covered. That 5.2% receive continuation benefits suggests that 58% of the retired population who would be at all likely to be covered by COBRA actually are. As knowledge about the availability of such coverage has become more widespread since 1988, this fraction may be higher today.

An alternative calculation is possible using figures reported in Flynn (1992). She uses data from a large firm that administers COBRA claims to estimate that 23% of individuals who qualified for COBRA coverage because of retirement elected to receive benefits. If we expected only the 30% of individuals in firms that offer health insurance but do not offer retiree health insurance to even consider purchasing COBRA insurance, this take-up rate implies that 75% of those most likely to be covered by continuation benefits actually are. Both of these calculations, therefore, suggest that retirees without an alternative source of health insurance coverage are quite likely to elect continuation coverage.

For all COBRA beneficiaries, the average length of time on COBRA was seven months (Flynn 1992). Individuals over age 61, however, maintained their coverage for a much longer period of time—about twelve months on average. This finding is not surprising for two reasons. First, younger individuals are more likely to find alternative coverage through a new job or a spouse's employment. Second, COBRA coverage provides a larger subsidy for older workers; with a lower relative price, they should therefore demand more coverage.

Table 4.8 compares the distribution of health insurance coverage in 1984, two years before COBRA was first implemented, and in 1989, two years after it had been phased in. Note that employment-based health insurance coverage is more prevalent after COBRA, and that this effect is confined to those who are not employed, exactly the group whom we would expect to be insured under COBRA. This finding is similar to evidence presented in Rogowski and Karoly (1992), who examined the primary source of insurance coverage after retirement, based on the source of insurance coverage before retirement, before and after COBRA. They find that in the pre-COBRA period, 72% of individuals who retired from jobs with employment-based health insurance continued to be covered by that insurance upon retirement. After COBRA, this figure rises to 78.5%.[10] Taken together, the evidence on take-up rates and the increase in the extent of employer-provided health insurance coverage among early re-

---

10. We present a stronger test of the effect of continuation coverage mandates on insurance coverage in section 4.6.

Table 4.8   Health Insurance Coverage before and after COBRA (%)

	All Individuals		Employed		Not Employed	
	25–54	55–64	25–54	55–64	25–54	55–64
Insurance coverage in 1984						
Any private health insurance	82.1	83.7	89.1	92.5	60.1	74.1
Health insurance in own name						
Employment-based	52.1	47.4	66.7	68.9	5.9	23.6
Not employment-based	5.1	12.5	5.1	10.4	5.2	14.7
Covered as a dependent	24.2	23.4	16.8	12.8	47.7	35.0
Insurance coverage in 1989						
Any private health insurance	82.4	84.3	88.6	92.1	57.3	74.9
Health insurance in own name						
Employment-based	54.7	49.2	66.4	68.1	7.1	26.6
Not employment-based	5.3	12.9	5.2	9.6	5.2	16.8
Covered as a dependent	22.0	21.8	16.4	14.4	43.7	30.6

Source: Authors' calculations using data from the Survey of Income and Program Participation, 1984 Wave 3 and 1987 Wave 7.

tirees after COBRA suggests that older workers who retire early and who do not have an alternative source of coverage actually avail themselves of the continuation benefits to which they are entitled.

4.3 Modeling the Effect of Health Insurance on Retirement

We present a simple graphical exposition of the effect of health insurance benefits on the retirement decision, along the lines of Burtless (1986) and Burtless and Moffitt (1984). We consider both retiree health insurance in general and continuation benefits more specifically. Figure 4.1 shows the budget constraint facing an older worker between the ages of 55 and 65. The horizontal axis represents the age of retirement. The vertical axis measures the certainty equivalent (CE) of consumption from age 55 onward. This differs from the earlier literature, which has typically considered the relationship between the age at retirement and the actual level of future consumption rather than the CE of future consumption. This departure is necessitated by our focus on the effect of insurance coverage.

We assume that workers receive health insurance on their current job but that they may or may not have retiree health insurance coverage. Firms that provide postretirement health insurance do so on the same basis for both workers and retirees, and these benefits cease upon eligibility for Medicare.[11] We also assume that once workers leave their current job, they will remain retired for the rest of their life. To simplify the analysis, we ignore the effects of both

---

11. In reality, most retiree health insurance plans do "top off" Medicare to some extent. This does not alter the main conclusions of this section.

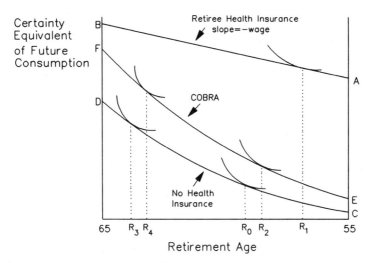

Fig. 4.1 Modeling the effect of continuation coverage on retirement

Social Security and pensions; they could, however, be easily incorporated into the analysis.

In the model, as in the real world, workers who retire without health insurance coverage have two options: they may purchase an individual policy, or go uninsured. In either case their out-of-pocket medical expenditures will be significantly higher than if they receive retiree coverage or have the option of continuing their group coverage. For a worker with retiree health insurance, the slope of the budget constraint will be the after-tax wage, which is depicted by line AB in figure 4.1. Since medical expenditures are insured, there is no uncertainty about future consumption.

For the worker without retiree coverage, the relative position and slope of the budget constraint depend on two factors. First, because individuals are risk averse, those without retiree health insurance will have a lower level of CE consumption; this places the no-health-insurance budget constraint below that of an insured worker.[12] Second, because both the mean and the variance of medical expenditures rise with age, a year of health insurance coverage is worth more at older ages. The cumulative reduction in CE consumption will be greater at younger retirement ages, but the incremental effect will be smaller. This latter effect gives curvature to the no-health-insurance budget constraint, line CD in figure 4.1. At age 65 there is a jump in the no-health-insurance budget constraint as Medicare equalizes the opportunities of all individuals.

If leisure is a normal good, retiree health insurance will lead to earlier retirement, at age $R_1 < R_0$, because such coverage makes individuals wealthier. As

---

12. Risk aversion in this model operates in a similar fashion to higher expected medical costs.

individuals are more risk averse, the wealth effect will increase as both the level of the no-health-insurance budget constraint falls and its slope becomes steeper.

Now consider the effect of a continuation coverage mandate that provides one year of subsidized insurance coverage relative to having no health insurance. For the risk-neutral worker, this is simply equivalent to an increment in wealth equal to expected medical costs for a year minus the cost of the group policy.[13] This increment rises in value as the worker ages, since expected medical expenditures increase with age. Thus, the budget constraint with a continuation coverage option, line *EF,* lies above the no-health-insurance constraint but below the retiree-coverage constraint. At younger ages, it is very close to the no-health-insurance constraint; at age 64, it differs from the retiree-coverage constraint by the cost of the group coverage. As workers become more risk averse and the no-health-insurance constraint becomes steeper, the distance between the no-health-insurance and the continuation coverage constraints will increase, and this increase will be greater at older ages. In this case the value of one year of coverage will equal expected medical costs minus the cost of the group policy plus the increase in CE consumption implied by eliminating uncertainty in that year.

The value of both retiree health insurance and continuation benefits will rise with the cost of being uninsured or the cost of buying individual insurance in the private market. The important difference between these two sources of coverage, however, is their age patterns: while retiree insurance coverage is of highest value to very early retirees, continuation benefits are more valuable at older ages. Because of this, we might expect continuation benefits to be used primarily by older workers seeking a "bridge to Medicare," which allows them to retire a certain number of months before age 65 without losing group coverage. If this is the case, we would expect the effect of continuation coverage on retirement to be greatest at older ages.

There are, however, a number of complications that cloud this basic intuition. The first is the empirical violation of one of our assumptions, namely, that retirement is permanent. Diamond and Hausman (1984) report substantial reentry rates for early retirees; among 55–64-year-olds, the one-year reentry rate is approximately 15%. Sueyoshi (1989) finds that one-third of the elderly "partially retire," moving from permanent employment to less than full-time work. To the extent that continuation coverage mandates facilitate movement across jobs, rather than permanent retirement, they may have larger effects at younger ages than was depicted above.[14]

In this analysis we have assumed that retiree health insurance offers pure

13. Once again, this amount is presumably positive even for a risk-neutral worker due to cross-subsidization of the group policy by younger coworkers.

14. One important consideration, of course, is whether this reentry is to jobs that offer health insurance; unfortunately, there is little evidence on this question.

rents to workers in the firms that offer this type of coverage. In labor market equilibrium, presumably at least a portion of these rents will be reflected in lower wages for workers with retiree coverage. The extent to which these compensating differentials offset the benefits of retiree health insurance at each age will be a function of the employer's ability to set relative age-specific wages freely,[15] the mobility of workers across firms at different ages, and the excess of the cost of continuation benefits over the group premium paid by the early retiree.[16] The existence of compensating differentials may affect both the location and the shape of the budget constraint facing the potential retiree; the net effect on retirement age will be a function of the nature of the compensating differential.[17]

Finally, we have ignored the possibility that workers may be liquidity constrained in making their retirement decisions. The fact that most retirees have few liquid assets (Diamond and Hausman 1984) implies that such liquidity constraints may be empirically important in determining retirement dates. This explanation is suggested in both Diamond and Hausman (1984) and Burtless and Moffitt (1984) in their discussion of why Social Security benefits do not seem to affect retirement until they actually become available at age 62. Samwick (1993) finds that much of the estimated increase in retirement probabilities attributed to Social Security occurs among those with pensions, suggesting that all workers would like to take advantage of these benefits early, but that only those with pensions can afford to do so. The presence of liquidity constraints could increase the effect of continuation benefits at younger ages, as the wealth increment that these benefits represent could be loosening these constraints.

4.4   Data and Regression Framework

4.4.1   Data

The data for this study must meet two key criteria. First, in order to exploit the variation in state and federal continuation coverage legislation, they must extend over a number of years before and after 1986. Second, there must be a

---

15. See Rosen (1986) for a discussion of the theory of compensating differentials. Gruber (1994a) provides some evidence that shifting the costs of employer-provided benefits to distinct demographic groups in the workplace is feasible.

16. Huth (1991) reports that the health insurance claims of COBRA recipients exceed those of active employees by 50%. This difference in cost is attributed to adverse selection; it is the sickest individuals who will find continuation coverage most attractive, and they will therefore be the ones most likely to take it up. Similar evidence is provided in Long and Marquis (1992).

17. For example, if the entire cost of the benefits is shifted to older workers, this will lower the slope of the budget constraint with continuation benefits (fig. 4.1) relative to the budget constraint without benefits (because wages for those with benefits fall), which will have both income and substitution effects on the retirement decision.

large sample size so that the effects of state-law changes on older workers can be identified. The data that best meet these two criteria are the Merged Outgoing Rotation Group (MORG) sample of the CPS. The CPS is a nationally representative survey that interviews over fifty thousand households each month. The MORG file contains information on demographic characteristics and labor force attachment during the survey week for one-quarter of each month's sample for each month of the year. This is the largest available annual data set on individual labor force behavior in the United States.

Recent studies of retirement behavior have focused on dynamic modeling of the transition into retirement. In this paper we instead use a static model of whether or not an individual is currently retired, since the only labor force information we have in the MORG is for the week of the interview. Evidence on the stock of retired persons can still be useful for considering the effect of continuation coverage mandates on retirement; if the laws are affecting flows, they should affect stocks as well.[18] Furthermore, dynamic modeling strategies for retirement decisions using survey data sets often suffer from an important econometric difficulty, known as dynamic sample selection bias (Diamond and Hausman 1984). In the case of continuation coverage laws, this bias arises from the fact that the set of individuals observed actually working after the law has been in place for a number of years would be less likely to retire in response to the law than would the entire population, because those most likely to respond will have already retired. When the sample is selected on the basis of those who are still working, the results will therefore be biased against finding an effect of the law.[19] In a multivariate setting, the bias cannot be signed a priori, and with time-varying covariates in the model, such as months of continuation coverage, it is impossible to correct for this "left-censoring."[20] Our static regressions, which include all 55–64-year-old males regardless of initial work status, do not suffer from this bias.

On the other hand, the major disadvantage of our static framework is that we cannot control for the characteristics of the job from which the individual has retired. This will be important if, for example, there is a systematic correlation between the passage of these mandates and the nature of the jobs in the states where they are passed. In the regression analysis we attempt to reduce any bias that results from this potential correlation by controlling for the time-

18. This is not strictly true if the mandates affect the number of persons who decide to work at all; in this case, both the numerator and denominator of the labor force participation rate would be increasing, and the effect on the stock would be ambiguous. This is not likely to be a problem for the sample of older males on which we focus.

19. An alternative way to see this point is to imagine a law that applied to a cohort rather than to an age group. The individuals who are most likely to respond to this law will do so in the first year. In the next year, by selecting on the set of individuals who have not yet retired, we will bias the results against finding an effect of the law. When the law applies to an age group, rather than a cohort, this effect is attenuated by the fact that new members arrive into the age group.

20. It is possible, however, to test for the magnitude of the bias; see Gruber and Madrian (1995).

invariant characteristics of the states that pass these mandates. In section 4.5 we will contrast our findings from this static regression with those from dynamic models that allow us to better control for the types of jobs held by individuals.

4.4.2   Regression Framework

We focus on two definitions of retirement: whether or not an individual reports being retired, and whether or not an individual is out of the labor force. Both are based on a CPS question that asks about the major activity in which an individual was engaged during the week before the survey. The latter definition is useful because *retirement* may be a subjective term that takes on different meanings for different individuals. These retirement definitions are clearly problematic along at least two dimensions. First, we are unable to contrast the effect of these regulations on both "full" and "partial" retirement, as is done in Burtless and Moffitt (1984) or Sueyoshi (1989). Second, we are unable to account for reentry into the labor market, as discussed in Diamond and Hausman (1984). Nevertheless, these measures should provide reasonable estimates of the effect of continuation coverage mandates on the propensity of older workers to remain employed.

Our sample consists of men between the ages of 55 and 64. Overall, 20% of the sample report being retired, and 35% are out of the labor force. The average level of education is twelve years, and 9.5% of the sample is nonwhite.

We estimate the following probit model of retirement:

$$(1) \quad Pr(Retired_{ijt}) = \Phi(\alpha + \beta_1 {\cdot} X_{ijt} + \beta_2 {\cdot} State_j + \beta_3 {\cdot} Time_t + \beta_4 {\cdot} Law_{jt}),$$

where i indexes individuals, j indexes states, and t indexes time. X_{ijt} is a set of individual demographic characteristics, $State_j$ is a set of state dummies, $Time_t$ is a set of year and month dummies, and Law_{jt} is the number of months of continuation coverage available in state j at time t.[21] The state fixed effects control for any time-invariant characteristics of a state that may be correlated with the state's propensity to pass continuation coverage legislation. We include a set of year dummies to control for national trends in retirement behavior that may be correlated with the passage of these laws, and month dummies to control for seasonal patterns in retirement behavior. Thus, the effect of the laws is identified in this model by changes in retirement behavior in states that passed the laws (or that were affected by the federal law), relative to those that did not, during the period after the laws were passed. Further identifying variation comes from differences across states in the number of months of

---

21. We exclude individuals from two states from our sample: Hawaii, which has mandated health insurance for all employees, and West Virginia, for which we were unable to definitively date the effective date of their continuation coverage mandate.

eligibility that these laws allow. Since we have monthly data, we phase in the federal law in twelve equal increments between July 1986 and June 1987.

4.5 Results

The basic regression results are reported in table 4.9. The first column reports the probit coefficients from the self-reported retirement equation, while the second column gives the marginal probabilities implied by these coeffi-

Table 4.9   **The Effect of Continuation Coverage on the Probability of Being Retired**

	Definition of Retired			
	Report Being Retired		Not in the Labor Force	
Independent Variable	Coefficient	Marginal Probability	Coefficient	Marginal Probability
Months of coverage	0.0036	.0107	0.0025	.0098
	(.0017)		(.0015)	
Married	−0.0154	−.0037	−0.0577	−.0187
	(.0010)		(.0009)	
Education	−0.0655	−.0162	−0.3427	−.1173
	(.0092)		(.0081)	
Nonwhite	−0.1204	−.0282	0.0918	.0305
	(.0121)		(.0104)	
55 years old	−1.205	−.1950	0.1180	.0392
	(.0503)		(.0443)	
56 years old	−1.097	−.1853	0.1935	.0646
	(.0502)		(.0443)	
57 years old	−1.016	−.1770	0.2435	.0816
	(.0501)		(.0443)	
58 years old	−0.9251	−.1669	0.3157	.1063
	(.0499)		(.0442)	
59 years old	−0.8115	−.1525	0.4094	.1385
	(.0498)		(.0442)	
60 years old	−0.6254	−.1254	0.5302	.1804
	(.0496)		(.0441)	
61 years old	−0.4903	−.1024	0.6394	.2187
	(.0496)		(.0442)	
62 years old	−0.0854	−.0203	0.9977	.3441
	(.0494)		(.0441)	
63 years old	0.1033	.0260	1.161	.3996
	(.0494)		(.0442)	
64 years old	0.1938	.0504	1.262	.4324
	(.0494)		(.0442)	

Notes: The table gives estimates from a probit equation for whether or not an individual is retired, using data from the 1980–90 Merged Outgoing Rotation Groups of the Current Population Survey. The sample comprises 214,508 men aged 55–64. Coefficients for year, month, and state dummies are not reported. Standard errors are in parentheses.

cients.[22] The same is done in the third and fourth columns, using "not in the labor force" as the definition of retirement. More education is associated with a slightly lower probability of being retired and a much lower probability of being out of the labor force. Being nonwhite is associated with a lower probability of retirement but a significantly higher probability of being out of the labor force. Individuals who are married are less likely to be either retired or out of the labor force. The age pattern of retirement propensities is familiar from the previous literature; there is a large jump in the probability of being retired at age 62, and individuals aged 64 are 25% more likely to be retired than individuals aged 55. This pattern is even more pronounced for being out of the labor force, as the probability at age 64 is 40% greater than the probability at age 55.

The availability of continuation coverage has a sizable and significant effect on the probability of being retired. One year of coverage raises the probability that an individual is retired by 1.1 percentage points, which is 5.4% of the baseline probability of being retired in this sample. For the not-in-the-labor-force regressions, the estimated effect of a year of continuation coverage is of approximately the same magnitude as in the retired equation (although the coefficient is only significant at the 10% level), and suggests an increase in the baseline probability of being out of the labor force of 2.8%.

The model described in section 4.3 suggests the possibility that the effect of continuation coverage mandates on retirement could vary with age; intuitively, it seemed that this effect should be strongest at older ages. In table 4.10, therefore, we free up the effect of months of continuation coverage by age. The second and fifth columns present the marginal probability derivatives of the probits. The third and sixth columns express these percentage-point increases in retirement propensities as a fraction of the baseline retirement rate at each age. This allows for a more natural interpretation of the percentage effects of continuation benefits on retirement at each age.

In both equations the coefficients rise with age and are statistically significant at ages 62 and above. The pattern of effects as a fraction of baseline retirement probabilities, however, is not uniformly supportive of the hypothesis suggested in section 4.3. For the retirement equation, there is actually a declining pattern of effects by age; for the not-in-the-labor-force equation, the effects are slightly increasing with age.

There are several possible explanations for this counterintuitive finding that the effects are not proportionately greatest at the ages near Medicare eligibility.

22. For dummy variables, the marginal probabilities are calculated by predicting the probability of retirement with the dummy equal to one for the entire sample, predicting the probability with the dummy set equal to zero for the entire sample, and taking the average of the difference in these predictions across all individuals. For continuous variables, the marginal probability is calculated by predicting the probability at the current level of the variable, predicting the probability by adding one to the variable, and once again taking the average of the difference in these predictions across individuals. The marginal probability on months of coverage is the probability increase associated with going from zero to twelve months of coverage.

Table 4.10   The Age-Specific Effect of Continuation Coverage on the Probability of Being Retired

	Definition of Retired					
	Report Being Retired			Not in the Labor Force		
Independent Variable	Coefficient	Marginal Probability	Percentage of Baseline	Coefficient	Marginal Probability	Percentage of Baseline
55*months	.0028	.0083	13.3	.0012	.0047	2.4
	(.0023)			(.0019)		
56*months	.0013	.0037	4.8	.0022	.0088	4.1
	(.0023)			(.0019)		
57*months	.0021	.0061	6.8	−.0005	−.0021	0.9
	(.0022)			(.0019)		
58*months	.0027	.0080	7.6	.0008	.0031	1.2
	(.0022)			(.0019)		
59*months	.0046	.0135	10.6	.0019	.0074	2.6
	(.0021)			(.0019)		
60*months	.0024	.0071	4.2	.0018	.0069	2.1
	(.0021)			(.0018)		
61*months	.0020	.0060	2.9	.0021	.0085	2.3
	(.0020)			(.0018)		
62*months	.0048	.0143	4.2	.0040	.0161	3.2
	(.0020)			(.0018)		
63*months	.0041	.0121	2.9	.0045	.0179	3.2
	(.0020)			(.0018)		
64*months	.0067	.0202	4.5	.0063	.0251	4.1
	(.0020)			(.0018)		

Notes: The table gives estimates from a probit equation for whether an individual is retired, using data from the 1980–90 Merged Outgoing Rotation Groups of the Current Population Survey. The sample comprises 214,508 men aged 55–64. Coefficients for year, month, age, and state dummies are not reported. Education, race, and marital status are also included. Standard errors are in parentheses.

The first is the set of theoretical issues we raised in section 4.3, such as the possibility that individuals may face liquidity constraints that are loosened by this temporary health insurance. The second reason is statistical: we may not have enough power to these probits to distinguish true larger effects at older ages from the effects at younger ages. Given the precision of our estimates, this seems an unlikely explanation for the unexpected age pattern of our results.

Alternatively, it may be that our result is spurious. One potential problem with our identification strategy is that the passage of these laws could be correlated with some other change in retirement behavior in these states. Alternatively, it could be that the laws themselves are endogenous responses to changes in retirement propensities among the population; that is, if more individuals are retiring, states may respond by mandating benefits that cover individuals after their retirement.

One form of potential endogeneity could be that the propensity of legislatures to mandate continuation coverage is correlated with long-term within-state trends in retirement behavior. In this case, even with state fixed effects included in the regression, there will be a spurious correlation between changes in retirement behavior within a state and the passage of a continuation coverage mandate. One possible control for such spurious causation is to include in the regression not only state effects but state-specific trend terms; that is, we interact each state effect with a trend for the ten-year period.[23] The results from this specification check are presented in table 4.11. For the not-in-the-labor-force regression, the age-specific coefficients are virtually unchanged from those in table 4.10; in the retirement equation, the coefficients are slightly larger, but once again the effects are very similar.

A further potential problem with these findings is that it may not be appropriate to compare the effects of the state and federal mandates. As we noted earlier, these mandates differ along a number of dimensions, the most important being that the state mandates do not apply to self-insured firms, while the federal mandate does not apply to small firms. In results not reported, we have rerun these regressions for the period prior to July 1986 in order to restrict our analysis to the effects of the state laws. The results are somewhat stronger than those in tables 4.10 and 4.11, although the age patterns are similar.

In related work (Gruber and Madrian 1995), we consider the effect of continuation benefits on transitions into retirement using two different data sets—the March files of the CPS, and the Survey of Income and Program Participation (SIPP). These data sources allow us to estimate dynamic retirement models and to control for some characteristics of the jobs from which individuals retire. The sample sizes are much smaller than we have with the MORG data, however, and we are confronted with the issue of dynamic sample selection, discussed above. Nevertheless, this study confirms the two key findings of the research reported above. First, there is a sizable and significant effect of continuation coverage on retirement behavior. Using one-year retirement transitions in the March CPS, we find that one year of continuation coverage raises retirement propensities by 1.4 percentage points. This is quite similar to the 1.1 percentage-point effect estimated in this paper using the MORG data. Furthermore, the implied effect on the hazard rate in both the March CPS and SIPP data is identical.

Second, despite the presumption that these laws should act as a "bridge to Medicare," the estimated effects in these dynamic models do not rise with age either. Figure 4.2 graphs the change in the propensity to be retired from having a year of continuation coverage estimated from the MORG regressions (column three of table 4.10) along with the percentage increase in retirement probabilities estimated using transition data from the March CPS (Gruber and

---

23. The trend is monthly, taking on values of 1 to 132. This type of "random growth" or "fixed trend" estimator is suggested by Heckman and Hotz (1988) and is used by Jacobson, LaLonde, and Sullivan (1992) and Gruber (1994b).

Table 4.11   **The Effect of Continuation Coverage on the Probability of Being Retired (fixed-trend included)**

Independent Variable	Definition of Retired					
	Report Being Retired			Not in the Labor Force		
	Coefficient	Marginal Probability	Percentage of Baseline	Coefficient	Marginal Probability	Percentage of Baseline
Age effects equal						
Months of						
coverage	.0045	.0133	6.7	.00027	.0105	3.0
	(.0020)			(.0017)		
Age-specific effects						
55*months	.0037	.0108	17.3	.0014	.0054	2.8
	(.0025)			(.0021)		
56*months	.0021	.0061	8.0	.0024	.0094	4.4
	(.0025)			(.0021)		
57*months	.0030	.0087	9.7	−.0003	−.0013	0.5
	(.0024)			(.0021)		
58*months	.0035	.0105	10.0	.0010	.0039	1.5
	(.0024)			(.0021)		
59*months	.0054	.0160	12.6	.0020	.0081	2.9
	(.0023)			(.0020)		
60*months	.0033	.0097	5.7	.0020	.0077	2.4
	(.0023)			(.0020)		
61*months	.0028	.0084	4.1	.0023	.0091	2.5
	(.0023)			(.0020)		
62*months	.0056	.0169	5.0	.0042	.0167	3.3
	(.0022)			(.0020)		
63*months	.0049	.0146	3.6	.0046	.0184	3.2
	(.0022)			(.0020)		
64*months	.0075	.0227	5.1	.0065	.0257	4.2
	(.0022)			(.0020)		

Notes: The table gives estimates from a probit equation for whether an individual is retired, using data from the 1980–90 Merged Outgoing Rotation Groups of the Current Population Survey. The sample comprises 214,508 men aged 55–64. Coefficients for year, month, age, and state dummies are not reported. Education, race, marital status, and state-specific trends are also included. Standard errors are in parentheses.

Madrian 1995).[24] To facilitate comparability, the two series are each normalized to take on a value of one at age 55. While the pattern of effects differs somewhat at the early ages, both series show a similar decline after age 59, and the effect at age 64 is approximately one-third as large as that at age 55. Thus, our two main findings from the static framework employed in this paper are borne out in the dynamic model that we employ elsewhere.

24. These latter coefficients come from the model that is most comparable to that used in this paper. See Gruber and Madrian (1995) for a number of extensions to this basic dynamic model.

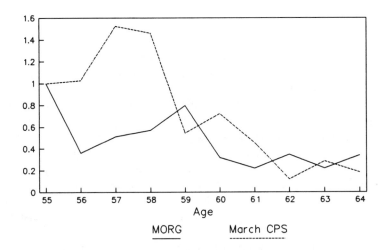

Fig. 4.2   **Relative age-specific effects of continuation coverage on retirement**

It is also interesting to consider what the magnitude of these findings imply about individual valuation of continuation benefits by comparing them to the estimated increase in retirement propensities following an increase in postretirement income. The results from a static probit model of retirement in Samwick (1993) suggest that a $5,000 increment to Social Security wealth increases the retirement hazard by approximately 8%. In a stochastic dynamic programming model employed by Stock and Wise (1990a, 1990b) and Lumsdaine, Stock, and Wise (1992, 1994), they find that a $5,000 increase in the value of pension wealth leads to an increase in the retirement hazard of between 10 and 13% for individuals between the ages of 55 and 64.[25]

The basic specification of Gruber and Madrian (1995) finds that one year of continuation coverage raises the retirement hazard by 32%. This implies that a year of continuation benefits is valued at between $12,300 and $15,000 in terms of postretirement wealth. Based on the cost information reported in section 4.2, a COBRA policy would save an older worker approximately $4,500 per year on the price of family coverage. Taken at face value, these results suggest that workers value the insurance received from continuation coverage policies at a somewhat higher level than its associated cost savings. This may reflect the fact that the individual policy we priced, as with most individual policies, excluded preexisting conditions for some period. Alternatively, it may be that a number of early retirees must pay substantially more for individual policies or are unable to obtain such policies at all.

25. We are grateful to Andrew Samwick, Robin Lumsdaine, and James Stock for performing these calculations for us.

4.6   Insurance Coverage

In this section we consider the effects of continuation coverage mandates on the insurance coverage of early retirees. If continuation coverage mandates are having an effect on the retirement decisions of older workers, then, by definition, they should be affecting their insurance coverage as well. Thus, evidence that such mandates increase insurance coverage among early retirees provides a necessary (but not sufficient) specification check of our result that these mandates affect retirement behavior. Furthermore, it is interesting to contrast the direct effects of these mandates on insurance coverage with their indirect effects on retirement behavior. To what extent do continuation coverage mandates affect the "inframarginal" individual, who would have retired in their absence, relative to the "marginal" individual whose retirement decision is made in response to their presence?

In order to investigate the effect of continuation coverage mandates on insurance coverage, we use data from the SIPP.[26] The SIPP is a nationally representative survey of households designed to collect information on the economic and demographic characteristics of individuals and their families. We use data from the 1984, 1985, 1986, and 1987 panels of the SIPP. Sample members are interviewed every four months for roughly two and a half years and asked to provide information about their labor market activity, income, and participation in welfare and transfer programs over the previous four months. The first interviews of the 1984 panel were conducted in October 1983, while the initial interviews for subsequent panels commenced in February of the corresponding calendar year. For previously cited reasons, we exclude individuals living in West Virginia and Hawaii. We also drop individuals from several other small states because, out of concern for confidentiality, the SIPP has grouped these states together, thereby making it impossible to assign the appropriate state laws to individuals in these states.[27]

We restrict our sample to men aged 55–64 who retired during the sample period. The SIPP does not ask individuals directly whether they have retired. We therefore use a measure of retirement based on length of time out of the labor force. This has the advantage, relative to point-in-time self-reported measures, of capturing transitions to nonwork rather than partial (but perceived) retirement. It has the disadvantage, however, of not allowing us to disentangle retirement from other reasons for a temporary absence from the labor force. Following Rogowski and Karoly (1992), we define retirement as a departure

26. To keep the sample of individuals comparable to the MORG data used in this paper, one could in principle use the March CPS to look at insurance coverage over a similar time period. Unfortunately, a 1988 change in the questionnaire that altered the reported coverage rates of older individuals who were not working (precisely the group of interest) precludes performing a reliable analysis with this data set.

27. These states are Alaska, Idaho, Iowa, Maine, Mississippi, Montana, New Mexico, North Dakota, South Dakota, Vermont, and Wyoming. The CPS results are similar if we restrict our CPS sample in the same fashion. See Gruber and Madrian (1995) for more detail on our SIPP sample.

Table 4.12 **Continuation Coverage and the Probability of Being Insured after Retirement**

Independent Variable	Coefficient	Marginal Probability
Married	.0820	.026
	(.1764)	
Black	−.8403	−.293
	(.2227)	
Education	.0381	.012
	(.0122)	
Age	.1788	−.020
	(.0903)	
Age^2	−.0001	—
	(.00006)	
Months of coverage	.0163	.005
	(.0084)	

Notes: The table gives estimates of the probability of being insured after retirement, using data from the Survey of Income and Program Participation. The sample comprises 527 men aged 55–64 who retired over the sample period. Coefficients for industry and occupation dummies are not reported. Standard errors are in parentheses.

from the labor force of five or more months.[28] Individuals who are not in the labor force for at least the first four months for which we observe them are excluded from the sample, and individuals who report being out of the labor force in the last five months of the panel are censored at the last month for which they are in the labor force.

Table 4.12 presents the results from a probit equation for whether or not an individual is covered by employer-provided health insurance after retirement. The key independent variable is the number of months of continuation coverage available at the time of retirement. The results suggest that an extra month of continuation coverage increases the probability of being insured after retirement by 0.5%. This implies that one year of coverage would increase the probability of being insured by 6%, while eighteen months would increase the probability of coverage by 9%, a result consistent with that found by Rogowski and Karoly (1992). The results of table 4.12 corroborate the evidence on take-up rates presented in section 4.2. As mentioned, Zedlewski (1993) estimates that 5.2% of retired individuals between the ages of 55 and 64 are covered by COBRA. This fraction is very similar to our 6% estimated increase in coverage from one year of continuation coverage, which is the average length of time for which older individuals receive COBRA (Flynn 1992).

28. Rogowski and Karoly (1992) actually impose a six-month rule for departure from the labor force. It turns out that almost all of the individuals who are out of the labor force for five months are actually out for six or more months. This definition of retirement helps alleviate the problem of measurement error in the reporting of individual labor force status; since individuals are interviewed every four months, they must report that they are out of the labor force in two consecutive interviews to be counted as retired. See Gruber and Madrian (1995) for further discussion.

Furthermore, we can reconcile this finding with our estimates of the effect of continuation coverage mandates on retirement. Our findings imply that one year of coverage raised the probability of being retired by about 1.1 percentage points, but that it raises the probability of being insured by 6 percentage points. This suggests that the primary effect of these mandates is "inframarginal." That is, they provide insurance coverage for individuals who would have retired in the absence of these mandates even though they would not have been covered by employer-provided health insurance. Thus, continuation coverage mandates may be policies with a sizable bang for the buck: they have a large and significant effect along their intended dimension, increased insurance coverage, with a relatively small effect along their unintended dimension, increased retirement.

4.7   Conclusion

A number of current policy proposals in the United States, such as increasing the age of Medicare eligibility to 67 or providing guaranteed health insurance coverage for all citizens, would affect the health insurance coverage of early retirees. Thus, it seems especially important at this time to understand the interaction between insurance coverage and the retirement decision. If retirement is very sensitive to insurance coverage, for example, it could have important public finance implications for policies that provide universal health insurance coverage; a spate of retirement may nontrivially lower the tax base on which new policies can be financed.

Our strategy for estimating the effect of health insurance on retirement has been to examine the effect of state and federal continuation coverage mandates on retirement propensities. We do this in a static regression framework, which allows us to exploit a very large data set and to avoid the problems of dynamic sample selection that plague other studies based on survey data. Our results suggest that continuation coverage mandates have a sizable and significant effect on retirement. Contrary to our basic intuition, however, the effects are not necessarily the strongest at older ages. Rather, taken in conjunction with evidence from dynamic models, we appear to find declining effects by age. We also found that one year of continuation benefits is associated with a 6% increase in insurance coverage levels, suggesting that these policies are not only inducing retirement, but are "inframarginally" covering those who would have retired anyway.

Our use of continuation coverage regulations as the source of variation for identifying the effect of insurance coverage on retirement has both advantages and disadvantages relative to looking directly at workers with and without employer-provided retiree health insurance. One potential problem with the latter strategy is that the researcher is unable to control for job characteristics that may be correlated with both the generosity of retiree health coverage and the incentives that these jobs offer for retirement. An obvious example is pensions (which are accounted for in both Lumsdaine, Stock, and Wise 1994 and Gustman and Steinmeier 1994). There may be a number of other ways in which firms encourage or discourage retirement, however, such as through the tasks that they assign older workers or the wage profile that these workers are offered. Furthermore, there may be sorting of workers by retirement propensities into the types of firms that do or do not offer retiree health insurance. To the extent that these are unobserved by the econometrician but correlated with both the offering of retiree coverage and the retirement decision, they will bias the estimated effect of such coverage on retirement. What is needed to identify the effect of retiree health insurance is exogenous assignment of such coverage to individuals that is independent of these other job characteristics. Continuation coverage mandates potentially provide such exogenous assignment.

The primary disadvantage of our strategy is that continuation benefits are more expensive to the early retiree than retirement health insurance and provide coverage only for a limited number of months. These differences may make it unreasonable to extrapolate our results to infer the effects of full retiree health insurance coverage. Future research should focus on combining a study of true employer-provided retiree coverage with an identification strategy that overcomes the omitted-variable bias problems described above.

References

Bazzoli, Gloria J. 1985. The Early Retirement Decision: New Empirical Evidence on the Influence of Health. *Journal of Human Resources* 20:214–34.
Bound, John, and Timothy Waidmann. 1992. Disability Transfers, Self-Reported Health, and the Labor Force Attachment of Older Men: Evidence from the Historical Record. *Quarterly Journal of Economics* 107:1393–1420.
Burtless, Gary. 1986. Social Security, Unanticipated Benefit Increases, and the Timing of Retirement. *Review of Economic Studies* 53:781–805.
Burtless, Gary, and Robert A. Moffitt. 1984. The Effect of Social Security Benefits on the Labor Supply of the Aged. In *Retirement and Economic Behavior,* ed. Henry J. Aaron and Gary Burtless. Washington, DC: Brookings Institution.
Congressional Research Service. 1988. *Costs and Effects of Extending Health Insurance Coverage.* Washington, DC: Library of Congress.
Diamond, Peter A., and Jerry A. Hausman. 1984. The Retirement and Unemployment Behavior of Older Men. In *Retirement and Economic Behavior,* ed. Henry J. Aaron and Gary Burtless. Washington, DC: Brookings Institution.
Employee Benefits Research Institute. 1990. *Employee Benefit Notes.* Washington, DC: Employee Benefits Research Institute, November.
Farley, Pamela J. 1986. *Private Health Insurance in the United States.* National Health Care Expenditures Study Data Preview 23, DHHS Publication (PHS) 86–3406. Washington, DC: U.S. Department of Health and Human Services, National Center for Health Services Research and Health Care Technology Assessment.
Flynn, Patrice. 1992. Employment-Based Health Insurance: Coverage under COBRA

Continuation Rules. In U.S. Department of Labor, Pension and Welfare Benefits Administration, *Health Benefits and the Workforce.* Washington, DC: Government Printing Office.

Gruber, Jonathan. 1994a. The Incidence of Mandated Maternity Benefits. *American Economic Review* 84:622–41.

———. 1994b. State Mandated Benefits and Employer Provided Health Insurance. *Journal of Public Economics* 55:433–64.

Gruber, Jonathan, and Brigitte C. Madrian. 1995. Health Insurance Availability and the Early Retirement Decision. *American Economic Review* 85.

Gustman, Alan L., and Thomas L. Steinmeier. 1994. Employer-Provided Health Insurance and Retirement Behavior. *Industrial and Labor Relations Review* 48:86–102.

Hausman, Jerry A., and David A. Wise. 1985. Social Security, Health Status, and Retirement. In *Pensions, Labor, and Individual Choice,* ed. David A. Wise. Chicago: University of Chicago Press.

Heckman, James, and V. Joseph Hotz. 1988. Choosing among Alternative Non-Experimental Methods for Estimating the Impact of Social Programs: The Case of Manpower Training. *Journal of the American Statistical Association* 84:862–80.

Hewitt Associates. 1985. *Continuation of Group Medical Coverage: A Study of State Laws.* Lincolnshire, IL: Hewitt Associates.

Hurd, Michael D. 1990. Research on the Elderly: Economic Status, Retirement, and Consumption and Saving. *Journal of Economic Literature* 28:565–637.

Huth, Stephen A. 1991. COBRA Costs Average 150% of Active Costs. *Employee Benefit Plan Review* 46:14–19.

Jacobson, Lewis S., Robert J. LaLonde, and Daniel G. Sullivan. 1992. Earnings Losses of Displaced Workers. Federal Reserve Bank of Chicago Working Paper 92–28. Chicago: Federal Reserve Bank of Chicago.

Long, Stephen H., and M. Susan Marquis. 1992. COBRA Continuation Coverage: Characteristics of Enrollees and Costs in Three Plans. In U.S. Department of Labor, Pension and Welfare Benefits Administration, *Health Benefits and the Workforce.* Washington, DC: Government Printing Office.

Lumsdaine, Robin L., James H. Stock, and David A. Wise. 1992. Three Models of Retirement: Computational Complexity versus Predictive Validity. In *Topics in the Economics of Aging,* ed. David A. Wise, 19–57. Chicago: University of Chicago Press.

———. 1994. Pension Plan Provisions and Retirement: Men and Women, Medicare, and Models. In *Studies in the Economics of Aging,* ed. David A. Wise, 183–220. Chicago: University of Chicago Press.

Madrian, Brigitte C. 1994. The Effect of Health Insurance on Retirement. *Brookings Papers on Economic Activity* 1:181–252.

Rogowski, Jeannette A., and Lynn A. Karoly. 1992. Retirement and Health Insurance Coverage. In U.S. Department of Labor, Pension and Welfare Benefits Administration, *Health Benefits and the Workforce.* Washington, DC: Government Printing Office.

Rosen, Sherwin. 1986. The Theory of Equalizing Differences. In *Handbook of Labor Economics,* vol. 1, ed. Orley Ashenfelter and Richard Layard. Amsterdam: North-Holland.

Samwick, Andrew A. 1993. The Joint Effect of Social Security and Pensions on the Timing of Retirement: Some New Evidence. Massachusetts Institute of Technology. Mimeo.

Stock, James H., and David A. Wise. 1990a. The Pension Inducement to Retire: An Option Value Analysis. In *Issues in the Economics of Aging,* ed. David A. Wise. Chicago: University of Chicago Press.

———. 1990b. Pensions, the Option Value of Work, and Retirement. *Econometrica* 58 (5): 1151–80.

Sueyoshi, Glenn T. 1989. Social Security and the Determinants of Full and Partial Retirement: A Competing Risks Analysis. NBER Working Paper no. 3113. Cambridge, MA: National Bureau of Economic Research.

Thompson Publishing Group. 1992. *Employer's Handbook: Mandated Health Benefits: The COBRA Guide.* Salisbury, MD: Thompson Publishing Group.

Zedlewski, Sheila R. 1993. Retirees with Employment-Based Health Insurance. In U.S. Department of Labor, Pension and Welfare Benefits Administration, *Trends in Health Benefits.* Washington, DC: Government Printing Office.

Comment   Richard J. Zeckhauser

Old workers who turn out the widget,
Here studied by Jon and by Brigitte,
     Their fondest desire
     Is just to retire,
But the cost of health care makes them fidget.

Legislation attuned to their plight:
Makes twelve months' insurance a right.
     With the cost now reduced,
     A five-point-four percent boost
In retirement rate is in sight.

Jonathan Gruber and Brigitte Madrian's carefully crafted article springs from the observation that health insurance is a pricey commodity for individuals of prime retirement age, due to adverse selection and transactions costs. Recognizing this, a number of states, and recently the federal government, have passed legislation requiring that companies sell continuing coverage to their departing employees. The price can't exceed the average employee's cost, plus a sliver. (The federal mandate now extends for eighteen months.)

Such coverage slashes the costs of health insurance. Not surprisingly, for each year of mandated coverage an additional 6% of retirees buy health insurance. The dramatic reduction in health insurance costs also makes retirement more attractive. Indeed, employing appropriate econometric wizardry, Gruber

Richard J. Zeckhauser is the Frank P. Ramsey Professor of Economics at the John F. Kennedy School of Government, Harvard University, and a research fellow of the National Bureau of Economic Research.

and Madrian (GM) infer that an additional 1.1% of the 55–64-year-old cohort choose retirement, which is 5.4% of its baseline value.[1]

The model implicit in figure 4.1 suggests that employees value the continued coverage by the certainty equivalent of the difference between the price for the extended insurance charge and a retiree's other health coverage options—either the selection-biased price of privately purchased insurance, or the highly variable costs of self-insurance. Since this difference grows as people get older and sicker, and health becomes more heterogeneous, the retirement inducement will grow with age. GM therefore predict that the older workers are, the more mandates for continuation of health coverage will increase retirement as a percentage of baseline. But they find the reverse.

GM might have made the opposite prediction if they had pushed the heterogeneity button a bit harder. Say potential retirees fall into two groups, Calibrators and Instinctuals. The Calibrators are the tribe traditionally studied by economists;[2] they leave the Instinctuals to the sociologists. The Instinctuals range from bon vivants, the silver-haired types pictured on a golf course in national media advertising, to those too sick to work. One feature unites the Instinctuals—their decision to retire is unaffected by the cost of health insurance.

Evidence on the incidence of illness by age, including some presented by GM, show a rapid acceleration with age. For this reason alone, we would expect many more Instinctuals to have retired at 64, say, than at 55. Conceivably the acceleration with age of Calibrators' induced retirements could be more than proportional to the Instinctuals' upsweep. But maybe not. It depends in part on the elasticity of Calibrators' retirement with respect to health costs at each age.

The curve showing the number of workers who will be induced to retire by various levels of health savings may resemble many textbook labor-supply curves, with a range that is relatively flat followed by a range that is fairly inelastic. When coverage costs are reduced, the "cheap retirers" will go early. And the escalation in benefits over time, as people get sicker, may not be sufficient to get "expensive retirers" to participate. For example, it is often found that companies' early retirement plans disproportionately push out those at the

1. The impact is actually greater than that, since many employers were presumably already offering coverage before the government mandated it. As the mandate increases, it becomes a binding constraint on an ever-increasing percentage of firms. Assuming all months of coverage have the same effect, as GM do, this would produce a built-in nonlinearity.

2. The Calibrators have quite a challenge, since the implicit calculations are quite complex, probably sufficiently complex to defeat a pride of NBER researchers. GM find, for example, that one year of continuation coverage saves a worker $4,500 and has the same retirement consequences as $17,000 in Social Security wealth. They conclude, with reservations about variability among workers, that the two are worth the same. The logic doesn't follow, since the former is a price effect, whereas the latter is an income effect. Pity the poor worker confronted with this problem. Amos Tversky might explain the worker's behavior better than Alfred Marshall.

bottom end of the qualifying age range. And so it may be with some retirement due to reduced health care costs.

Retirement is a complex decision, involving health, location, and friends, as well as dollar costs and benefits, and we should be cautious before predicting the age-specific effects of inducements. We should be more cautious still when making predictions relative to baselines, given the array of reasons why workers retire.

GM are moving on to dynamic assessments of the transition to retirement in forthcoming work. They have already shown they can do the econometric nip-ups required to deal with sample selection issues. A bit of dextrous modeling as an accompaniment would now help them distill more about who retires and why.

GM complement an informative compilation of background data—age-specific patterns of health, expenditures, and coverage—with sound empirical methods to reach intuitive results. Embracing these results, what shall we make of mandates that require employers to sell health insurance to their retirees at a subsidized price? The economist's first concern—excess consumption—is hardly a problem: rational retirees would buy the insurance even at fair actuarial prices.

What of distributional consequences? Until wage adjustments work through the system—which could take quite a while, given that the system shock is a government mandate—these impositions represent a transfer from continuing workers to retirees. In the long run, wages will be pushed down to pay for this new mandated benefit, which thus becomes an imposed subsidy of one group by another.

What are the welfare consequences of this imposed subsidy? Should rational employers dealing with rational workers offer such coverage voluntarily? At least to deal with the adverse selection problem, it might seem so. Subsidized insurance is a second-best remedy to the hidden information problem. Add to this the labor economist's belief that age-earnings profiles are steeper than productivity profiles, which implies that older workers don't earn their keep. A subsidy for retirement may promote efficiency in the composition of a company's labor force, quite apart from saving the company money.

The company should also be concerned about who decides to retire in return for this small health coverage benefit. (The federally mandated eighteen months saves the retiree roughly $7,000, but costs the company far less, since it also subsidizes health coverage for older workers who do not retire.) If the most talented workers, who are presumably underpaid given bureaucratic constraints at firms, dash to retire (perhaps due to confidence that they can get another job), this will be poor policy. But if the sickly take off, reassured by coverage for a period in retirement, it looks more promising. In any deliberation by the firm, it should recognize, as GM find, that an extension of coverage induces about 5.5 times as many people to buy insurance as it does to retire.

In the short run, this multiplies the cost enormously. In the long run, downward wage adjustments wash out this effect. In sum, particularly in an era when many established firms are downsizing, continued health coverage in retirement may be an inexpensive way around a range of labor market rigidities.

What of the government's interest in promoting health coverage continuation? Some would argue that the government needs to step in due to market imperfections in the insurance market for older workers. But firms already have an incentive to address this problem on their own. The intensity of government action in this area is probably due to a desire to provide a subsidy to a specified group of workers—those about to retire—leaving till later the worry about who will ultimately pay.

The government's major concern should be whether we want workers to retire. If you think the size of the labor force is relatively fixed, a popular but noneconomic viewpoint, then you might promote retirement to spread things around. An economist would urge the government to consider the relationship of expected Social Security less taxes to retirement age. Since the relationship is strongly negative, the government should be in the business of delaying, not promoting, retirement.

These are revolutionary times in health insurance. Market conditions are forcing firms to drastic action. The federal government may soon make dramatic moves. GM demonstrate that even comparatively modest changes in government health coverage regulations have significant effects on retirement behavior. Their paper offers a more general lesson: health insurance interventions by the government have significant effects on the operation of labor markets.

II Health Care

5   Medicare Reimbursement and Hospital Cost Growth

Mark B. McClellan

In 1984, the Health Care Financing Administration implemented the prospective payment system (PPS) to reimburse hospitals for treating Medicare patients. PPS features payment on the basis of the diagnosis-related group (DRG), an essentially fixed payment for the entire bundle of medical services produced during a hospital admission. DRG outlier payments provide some insurance to hospitals for treating patients with extraordinarily high costs or long stays within the DRG. Other DRG adjustments, such as higher DRG payments for patients with versus without "complicating conditions" and higher payments for teaching hospitals, provide limited opportunities for hospitals to receive additional compensation for higher costs of care. But DRGs have been thought to provide high-powered incentives for efficient production of hospital care: reimbursement for an admission in a given DRG should not change much as input use varies.

In many respects, Medicare's actual experience with hospital costs under PPS has not worked out as hoped. Most troubling has been a continued steady increase in intensity per admission, and consequently in average per capita expenditures for hospital services in the Medicare program. Between 1984 and 1990, the Prospective Payment Assessment Commission (1991) estimated that the case-mix index per discharge increased by almost 20%, after adjusting for price updates and other policy changes. A 1% increase in the case-mix index translates into an additional $750 million per year in Medicare payments; this increase in intensity accounts for the bulk of Medicare hospital expenditure increases. As the Prospective Payment Assessment Commission (1993) has

Mark B. McClellan is professor of economics and medicine at Stanford University and a faculty research fellow of the National Bureau of Economic Research.

The author thanks Jonathan Feinstein, Joseph Newhouse, Andrew Samwick, and Jonathan Skinner for useful discussions, and the Agency for Health Care Policy Research (grant R03-HS07638-01) and the National Institute on Aging (grant 5-R29-AG11706-02) for financial support.

noted, growth in the case mix index is the principal determinant of hospital payment growth; its effect has been "greater than the combined effect of . . . all other policy changes implemented under PPS" (20–21).

From the standpoint of controlling Medicare hospital expenditure growth, the PPS experience has clearly been disappointing. In a related paper (McClellan 1993), I have argued that a few basic implications of the nature of DRG payments, coupled with some understanding of the internal organization of hospital production, can explain the "puzzles" of PPS in the context of a standard analysis of production incentives with price regulation. Here I review and expand the previous analysis, describing some distinctive institutional features of hospital production in more detail and summarizing the results of the static model of hospital production designed to capture these features. I then develop a dynamic framework to describe how price and cost growth interact in hospital production, which suggests that a reimbursement system such as PPS may encourage technological change endogenous to the payment rules. Finally, I turn to some preliminary evidence on the nature of expenditure-increasing technological change in the Medicare program, which appears to be consistent with the dynamic framework.

5.1   Institutional Characteristics of Hospital Production

This section addresses two related topics that have received limited attention in the literature on hospital behavior: the appropriate definition of the "good" produced for patients demanding hospital care, and the nature of the internal organization of hospitals. These issues have important implications for the production and regulation of medical care.

Patients do not demand hospital treatments per se; they demand treatment for their particular health problems. "Production" of health care involves both diagnostic and therapeutic treatments, the most intensive of which are administered to patients who have been admitted to a hospital. For most health problems, many technological choices exist, and hence many alternative treatment intensities are possible. As a result, a hospital admission per se does not constitute a well-defined product. The following examples, drawn from some of the most common and costly diseases in the elderly, illustrate that (1) hospitalizations may or may not be required for treatment; (2) when a patient is hospitalized, multiple treatment courses involving quite different medical technologies are possible; and (3) these treatment courses can result in different payment levels, even in "prospective" reimbursement systems such as Medicare PPS. The brief clinical summaries are not intended to imply that all patients with each of the health problems are equally appropriate candidates for all treatment alternatives. However, the net benefits of more intensive treatment may be modest or uncertain for a considerable fraction of patients with a health problem, providing considerable opportunities for physician discretion in treatment choices (Park et al. 1986; McClellan and Brook 1992).

Coronary heart disease. Coronary heart disease is the leading cause of death in the United States. In most cases, death is directly or indirectly related to a heart attack, or acute myocardial infarction (AMI). Patients with symptoms of a heart attack such as crushing chest pain will be treated at a hospital to "rule out" AMI or to manage its complications. The diagnostic and therapeutic management of all heart disease patients may include several intensive procedures: cardiac catheterization, percutaneous transluminal coronary angioplasty (PTCA), and coronary artery bypass graft (CABG) surgery. These technologies are substantially more costly than the less intensive alternatives, which involve noninvasive diagnostic studies, drug treatments, and lifestyle counseling.

Cancer. Treatment modalities for most types of cancer involve some combination of surgery, radiation therapy, and chemotherapy. For example, for localized breast cancer, treatment may involve total or partial mastectomy, followed by radiation or chemotherapy. Various cancer treatment regimens have different requirements for the intensity of these treatments and for the frequency of inpatient hospital stays.

Hip fracture. Patients with hip fracture will be admitted to the hospital. Depending on the nature of the fracture, the treatment for setting the fracture may involve open reduction (a surgical procedure) or closed reduction (a nonsurgical procedure).

Gall bladder disease. Patients with chronic cholecystitis (gall bladder disease) can be managed "medically," with drugs and dietary modification, or "surgically," with removal of the gall bladder. For patients managed surgically, several types of cholecystectomy procedures are possible. Cholecystectomy may include intraoperative radiographic imaging of the biliary ducts with contrast dye enhancement to identify any remaining gallstones. An alternative cholecystectomy technique for uncomplicated cases, laparoscopic cholecystectomy, involves a more limited surgical incision and potentially shorter postoperative recovery.

Benign prostatic hypertrophy. Enlargement of the prostate gland, leading to urinary retention, frequency, and hesitancy, is extremely common in elderly males. One treatment is prostatectomy (primarily transurethral prostatectomy) to remove gland tissue. Alternatively, especially in milder cases, patients can simply endure symptoms (e.g., having to get up to urinate in the middle of the night). Patients who choose not to have surgery require hospitalization only for severe complications.

Back pain. Back pain is an extremely common chronic health problem. Surgical treatments to reduce symptoms include spinal decompression (for pain, tingling, or numbness arising from nerve compression), intervertebral diskectomy and spinal fusion, and laminectomy. Patients who are managed without these surgical procedures (through drugs, musculoskeletal therapies, and other regimens) may require hospital treatments such as traction only for severe complications.

Arthritis. Rheumatoid arthritis and osteoarthritis are leading causes of functional limitations in the elderly, especially elderly females. Many drug regimens of increasing strength (and side effects), as well as other nonsurgical treatments such as heat baths, are available to reduce pain and limit deterioration in affected joints. These treatments generally do not require hospitalization. A more intensive hospital-based alternative is surgical replacement of the knee or hip.

The preceding illustrations, representing a spectrum of common diseases, demonstrate that any analysis of hospital production should consider incentives for treatment of a health problem rather than for production of a particular kind of treatment. However, virtually all of the alternative treatments just described lead to different DRG classifications. The structure of DRGs consequently supports a form of indirect cost sharing, in which payments depend not on reported costs but on actual use of particular technologies that have important implications for the cost of an admission. In this sense, the DRG system continues a historical trend in hospital payment mechanisms toward dependence on real measures of resource use. Indeed, hospital payments under the Tax Equity and Fiscal Responsibility Act (TEFRA) system that PPS replaced were primarily based on allowed per diems, that is, hospital payments that depended on the number of days provided. While PPS moved further toward an admission-based payment system, it retained some features of intensity-related payment.

Why is PPS structured so that use of specific intensive procedures for a health problem leads to more generous reimbursement? If health care were produced competitively, then additional payments would not be required to encourage hospitals to produce enough intensive treatments that are valued by patients. A fixed payment per admission or even per individual would be adequate; hospitals would simply maximize (costly) intensity subject to the budget constraint implied by the payment level. Cost sharing implies a concern about imperfect competition: for whatever reason, hospitals would tend to underproduce intensity unless incentives were softened. Myriad reasons for market failures have been proposed in health care, and it is beyond the scope of this paper to review all of them here. I concentrate on one important tension that has been noted by a few other researchers: on one hand, the tension between physician incentives, financial and otherwise, to maximize patient welfare and, on the other, hospital incentives to maximize financial and other rents.

Theoretical papers on the optimal regulation of hospitals have mostly assumed that the incentives facing hospitals match the incentives of the physicians practicing in them, at least up to the (costly) implementation of appropriate internal incentives.[1] One exception is Harris (1977), who describes hospital production as a noncooperative game between physicians engaged in specific relationships with patients on the one hand and hospital managers making investment decisions involving capacity, equipment, and staff hiring on the other. Physicians generally are not employees of the hospital,[2] but rather are participants in highly incomplete contracts with both the hospital and their patients. When a patient seeks care for a health problem, the patient contracts for "appropriate" medical treatment, whatever the health problem turns out to be. Because these treatment contingencies are too numerous to describe ex ante or to verify ex post, patients and physicians cannot sign a complete contract that specifies how the physician will treat every possible medical contingency that may arise in the course of the treatment episode. Just as contingent production decisions are not specified in the contract between a medical expert and a patient, they are not specified in the physician's contractual arrangement with the hospital. Hospital contracts for admitting privileges specify few explicit restrictions on the use of hospital capital that is within the purview of the physician's specialty.

Harris emphasizes the transactions costs of all these treatment intensity decisions and the importance of physician preferences (as opposed to those of hospital managers) in resource allocation decisions for individual patients. But the problem is even more fundamental than transactions costs. Specific investments are substantial: a physician treating a particular patient develops detailed knowledge of the idiosyncrasies of the patient's case. In theory, physicians or hospital managers could hold up patients for the value of these specific investments at critical junctures in the course of treatment, when the patient's life may literally be at stake. These characteristics of hospital production suggest that markets or explicit contracts would represent costly approaches to fostering efficient production.

In this view, the traditional organizational structure of the hospital may rep-

---

1. An exception is Ellis and McGuire (1986), who model hospital production as a reflection of treatment decisions by physicians. However, the marginal rate of substitution between patient and hospital objectives (that is, the relative weight placed on maximizing hospital profits versus maximizing patient welfare) and hence the extent of the agency problem is treated as exogenous in the model, there is no role for hospital investment decisions in influencing physician decisions, and hospital payment is modeled as fixed regardless of treatment choice. These features may have important implications for hospital production decisions.

2. The physicians that tend to be contractual employees—radiologists, anesthesiologists, and pathologists—prove the rule, since these physicians specialize in technical aspects of hospital production rather than making decisions as agents for particular patients.

resent not so much a reflection of physicians' desire for autonomy in treating patients (Starr 1984) as an institutional mechanism to limit the power of incentives in the physician's other role, as an agent for the hospital. Physicians do not control investment decisions for the hospital or own hospital capital, but they largely retain the rights of control for utilization of hospital capital equipment and other resources.[3] Altering these residual rights of control over treatment decisions, for example through direct employment relationships between physicians and hospitals, would probably alter these residual rights of control and hence treatment decisions for hospitalized patients.[4]

Thus, if a hospital finds that treating patients in the DRG for congestive heart failure (CHF) is unprofitable, it cannot order its admitting physicians not to treat patients with CHF. Physicians control specific admission decisions. Even if such a prohibition were technically possible, it might impose considerable externalities on hospital production. Many patients with CHF initially arrive at the emergency department with shortness of breath, water weight gain, feelings of weakness and lightheadedness, or even vaguer symptoms. Only after some evaluation of the specific case can the diagnosis of CHF be made and treatment initiated. By this time, physicians practicing at the hospital have invested in a relationship with the patient that involves some specific knowledge of the idiosyncrasies of the case. Similarly, CHF is a problem that frequently accompanies other common diseases—such as a recent heart attack, diabetes, or hypertension—which also may require hospitalization (possibly at the same time) and which may represent relatively profitable DRGs for the hospital. Prohibiting or restricting admissions for the diagnosis would limit gains from relationship-specific investments between the patient and physicians that permit the delivery of more effective care for many other diagnoses.

Hospital managers can, however, affect the environment in which physicians make these specific treatment decisions. For diseases such as CHF that involve "nonspecific" technologies, hospital choices about capacity investments in hospital beds, laboratory equipment, and support staffing levels may indirectly affect physician decisions on treatment intensity, but only at the cost of affecting treatment decisions for many health problems. In contrast, for diagnoses and procedures requiring investments in specific capacity, the choices of hospital managers can significantly affect use of the treatments and admissions at the DRG level. For example, if a hospital finds cardiac catheterization unprofitable, it need not prohibit its physicians from catheterizing specific patients. It need only close its catheterization laboratory. By deciding its invest-

3. Some other capital-intensive professions in which the appropriateness of specific production decisions is difficult for managers to observe have similar arrangements. In many research laboratories, for example, the capital equipment may belong to the academic institution, but the researchers who use it are paid largely through grants obtained independently rather than through employee relationships.

4. The consequences of the nature of the employment relationship for production choices and efficiency are examined in detail in Grossman and Hart (1986), which provides some of the foundation for this discussion.

ment level in the technologies needed to produce catheterization, the hospital can effectively specialize or not in catheterization DRGs. Similarly, by determining whether to provide the specialized equipment and personnel required for cancer treatments or particular kinds of surgical procedures, hospital managers can significantly influence admissions in these DRGs.

Regardless of the nature of medical technologies, the physician faces inherent agency conflicts when patient and hospital interests do not coincide. They will not coincide if intensive treatments are costly and if hospitals are not fully insured against costs of care. Vesting the residual rights of production decisions in the physician, and separating physician reimbursement incentives from hospital reimbursement incentives, clearly reduces the strength of the physician-hospital agency relationship. To the extent that physicians are reimbursed at cost for the services they provide, so that the trade-offs they face between patient welfare and their own net profits (including effort costs) are minimized, then physician agency for patients may be much stronger than physician agency for the hospital at the margin.

Whether this allocation of noncontractible rights of control is optimal depends on hospital and patient incentives and on the nature of the alternative technologies that may be involved in patient care. Today, it is easy to consider other allocations of residual control. However, in both traditional insurance arrangements and most managed-care plans, patients typically face limited out-of-pocket prices for medical services; Medicare inpatient services are approximately fully insured.[5] If patients were fully informed and controlled marginal treatment decisions, they would consequently demand all services with positive net benefits. The implication is that residual control by physicians—supported by loose contractual relationships with hospitals and physician payment systems in which the physician tends not to be the residual claimant for substantial costs—strengthens patient agency, leading physicians to prefer more intensive treatment patterns than hospital managers prefer under fixed-price reimbursement.[6]

Together, these institutional characteristics imply that a model of the internal organization of hospital production decisions must incorporate the following features (McClellan 1993):

1. Physicians—who have the most knowledge about the benefits of alterna-

5. The Part A deductible is limited to the cost of one hospital day. While Part B insurance covers only 80% of physician allowed charges, over 80% of beneficiaries have supplemental insurance that eliminates this residual cost sharing.

6. Another advantage of explicitly modeling the internal organization of hospital production is that the consequences of other employment arrangements can be considered explicitly. Strong residual control by physicians has other costs besides limiting the power of hospital managers to influence use of some hospital technologies. For example, the costs of coordinating treatment for an illness beyond the level of an admission may be higher than it would be if the hospital (or HMO) employed all physicians involved in treating the illness. The costs and benefits of the various possibilities for vertical and horizontal integration in the production of treatment for an illness have not been explored much by economists. In this paper, I consider only "traditional" arrangements, which currently describe the production of care for most Medicare beneficiaries.

tive medical technologies for specific patients—are dual agents, for patients in the production of medical treatments and for hospitals in the use of hospital capital. The incomplete contractual arrangements that form the basis for specific production relationships between physicians and patients, and between physicians and hospitals, leave the residual rights of control for decisions to fulfill these production relationships primarily to the physician.

2. These open-ended contractual arrangements, coupled with generous demand-side insurance and a physician payment system that is largely independent of hospital profits, suggest that physicians involved in specific agency relationships with patients weigh patient welfare more than hospital profits, and in any case more than hospital managers weigh patient versus hospital objectives.

3. The nature of the medical technologies used to treat particular illnesses influences how hospital payment incentives influence equilibrium production decisions. For treatments dependent on specific hospital investments, hospital managers have more control over production levels; for treatments involving nonspecific technologies that are difficult to ration, physicians have more control.

5.2   A Model of the Production of Medical Treatment Intensity

McClellan (1993) formalizes the noncooperative game of hospital production described in the previous section. Here I sketch the main results for investment in a "simple" intensive technology, one that may be used in the treatment of a single health problem. There are four parties: fully insured *patients* with a health problem who decide which hospital to visit for treatment; *physicians* who learn the patient's expected benefits from alternative treatments and make treatment intensity decisions; *hospitals* that provide medical technologies for treatment; and a *regulator* who sets the price schedule for hospitals. The structure of the game is as follows:

1. The regulator sets prices for less intensive treatment (without the intensive technology) and more intensive treatment for the health problem.

2. The hospital invests in medical technologies that constitute the environment for medical treatment.

3. Physicians observe hospital investment choices, contract with hospitals to provide medical services, and define their equilibrium treatment intensity choices.

4. Patients observe some measure of hospital quality related to its investment decisions and, possibly with guidance from physicians, choose a hospital for treatment.

5. The physician observes the patient's expected benefit from alternative treatments and chooses treatment intensity. There are two treatment intensity choices, $r = 0$ (less intensive) and $r = 1$ (more intensive). The performance of

$r = 0$ or $r = 1$ is observable and verifiable, and hence can be used as the basis for a reimbursement contract.

6. Patients receive treatment and hospitals are reimbursed for services.

Suppose that the nature of the technology is such that the hospital can choose a capacity level; for example, staffing and equipment choices in a cardiac catheterization laboratory can effectively determine the number of patients with heart disease who receive catheterization. Because investment in the capacity to produce the intensive treatment is costly, hospital managers will invest in intensive capacity until the marginal benefits of investment (in terms of additional demand attracted and patients treated profitably) equal the marginal costs (in terms of the costs of additional capacity and the potential losses on the fraction of patients treated intensively). In turn, as more capacity becomes available, physicians are able to treat more patients intensively (the "marginal" patient treated intensively has a lower perceived benefit), and more intensive treatment patterns attract more patients. Denote the regulated payment level as $\bar{p}^0$ and $\bar{p}^1$ as the regulated prices for less intensive and more intensive treatment, c^0 and c^1 as the corresponding marginal costs, I^1 as the hospital investment in intensive capacity, $\hat{\theta}(I^1)$ as the expected net benefit (perceived by the physician) of more intensive treatment for the marginal patient receiving it, $F(\hat{\theta})$ denotes the share of patients treated with $r = 0$, and $q(\hat{\theta})$ denotes aggregate demand (decreasing in $\hat{\theta}$, i.e., increasing in intensity). The hospital will choose capacity I^1 such that

$$\frac{1}{\eta_{0\theta}}\cdot[\bar{p}^0 - c^0] + \frac{1}{\eta_{1\theta}}\cdot[\bar{p}^1 - c^1] = \frac{1}{\eta_{q\theta}}\cdot[(\bar{p}^0 - c^0) - (\bar{p}^1 - c^1)],$$

where $\eta_{0\theta} = (\partial F/\partial\theta)\cdot(\theta/F)$ is the elasticity of treatment with $r = 0$ with respect to $\hat{\theta}$; $\eta_{1\theta} = -(\partial(1 - F)/\partial\theta)\cdot(\theta/(1 - F))$ is the elasticity of treatment with $r = 1$ and with respect to $\hat{\theta}$; and $\eta_{q\theta} = -q'\cdot\theta/q$ is the elasticity of demand with respect to intensity $q(I)$. All of these "quality elasticities" are defined to be positive.[7]

The equation shows that equilibrium intensity increases and equilibrium profits[8] decrease as the elasticity of demand with respect to intensity increases. In the extreme case of perfectly elastic demand, the zero-profit constraint holds and intensity is maximized subject to the price constraints. For a given $\bar{p}^0$, equilibrium intensity also increases as $\bar{p}^1$ increases, and the difference in margins $[\bar{p}^0 - c^0] - [\bar{p}^1 - c^1]$ decreases (if $\bar{p}^0$ is set high enough for production to occur). Equilibrium intensity will only be first-best for a particular combination of prices, and actual intensity would vary across markets as a function of demand elasticity.

This model of equilibrium intensity choices for hospital investment in a specific technological capacity demonstrates that the quality and cost of hospital

---

7. McClellan (1993) describes the technical properties of this solution in more detail.
8. For nonprofit hospitals, economic rents are possible even if profits are not.

production need not depend on *physician* preferences in any direct way. However, it is easy to imagine other kinds of medical technologies where physician preferences would be much more important in determining equilibrium choice. Specific investments in capacity are an extreme case; for other technologies, physician objectives are more relevant to equilibrium intensity choices.

Many technologies involve a more or less binding capacity choice but are not specific to the treatment of a particular health problem. For example, hospital managers typically make decisions about opening a hospital bed, purchasing a computerized tomography (CT) scanner, or providing a chemical analyzer for laboratory tests, but they have much less control over how these technologies are used in practice. Because the hospital cannot direct their use to specific kinds of patients, it can only choose an optimal aggregate intensity level for all the health problems. It does so considering how physicians will allocate marginal units of capacity among patients with the various health problems, and the implications of these decisions for profits. In addition, some specific and nonspecific investments by hospitals may represent "line of business" decisions rather than capacity choices. For example, a hospital can decide whether to stock specific drugs such as thrombolytic agents (for heart attacks) or less specific drugs such as antihypertensive and pain-reducing drugs (for many types of patients), but it cannot easily choose a capacity for these treatments. Hospitals can make binary choices about whether to adopt these technologies, knowing that physicians will choose the treatment pattern that they prefer.

McClellan (1993) formalizes a model of these hospital investment decisions as well. For example, in deciding whether to adopt a "line of business" technology, the hospital's adoption decision is based on profits if it does or does not adopt; if the hospital adopts, then physician preferences and not hospital preferences determine equilibrium intensity levels for use of the technology. Even if hospital production is not very competitive, physician decisions can thus lead to more intensive treatment (i.e., lower rents and more spending on desired technology) than hospital managers would prefer.

Most medical technologies involve physician effort costs between the extremes of investments in fixed capacity and in a line of business. For example, congestion may make physician effort costs an increasing function of their intensity choice, as scanners or operating rooms become more crowded. Hospitals must trade off higher unit production costs associated with congestion against the effects of congestion on limiting resource use; the model is qualitatively similar to the capacity-constraint case. Hospitals may also make costly investments in technologies that influence physician use of other technologies. For example, hospitals may invest in monitoring systems that require physicians to justify particular admissions or long stays, in computer technologies that make it easier to order certain tests or drugs but harder to order others, and other "utilization management" investments that are not only costly to the hospital but also to the physician. Such investments are not first-best, but may be the best available option to hospital managers when their preferences conflict with those of the physicians.

This discussion suggests that optimal regulation of medical prices should consider not only price levels but also the extent of price aggregation. *Any* administered price system will lead to efficient production of the particular bundles of services for which prices are set exogenously: the fixed price makes the producer the residual claimant for all savings resulting from cost minimization in production of the services. However, disaggregating payments for treatment of a particular health problem so that the more intensive treatment receives a higher payment encourages more use of the intensive treatment than would be supported by a single, aggregated price. Administered price systems for medical care, as for other industries, are not new. The so-called cost-based hospital reimbursement system that Medicare PPS replaced was such a disaggregated administered price system. Hospitals could not charge any desired price for services billed to Medicare; instead, hospital regulators reviewed reported hospital costs for their "reasonableness" in relation to the services provided. Many large private insurers continue to rely on such disaggregated administered price systems today for hospital services; they are also widely used for reimbursement of physician services. At the opposite extreme, some health maintenance organizations (HMOs) use fixed-price per capita contracts with hospitals or physicians for providing all medical services for a given population.

Medicare PPS is between these extremes. The system provides a single payment per hospitalization, which is a more aggregated level of administered prices than the cost-based reimbursement system that it replaced. However, some particular treatments or types of treatments—primarily intensive surgical procedures—still define administered price groups. In contrast to the current DRG system, one can imagine a more aggregated DRG system at the level of diagnoses only.[9]

If hospitals have market power and can effectively control treatment intensity, increasing the aggregation of the pricing system reduces the costs of producing care for a health problem through intensity reductions. Such incentives may be too high-powered. On the other hand, setting price equal to cost for each alternative treatment provides no financial incentive for the hospital to limit treatment intensity; this is the same kind of problem that "prospective" payment was intended to address. There is no conflict between physician agency for patients and for hospitals with respect to the intensity choices that are each reimbursed at cost. Thus, pricing admissions for an intensive treat-

---

9. Diagnoses themselves may also be more or less aggregated. DRGs for most major diagnostic categories include a number of specific diagnoses (e.g., AMI, deep venous thrombophlebitis), some less specific diagnoses (e.g., chest pain), and catchall residual categories (other circulatory system diagnoses). Here I focus on the effects of allowing DRG classification to depend on treatment intensity decisions.

ment at its cost will tend to encourage its use to the point that marginal benefits are close to zero, though the treatment itself will be produced efficiently.

An intuitive solution to this dilemma is for the regulator to "split the difference" in setting prices for the alternative treatments. If regulators have some knowledge of the demand function and the distribution of net benefit levels from more intensive treatment, they can use the equation derived in McClellan (1993) to solve for the set of prices that implements the desired intensity level. Returning to the notation of the model, since treatment intensity is increasing in ($\bar{p}^1 - \bar{p}^0$), this procedure involves setting a price for $r = 0$ (the less intensive treatment) greater than c^0 and a price increment for $r = 1$ less than the cost difference ($c^1 - c^0$). While such a "first-best" rule seems to have strong informational requirements, changes in the Medicare price structure that are clearly welfare-improving can presumably be accomplished with much more limited information. In particular, moving away from paying the full cost differential (on average) for a more intensive treatment should reduce incentives to provide the more intensive treatment in cases of minimal expected benefit.

5.3   Medicare Price Regulation and the Dynamics of Medical Treatment Intensity

In this section, I illustrate the dynamic implications of the Medicare price rule based on the model reviewed in section 5.2. I assume no exogenous changes in technology over time to focus on endogenous technological change resulting from the PPS price rules. These DRG pricing rules include unbundled DRGs for some intensive treatments, and price updates that essentially make the current DRG price a function of average charges for patients in the DRG in a previous year (lagged "yardstick" competition).

The dynamic implications can be illustrated qualitatively with phase diagrams. Consider a true DRG; that is, reimbursement is a fixed price for the diagnosis regardless of the treatment intensity level chosen. Figure 5.1 illustrates the current Medicare pricing rule for a DRG of setting $\bar{p}_{t+1} = c_t$, where c_t is the average cost in the DRG in period t.[10] If there are a large number of identical hospitals, the impact of intensity choices by a particular hospital will have no effect on price in subsequent periods, so hospitals will not behave strategically, and all will choose the same equilibrium intensity and cost for a given price. At X, $p_t(X)$ is lower than $c_t(X)$, so $p_{t+1}(X)$ increases to offset the difference. At Y, $p_t(Y)$ is higher than $c_t(Y)$, so $p_{t+1}(Y)$ falls to offset the difference. At Z, $p_t(Z)$ equals $c_t(Z)$, so $p_{t+1}(Z)$ is unchanged. Assuming for now that regulators can measure hospital costs accurately, it is evident that a line with

10. The actual Medicare pricing rule is to set price equal to a conversion factor times the relative weight of a particular DRG, where the weight is determined by the ratio of charges in the DRG to average charges for all Medicare patients in year $t - 2$. The conversion factor is set to achieve a particular total expenditure target. Thus the price update rule is exact only if the conversion factor updates hospital output prices by the rate of increase in hospital input prices.

unitary slope through the origin traces out the set of (p_t, c_t) combinations for which p_{t+1} will be unchanged; this is the $dp/dt = \dot{p} = 0$ equilibrium line. To the northwest, $\dot{p} > 0$; to the southeast, $\dot{p} < 0$.

Figure 5.2 illustrates a complementary relationship for the dynamics of equilibrium cost. If cost happened to be very low in a period when a very high price was offered, cost will increase (the higher price increases the returns to attracting more demand). Thus, in the southeast corner of figure 5.2, for example at point Y, $c_{t+1}(Y) > c_t(Y)$. In contrast, if equilibrium cost happened to be very high and a low price were introduced, cost would fall through intensity reductions. Thus, in the northeast corner, for example at point X, $c_{t+1}(X) < c_t(X)$. At point Z, cost and price are such that no equilibrium adjustment is necessary, so $\dot{c} = 0$. A sample $\dot{c} = 0$ line is traced out in the figure; the line reflects an equilibrium cost function that becomes less sensitive to price at higher price levels. Different demand functions, intensity costs, distributions of expected net benefits to patients, and degrees of physician control over intensity choices will generate different forms for $\dot{c} = 0$. Intensity is increasing in costs, so the $\dot{c} = 0$ mapping also implies an equilibrium intensity level $\hat{\theta}$ as a function of price.

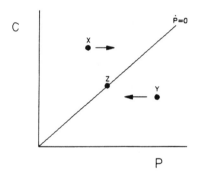

Fig. 5.1   Dynamics of Medicare DRG prices

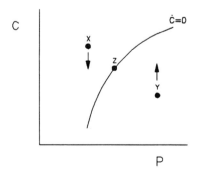

Fig. 5.2   Dynamics of hospital costs: an example

Combining the $\dot{c} = 0$ and $\dot{p} = 0$ relationships, as in figure 5.3, illustrates how the PPS might influence the dynamics of equilibrium cost and intensity levels in the DRG. In this example, two points comprise equilibrium price-cost relationships, A and B. A is an unstable equilibrium, since any perturbation away from A will tend to move farther from A. B is a stable equilibrium, since local perturbations tend to return to B. A key feature is that at B the slope of the $\dot{p} = 0$ function is greater than that of the $\dot{c} = 0$ function. The phase diagram does not depict time to convergence, but the time course of a sample intensity path from point W to point B is illustrated in figure 5.4. Cost and intensity first fall then rise to converge on B (that is, intensity first rises, then falls).

Note that, if costs are measured accurately, the $\dot{p} = 0$ line also comprises the zero-profit line for hospital production. One feature of figure 5.5, that $\dot{c} = 0$ equilibria could occur in a range where $p > c$, may seem implausible. However, it is possible if cross-subsidies exist (e.g., hospital investments are

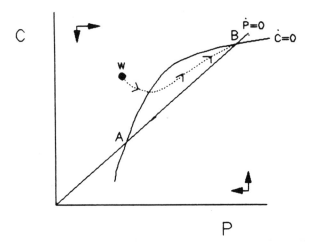

Fig. 5.3   Stable dynamic equilibrium

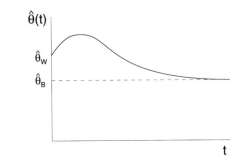

Fig. 5.4   Intensity choice over time

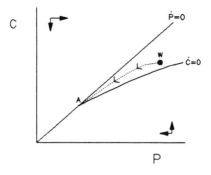

Fig. 5.5   Low-intensity dynamic equilibrium

nonspecific), if hospital costs are subsidized from other sources (e.g., separate reimbursement of capital costs, as described below, or subsidies from non-Medicare patients), if hospital-reported cost estimates are biased upward, or if other arguments in the hospital objective function besides patient welfare can be disguised as necessary costs of care. I return to some of these possibilities momentarily.

If none of these possibilities exist, figure 5.5 represents a more realistic path in the case where hospitals have market power. Point A represents a stable equilibrium, occurring at the *minimal* intensity level. At any given price, a hospital with market power can earn positive price-cost margins on average by decreasing quality slightly below the level that maximizes consumer welfare (and earns zero profits). Consequently, average cost is less than price. Thus the $\dot{c} = 0$ curve will generally have a flatter slope and be located to the right of the $\dot{p} = 0$ curve over the range of prices in which hospitals can choose intensity levels above the minimum. The updated price (equal to observed cost in the previous period) will be lower, leading to a lower optimal intensity level, and this downward spiral continues until the minimum intensity level is reached. In practice, of course, there is no distinct minimal intensity level of medical care; at the extreme, hospital care would simply move to an outpatient setting.

However, higher equilibrium intensity levels (or at least a slower rate of decline) are possible if the technologies used at equilibrium are such that physicians acting as patient agents control intensity or if hospitals face near-perfect competition. Whenever hospital demand is perfectly elastic or hospitals maximize patient welfare for other reasons, *any* point along the $\dot{p} = 0$ line is a stable equilibrium. Intensity is maximized subject to the zero-profit constraint, so price equals cost for *any* price at least as high as the minimum intensity level of hospital production requires. Thus, as shown in figure 5.6, an infinite number of stable equilibria are possible; the particular equilibrium that exists depends only on the initial price level.

Perfect competition or physician choices leading to intensity maximization for a given price result in stable equilibria. In contrast, figure 5.7 presents a

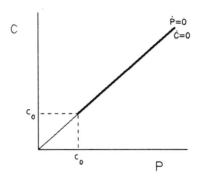

Fig. 5.6   Multiple dynamic equilibria with perfect competition

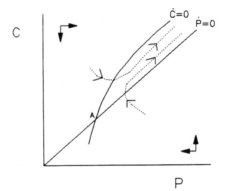

Fig. 5.7   Unstable dynamic intensity growth

more worrisome situation, in which the price rule encourages dynamic increases in intensity. The equilibrium $\dot{c} = 0$ curve is above the equilibrium $\dot{p} = 0$ curve in the relevant range of prices and costs. Equilibrium A is unstable: from any initial condition with cost or price beyond A, cost and price will continue to increase over time as long as the $\dot{c} = 0$ line is above the $\dot{p} = 0$ line. This instability is a general characteristic of pricing rules that increase the steepness of the $\dot{c} = 0$ line. Three scenarios that tend to lead to such relationships are considered below: separate cost-based reimbursement of specific dimensions of intensity, nonprofit hospital objectives, and overestimation of hospital marginal production costs in the reimbursement formulas.

In some respects the Medicare pricing rule is less high-powered than suggested by the fixed-price rules described in the preceding figures. Consider the extreme case of disaggregated pricing at average cost for each treatment, preserving the incentive to produce the treatment efficiently but making hospital profits zero regardless of intensity choice. Then every point on the $\dot{c} = 0$ line can be a dynamic equilibrium. (In fact, any intensity level in which price equals cost is sustainable.) Medicare actually reimburses only certain dimensions of treatment intensity separately, but this can still encourage broader intensity and cost increases in the treatment of a disease. In general, as the previous discussion indicated, increasing the price differential between alternative intensity levels appears to increase the steepness of the market equilibrium ($\dot{c} = 0$) curve, increasing the probability of unstable cost growth.[11]

Another possible cause of unstable intensity growth, even if measured costs are correct, is the existence of nonprofit objectives in hospital objective functions. Only a small fraction of hospitals are for-profit, so that most hospitals should not be expected to show much total accounting profit. To the extent that such nonprofit objectives translate into higher observed costs of treating Medicare patients, they will tend to push hospital $\dot{c} = 0$ curves toward—if not above—the $\dot{p} = 0$ curve, increasing the probability of dynamic cost and intensity increases in the absence of technological change.

An additional potential source of instability is mismeasurement of marginal production costs. A large literature documents the difficulty of correctly estimating "true" production costs in multiproduct firms in other industries. Fundamental cost estimation problems such as allocating costs in joint production or calculating true economic depreciation rates for assets that may be expensed or depreciated according to standard accounting formulas are no different for hospitals. Such detailed cost estimation is practically infeasible anyway. Medicare's cost estimates for setting DRG prices are obtained from "ghost" bills for hospital charges that would have been generated if the beneficiary were a private patient.[12] Further, because DRG prices are updated based on average charges in the DRG relative to national average charges,[13] the reimbursement system tends to favor treatments for which true cost-to-charge ratios are low.

In particular, the reimbursement system favors DRGs that rely more heavily on capital-intensive treatments such as operative procedures or laboratory tests. These DRGs have the lowest measured cost-to-charge ratios (Rogowski and Byrne 1991). Other features of PPS also favor more capital-intensive treatments. Teaching hospitals receive an indirect medical education adjustment to their DRG payments proportional to their ratio of interns and residents to hospital beds. Since the adjustment is proportional, it provides larger increments to reimbursement for admissions in more intensive DRGs. Finally, Medicare payments for hospital capital expenditures were cost-based through 1991:

11. Of course, reimbursing some dimensions of treatment intensity at higher levels also affects the form of the $\dot{p} = 0$ curves for treatment of the health problem in ways that cannot easily be captured in a two-dimensional phase diagram. In general, as the static model indicated, smaller intensity price differentials lead to higher equilibrium intensity levels; if the resulting cost increases lead to further average price increases, the cycle may continue over time.

12. The relationship of hospital charge data to "true" costs may be declining. Most hospitals provide special discounts to many large payers (e.g., Blue Cross, HMOs, preferred provider organizations [PPOs]). Charges to residual third-party payers may be higher as a result, and in any event may bear less of a direct relationship to actual hospital costs of care.

13. Charge-based weights were first used in the fiscal year 1988 PPS DRG updates. Prior to that, cost-based weights were used, where costs were calculated from reported hospital charges using hospital-specific cost-to-charge ratios.

Medicare reimbursed hospitals for 85% of its "share" of capital purchases (i.e., 0.85 times the proportion of Medicare admissions at the hospital times the capital purchase). The pass-through payment system for capital costs is being gradually phased out over a ten-year period ("prospective" capital payments will be included in DRG payments), but pass-throughs will still be larger for the more intensive, treatment-based DRGs. Thus, particularly for intensive DRGs requiring substantial investments in equipment, reported costs (and prices) may be greater than true marginal costs to the hospital.

The dynamic instability of treatment intensity is further complicated by the mechanism for updating Medicare prices. The "conversion factor" between DRG relative weights and dollar payment levels is set so that if the current period's DRG admission patterns are identical to the prior period's DRG admission patterns, aggregate hospital payments will increase at a target growth rate. This updating mechanism has consequences for the dynamic reallocation of resources to health problems between single-DRG health problems and health problems for which DRGs are available for multiple intensity levels. Suppose that all treatments for health problem A are aggregated into a single DRG at price $\bar{p}_A(t)$, and that treatments for health problem B are divided into a less intensive DRG at price $\bar{p}_B^0(t)$ and a more intensive DRG at price $\bar{p}_B'(t) > \bar{p}_B^0(t)$. Assume that the number of patients with the health problem in each period n_A and n_B is fixed and that production of care for A is competitive, so that $\hat{c}_A(t) = \bar{p}_A(t)$ (the dynamic problem is worse if it is not). Assume that the current (price, cost) state is such that the use of the more intensive treatment for problem B is increasing (that is, $\hat{\theta}_B$ is decreasing). The current price for a DRG is a function of its relative weight $\omega(t-1)$ in the previous period (average cost per admission in the DRG divided by the average cost of all admissions) times the conversion factor $\phi(t)$, which solves

$$\phi(t) \cdot \{n_A \cdot \omega_A(t-1) + n_B \cdot [F(\hat{\theta}_B(t-1)) \cdot \omega_B^0(t-1)] \\ + [1 - F(\hat{\theta}_B(t-1))\omega_B^1(t-1)]\} = \hat{c}(t-1) \cdot g(t),$$

where $\hat{c}(t-1)$ is total cost in the previous period, and $g(t)$ is the exogenous target growth rate for the current period. If the rate of change of $F(\hat{\theta}_B) \cdot (c_B^1 - c_B^0)$ exceeds g, then $\phi(t)$ will decrease over time, leading to a decline in price (and cost) for treatment of health problem A and a reallocation of resources to health problem B. Even if the production of A is competitive, the intensity of treatment for problem A will decline over time due to an externality effect of increasing intensity for problem B induced by the update rule.[14]

This theoretical evaluation of intensity dynamics indicates that PPS rules are unlikely to lead to dynamic cost-intensity equilibria with any particularly

14. In recent years, PPS updates have been based on target growth rates lower than measured hospital cost inflation. To the extent that this reflects true price ratcheting, it can be captured in the phase diagrams above by a counterclockwise rotation of the $\dot{p} = 0$ line. Thus it tends to lead to treatment equilibria at lower intensity levels and is less likely to result in unstable growth; the qualitative conclusions are unchanged.

desirable properties, if they lead to cost equilibria at all. The next section presents some preliminary empirical evidence consistent with the model of reimbursement dynamics suggested here.

5.4   Preliminary Empirical Evidence

The model developed in sections 5.2 and 5.3 has a number of empirical predictions. In this section, I describe preliminary evidence on two of them. First, facing some competitive pressures, hospitals have minimal incentives to limit dimensions of treatment intensity that involve technologies reimbursed through treatment-based DRGs; if the treatments themselves are produced efficiently, these costs will be shared almost completely. Second, if demand for hospital services is not perfectly elastic in intensity, dynamic changes in treatment intensity are likely to occur *independently* of any exogenous technological change. In particular, dynamic intensity growth is likely for health problems where reimbursement differences reflect cost differences, leading to steeper equilibrium price-cost relationships, or where measured marginal production costs overstate true costs. Conversely, for health problems grouped into true diagnosis-based DRGs, declines in intensity over time are likely because the PPS price update mechanism tends to increase the share of reimbursement devoted to health problems in which cost increases can occur through shifts to more intensive DRGs.

To illustrate the practical consequences of the structure of the DRG reimbursement system, I first present evidence on one particular health problem, AMI. This very common health problem in the elderly accounts, directly or indirectly, for much of the mortality and hospital use associated with coronary heart disease. The data are derived from all hospital discharge abstracts filed over a two-year period by all elderly Americans hospitalized with a new AMI in 1987. The sample thus includes data from 522,506 hospitalizations for 205,021 elderly AMI patients (see McClellan and Newhouse 1993 for details of the data-set creation process). Table 5.1 summarizes demographic characteristics and some important treatment intensity decisions for these patients. In 1987, approximately 23% of elderly AMI patients underwent cardiac catheterization, an invasive procedure, and approximately 13% of these patients underwent a further intensive revascularization procedure, PTCA, or CABG surgery. Approximately 87% of patients spent at least one day in a specialized coronary- or intensive-care-unit bed (CCU/ICU), including 84% of patients who did not undergo any invasive procedure (second column).

These intensive treatments have different implications for hospital reimbursement. Admissions for AMI patients who do not undergo intensive procedures are categorized into DRG 121 (AMI with complicating conditions), 122 (AMI without complicating conditions), or 123 (AMI, expired). The three DRGs differ somewhat in reimbursement levels, reflecting patient disease severity (ideally independent of hospital treatment choices) that is correlated

Table 5.1   Characteristics and Technology Use for Elderly Patients with Acute Myocardial Infarction (%)

	All Patients (N = 205,021)	No Procedures (N = 155,880)	Catheterization Only (N = 22,902)	Catheterization and PTCA[a] (N = 10,837)	Catheterization and CABG[b] (N = 15,402)
				Use of Invasive Procedures	
Patient characteristics					
Female	50.36	53.75	41.07	41.02	36.37
Black	5.65	6.08	5.69	3.19	2.96
Age in years	76.11	77.49	71.71	71.51	71.47
(standard deviation)	(7.26)	(7.28)	(5.11)	(5.15)	(4.79)
Rural	29.45	30.56	26.40	24.45	26.32
Technology use					
Catheterization within 90 days	22.81	0	100.0	100.0	100.0
Percutaneous transluminal coronary angioplasty within 90 days	5.30	0	0	100.0	0
Coronary artery bypass graft within 90 days	7.74	0	0	0	100.0
Acute treatment in coronary care unit	86.56	83.99	92.07	96.70	97.21

[a]Percutaneous transluminal coronary angioplasty.

[b]Coronary artery bypass graft.

with cost of care. Both revascularization procedures, PTCA (DRG 112) and CABG (DRGs 106 and 107), involve distinct DRGs with much higher reimbursement levels that reflect the incremental costs of the intensive treatments. In contrast, although one might imagine a DRG for "AMI with CCU admission," there is no incremental reimbursement for treatment involving specialized CCU beds. The implications for DRG classification of the initial hospitalizations of AMI patients are presented in table 5.2, which shows that only 92% of all AMI patients and only 88% of male patients aged 65–74 years were initially hospitalized in an AMI-related DRG. The other AMI patients were mostly categorized in more intensive DRGs based on the use of invasive or surgical treatments. Table 5.2 also shows that the share of treatment-based DRGs is even larger when all hospitalizations within thirty days of the AMI are considered. AMI patients are specifically excluded from the catheterization DRGs (124 and 125), but over 1% of patients are hospitalized in these DRGs within a month of their AMI.

Table 5.3 reports means and standard deviations for hospital utilization, reported hospital costs, and reimbursement for AMI patients grouped by which treatments they received. These statistics are reported for all hospital admissions during three time intervals after AMI: within thirty days, within ninety

Table 5.2	Distribution of Admissions for Acute Myocardial Infarction among Diagnosis-Related Groups			
	All Patients ($N = 205,021$)		Male Patients Aged 65–74 ($N = 55,570$)	
Diagnosis-Related Groups	Initial AMI Admission ($N = 205,021$)	All Admissions within 30 Days ($N = 251,575$)	Initial AMI Admission ($N = 55,570$)	All Admissions within 30 Days ($N = 72,006$)
Acute myocardial infarction (AMI) (121, 122, 123)	92.0	81.1	88.1	75.4
Coronary artery bypass graft (106, 107)	2.2	4.9	4.1	8.5
Percutaneous transluminal coronary angioplasty (112)	2.8	3.9	4.7	6.1
Catheterization without acute myocardial infarction (124, 125)	0	1.2	0	1.9
Other cardiovascular procedures (mainly 109, 115)	2.5	2.8	2.7	3.0
Other	0.5	6.1	0.4	5.2

Table 5.3   Hospital Utilization, Costs, and Reimbursement for Elderly Patients with Acute Myocardial Infarction

Time Interval after AMI	All Patients (N = 205,021)	Use of Invasive Procedures			
		No Procedures (N = 155,880)	Catheterization Only (N = 22,902)	Catheterization and PTCA[a] (N = 10,837)	Catheterization and CABG[b] (N = 15,402)
Hospital admissions[c]					
Within 30 days	1.22	1.12	1.46	1.53	1.71
	(0.48)	(0.35)	(0.62)	(0.67)	(0.69)
Within 90 days	1.46	1.29	1.83	1.90	2.23
	(0.77)	(0.63)	(0.90)	(0.94)	(0.97)
Within 1 year	1.95	1.78	2.38	2.42	2.67
	(1.39)	(1.31)	(1.53)	(1.48)	(1.46)
Hospital days[c]					
Within 30 days	12.06	10.85	13.46	13.43	21.31
	(10.59)	(9.92)	(8.99)	(9.24)	(14.50)
Within 90 days	14.13	12.45	15.91	15.91	27.22
	(13.70)	(12.76)	(12.27)	(11.93)	(17.90)
Within 1 year	18.38	16.76	20.37	19.64	30.93
	(19.69)	(19.19)	(18.62)	(16.93)	(22.87)
ICU/CCU days[c]					
Within 30 days	5.28	4.46	6.48	6.98	10.59
	(6.09)	(5.11)	(6.46)	(6.03)	(10.10)
Within 90 days	5.83	4.80	7.24	7.88	12.62
	(6.92)	(5.66)	(7.57)	(7.34)	(11.26)
Within 1 year	6.77	5.73	8.47	8.92	13.35
	(8.27)	(7.15)	(9.24)	(8.94)	(12.15)

Total hospital costs ($)[d]					
Within 30 days	7,702	6,073	8,992	11,413	19,663
	(7,529)	(5,505)	(6,880)	(7,136)	(12,634)
Within 90 days	9,096	6,953	10,697	13,614	25,221
	(9,188)	(6,694)	(8,699)	(8,985)	(13,285)
Within 1 year	11,364	9,198	13,416	16,024	26,964
	(7,529)	(9,878)	(12,187)	(11,958)	(15,456)
Total hospital reimbursement ($)[e]					
Within 30 days	6,810	5,418	7,141	9,880	18,235
	(5,704)	(3,501)	(4,985)	(5,471)	(9,690)
Within 90 days	8,098	6,177	8,749	12,146	23,708
	(7,066)	(4,443)	(6,384)	(6,888)	(8,794)
Within 1 year	10,078	8,118	11,155	14,479	25,208
	(9,196)	(7,338)	(9,161)	(9,425)	(10,497)

Note: Standard errors in parentheses.

[a]Percutaneous transluminal coronary angioplasty.

[b]Coronary artery bypass graft.

[c]Number of admissions, number of total hospital days, and number of ICU or CCU days were calculated from Medicare claims.

[d]Reported departmental costs for each hospitalization were calculated by multiplying the reported departmental charges for a hospitalization by the PPS cost-to-charge ratio for that hospital department and summing the resulting cost estimates across all departments. Reported routine costs were calculated by determining the average accounting cost per day for Medicare patients by bed type (standard, ICU, CCU) and multiplying by the number of days spent in each bed type during the admission. Total reported operating costs are the sum of these two components; DRG payments are intended to reimburse hospitals for these operating costs. As noted above, these reported costs are not perfect measures of "true" average incremental costs to the hospital and so should only be interpreted qualitatively.

[e]Reimbursement rates were calculated for each admission by summing DRG-based payments and DRG outlier payments (if any).

days, and within one year. Compared to patients not undergoing invasive procedures, patients undergoing one or more of the procedures used hospitals more intensively (in terms of number of admissions, total days, and intensive-care days) and incurred substantially higher costs. But reimbursement totaled a relatively constant proportion of reported costs, regardless of procedure use. For example, within ninety days of AMI, total DRG reimbursement for patients not undergoing procedures was 89% of reported costs ($6,177 versus $6.953 on average), for patients undergoing catheterization only was 82% of costs ($8,749 versus $10,697), for patients undergoing catheterization and PTCA was 89% of reported costs ($12,146 versus $13,614), and for patients undergoing catheterization and CABG was 94% of reported costs ($23,708 versus $25,221). Thus, for these intensive procedures used in the management of AMI patients, PPS reimbursement tracks costs quite closely on average.[15]

In contrast, table 5.4 reports summary statistics for patients grouped on the basis of whether or not they stayed in a specialized CCU or ICU bed for more than two days during their acute AMI treatment. Patients with acute CCU/ICU stays of two days or less had costs significantly lower than those of patients with stays over two days. Reimbursement differences between the two groups were much more modest, however, so that patients receiving two days or less of CCU/ICU treatment had average reimbursement levels 29% higher than average hospital costs within ninety days of AMI ($5,133 versus $3,971), while average reimbursement was only 77% of costs for patients receiving more than two days' CCU/ICU treatment ($6,802 versus $8,855). Such a pattern is expected under prospective payment—patients requiring more CCU/ICU days are sicker than those who do not—but the pattern differs markedly from that observed for intensive technologies with separate DRGs. Because DRG payments are largely independent of CCU/ICU use, additional CCU days lead to relatively little additional hospital reimbursement.

The association between reimbursement and treatment intensity for AMI illustrates the financial incentives for hospital investments in medical technologies. Implementing the capacity to perform CABG, PTCA, or cardiac catheterization, as well as choosing the quantity of CCU beds to support, are all hospital investment decisions that may have substantial effects on physician decisions for AMI treatment. As noted in section 5.1, analogous intensive hospital treatments and treatment-based DRGs exist for many other health problems, providing similar relatively low-powered incentives for investments in the capacity to perform treatments.

Table 5.5 suggests that these incentives have had a fundamental effect on the

15. The slightly lower proportion of cost sharing for patients undergoing catheterization only is likely to be a reflection of DRG structure as well. For patients admitted with AMI, only if catheterization occurs during a subsequent admission does it provide additional reimbursement for the hospital. Table 5.2 demonstrates that some patients are readmitted soon after their initial AMI admission to undergo catheterization, which then constitutes a non-AMI DRG.

Table 5.4   **Hospital Utilization, Costs, and Reimbursement for Elderly Patients with Acute Myocardial Infarction, 1987**

Time Interval after AMI	All Patients (N = 205,021)	Acute Coronary Care/Intensive Care Unit	
		Two Days or Less (N = 60,707)	More Than Two Days (N = 95,103)
Hospital admissions			
Within 30 days	1.22	1.06	1.16
	(0.48)	(0.26)	(0.40)
Within 90 days	1.46	1.19	1.39
	(0.77)	(0.52)	(0.68)
Within 1 year	1.95	1.58	1.91
	(1.39)	(1.16)	(1.37)
Hospital days			
Within 30 days	12.06	7.08	13.30
	(10.59)	(7.97)	(10.29)
Within 90 days	14.13	8.24	15.13
	(13.70)	(10.96)	(13.10)
Within 1 year	18.38	11.67	20.01
	(19.69)	(17.24)	(19.66)
CCU/ICU days			
Within 30 days	5.28	0.87	6.75
	(6.09)	(0.83)	(5.38)
Within 90 days	5.83	1.03	7.21
	(6.92)	(1.60)	(5.99)
Within 1 year	6.77	1.53	8.40
	(8.27)	(3.22)	(7.66)
Total hospital costs ($)			
Within 30 days	7,702	3,379	7,791
	(7,529)	(2,789)	(6,090)
Within 90 days	9,096	3,971	8,855
	(9,188)	(4,025)	(7,332)
Within 1 year	11,364	5,673	11,446
	(7,529)	(7,452)	(10,555)
Total hospital reimbursement ($)			
Within 30 days	6,810	4,637	5,915
	(5,704)	(2,314)	(4,002)
Within 90 days	8,098	5,133	6,802
	(7,066)	(3,245)	(4,960)
Within 1 year	10,078	6,695	9,023
	(9,196)	(6,120)	(7,885)

Note: Standard errors in parentheses.

nature of hospital expenditure growth since the adoption of PPS. The table summarizes changes in admissions and hospital treatment intensity between 1983 and 1988 for some common health problems for which alternative diagnosis- and treatment-based DRGs exist. The table includes all health problems that are indications for the principal inpatient surgical procedures reim-

Table 5.5 **Changes in Hospital Treatment Patterns for Common Health Problems in the Elderly**

Diagnosis-Related Group	Surgical Treatment Diagnosis-Related Groups			Diagnosis-Related Group	Alternative Nonsurgical Diagnosis-Related Groups		
	Description	Relative Weight	1988 Discharges (% change from 1983 base)		Description	Relative Weight	1988 Admissions (% change from 1983 base)
Spinal Nerve Compression							
4	Decompression of spinal canal	2.59	4,970 (+46.2)	9	Spinal disorder/injury	1.24	2,570 (−36.9)
					Medical treatment outside hospital		
Cerebrovascular Disease							
5	Carotid endarterectomy[a]	1.57	47,530 (+8.3)	14	Specific cerebrovascular disorder (except transient ischemic attack)	1.24	328,900 (+9.8)
				15	Transient ischemic attack	0.62	150,395 (−5.3)
				16	Nonspecific cerebrovascular disorder (except transient ischemic attack) with complicating conditions	1.03	
				17	Nonspecific cerebrovascular disorder (except transient ischemic attack) without complicating conditions	0.63	18,470 (−63.9)
					Medical treatment outside hospital	—	

Coronary Heart Disease

106	Coronary artery bypass graft with catheterization	5.54	61,815 (+1,260.1)	121	Acute myocardial infarction with complicating conditions	1.72	
107	Coronary artery bypass graft without catheterization	3.99	44,790 (−11.0)	122	Acute myocardial infarction without complicating conditions	1.20	333,540 (+16.3)
112	Percutaneous transluminal coronary angioplasty[b]	1.89	109,830 (+211.5)	123	Acute myocardial infarction, expired	1.40	
124	Non–acute myocardial infarction cardiac catheterization with complicating conditions	1.18	197,175 (+414.5)	140	Angina pectoris (cardiac-related chest pain)	0.67	367,585 (+34.5)
125	Non–acute myocardial infarction cardiac catheterization without complicating conditions	0.69		132	Atherosclerosis with complicating conditions	0.80	23,420 (−92.0)
				133	Atherosclerosis without complicating conditions	0.60	

(continued)

Table 5.5 (continued)

Surgical Treatment Diagnosis-Related Groups				Diagnosis-Related Group	Alternative Nonsurgical Diagnosis-Related Groups		
Diagnosis-Related Group	Description	Relative Weight	1988 Discharges (% change from 1983 base)	Diagnosis-Related Group	Description	Relative Weight	1988 Admissions (% change from 1983 base)
				Cardiac Rhythm Irregularity			
115	Pacemaker implantation with complicating conditions[a]	4.05	58,300 (+6.5)	138	Cardiac arrhythmia with complicating conditions	0.85	254,705 (+11.2)
116	Pacemaker implantation without complicating conditions[a]	2.77		139	Cardiac arrhythmia without complicating conditions	0.59	
				Cardiac Valvular Disease			
104	Cardiac valve procedure with pump and cardiac catheterization	7.34	12,015 (+1,869.5)	135	Cardiac congenital and valvular disorders with complicating conditions	0.92	9,140 (−67.1)
105	Cardiac valve procedure with pump, without catheterization	5.78	12,010 (+18.0)	136	Cardiac congenital and valvular disorders without complicating conditions	0.61	
				Small and Large Intestinal Disorders			
148	Major small and large bowel procedures with complicating conditions	3.24	142,750 (+53.1)		None		
149	Major small and large bowel procedures without complicating conditions	1.83					

DRG	Description	Weight	Cases (% change)
	Gall Bladder and Biliary Disorders		
195	Total cholecystectomy with contrast dye enhancement with complicating conditions[c]	2.39	28,285 (+284.3)
196	Total cholecystectomy with contrast dye enhancement without complicating conditions[c]	1.69	
197	Total cholecystectomy without contrast dye enhancement with complicating conditions[c]	1.88	102,860 (+9.7)
198	Total cholecystectomy without contrast dye enhancement without complicating conditions[c]	1.12	
207	Biliary tract disorder with complicating conditions	0.92	52,475 (−22.9)
208	Biliary tract disorder without complicating conditions	0.58	
	Medical treatment outside hospital	—	
	Inguinal/Femoral Hernia		
161	Inguinal/femoral hernia repair with complicating conditions	0.75	78,150 (−31.2)
162	Inguinal/femoral hernia repair without complicating conditions	0.50	
	None		

(continued)

Table 5.5 (continued)

	Surgical Treatment Diagnosis-Related Groups			Diagnosis-Related Group	Alternative Nonsurgical Diagnosis-Related Groups		
Diagnosis-Related Group	Description	Relative Weight	1988 Discharges (% change from 1983 base)		Description	Relative Weight	1988 Admissions (% change from 1983 base)
				Arthritis of Hip			
209	Hip replacement	2.42	209,080 (+78.0)		Medical treatment outside hospital	—	
				Hip Fracture			
210	Open reduction of hip/femur fracture with complicating conditions	2.18	139,310 (+29.3)	235	Fracture of femur	1.21	47,110 (−23.0)
211	Open reduction of hip/femur fracture without complicating conditions	1.61		236	Fracture of hip	0.90	
				Back Pain			
214	Intervertebral diskectomy with complicating conditions	2.14	62,550 (+87.1)	243	Back problem	0.67	129,050 (−38.2)
215	Intervertebral diskectomy without complicating conditions	1.38			Medical treatment outside hospital	—	

(continued)

Breast Cancer

257	Total mastectomy with complicating conditions	1.04	59,155 (+44.1)	None	
258	Total mastectomy without complicating conditions	0.85			
259	Subtotal mastectomy with complicating conditions	1.00	7,700 (−28.1)		
260	Subtotal mastectomy without complicating conditions	0.60			

Benign Prostatic Hypertrophy

336	Transurethral prostatectomy with complicating conditions	1.08	207,570 (+35.5)	348	Benign prostatic hypertrophy with complicating conditions	0.66	8,685 (−82.3)
347	Transurethral prostatectomy without complicating conditions	0.75		349	Benign prostatic hypertrophy without complicating conditions	0.40	
					Medical treatment outside hospital	—	

Table 5.5 (continued)

	Surgical Treatment Diagnosis-Related Groups			Alternative Nonsurgical Diagnosis-Related Groups			
Diagnosis-Related Group	Description	Relative Weight	1988 Discharges (% change from 1983 base)	Diagnosis-Related Group	Description	Relative Weight	1988 Admissions (% change from 1983 base)
	Cancer (nonsurgical treatments)						
409	Radiotherapy[d]	1.08	8,530 (+85.8)	None			
410	Chemotherapy[d]	0.47	137,890 (+248.3)				
	Surgical discharge rate per 1,000 elderly		191 (+33.6)		Nonsurgical discharge rate per 1,000 elderly		121 (−50.0)

Note: Standard errors in parentheses.

[a]During the time period, new clinical evidence suggested these procedures are often ineffective.

[b]Some other surgical procedures for coronary heart disease account for a small proportion of admissions in this DRG.

[c]Contrast dye enhancement is an intraoperative radiological procedure.

[d]Though these cancer therapies comprise treatment-based DRGs, they are not surgical procedures.

bursed separately under PPS, as well as the alternative nonsurgical DRGs.[16] In general, the use of technologies that constituted treatment-based DRGs for each of these health problems increased substantially between 1983 and 1988. For example, the use of CABG and PTCA as intensive treatments for heart disease doubled between 1983 and 1988, reflecting the increased investment in cardiac surgery capacity and the complete cost sharing documented above. Other intensive DRG-based treatments for health problems that showed substantial increases in utilization rates included valve-replacement procedures as a treatment for heart valve diseases, cholecystectomy as a treatment for gall bladder disease, open reductions in the treatment of hip fracture, diskectomy in the treatment of back pain, and prostatectomy in the treatment of benign prostatic hypertrophy. Hospitalizations in treatment-based DRGs for diseases without alternative hospital treatments—such as joint replacement for arthritis and chemotherapy for cancer—also increased substantially. Altogether, the surgical admission rate for elderly Medicare beneficiaries increased by a third between 1983 and 1988, while the nonsurgical admission rate fell by one-half.

Table 5.6 summarizes changes in admissions and intensity between 1983 and 1988 for some common "single DRG" diseases, those that do not have distinct DRGs for more intensive treatments. Three of these health problems— chronic obstructive pulmonary disease, pneumonia and pleurisy, and bronchitis and asthma—show intensity increases, though the large changes in admission rates for these respiratory diseases imply that underlying coding changes make it difficult to compare the 1983 and 1988 populations. For most of these health problems, however, average intensity was virtually unchanged or fell, and total admissions declined. Treatment intensity growth thus appears much more modest for health problems where hospitals face single prices regardless of intensity decisions.

McClellan (1993) reviews more comprehensive evidence on these intensity trends, confirming that actual hospital expenditure growth appears to reflect the reimbursement incentives illustrated here. In particular, more use of specific intensive procedures (especially surgical procedures) appears to account for all Medicare hospital expenditure growth. These trends do not appear to be part of a general technological imperative toward more intensive treatment. For example, the reimbursement incentives for AMI illustrated that ICU and CCU bed use is associated with relatively little additional reimbursement, and in fact the total number of ICU and CCU beds has been relatively flat since PPS was adopted. These findings, based entirely on aggregate statistical data

16. For many DRGs, separate groups exist for cases with and without "complicating conditions." The DRGs with complications are reimbursed at somewhat higher rates than those without, with the goal of providing "fair" reimbursement for sicker patients within the diagnosis group as well as incentives for upcoding or "DRG creep." Both prices influence hospital investments in intensive technologies. To abstract from coding instability that severely affected admission patterns in DRGs with versus without complicating conditions during this period, I group DRGs with and without complicating conditions together in the descriptive tables.

Table 5.6   Trends in Intensity and Admissions for Health Problems without
                   High-Intensity Treatment Diagnosis-Related Groups

Diagnosis-Related Group	Description	1983 Intensity (DRG weight)	1988 Intensity (DRG weight)	Change in Intensity, 1983–88	1988 Admissions (% change from 1983)
11	Multiple sclerosis/cerebellar ataxia	1.01	0.93	−.08	4,785 (−23.5)
12	Degenerative nervous system disorders	1.11	0.95	−.16	28,840 (−54.9)
22	Hypertensive encephalopathy	0.79	0.70	−.09	11,925 (+15.6)
87	Pulmonary edema and respiratory failure	1.55	1.57	+.02	68,265 (+7.4)
88	Chronic obstructive pulmonary disease	1.04	1.13	+.09	92,275 (−66.2)
89–90	Simple pneumonia/pleurisy	1.08	1.21	+.13	405,760 (+26.7)
96–97	Bronchitis/asthma	0.78	0.93	+.15	266,450 (+31.2)
127	Heart failure/shock	1.04	1.02	−.02	537,875 (+17.6)
128	Deep venous thrombophlebitis	0.86	0.85	−.01	30,725 (−19.0)
174–75	Gastrointestinal hemorrhage	0.91	0.92	+.01	168,810 (+22.0)
176–78	Peptic ulcer disease	0.79	0.80	+.01	38,610 (−34.2)
316	Renal failure	1.33	1.28	−.05	39,935 (−27.7)

on Medicare hospital utilization, are obviously preliminary. But they suggest
that hospitals have responded quite dramatically to actual PPS incentives for
treatment intensity.

5.5   Conclusions

Exogenous technological progress is viewed as a principal cause of growth
in health care costs (Newhouse 1992), and the adoption and diffusion of new
technologies desired by patients clearly represents a major component of
Medicare hospital expenditure growth. In this paper, however, I have argued
that technological change may in fact be endogenous to reimbursement incentives. This argument required a review of the details of hospital production and
of a model for capturing static reimbursement incentives adequately, as well

as the development of arguments for why the current structure of PPS reimbursement rules may lead to changes in equilibrium intensity choices over time. While the development of a formal model of hospital technology adoption decisions in the context of the model presented here awaits further work,[17] some important implications for technology diffusion are evident. For health problems with multiple DRGs for different levels of treatment intensity, innovations are favored that shift the net benefit distribution to permit "marginal" patients to be treated in more intensive DRGs. For example, innovations that reduce operative mortality and morbidity for specifically reimbursed surgical procedures will be adopted and will lead to dynamic cost increases through more intensive treatment of the disease. For diseases without intensive treatment-based DRGs, such technologies are less likely to be adopted. In these cases, the adoption of cost-reducing technologies may complement the dynamic decline in costs outlined previously.

   The theoretical and empirical results presented here suggest that current PPS incentives are unlikely to achieve stated policy goals. In particular, they probably will not limit the use of intensive treatments with small marginal expected benefits. As the previous section and McClellan (1993) suggested, improvements in these incentives appear feasible through simple reforms in the DRG payment structure. First, for health problems for which production is competitive or for which physician incentives are likely to determine equilibrium intensity choices, the regulator's basic goal should be to set a single price for all alternative treatments for the health problem. Indeed, the regulator need only get the aggregate price level right for the set of health problems that rely on similar hospital technologies. Concerns about hospitals engaging in more patient-selection behavior if incentives really were high-powered, or about hospitals going out of business because of the high resulting variance in payments, are legitimate reasons for providing some cost sharing through DRG structure. Such concerns can be addressed by allowing partial but not complete price differentials for DRGs that lead to payment variation based on intensity within a diagnosis. Alternatively, they might be addressed through other features of the payment system. The present system uses "outlier" payments,

---

17. Most biomedical research is conducted not by the clinical divisions of hospitals but by their biomedical research divisions and separate research organizations. Funding for biomedical research, primarily from the federal government, is largely independent of Medicare funding for patient care. Consequently, technology diffusion rather than innovation itself has greater consequences for medical costs. In a standard model of diffusion, the firm compares its expected profit stream from investing in the innovation during this period to the expected profit stream associated with waiting until the next period (Reinganum 1989). Firm heterogeneity leads to heterogeneity in observed adoption times and frequency of use. Incentives for technology adoption include the reimbursement rules and demand responses associated with the technology. Thus the intuitive prediction of the model developed here is that technological diffusion will tend to be more rapid for the types of technologies favored by the DRG system.

which are essentially supplemental cost-sharing payments for very expensive admissions, to address these issues.

Second, if hospitals have more control over equilibrium intensity for a health problem *and* they face upward-sloping demand curves, then separate intensity-based DRGs may be optimal. However, these DRGs should not be designed to reflect completely the cost differential of producing the more intensive treatment, unless demand is completely inelastic (which seems improbable). Instead, the price differential should partially reflect the cost differential, and the price of the low-intensity treatment can be increased as needed to assure that hospitals will not find it more profitable to forgo treating patients altogether.

References

Ellis, Randall, and Thomas McGuire. 1986. Provider Behavior under Prospective Reimbursement: Cost Sharing and Supply. *Journal of Health Economics* 5:129–52.

Grossman, Sanford J., and Oliver D. Hart. 1986. The Costs and Benefits of Ownership: A Theory of Vertical and Lateral Integration. *Journal of Political Economy* 94 (4): 691–719.

Harris, Jeffrey. 1977. The Internal Organization of Hospitals: Some Economic Implications. *Bell Journal of Economics* 8:467–82.

McClellan, Mark B. 1993. The Effects of Hospital Characteristics on Medical Treatment Intensity. Massachusetts Institute of Technology. Mimeo.

McClellan, Mark B., and Robert H. Brook. 1992. Appropriateness of Care: A Comparison of Global and Outcome Methods to Set Standards. *Medical Care* 30:565–86.

McClellan, Mark B., and Joseph P. Newhouse. 1993. The Marginal Benefits of Medical Treatment Intensity: Acute Myocardial Infarction in the Elderly. NBER Working Paper. Cambridge, MA: National Bureau of Economic Research.

Newhouse, Joseph P. 1992. The Basis of Reimbursing Health Providers. Harvard University. Mimeo.

Park, Rolla Edward, et al. 1986. Physician Ratings of Appropriate Indications for Six Medical and Surgical Procedures. *American Journal of Public Health* 76:766–72.

Prospective Payment Assessment Commission. 1993. *Report and Recommendations to the Congress.* Washington, DC: Prospective Payment Assessment Commission.

Reinganum, Jennifer F. 1989. The Timing of Innovation: Research, Development, and Diffusion. In *Handbook of Industrial Organization,* ed. Richard Schmalensee and Robert Willig. Amsterdam: North-Holland.

Rogowski, Jeannette R., and Daniel J. Byrne. 1991. Comparison of Alternative Weight Recalibration Methods for Diagnosis-Related Groups. *Health Care Financing Review* 12:87–101.

Starr, Paul. 1984. *The Social Transformation of American Medicine.* New York: Basic Books.

Comment   Thomas E. MaCurdy

Reduced to its essence, McClellan's paper represents the beginnings of a research effort designed to address the following issue: viewing the prospective payment system (PPS) as regulatory structure, how should one define diagnostic groups (DRGs) to provide the prerequisite amount of health care while simultaneously controlling costs? To highlight the paper's achievements in confronting this issue, my comment first outlines the basic economic model proposed to describe behavior in the health care industry. I next explain how the paper interprets PPS as a regulatory system. Finally, I offer an annotated list of major enhancements needed to develop a richer framework that offers a basis for understanding the critical factors relevant in fashioning PPS to govern the provision of health care.

Basic Behavioral Model

McClellan's basic economic model operates as follows. Patients develop health conditions of unknown severity. For each illness, two medical procedures are available as treatment: intensive and nonintensive. Patients choose hospitals based on the likelihood of receiving intensive treatment. The intensity of treatment offered by a hospital is determined solely by its investment in technology, with higher investment raising the likelihood of intensive treatment. Hospitals act to maximize profits in a way that balances the expense of investment with the extent to which investment attracts patients. Physicians play a purely passive role. Assigned to hospitals in an unspecified manner, they observe the severity of the health condition afflicting each patient. They mechanically act to provide intensive treatment when a patient's illness reaches a sufficiently high level of severity.

To describe the formal framework in greater detail, initially consider the behavior of the patients. For their health conditions, they can receive one of two treatments: nonintensive, indicated by the discrete variable r taking the value $r = 0$; and intensive, indicated by $r = 1$. The outcome from treatment is a random variable y (my notation) generated by the following rule: $y = y^*$ when $r = 0$; $y = y^* + \theta > y^*$ when $r = 1$, where y^* is a latent variable with a mean equal to μ, and θ is a random variable whose cumulative distribution function is $F(\theta)$, with $F(0) = 0$ (i.e., Prob$(\theta > 0) = 1$). Both y^* and θ are unobserved by the patient. The outcome expected by the patient when he or she enters a hospital for treatment is

$$E(y) = \mu + E(\theta \mid r = 1)\, p(r = 1).$$

The patient chooses that hospital offering the highest expected value.

Physicians play a routine role. In effect, they act to maximize patients' wel-

Thomas E. MaCurdy is professor of economics at Stanford University and a research associate of the National Bureau of Economic Research.

fare subject to a hospital's treatment capacity. They observe θ and implement $r = 1$ whenever $\theta > \Delta$, where $\Delta = \Delta(I)$ is a threshold defined by a hospital's level of investment, I, in capital and technology. With this mechanism, the expected value of an outcome perceived by a patient becomes

$$E(y) = \mu + E(\theta \mid \theta > \Delta) \, \text{Prob}(\theta > \Delta).$$

The function $\Delta = \Delta(I)$ is a declining function of I. So a hospital makes itself more attractive to patients by raising the value of I and thereby lowering the value of Δ.

Finally, the hospital's behavior receives extensive consideration covering several circumstances. In all of these circumstances, a hospital's objective is to choose a level of investment I (or equivalently the value of Δ) to maximize its net revenue. Consider the two types of procedures. The nonintensive treatment receives revenue equal to p_0 at a cost equal to c_0, and the intensive treatment receives revenue p_1 at a cost c_1. The costs c_0 and c_1 may be nonincreasing functions of I. Higher levels of investment make the use of the intensive treatment more likely by lowering the value of Δ. McClellan considers four categories of investment or choices of technology.

1. In the case of "specific fixed capacity," the hospital chooses I to maximize profits given by

$$\Pi(I) = [F(\Delta)(p_0 - c_0) + (1 - F(\Delta))(p_1 - c_1)]q(\Delta) - bI,$$

where $\Delta = \Delta(I)$, $F(\Delta)$ is the fraction of patients who receive the nonintensive treatment, q is demand for the hospital's services and equals the number of patients, and b is the cost of a unit of investment. In optimizing this problem, the number of treatments cannot exceed a fixed capacity; satisfaction of the constraint $(1 - F(\Delta))q(\Delta) \leq I$ captures this condition. The demand q is a declining function of Δ, and therefore it is an increasing function of I.

2. In the case of "nonspecific fixed capacity," investment is a joint input into treating several classifications of health conditions. Using index k to designate these classifications, the hospital chooses I to maximize

$$\sum_k \Pi_k(I),$$

where each Π_k takes a form analogous to Π in the previous expression. In this optimization problem, satisfaction of the constraint $\sum_k (1 - F_k(\Delta))q_k(\Delta) \leq I$ ensures that the number of procedures does not exceed a fixed capacity for all available treatments.

3. In the case of the "line of business," investment is lumpy and is either undertaken at the level $\bar{I}$ or not at all. Thus, the hospital chooses $I = \bar{I}$ if $\Pi(\bar{I}) > \Pi(0)$, and $I = 0$ otherwise, where Π once again looks like the specification in category 1.

4. Finally, the "intermediate technology" case is an unspecified variant of cases 1 and 3.

The first-order conditions associated with the optimization of categories 1–3 provide the primary motivation for the behavioral claims made in the paper.

Regulatory Structure

The basic regulatory problem in PPS is to define DRGs in a way that balances the provisions of health care with the costs of supplying this care. Within the framework outlined so far, there are two options for specifying DRGs. One can combine the intensive and the nonintensive procedures into a single DRG. This means that the hospital receives the same revenue regardless of which treatment prevails, and therefore, $p_0 = p_1$. Alternatively, one can categorize the two treatments as distinct DRGs, in which case $p_1 > p_0$.

Many health-policy decision makers and researchers believe that DRGs associated with a particular illness are primarily covered by the first option, where compensation does not depend on the intensity of treatment. However, McClellan usefully points out that in fact a large fraction of DRGs represent applications of the second option. This is especially true when considering surgical treatments. A surgical procedure often is defined as its own DRG. McClellan uses heart attacks as an illustration. A patient experiencing heart attacks can be categorized into any one of many DRGs: three represent varying degrees of intrusive treatments involving cardiac surgery and an even greater number represent nonintensive classifications such as drug treatments. The resulting practice looks very much like a cost-based reimbursement system, which PPS was designed to replace.

McClellan provides some intriguing evidence suggesting that this feature of the current system is a major factor in explaining the growth in health costs since the introduction of PPS. A related paper (McClellan 1996) provides stark evidence supporting this argument. Around the time of the introduction of PPS in the early 1980s, the trend in nonsurgical discharges for the elderly reversed direction from a continuous increase to a steady decline. At the same time, surgical discharges rose steadily and at a higher rate after the introduction of PPS. Because nonsurgical treatments tend to receive lower reimbursements on average, such evidence supports the view that medical practitioners treat patients using intensive procedures in order to justify a more lucrative DRG classification. McClellan further notes that the number of DRGs assigned to each admittee has steadily increased, with index per beneficiary rising by 20% in recent years.

The problem of creating an optimal classification scheme for DRGs is quite complicated, and it receives only peripheral discussion in the paper. The trade-offs are clear. Grouping various medical procedures into one DRG means that the more expensive treatment will only be applied if there are substantial advantages to its implementation compared to other alternatives in the DRG for the patient in question. On the other hand, such a grouping lowers the incentives of hospitals to invest in the technology needed for more intensive procedures, which lessens their use for marginal patients who could benefit. The model provided in McClellan's paper does not offer a rich enough structure to solve the problem of defining DRGs from a regulatory perspective. In particular, the model needs to specify the willingness of informed patients to pay for more intensive treatments.

Proposed Development

McClellan's research to date provides a preliminary structure to assess how DRG definitions balance the trade-offs between costs and the provision of health care. However, there are several obvious dimensions for augmenting the current model to better address the basic regulatory problem of reforming PPS. I briefly mention four such enhancements.

1. McClellan's existing formulation is a partial equilibrium model. It is incomplete in two important respects: first, it does not specify the factors determining the demand for health care q; and, second, it is silent about the industrial organization underlying the behavior of medical service providers.

In McClellan's model, the demand for medical care is determined by the function q, which in turn depends only on the likelihood of receiving intensive care. Such a formulation may have some appeal in describing Medicare demand in the current system, because in theory price does not influence the demand for medical care by Medicare patients. However, even in defining DRGs in the current system, it is necessary to introduce a demand for health care that specifies patients' willingness to pay for various procedures. Without it, one has no basis for comparing the merits of alternative structures. The need to elaborate the demand side becomes even more obvious when one considers additional aspects of the regulatory problem such as copayments.

Adding an industrial-organizational component to the model specifies hospitals' assumptions about the actions of other health care providers. There are several standard formulations, including perfect competition or oligopoly models (e.g., Cournot). A broader range of formulations may be appropriate for describing the behavior of nonprofit hospitals. Industrial organization will play a critical role in any consideration of the regulatory problem of the health care industry. It will not only determine the tendency of hospitals to overinvest in technology from a societal perspective—as happens in patent races, a well-known example in the industrial-organizational literature—but it will also play a key role in determining the specification of the demand curves (q) faced by individual health care providers.

2. McClellan's current model does not adequately specify the behavior of physicians. Physicians are not robotic agents acting to maximize patients' welfare subject to hospitals' costs conditions. Instead, physicians act to optimize their own benefits, and indeed their actions may sacrifice the welfare of both the patients and the hospitals. One often suspects that the use of particular medical procedures may primarily reflect the compensation received by doc-

tors, with only a peripheral link to patients' welfare or to hospitals' costs. Critics of such behavior often cite unnecessary surgery as a prime example.

Introducing physicians' incentives into McClellan's model is not straightforward and will undoubtedly result in significant changes in behavioral implications. A conflict arises among patients', physicians', and hospitals' incentives. Since hospitals do not observe θ or aspects of Δ, they face a principal-agent problem in their interactions with physicians, with the hospital playing the role of the principal. Similarly, patients face a principal-agent problem in their interactions with physicians and hospitals. These are important behavioral relationships that are central to understanding the effectiveness of PPS regulations.

3. Accounting for the multiproduct nature of hospitals would provide another important enhancement to McClellan's model. Most medical providers, and certainly hospitals, produce an array of products simultaneously. Such considerations introduce significant complications in the analysis when properly incorporated into an economic framework. The section of the paper dealing with nonspecific fixed-capacity investment highlights the added complications of considering multiple products produced by hospitals. Because many technologies affect the availability of a spectrum of medical procedures, not only is it true that investment enriches the capability of a hospital to perform a group of sophisticated procedures, but it is also true that a substantial degree of substitutability may arise among the procedures making up this group. Even more important, the multiproduct nature of hospitals makes it exceedingly difficult to assign or measure costs of particular treatments, a critical assumption maintained throughout McClellan's formulation.

4. Finally, introducing an explicit formulation for the economic problem faced by regulators is vital if one wants to study the consequences of alternative PPS schemes. This involves specifying the overall objectives that regulators, patients, physicians, and hospitals act to optimize, as well as the information sets available to all agents. The resulting problem faced by the regulator is quite complicated, with several game-theoretic and principal-agent structures possible to describe behavior in the health care industry. Analyses of alternative PPS schemes will undoubtedly depend on the particular formulation for the regulatory problem. The optimal structure for DRG categories under the assumption that physicians act to maximize patients' welfare and hospitals act to maximize profits will look quite different than under the assumption that agents act to satisfy other objectives. A vast literature exists on the regulation of public utilities (e.g., *A Theory of Incentives in Procurement and Regulation* by Jean Laffont). This body of research offers a rich source for analyzing alternative PPS structures.

Conclusion

McClellan's paper is an enlightening contribution to a topic that is central to the upcoming debate on the financing of health care. I know that McClellan is planning to continue with this research project, and I view it as some of the most promising work in the health-economics area. In my comments, I have taken a time-honored approach of suggesting generalizations of the approach proposed in the paper. Introducing these generalizations will undoubtedly require significant effort and a comprehensive long-term research plan, but I expect large payoffs from this activity.

Reference

McClellan, Mark B. 1996. Why do hospital costs keep rising? A model of hospital production and optimal payment regulation. NBER Working Paper. Cambridge, MA: National Bureau of Economic Research. Forthcoming.

III   Housing and Living Arrangements

6   Living Arrangements: Health and Wealth Effects

Axel Börsch-Supan, Daniel L. McFadden, and
Reinhold Schnabel

6.1 Introduction

The choice of a living arrangement—as an independent household, with
adult children or other related or unrelated persons, or in an institution—has
many implications for the well-being of an elderly person. Changes in living
arrangements are likely to be associated with changes in the level of care and
assistance received by the elderly. Living with other family members eases
situations of illness; living alone makes coping with illnesses harder. Thus,
the choice of living arrangements has many external effects. Moreover, living
arrangements commonly affect the elderly's eligibility for certain types of government assistance, such as food stamps and supplemental Social Security, and
induces demand for social support services such as district nursing, meals-on-
wheels, and so forth. Finally, the change of living arrangements frequently
involves the sale of the home by the elderly and may therefore dramatically
change the liquid wealth of the elderly. On the other hand, if the elderly tend to
live longer independently, the balance of the housing market changes because
housing becomes relatively more scarce due to the increased length of stay in
the family home by the older generation. In short, it is important to understand
the determinants of the living arrangement choice.

Axel Börsch-Supan is professor of economics at Mannheim University and a research associate
of the National Bureau of Economic Research and of the Center for Economic Policy Research,
London. Daniel L. McFadden is professor of economics at the University of California at Berkeley
and a research associate of the National Bureau of Economic Research. Reinhold Schnabel is a
research associate in the department of economics and statistics at Mannheim University.

The first author appreciated the hospitality at the University of California at Berkeley during
his sabbatical. Financial assistance was provided by the National Institute on Aging, grant 3-PO-
AG05842-01. The authors thank Ed Norton, who cleaned up the NBER Economic Supplement,
and Angus Deaton, Steven Venti, and David Wise for their helpful comments. Any opinions expressed are those of the authors and not necessarily those of the National Bureau of Economic
Research.

There is a long line of literature investigating the determinants of living arrangements of the aged. Schwartz, Danziger, and Smolensky (1984) employ the Retirement History Survey (RHS) to estimate a binary choice model between living independently and dependently. Their empirical results were mixed, and neither health nor income effects are very strong. Börsch-Supan (1989) estimates a multinomial logit model of living arrangements using data from the Annual Housing Survey (AHS). As in the paper by Schwartz, Danziger, and Smolensky, the data preclude an analysis of institutionalization. In contrast, Garber (1990) and Greene, Lovely, and Ondrich (1993) concentrate on the determinants of institutionalization and its duration, using the channeling demonstration, while Kotlikoff and Morris (1987, 1990) and Börsch-Supan, Gokhale, Kotlikoff, and Morris (1992) analyze the importance of family links in forming multigenerational households.

Papers by Ellwood and Kane (1990), Börsch-Supan (1990), and Börsch-Supan, Hajivassiliou, Kotlikoff, and Morris (1992) represent more comprehensive analyses of living arrangements that include both institutionalized and noninstitutionalized elderly. All three papers find an increasing proportion of elderly living alone and attribute this to the positive income elasticity of privacy.

These studies leave several questions unanswered. First, most studies of living arrangements suffer from a less than satisfactory description of health. This is partly due to lack of data, but the problem is deeper: even when health is measured by indicators such as activities of daily living (ADLs) and instrumental activities of daily living (IADLs), or by the presence of conditions such as cancer or Alzheimer's disease, or by simply asking the elderly how they feel, we do not really measure health but a concoction of subjective feelings and objective states that are correlated with health. In the language of econometrics, health is a latent, unmeasurable variable, for which we only observe a set of indicators. One goal of this paper is to develop an econometric framework in order to model this errors-in-variables problem in the discrete decision of living arrangements. We relate latent health to ADLs and IADLs by a nonlinear version of a multiple-indicator, multiple-cause (MIMIC) model, which explicitly considers the categorical measurement of the health indicators. We estimate this model using data from the Longitudinal Study on Aging (LSOA).

Another important question that has not been answered is the role of wealth. Does housing wealth tie the elderly to their homes? This question extends the lock-in discussion (Feinstein and McFadden 1989; Venti and Wise 1990) to household formation. What is the role of financial wealth in the demand for old-age institutions? Wealth data are rarely available in elderly surveys, and if so, their value may be questionable. We will explore in this respect the National Bureau of Economic Research (NBER) Economics Supplement of the LSOA, which contains information on income and assets of the LSOA sample persons in 1990.

The paper is set up as follows. Section 6.2 introduces the data sources and presents descriptive statistics of our working sample. Estimates based on a standard discrete choice model are briefly described in section 6.3. In section 6.4 we discuss the econometric model and address the issues of identification and estimation, while section 6.5 presents the results and section 6.6 concludes.

6.2 The Longitudinal Study on Aging and the NBER Economic Supplement

The LSOA is a panel survey based on the 1984 Supplement on Aging (SOA) to the National Health Interview Survey (NHIS). The NHISs are continuing surveys comprising each year about 100,000 noninstitutionalized persons of all ages in about 40,000 households (see Kovar and Poe 1985). Interviews are held every week throughout the year. The SOA was added to the NHIS during the 1984 interviews. The SOA included questions on

- family structure,
- community and social support,
- occupation and retirement,
- conditions and impairment, ADLs and IADLs,
- structural characteristics of housing,
- regular medical care and nursing home stay, and
- health opinions and behavior

to all NHIS sample persons aged 65 years and over.[1] The questions were similar to those in the 1984 National Nursing Home Survey (NNHS), so that when the two data sets are combined, estimates for the total elderly population are possible.

The SOA was explicitly designed to be the first wave of the LSOA. In 1986, 1988, and 1990, all persons aged 70 and above in the 1984 SOA were reinterviewed by computer-assisted telephone interviews with mail follow-ups (National Center for Health Statistics 1991).

Records for participants who gave permission were also matched with the National Death Index maintained by the National Center for Health Statistics and the Medicare files maintained by the Health Care Financing Administration. While the first wave does not include the institutionalized elderly, sample persons were interviewed in the later waves even when they entered a nursing home or another institution.

In 1990 the NBER added an Economics Supplement to the LSOA. This supplement included a detailed account of personal income sources for each sample person, an inventory of assets including financial and real wealth, and

---

1. See Fitti and Kovar (1987). The response rate to the SOA was 96.7%.

questions about structural housing characteristics. Response rates to these
questions were smaller than to the standard LSOA questions, and particularly
small to the wealth questions.[2]

As a working sample, we selected only single elderly because almost all
married elderly are living independently. In the 1990 cross-section this working sample consists of 2,193 elderly between age 76 and 102. The average age
in 1990 was almost 83 years.

Table 6.1 presents descriptive statistics of the most important variables.
Even in this sample of the very old and nonmarried, 63% live by themselves;
28.7% live with their children, other relatives, or nonrelatives, and 8.2% live
in institutions. Women make up 81.4% of the sample. The nonwhite population
is underrepresented with only 9.2%. On average, the sample persons have two
children still living.

The economic variables comprise income and wealth. Income is very low:
the median is below $2,400, and 27.6% report no income at all. On the other
hand, 63.4% have their own home, and except for less than 15% of the homeowners, this home is free and clear of mortgages. The median value of the
home is $31,000, and the average value is about $50,000. The discrepancy
between mean and median is much larger for financial assets. The median financial assets sum up to only $3,500, while the mean is ten times as large.
These numbers are approximately in line with results from the Survey of Income and Program Participation (SIPP) and other surveys (Venti and Wise
1991).

Table 6.1 also reports on a set of health indicators. We restrict our attention
to functional health measures such as the ADLs and the IADLs, which are
measured in four categories (no, some, severe problems in doing xyz, and cannot do xyz at all). The variables are coded such that *higher* values for ADLs
and IADLs indicate *less* capability. Functional health indicators have been
found most appropriate in describing living arrangements, and superior to subjective health ratings or indicators for the presence and severity of diagnosed
conditions (Börsch-Supan, Kotlikoff, and Morris 1991). Table 6.1 lists the percentages of sample persons who have no problems in performing a set of ten
activities. IADLs were asked only for the noninstitutionalized, ADLs for all
sample persons. The pattern is familiar: most problems occur with walking,
and the fewest with eating.

6.3   The Standard Approach: Multinomial Logit Analysis

Tables 6.2 and 6.3 present results of a simple multinomial logit model, relating the choice of living arrangements to demographic, economic, and—in

---

2. The response rate to financial assets was 63.5%. Missing values were assigned by Edward
Norton, using a hot-deck method.

Table 6.1   **Description of Variables: Longitudinal Study on Aging 1990**

Dependent variable (living arrangements) (%)

LIVARG	Living independently	63.0	
	Living with others	28.7	
	Living in an institution	8.2	

Demographic exogenous variables

AGE90	Age in 1990 (years)	82.6	
EDUC	Highest grade completed (years)	10.1	
RACE	Black and Hispanic = 1 (%)	9.2	
GENDER	Female = 1 (%)	81.4	
DAUGHTERS	Number of living daughters	1.07	
SONS	Number of living sons	1.01	

Economic exogenous variables

OWN	Homeownership = 1 (%)	63.4	
MORTG	Home free and clear = 1	85.7[a]	

		Mean	Median
FIN	Financial assets ($)	36,012	3,500
	Stocks, bonds, mutual funds	16,517	
	Savings, other bank accounts	19,495	
INCPERS	Annual personal income ($)	7,748	2,394
HOME	House value, all ($)	38,113	20,000
	House value, owners ($)	49,684	31,000

Health indicators (%)

Activities of daily living: sample person without difficulties

BATH	Bathing	74.4	
DRESS	Dressing	82.5	
EAT	Eating	92.1	
GETUP	Getting up from bed/chair	76.6	
WALK	Walking	58.8	
OUTSD	Getting outside	75.9	
TOIL	Toileting	86.4	

Instrumental activities of daily living: sample person without difficulties[b]

HOUSEW	Doing light housework	77.9	
SHOP	Shopping	68.9	
MEALS	Preparing meals	75.0	

Source: Longitudinal Study on Aging 1990.

Note: Means and medians were computed on the working sample of 2,193 elderly.

[a]Percentage of owners.

[b]Asked only for elderly persons in households.

table 6.3—health indicators. Both versions of the discrete choice model show that educated persons are less likely to live with others or in nursing homes, and that the probability of living with others (mainly children) increases with the number of daughters but not significantly with the number of sons. Higher wealth increases the likelihood of living with children, while there is no significant wealth effect in institutionalization, except that ownership of a house reduces the probability of entering a nursing home.

The contribution of the health indicators in table 6.3 is highly significant—

Table 6.2   **Multinomial Logit Model: Estimation Results**

| | Probability to . . . Rather Than to Live Independently | | | |
| | Live with Children or Others | | Live in an Institution | |
	Coefficient	t-Value	Coefficient	t-Value
CONSTANT	−3.51220	−3.98	−11.35623	−7.90
AGE90	0.04896	4.82	0.13259	8.24
EDUC	−0.09395	−6.07	−0.08393	−3.22
RACE	0.59230	3.61	−1.09008	−2.24
GENDER	−0.17913	−1.32	−0.09591	−0.39
DAUGHTERS	0.15276	3.74	0.06029	0.80
SONS	0.03730	0.88	−0.05156	−0.63
OWN	0.33773	3.02	−1.82145	−8.94
MORTG	−0.95982	−5.85	−0.25593	−0.75
FIN	0.00124	2.41	0.00100	1.04
HOME	0.00157	1.91	0.00249	1.69
INCPERS	0.00037	0.14	−0.00282	−0.53

Source: Longitudinal Study on Aging 1990.
Notes: Sample size = 2,193 elderly. Log likelihood = −1,657.1.

the log likelihood increases considerably, and the likelihood ratio test statistic is 718.2. However, the inclusion of so many indicators results in multicollinearity and low *t*-statistics among the individual ADLs. This is one reason to contemplate using factor analysis in describing the effect of the health indicators. Exploratory factor analysis, taking the health indicators as if they were continuous indicators, shows that more than three-quarters of the variance can be explained by only two factors.

The inclusion of the health indicators does not change the other parameters by a lot. The main exception is age, which becomes insignificant once the functional health measures are taken into account. In turn, personal income, which was insignificant when the health indicators were left out, increases in statistical importance, with a negative effect on institutionalization and living with others.

These results essentially reproduce the estimates of Börsch-Supan, Kotlikoff, and Morris (1991). This is helpful to know because the latter estimates were obtained from a geographically very restricted sample of Massachusetts elderly, the Hebrew Rehabilitation Center for the Aged (HRCA) sample. Knowing that the HRCA sample is representative at least in the respect of choosing living arrangements gives confidence in the other analyses that have been performed on the basis of this rich data set.[3]

3. Kotlikoff and Morris (1987, 1990); Börsch-Supan, Kotlikoff, and Morris (1991); Börsch-Supan, Gokhale, Kotlikoff, and Morris (1992); Börsch-Supan, Hajivassiliou, Kotlikoff, and Morris, (1992).

Table 6.3   **Multinomial Logit: Estimation Results with Activities of Daily Living and Instrumental Activities of Daily Living**

| | Probability to ... Rather Than to Live Independently | | | |
| | Live with Children or Others | | Live in an Institution | |
	Coefficient	t-Value	Coefficient	t-Value
CONSTANT	−1,97921	−2.10	−10.39988	−4.15
AGE90	0.01790	1.61	0.00993	0.39
EDUC	−0.07186	−4.42	−0.02114	−0.52
RACE	0.50494	2.91	−1.49199	−2.56
GENDER	−0.24538	−1.74	−0.33389	−0.85
DAUGHTERS	0.14204	3.34	0.07087	0.65
SONS	0.04433	1.00	−0.03871	−0.33
OWN	0.31200	2.68	−1.87982	−6.79
MORTG	−0.90636	−5.30	−0.18384	−0.38
FIN	0.00150	2.77	0.00249	1.87
HOME	0.00155	1.83	−0.00113	−0.50
INCPERS	−0.00176	−0.60	−0.01341	−2.06
BATH	−0.02732	−0.29	0.04103	0.24
DRESS	−0.09357	−0.74	−0.04878	−0.27
GETUP	−0.04733	−0.42	0.02812	0.14
WALK	−0.02884	−0.34	−0.09203	−0.49
OUTSD	0.00642	0.06	0.01751	0.09
HOUSW	0.22450	2.52	1.63224	5.49
MEALS	0.38729	4.52	0.95070	3.87
SHOP	0.13567	1.98	0.57994	1.76

Source: Longitudinal Study on Aging 1990.
Notes: Sample size = 2,193 elderly. Log likelihood = −1,298.0.

6.4   An Econometric Model of the Influence of Latent Health

6.4.1   Model Specification

Obviously, the contribution of the health indicators in table 6.3 is highly significant. However, one might doubt that these indicators directly affect the choice of living arrangements. Rather, one might argue that it is the underlying but unobservable health status that affects both, the choice of living arrangements *and* the set of indicators. The problem boils down to the question of causal links among four groups of variables:

- the choice among N_a living arrangements, denoted by u,

- the latent health status, denoted by h^*, N_h-dimensional,

- the health indicators (ADLs and IADLs), denoted by y_k, $k = 1, \ldots, N_y$, and

- the demographic and economic exogenous variables, denoted by z_j, $j = 1, \ldots, N_z$.

Figures 6.1 and 6.2 visualize the two approaches, using the above notation for the four variable groups, and distinguishing latent from observable variables by an asterisk. In addition to latent health, we have two more latent variables. First, the choice between the discrete alternatives u depends on the unobserved utility levels u_i^*, $i = 1, \ldots, N_a$. In our case N_a equals three (living independently, with others, or in an institution). A person chooses the living arrangement that yields the highest utility level u_i^*;

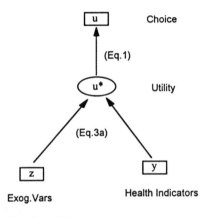

Fig. 6.1   Multinomial logit model

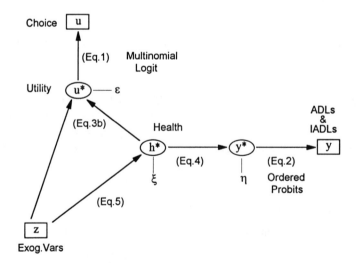

Fig. 6.2   Nonlinear MIMIC model

(1) $u = i \iff u_i^* = \max(u_j^*, j = 1, \ldots, N_a).$

This is the conventional random utility-maximization hypothesis underlying discrete choice. Second, we also do not precisely observe the health indicators because the sample persons are asked to report their performance in each activity using S_k ordinal categories (e.g., no, some, severe problems in walking, and cannot walk at all) rather than a continuous scale. The relation between the kth observed health indicator y_k and the underlying continuous y_k^* is described by thresholds $\mu_{k,j}$, which will be estimated:

(2) $y_k = j \iff \mu_{k,j-1} < y_k^* < \mu_{k,j}, \qquad k = 1, \ldots, N_y, j = 1, \ldots, S_k.$

In the discrete choice model of the preceding section, the choice of living arrangements is directly linked to the ordinal health indicators and to the exogenous variables (fig. 6.1). Moreover, the transmission between ordinal measurement and continuous indicators (equation 2) is ignored. The unobserved utility levels u_i^* are therefore given by

(3a) $u_i^* = \tilde{\beta}_i' z + \tilde{\gamma}_i' y + \tilde{\varepsilon}_i, \qquad i = 2, \ldots, N_a,$

where $\tilde{\varepsilon}_i$ denotes an additive error term in the utility of alternative i. Alternative 1 (living independently) is taken as the reference alternative.

The MIMIC model endogenizes the indicators y_k. Latent health determines both indicators and living arrangement choice. The model also takes the categorical measurement of the health indicators and the choice decision into account. Moreover, our MIMIC model distinguishes between the direct influence of the exogenous variables on the living arrangement choice, and the indirect influence via the latent health status.

The unobserved utility levels u_i^* are now determined by

(3b) $u_i^* = \beta_i' z + \gamma_i' h^* + \varepsilon_i, \qquad i = 2, \ldots, N_a.$

Rather than taking the health indicators as given, we determine them now by the health status in a factor-analytic model:

(4) $y_k^* = \lambda_k' h^* + \eta_k, \qquad k = 1, \ldots, N_y.$

Finally, a set of equations expresses the influence of the exogenous variables on the latent health status:

(5) $h_m^* = \delta_m' z + \xi_m, \qquad m = 1, \ldots, N_h,$

or in stacked form,

$$h^* = \Delta' z + \xi.$$

One may interpret relation 5 as a production function of health. Due to progress in medical science, this function may change over time.

The three sets of equations 3b, 4, and 5 form a nonlinear version of a LISREL model.[4] It is nonlinear in two respects. First, the main dependent variable, the choice of living arrangements, is described by a nonlinear discrete choice model that links the observed choices u to the latent utilities u^* (equation 1). McFadden (1988) introduced this case of factor analysis in the presence of a discrete choice equation, and Morikawa, Ben-Akiva, and McFadden (1990) present an application to travel demand.

Our model introduces a second nonlinearity with the additional complication of categorical indicators. The measurement equations 4, which link the indicators y^* with the health status h^* via the factor loadings λ_k, are described by ordered probit models if we assume the η_k to be normally distributed.

By inserting equation 5 into 3b and 4, we eliminate the health production equation and obtain two sets of reduced-form equations on which our estimation will be based:

$$(6) \qquad u_i^* = \beta_i'z + \gamma_i'(\Delta'z + \xi) + \varepsilon_i, \qquad i = 2, \dots, N_a$$

$$= \pi_i'z + \gamma_i'\xi + \varepsilon_i,$$

and similarly for the factor-analysis equations that determine the health indicators:

$$(7) \qquad y_k^* = \lambda_k'(\Delta'z + \xi) + \eta_k, \qquad k = 1, \dots, N_y$$

$$= \psi_k'z + \lambda_k'\xi + \eta_k,$$

where the reduced-form parameters π_i and ψ_k are

$$(8) \qquad\qquad \pi_i' = \beta_i' + \gamma_i'\Delta' \quad \text{for } i = 2, 3$$

and

$$\psi_k' = \lambda_k' \Delta' \quad \text{for } k = 1, \dots, N_y.$$

6.4.2 The Likelihood Function

We assume that the three groups of error terms ξ, ε, and η are mutually independent. Moreover, we assume that the ε are extreme-value distributed, resulting in a logit model for the choice equation 6. The η are assumed to be normal, resulting in N_y ordered probit models for the health indicators. The likelihood of an individual who has chosen alternative i and is characterized by the values of the health indicators j_k, $k = 1, \dots, N_y$, conditional on ξ, the

---

4. See Jöreskog and Sörbom (1988) for a description of LISREL (analysis of linear structural relationships).

errors of the health equation, is therefore a product of the probabilities of a logit model and N_y ordered probit models:[5]

(9)

$$
\begin{aligned}
L(\beta, \gamma, \Delta, \lambda, \mu \mid \xi) &= \frac{\exp(\beta_i'z + \gamma_i'\Delta'z + \gamma_i'\xi)}{1 + \sum_{j=2}^{N_a} \exp(\beta_j'z + \gamma_j'\Delta'z + \gamma_j'\xi)} \\
&\quad \times \prod_{k=1}^{N_y} \Bigg(\Phi(\mu_{k,j_k} - \lambda_k'\Delta'z - \lambda_k'\xi) \\
&\qquad - \Phi(\mu_{k,j_k-1} - \lambda_k'\Delta'z - \lambda_k'\xi) \Bigg) \\
&= LOGIT(i,\, z,\, \xi) \prod_{k=1}^{N_y} ORDPROBIT(j_k,\, z,\, \xi).
\end{aligned}
$$

We now have to eliminate the error terms ξ in equation 9, which represent the latent components of the health status. We accomplish this by integrating over the N_h-dimensional error term, assuming that the ξ are jointly standard normally distributed, possibly with correlations $\rho(\xi_m, \xi_m')$. The unconditional likelihood function is therefore

(10) $L(\beta, \gamma, \Delta, \lambda, \mu, \rho) =$
$$
\int_{-\infty}^{\infty} LOGIT(i,\, z,\, \xi) \prod_{k=1}^{N_y} ORDPROBIT(j_k,\, z,\, \xi)\, \phi(\xi,\, \rho)\, d\xi.
$$

We estimate the nonlinear MIMIC model by maximizing the sum of the individual log-likelihood contributions over the coefficients β, γ, Δ, and λ, over the thresholds $\mu_{k,j}$, and over the correlations ρ among the latent health components.

6.4.3 Identification and Estimation

In order to check the identification of the system, we start by inspecting the set of equations 7, which make up the ordered probit part of the likelihood function.[6] Maximizing equation 10 directly identifies the absolute value of the factor loadings λ_k attached to ξ through the term $\lambda_k'\xi$ in the case of orthogonal ξ. The signs are not identified because the thresholds $\mu_{j,k}$ of the ordered probit can be ordered either way. By counting the elements of δ_m, the coefficients of the exogenous variables in the health equations, and the elements of the reduced form parameters ψ_k in the ordered probit part

---

5. For notational convenience the index for individual observations is left out.
6. In the sequel we consider uncorrelated ξ. If the ξ are correlated, the ρ have to be estimated and additional identification restrictions are required.

$$
(11) \quad
\begin{pmatrix} \psi_{1k} \\ \psi_{2k} \\ \vdots \\ \vdots \\ \psi_{N_zk} \end{pmatrix}
= \lambda_{1k}
\begin{pmatrix} \delta_{11} \\ \delta_{21} \\ \vdots \\ \vdots \\ \delta_{N_z1} \end{pmatrix}
+ \lambda_{2k}
\begin{pmatrix} \delta_{12} \\ \delta_{22} \\ \vdots \\ \vdots \\ \delta_{N_z2} \end{pmatrix}
\quad \text{for } k = 1, \ldots, N_y,
$$

it becomes clear that the structural coefficients δ_m are identified only if $N_y \geq N_h$. Hence, the number of indicators y_k has to be at least as large as the number of latent health dimensions h^*. Since in typical applications the number of indicators tends to be large compared to the number of underlying factors, identification of λ and δ is easily achieved.

In contrast to the factor loadings λ_k in equations 7, the coefficients of health in the choice of living arrangements, γ_i, are not identifiable through the term $\gamma_i' \xi$ because the scale in the discrete choice model is undetermined. Moreover, the coefficients of the exogenous variables in the choice of living arrangements, β_i, are also not directly identifiable even though δ_m is given:

$$
(12) \quad
\begin{pmatrix} \pi_{1i} \\ \pi_{2i} \\ \vdots \\ \vdots \\ \pi_{N_zi} \end{pmatrix}
=
\begin{pmatrix} \beta_{1i} \\ \beta_{2i} \\ \vdots \\ \vdots \\ \beta_{N_zi} \end{pmatrix}
+ \gamma_{1i}
\begin{pmatrix} \delta_{11} \\ \delta_{21} \\ \vdots \\ \vdots \\ \delta_{N_z1} \end{pmatrix}
+ \gamma_{2i}
\begin{pmatrix} \delta_{12} \\ \delta_{22} \\ \vdots \\ \vdots \\ \delta_{N_z2} \end{pmatrix}
\quad \text{for } i = 2, \ldots, N_a.
$$

The number of elements in β_i equals the number of reduced-form parameters in π_i. Since γ_i is not identifiable, there is an excess number of structural parameters equal to the number of elements in γ_i, the number of health dimensions. Hence, β_i and γ_i can be identified only by imposing further restrictions.

We explore two possibilities of identifying β_i and γ_i:[7] identification in a cross-section with N_h parameter restrictions on each β_i, and identification in repeated cross-sections exploiting parameter differences in Δ over time.

In the first case we impose the assumption that at least N_h exogenous variables influence the choice of living arrangements only indirectly via their influence on health, but not directly. This pins down the parameters γ_i, the impact of health on choice. With γ_i given, the remaining β_i are just identified.[8]

In the second approach we impose the assumption that the coefficients of the main choice equation 3b do not change over time but that technical progress in medical science changes the health production function (equations 5). With two cross-sections t_1 and t_2, we first estimate the reduced form coefficients:

---

7. Other identification approaches are possible with panel data.
8. Identification of factor analytic models through linear parameter restrictions has been introduced by Jöreskog (1967).

(13)
$$\hat{\pi}'_{i(t_1)} = \beta'_i + \gamma'_i \hat{\Delta}'_{(t_1)};$$

$$\hat{\pi}'_{i(t_2)} = \beta'_i + \gamma'_i \hat{\Delta}'_{(t_2)}.$$

Then γ_i can be estimated from

(14)
$$\hat{\pi}'_{i(t_1)} - \hat{\pi}'_{i(t_2)} = \gamma'_i (\hat{\Delta}'_{(t_1)} - \hat{\Delta}'_{(t_2)}),$$

provided that $N_z \geq N_h$.

In either approach to identification, we first estimate the reduced form parameters by maximizing equation 10 using equations 8. In a second step we compute the structural parameters by a minimum-distance method (nonlinear generalized least squares) applied to equations 8.

Given the results from the exploratory factor analysis, we assume that two dimensions suffice to describe the latent health status. For simplicity we also impose $\rho(\xi_1, \xi_2) = 0$, although other factor structures can be thought of. Even with $\rho = 0$, the integral in equation 10 does not factor easily due to the functional form. In order to evaluate the integral we therefore employ two-dimensional Gauss-Hermite integration.

6.5   Estimation Results

Table 6.4 presents the reduced form estimates of the nonlinear MIMIC model. The first panel refers to the discrete choice submodel (equations 6) with parameters π, while the second panel represents estimates of the ordered probit submodel (equations 7) with parameters ψ_k, λ_k, and μ_k. In addition to the factor loadings γ_k for the two latent health status variables and the switch points μ,[9] some of the structural parameters β_{ik} in the living arrangement choice (equations 3b) can directly be identified because the corresponding δ_{nk} (equations 5) are zero. These are the coefficients of those exogenous variables that appear in the upper but not in the lower panel. The corresponding rows of coefficients are marked by $\beta = \pi$.

The results are encouraging. The large t-values of π and ψ show that the causal links in figure 6.2 are significant. The values of the "thresholds" μ_2^* and μ_3^* and the corresponding t-statistics have to be interpreted with care: large negative values and t-values indicate that the difference between adjacent thresholds is small, while t-values close to zero indicate that the null (i.e., $\exp(0) = 1$) cannot be rejected. We proceed in estimating the structural coefficients. We first pursue identification through parameter restrictions.

---

9. The proper ordering of the thresholds has been enforced by the parameterization: $\mu_2 = \mu_1 + \exp(\mu_2^*)$ and $\mu_3 = \mu_2 + \exp(\mu_3^*)$. This ensures $\mu_1 < \mu_2 < \mu_3$. In the tables we display μ_1, μ_2^* and μ_3^*.

Table 6.4   **Multiple-Indicator, Multiple-Cause Model: Reduced Form 1990**

Living Arrangement Choice (equations 6)

Probability to . . . Rather Than to Live Independently

	Live with Children or Others		Live in an Institution		
	Coefficient	t-Value	Coefficient	t-Value	
CONSTANT	−5.07076	−4.40	−12.87920	−6.68	
AGE90	0.07081	5.37	0.15511	7.28	
EDUC	−0.12157	−6.12	−0.12186	−3.65	
RACE	0.87069	3.74	−0.76198	−1.45	
GENDER	−0.28649	−1.60	−0.15910	−0.49	
DAUGHTERS	0.21032	3.82	0.12253	1.35	($\beta=\pi$)
SONS	0.02979	0.55	−0.04329	−0.42	
OWN	0.27072	1.91	−1.85104	−7.63	
MORTG	−1.18610	−5.13	−0.56230	−1.24	($\beta=\pi$)
FIN	0.00173	2.28	0.00119	1.11	($\beta=\pi$)
HOME	0.00197	2.00	0.00243	1.20	($\beta=\pi$)

Health Measurement (equations 7)[a]

	Bathing		Dressing		Getting Up		Walking	
AGE90	0.114	13.00	0.129	11.26	0.104	9.32	0.103	11.73
EDUC	−0.034	−2.55	−0.040	−2.74	−0.043	−2.92	−0.050	−4.26
RACE	0.968	5.49	1.193	6.21	0.799	4.65	0.652	4.90
GENDER	0.059	0.41	−0.208	−1.48	0.189	1.35	−0.007	−0.06
OWN	−0.324	−3.02	−0.517	−4.55	−0.479	−4.53	−0.406	−4.79
HEALTH1	−1.084	−13.10	−1.210	−13.74	−1.322	−13.67	−1.123	−14.27
HEALTH2	−1.717	−18.30	−1.702	−18.45	−1.493	−18.49	−1.260	−20.63
MU1	13.254	13.36	12.339	12.28	9.870	9.91	8.367	11.26
MU2*[b]	−0.138	1.89	−0.050	−0.63	0.162	2.27	0.231	4.62
MU3*[b]	−0.785	−6.63	−0.478	−3.58	−0.167	−1.43	−0.118	−1.68

	Going Outside		Light Housework		Preparing Meals		Shopping	
AGE90	0.186	13.92	0.199	11.28	0.208	12.40	0.223	14.97
EDUC	−0.077	−4.89	−0.102	−5.43	−0.135	−6.94	−0.127	−7.50
RACE	1.118	5.82	1.153	5.27	1.264	6.01	1.154	6.15
GENDER	0.163	1.04	−0.225	−1.39	−0.029	−0.17	0.420	2.51
OWN	−0.574	−4.69	−0.852	−5.95	−0.832	−5.84	−0.726	−5.85
HEALTH1	−1.376	−13.33	−0.761	−8.31	−0.625	−7.21	−0.718	−9.62
HEALTH2	−2.035	−17.06	−2.621	−14.88	−2.689	−15.55	−2.308	−16.68
MU1	16.645	14.16	17.485	11.51	17.852	12.44	18.791	14.80
MU2*[b]	−0.272	−3.19	−0.749	−6.30	−0.496	−4.47	−0.867	−7.97
MU3*[b]	−0.422	−3.94	−1.078	−6.48	−0.884	−5.99	−1.098	−8.49

Source: Longitudinal Study on Aging 1990.

Notes: Sample size = 2,193 elderly. Log likelihood − −8,122.

[a]Left-hand columns are coefficients, right-hand are t-values.

[b]μ_2^* and μ_3^* are defined by $\mu_2 = \mu_1 + \exp(\mu_2^*)$ and $\mu_3 = \mu_2 + \exp(\mu_3^*)$.

In selecting possible restrictions, the main question is which variables are most likely to influence the living arrangement decision only by their indirect impact on health without directly influencing the living arrangement choice. Of the variables included, age per se as well as education certainly does effect the health status but is less likely to directly affect living arrangement choices. This is also clear from the exploratory logit analysis, table 6.3, where age in both columns and education in the second column become insignificant after including the health indicators. The estimated coefficient of education, although still significant in the first column, decreases in magnitude and its significance level.

Table 6.5 presents the estimates. The upper panel displays the living arrangement choice equation. The demographic variables are weaker than in the multinomial logit estimation, table 6.3, except for the "daughters' effect." Living with children is strongly correlated with the number of daughters who can take care of the elderly. There is no corresponding "sons' effect."

Higher financial and housing wealth significantly increases the likelihood to live with children, while the ownership of a house reduces the probability of entering a nursing home. The positive correlation between wealth of the elderly and living together appears to be evidence in favor of the "bribery hypothesis" of Kotlikoff and Morris (1990)—wealthy elderly who like to be taken care of by their children are able to bribe the children, who would rather live by themselves, if it weren't for the shared wealth. Unfortunately, we do not know the wealth of the children to shed more light on this issue. Because the wealth of children is commonly highly correlated with the wealth of the parents, the coefficients may also express a supply effect: only wealthy children can take their parents in. As a caveat, we note that reported wealth may reflect household wealth including the younger generation's wealth, although the question in the survey instrument was intended to record the personal wealth of the elderly sample person.

The strong negative and significant coefficient on the *MORTG* variable tells us that the few elderly who still have mortgages on their home are unlikely to move to their children's home (or, though not significantly, into a nursing home). This is easily explained by the fact that almost all elderly with a mortgage are recent movers and unlikely to move again.

The main point of the MIMIC model was capturing the influence of health. Both health variables significantly affect the choice to live with children. While the first factor affects only the probability of living with children, a higher value of the second health factor, indicating a healthier elderly person, makes both dependent living arrangements less likely than living independently.

What are the two health factors? If we look at the next block of results—pertaining to the health measurement equations 4—we see that the second factor is strongly associated with the IADLs, while the first factor is more related to the first four ADLs. Looking at the health production function—lower panel of table 6.5, compare equations 5—we see that the second factor

Table 6.5   **Structural Parameters of the Multiple-Indicator, Multiple-Cause Model**

Living Arrangement Choice (equations 3b)

	Probability to . . . Rather Than to Live Independently			
	Live with Children or Others		Live in an Institution	
	Coefficient	t-Value	Coefficient	t-Value
CONSTANT	−5.21285	−4.60	−12.49175	−6.59
RACE	1.06272	3.38	−1.09591	−1.69
GENDER	−0.01280	−0.04	0.18139	0.47
DAUGHTERS	0.22783	4.18	0.14136	1.58
SONS	0.03278	0.62	−0.03544	−0.34
OWN	0.56104	2.33	−1.34210	−4.55
MORTG	−1.31190	−5.74	−0.52219	−1.17
FIN	0.00150	1.99	0.00094	0.88
HOME	0.00189	1.94	0.00190	0.95
HEALTH1	−2.72910	−2.16	−1.28417	−0.86
HEALTH2	−0.76748	−2.93	−1.67740	−5.43

Health Measurement (equations 4)[a]

	Bathing		Dressing		Getting Up		Walking	
HEALTH1	−1.057	−13.15	−1.179	−13.78	−1.333	−14.18	−1.154	−15.17
HEALTH2	−1.635	−19.07	−1.616	−19.30	−1.440	−18.52	−1.273	−21.38
MU1	12.390	16.28	13.005	16.85	11.284	14.75	8.976	14.86
MU2*[b]	−0.164	−2.28	−0.048	−0.63	0.169	2.41	0.270	5.54
MU3*[b]	−0.805	−6.94	−0.506	−3.87	−0.146	−1.27	−0.091	−1.31

	Going Outside		Light Housework		Preparing Meals		Shopping	
HEALTH1	−1.370	−13.66	−0.772	−8.55	−0.638	−7.54	−0.711	−9.66
HEALTH2	−2.039	−17.53	−2.490	−14.97	−2.654	−16.01	−2.369	−17.46
MU1	15.540	15.32	18.795	14.14	19.631	14.84	16.976	14.99
MU2*[b]	−0.242	−2.89	−0.763	−6.35	−0.479	−4.41	−0.895	−8.39
MU3*[b]	−0.461	−4.39	−1.118	−6.84	−0.899	−6.21	−1.160	−9.16

Health Production (equations 5)

	HEALTH1		HEALTH2	
AGE 90	−0.00216	−0.31	−0.08708	−20.15
EDUC	0.02881	2.97	0.05623	9.56
RACE	0.20709	1.85	−0.42710	−6.83
GENDER	0.04999	0.55	0.01938	0.34
OWN	0.02259	0.31	0.32748	7.24

Source: Longitudinal Study on Aging 1990.

Notes: Sample size = 2,193 elderly. Identification is by parameter restrictions.

[a]Left-hand columns are coefficients, right-hand are t-values.

[b]μ_2^* and μ_3^* are defined by $\mu_2 = \mu_1 + \exp(\mu_2^*)$ and $\mu_3 = \mu_2 + \exp(\mu_3^*)$.

is mainly determined by age, while the most important determinant for the first factor is education. The first health factor works more like a random effect, while the second factor carries the deterministic component associated with the exogenous variables.

The coefficients of the sociodemographic variables in table 6.5 have a pattern similar to the coefficients in table 6.3. However, some of the magnitudes change considerably. For example, the coefficients of the *RACE* and the *OWN* variables in the first column almost double in magnitude compared to table 6.3. In general, the changes are largest for those variables that appear in several equations of the system and not only in the choice equation. If we believe in the a priori assumptions underlying the MIMIC model, we must conclude that the multinomial logit model yields biased parameter results.

One may also be interested in seeing whether the nonlinear MIMIC model predicts better than the simple multinomial logit model. This is a weak test of the a priori assumptions underlying the MIMIC model. It is weak because the real strength of the structural model is the prediction of the effect of structural changes. However, the data do not provide such an experiment.

In order to test the out-of-sample performance, we used the 1986 and 1988 waves of the LSOA. We restricted attention to the unmarried elderly, so the 1986 and 1988 samples are smaller than the 1990 sample due to those elderly who were still married in 1986 or 1988. Table 6.6 shows the results.

In the in-sample prediction, the multinomial logit model fits the sample better than the nonlinear MIMIC model. It produces better estimates of the institutionalization probability, and it has an overall higher success rate. This might be expected from an atheoretical model designed to describe the data. The balance changes in the out-of-sample prediction. Now the nonlinear model has a better overall performance, and it is closer in predicting living with others. Again, this reversal is exactly what an econometrician wishes for a model that may mine the sample worse but capture the true structure better. The improvement, however, is rather modest. It would be helpful to have a holdout sample that consists of different elderly persons rather than of the same persons two years prior to the estimation period.

We also pursued the second method to identify the structural parameters in exploiting the variation in the health production function over time; see equation 14. We use the difference between the matrices Δ_{1988} and Δ_{1990}, estimated for the 1988 and 1990 waves, maintaining that the structural coefficients of the choice equation (β, γ) remain constant. It would be preferable to estimate the second set of coefficients from a cross-section as far away from 1990 as possible in order to capture a sufficient change in health technology, rather than using 1988. However, the 1986 wave has very few institutionalized persons, and the 1984 wave has none. The results are disappointing because the difference between Δ_{1988} and Δ_{1990} turns out to be virtually random: two years are too short to induce significant changes in health technology.

Table 6.6   Prediction Performance of the Two Alternative Models (%)

	Observed	Multinomial Logit	Nonlinear MIMIC Reduced Form	Nonlinear MIMIC Structural Form
In-sample 1990				
Alone	64.02	79.30	82.58	73.83
With others	28.45	13.41	15.18	23.16
Institution	7.52	7.30	2.33	3.01
% correct		74.15	69.08	63.61
Out-of-sample 1988				
Alone	67.50	87.32	86.70	76.97
With others	28.63	9.44	12.07	21.65
Institution	3.87	3.24	1.22	1.38
% correct		68.19	70.96	64.85
Out-of-sample 1986				
Alone	70.96	90.30	89.66	78.40
With others	27.62	8.50	10.12	21.18
Institution	1.42	1.20	0.2	0.42
% correct		74.86	72.8	67.07

Source: Longitudinal Study on Aging 1986, 1988, and 1990. Sample size is 1,412, 1,963, and 2,193 elderly, respectively.

6.6   Conclusions

Like the entire paper, the conclusions address econometric methodology as well as economic substance. We start with econometrics.

This paper is a classical exercise in what econometrics is supposed to do—and where the problems of sophisticated econometrics are. It uses a priori knowledge drawn from economics (and from common sense) in order to structure the inference we draw from the data. The multinomial logit model is atheoretical in the sense that it makes no usage of the causal links depicted in figure 6.1. In turn, the MIMIC model in figure 6.2 employs a rather involved superstructure to guide our inference.

The main problem with this model is of course identification. After all, the MIMIC model uses the same information as the simple multinomial logit model, and only introduces a potentially large number of latent variable constructs. In addition to postulating causal links as in figure 6.2, additional parameter restrictions were required. In the first case identification via exclusion restrictions is pretty much in the spirit of conventional simultaneous equation models. In the second case we assumed that some parameters change over time while others stay constant. Both identifying assumptions can easily be criticized. If the identifying assumptions are false, our estimates are inconsistent. If they are true, we have gained efficiency and have learned more about those structural coefficients that we have estimated.

Our panel data could identify the coefficients of the latent health variables much better than the cross-section models of section 6.5. The latent health variables have a function very similar to random effects. This is the reason they are so hard to identify in cross-sections. By exploiting the panel structure, we could identify, say, two latent health statuses in 1988 as well as in 1990, possibly correlated over time. The likelihood function would be similar to equation 10 but would require higher dimensional integration. In further research we will estimate this model by employing simulation methods for the computation of these integrals, such as the smooth simulated maximum-likelihood approach of Börsch-Supan and Hajivassiliou (1993).

As for economic substance, the coefficients of our main interest were health and wealth. While wealth is an important economic variable in the choice of living arrangements, income has proven to be of little relevance once wealth is included. Health is one of the main predictors of living arrangement choices. This is to be expected. Health is well captured by two factors, one associated with independent activities and strongly related to age, while the other, more person-specific factor is associated with more basic capabilities. Living with others, mainly children, is positively affected by financial and housing wealth, while homeowners are less likely to become institutionalized.

References

Börsch-Supan, A. 1989. Household Dissolution and the Choice of Alternative Living Arrangements among Elderly Americans. In *The Economics of Aging,* ed. David A. Wise. Chicago: University of Chicago Press.
———. 1990. A Dynamic Analysis of Household Dissolution and Living Arrangement Transitions by Elderly Americans. In *Issues in the Economics of Aging,* ed. David A. Wise. Chicago: University of Chicago Press.
Börsch-Supan, A., J. Gokhale, L. Kotlikoff, and J. Morris. 1992. The Provision of Time to the Elderly by Their Children. In *Topics in the Economics of Aging,* ed. David A. Wise. Chicago: University of Chicago Press.
Börsch-Supan, A., and V. Hajivassiliou. 1993. Smooth Unbiased Multivariate Probability Simulators for Maximum Likelihood Estimation of Limited Dependent Variable Models. *Journal of Econometrics* 58:347–68.
Börsch-Supan, A., V. Hajivassiliou, L. Kotlikoff, and J. Morris. 1992. Health, Children, and Elderly Living Arrangements: A Multiperiod-Multinomial Probit Model with Unobserved Heterogeneity and Autocorrelated Errors. In *Topics in the Economics of Aging,* ed. David A. Wise. Chicago: University of Chicago Press.
Börsch-Supan, A., L. Kotlikoff, and J. Morris. 1991. The Dynamics of Living Arrangements of the Elderly: Health and Family Support. In *The Economics of Care of the Elderly,* ed. J. Pacolet and C. Wilderom. London: Avebury Aldershot.
Ellwood, D. T., and T. J. Kane. 1990. The American Way of Aging: An Event History Analysis. In *Issues in the Economics of Aging,* ed. David A. Wise. Chicago: University of Chicago Press.
Feinstein, J., and D. McFadden, 1989. The Dynamics of Housing Demand by the El-

derly. In *The Economics of Aging,* ed. David A. Wise. Chicago: University of Chicago Press.

Fitti, J. E., and M. G. Kovar. 1987. The Supplement on Aging to the 1984 National Health Interview Survey. National Center for Health Statistics working paper. Washington, DC.

Garber, A. M. 1990. Predicting Nursing Home Utilization among the High-Risk Elderly. In *Issues in the Economics of Aging,* ed. David A. Wise. Chicago: University of Chicago Press.

Greene, V. L., M. E. Lovely, and J. I. Ondrich. 1993. Do Community-Based, Long-Term-Care Services Reduce Nursing Home Use? A Transition Probability Analysis. *Journal of Human Resources* 28 (2): 297–317.

Jöreskog, K. G. 1967. Some Contributions to Maximum Likelihood Factor Analysis. *Psychometrica* 32:443–82.

Jöreskog, K. G., and D. Sörbom. 1988. LISREL 7: A Guide to the Program and Applications. Chicago: SPSS Inc.

Kotlikoff, L. J., and J. Morris. 1987. How Much Care Do the Aged Receive from their Children? A Bimodal Picture of Contact and Assistance. NBER Working Paper no. 2391. Cambridge, MA: National Bureau of Economic Research.

———. 1990. Why Don't the Elderly Live with their Children? A New Look. In *Issues in the Economics of Aging,* ed. David A. Wise. Chicago: University of Chicago Press.

Kovar, M. G., and G. S. Poe. 1985. The National Health Interview Survey Design, 1973–1984, and Procedures, 1975–1983. National Center for Health Statistics working paper. Washington, DC.

McFadden, D. 1988. Discrete Response to Unobserved Variables for Which There Are Multiple Indicators. Massachusetts Institute of Technology. Mimeo.

Morikawa, T., M. Ben-Akiva, and D. McFadden. 1990. Incorporating Psychometric Data in Econometric Travel Demand Models. Massachusetts Institute of Technology. Mimeo.

National Center for Health Statistics. 1991. The Longitudinal Study on Aging. Version 4. Washington, DC. Mimeo.

Schwartz, S., S. Danziger, and E. Smolensky. 1984. The Choice of Living Arrangements by the Elderly. In *Retirement and Economic Behavior,* ed. H. J. Aaron and G. Burtless. Washington, DC: Brookings Institution.

Venti, Steven F., and David A. Wise. 1990. But They Don't Want to Reduce Equity. In *Issues in the Economics of Aging,* ed. David A. Wise. Chicago: University of Chicago Press.

———. 1991. The Saving Effect of Tax-Deferred Retirement Accounts: Evidence from SIPP. In *National Saving and Economic Performance,* ed. B. D. Bernheim and J. B. Shoven. Chicago: University of Chicago Press.

Comment   Steven F. Venti

Axel Börsch-Supan, Daniel McFadden, and Reinhold Schnabel present and estimate a model of the effects of health and wealth on the living arrangements of the elderly. Most of my discussion will deal with wealth effects on living

Steven F. Venti is professor of economics at Dartmouth College and a research associate of the National Bureau of Economic Research.

arrangements. This is a bit unfair, since the principal objective of the paper is to obtain better estimates of the effect of health on living arrangements. Let me say at the outset that this objective has been met. I thus have little to add, either critically or constructively, to their comprehensive and thorough analysis of health effects. Instead I will focus on some other implications of their work I find interesting.

For the benefit of those who have not followed this area of research closely, let me briefly review some of the dramatic changes in living arrangements over the past two or three decades. If we concentrate attention on unmarried persons, age 75–79, we find that the percentage living independently has approximately doubled over the period 1960–90. Over the same period the percentage living with relatives has fallen by half, and the percentage living in nursing homes, although still small (about 7%), has doubled. The last few decades have also witnessed substantial growth of the wealth of the elderly. The explosion in house prices in the 1970s and early 1980s, the run-up in the stock market, the favorable "deal" received by the current retirement generation on their Social Security investment, and the increasing pension coverage of recent retirement cohorts have all contributed to this trend.

It seems natural to consider whether these two trends—rising wealth and an increase in the likelihood of independent living—are related. There is what I will call the "conventional view" (see the references in Schwartz, Danziger, and Smolensky 1984). This view suggests the trend toward independence is an indicator of increasing well-being of the elderly. The assumption, either implicit or explicit, is that the elderly clearly prefer living independently to either living with relatives or in an institution. Thus recent trends are a sign that the elderly today are more likely to be free of the health and wealth limitations that in the past "forced" them into alternative living arrangements. Independent living simply reflects a high income elasticity of privacy, according to this view. Empirical research, mostly based on cross-section studies, has generally been supportive. Wealth, good health, and income have all been found to be positively associated with the choice of an independent living arrangement.

There is, of course, an alternative view of the trend toward independent living (see, for example, Börsch-Supan 1990). For whatever reason—the entry of more women into the labor force is often cited—it may be that living with relatives is no longer a viable alternative for many of the elderly. The trend to independence is a trend to isolation, reflecting constraints rather than preferences, and the implications for the rising well-being of the elderly are ominous.

This study doesn't do great damage to the conventional view of living arrangements, but it is suggestive that some recent trends may be the result more of constraints than of preferences. The authors' work is the first on living arrangements to be based on the LSOA and the associated NBER Economics Supplement. These data are very recent (1990), which is important, given the pace of change. Much prior work was based on the Retirement History Survey, which spanned the period 1969–79 and thus predates some of the current trends. The LSOA data also have good information on health and wealth, probably superior to anything else available for this purpose. The one shortcoming of these data is the absence of information on the proximity and financial resources of kin, which would permit us to better ascertain the set of feasible alternative living arrangements for elderly persons in the sample.

The authors begin by estimating a conventional multinominal logit model of the choice between living independently, living with relatives or others, and living in an institution. Among the explanatory variables are five measured ADLs and three IADLs. As a group these variables provide a great deal of explanatory power, although the five ADLs are individually not significant, thus suggesting that the effect of health may be reasonably captured in fewer dimensions in the ensuing latent-variable model. Age, education, and the number of sons and daughters have the expected effects. There is surprisingly little effect of income, due perhaps to the presence of very good measures of wealth. It is these wealth effects that I find most intriguing. The three measures of wealth—homeownership, financial assets, and housing assets—are all associated with an increase in the likelihood of living with relatives or others.

To uncover the true effects of health, which cannot be directly measured, the authors adopt the MIMIC framework. Essentially they face an errors-in-variables problem because ADLs and IADLs only imperfectly measure true health. This gives rise to a two-factor latent-variable parameterization of health. Moreover, the observed health indicators are categorical. This requires an ordered probit model of the health indicators as functions of the latent health variables. Thus estimation of this model requires "integrating out" the two latent health variables from a likelihood function comprising the product of logit choice equations and probits. This is a formidable task that is successfully executed.

If the question is, "Why do some elderly live independently and others in alternative living arrangements?" then the structural MIMIC model clearly implicates health as the answer. Estimates of the two latent health factors are large and significant. One of these factors is clearly capturing the general deterioration of health associated with aging. The other is more of a puzzle, having an unexpected negative sign in the health indicator equations.

The wealth effects are similar to those estimated in the earlier specification and imply that the wealthier elderly are more likely to live with relatives or others. There are several possible explanations for this curious result. The authors suggest a "bribery" effect where wealthy parents are able to get their children, who would otherwise choose to live alone, to take them in. This explanation suggests wealthy parents are living in the homes of their children.

Alternatively, the children may be living in the homes of their parents. This "wealth attracts kids" phenomenon has been observed by others (Schwartz, Danziger, and Smolensky 1984) in the Retirement History Survey. In these data, we cannot distinguish this explanation from the bribery hypothesis. However, the fact that more elderly persons own homes than live independently in this sample suggests this explanation may be reasonable.

A final explanation focuses on the "others" in the choice category "living with relatives or others." A possibility here is what Feinstein (chap. 9 in this volume) calls transitional living arrangements. This form of housing—somewhere between independent and institutional—includes many varieties such as congregate housing, life-care communities, and other arrangements where the elderly generally do not own their housing unit, but are also not part of an institutional arrangement. Such facilities are typically characterized by the presence of on-site dining facilities, availability of nursing or personal care, and perhaps housekeeping or laundry services. It is difficult to assess how prevalent such arrangements are because, as a group, they are only vaguely defined. In particular, it is not clear how survey respondents in transitional arrangements would classify their own living arrangements. About the only data I have been able to uncover on these arrangements is a 1988 Congressional Budget Office report indicating that the percentage of elderly living with "unrelated others" approximately doubled between 1980 and 1984. The results of Börsch-Supan, McFadden, and Schnabel may suggest that, once health limitations set in, these transitional facilities are the *preferred* next step for wealthy families that are either unable to or prefer not to live with relatives. More disaggregated information on living arrangements would be useful to address this point.

I have one final comment on the econometric innovation at the core of this paper. I agree with the authors that, because health is not measurable, a latent-variable framework is important to deal with the errors-in-variables problem posed by using observed health indicators such as ADLs and IADLs. However, it may also be that, in some sense, the "errors" themselves may be of interest. For instance, given true health, the choice of living arrangements may depend on whether an elderly person perceives himself or herself to be limited in the ability to provide, say, meals (one of the IADLs). It is conceivable that two persons with the same health may differ in this ability. In this case, the measured ADLs and IADLs may provide useful additional information not captured by the true latent health variables. Thus it may make sense to include both measured and latent health in the choice specification.

In summary, the authors have made a significant methodological and substantive contribution to our understanding of the determinants of the living standards of the elderly. Their latent-variable characterization of health will help us better understand the complex relationship between health limitations and housing choice. And their results on wealth effects suggests great care should be exercised interpreting the trend to independent living as an indicator of the rising well-being of the elderly.

References

Börsch-Supan, Axel. 1990. A Dynamic Analysis of Household Dissolution and Living Arrangement Transitions by Elderly Americans. In *Issues in the Economics of Aging,* ed. David A. Wise. Chicago: University of Chicago Press.
Schwartz, Saul, Sheldon Danziger, and Eugene Smolensky. 1984. The Choice of Living Arrangements by the Elderly. In *Retirement and Economic Behavior,* ed. H. Aaron and G. Burtless. Washington, DC: Brookings Institution.

IV   Saving and Wealth

7   Do 401(k) Plans Replace Other Employer-Provided Pensions?

Leslie E. Papke, Mitchell Petersen, and James M. Poterba

The rapid growth of 401(k) plans is one of the most striking trends in retirement saving during the last decade. These plans allow employees to defer income, to take advantage of generous employer matching provisions on some contributions, and to accumulate assets at the pretax rate of return. Strong employee demand for 401(k) plans is undoubtedly part of the explanation for their expansion during the 1980s. So too are various changes in the tax and regulatory treatment of defined-benefit (DB) pension plans that were enacted in the 1981 and 1984 tax reform bills and especially in the 1986 tax reform bill. These changes reduced employers' willingness to provide DB plans for their employees and contributed to the growth of defined-contribution (DC) pension plans, including 401(k)s.

A growing body of evidence suggests that 401(k) contributors do not offset their contributions by reducing their accumulation of other financial assets (see Poterba, Venti, and Wise 1994, 1995). This does not *necessarily* mean that 401(k) contributions represent net additions to private saving, however, since they could be offset by reduced contributions to other pension plans. In particular, if 401(k) plans have replaced other types of private pension arrangements, then their net effect on private saving may be smaller than the contribution flow to these plans would otherwise suggest.

To investigate the degree of substitution between 401(k) plans and other

Leslie E. Papke is associate professor of economics at Michigan State University and a faculty research fellow of the National Bureau of Economic Research. Mitchell Petersen is assistant professor of finance at Northwestern University. James M. Poterba is professor of economics at the Massachusetts Institute of Technology and director of the Public Economics Research Program at the National Bureau of Economic Research.

The authors are grateful to James Zolnierek for outstanding research assistance, to Jonathan Gruber, Andrew Samwick, Richard Thaler, and Steven Venti for many helpful comments on an earlier draft, and to the National Institute on Aging, the National Science Foundation, and the James Phillips Fund for research support.

employer-provided retirement saving arrangements, and to obtain firm-level information on these plans more generally, we surveyed a stratified random sample of firms with 401(k) plans in 1987. We asked 401(k) plan administrators about the origins of their plan, in particular whether it replaced another pension plan for covered employees. We also inquired about various detailed provisions of the plan, including participation rates, employer matching rules, loan and hardship withdrawal provisions, and whether the plan had been affected by antidiscrimination rules.

This paper, which summarizes the results from our survey, is divided into six sections. Section 7.1 summarizes aggregate trends in contributions to 401(k) plans and other employer-provided pension plans, and describes the changing institutional environment in which firms select DB and DC pension plans. Section 7.2 explains our sample survey design, and presents summary statistics on the set of 401(k) plans in our sample. Section 7.3 reports our findings on the interaction between 401(k) plans and other retirement plans. We find that 401(k) plans do not appear to have displaced previous DB plans for many workers, but that these plans did in many cases replace preexisting DC thrift and profit-sharing plans.

The next two sections summarize the characteristics of 401(k) plans in our sample. Section 7.4 describes the pattern of participation rates and employer matching rates over time, and explores the links between these plan attributes. Section 7.5 explains the structure of antidiscrimination rules, describes their changes over time, and summarizes their effects on the 401(k) plans in our sample. There is a brief conclusion.

7.1   Trends in Defined-Benefit and Defined-Contribution Pension Plans

The 1980s witnessed a substantial change in the relative flows of contributions to DB and DC pension plans. This was the result of at least two coincident developments. First, Bernheim and Shoven (1988) argue that high investment returns on existing DB plans reduced required contributions to DB plans in the mid-1980s. A second factor, explored in Chang (1991), Kruse (1995), and Silverman (1993), was the changing regulatory and tax environment in the 1980s.

The changing regulatory treatment of DB and DC pension plans began with the Employee Retirement and Income Security Act of 1974 (ERISA).[1] ERISA imposed minimum plan standards for participation, vesting, and retirement, as well as requirements for funding past-service liability. It also established the Pension Benefit Guaranty Corporation (PBGC) to insure pension benefits to employees in DB plans, and financed this insurance program with taxes on existing plans. ERISA placed a lower regulatory burden on DC plans, which were subject only to the minimum plan standards that also affected DB plans.

---

1. Clark (1987) and Beller and Lawrence (1992) discuss these issues in more detail.

Legislation since ERISA has raised PBGC premiums, required faster funding of liabilities, and penalized employers for claiming excess assets of terminated DB plans. The Tax Equity and Fiscal Responsibility Act of 1982 imposed faster vesting schedules for lower-paid employees in so-called top-heavy plans. The Tax Reform Act of 1986 (TRA86) imposed an excise tax of 10% on excess pension plan assets that revert to an employer upon termination of a pension plan. Subsequent legislation raised this tax to 20%, effective in 1990, and to 50% if the employer does not transfer a portion of the excess assets to a replacement plan, or increase benefits under the terminating plan.

The 1987 Omnibus Budget Reconciliation Act increased the basic PBGC premium from $8.50 to $16.00 per participant, and added a variable premium that depends on the plan's degree of underfunding. It also limited the tax deduction for plan contributions to 150% of the plan's termination liability; this had the effect of reducing employer contributions to DB plans (see Chang 1993). The net effect of these tax and regulatory changes has been a marked increase in the administrative cost, and a decrease in the benefits to employers from establishing DB pension plans.

Table 7.1 reports the number of DC and DB pension plans, the number of participants in these plans, and the level of contributions to these plans from 1975 to 1989. The table shows that the number of DC plans more than doubled between 1975 and 1982, and then rose by 50% again between 1982 and 1989. The number of DB plans increased during 1975–82, but the increase was slower than that for DC plans. Between 1982 and 1989, however, the number of DB plans actually *declined*. The second column in table 7.1 shows the total number of participants in DB and DC plans, which includes both working and retired participants. The number of participants in DB plans peaked in 1984 and has declined slightly in subsequent years. The number of *active* participants, current employees participating in DB plans, peaked in 1981, and has declined by several million since then. In contrast, the number of DC plan participants increased throughout the 1980s, although not as quickly as the number of DC plans. This reflects the growth of relatively small DC plans, particularly 401(k) plans, in recent years.

The last column in table 7.1 tracks contributions to DC and DB pension plans. The disparity between the contribution series is even more dramatic than that between the number of participants or the number of plans. DC plan contributions increased from $23.5 billion in 1980 to $80.1 billion in 1989, with $46.1 billion of the 1989 total accounted for by 401(k) contributions. Contributions to DB plans, however, peaked at $48.4 billion in 1982, and then declined to only $24.9 billion by 1989. The rapid growth in contributions to DC plans is largely due to the growth of 401(k) plans. Without them, contributions to DC plans would have been only $34 billion in 1989.

There are at least two reasons why 401(k) plans may have grown faster than other DC plans during the 1980s. First, 401(k)s offered tax advantages relative to the profit-sharing and thrift plans that they often replaced. The opportunity for employees to defer tax on a substantial share of their salary was, and contin-

Table 7.1		Trends in Pension Plans, Participants, and Contributions	
Year	Plans (thousands)	Participants (millions)	Contributions (billions of $)
Defined-Contribution Plans (401 (k) in parentheses)			
1975	207.7	11.5	12.8
1976	246.0	13.5	14.2
1977	281.0	15.2	15.9
1978	314.6	16.3	18.4
1979	331.4	18.3	20.7
1980	340.8	19.9	23.5
1981	378.3	21.7	28.4
1982	419.5	24.6	31.1
1983	426.6 (1.7)	29.1 (4.4)	36.1
1984	435.4 (17.3)	32.9 (7.5)	43.4 (16.3)
1985	462.0 (29.9)	35.0 (10.3)	53.2 (24.3)
1986	545.0 (37.4)	36.7 (11.6)	58.3 (29.2)
1987	570.0 (45.1)	38.3 (13.1)	62.3 (33.2)
1988	584.0 (68.1)	37.0 (15.5)	64.9 (39.4)
1989	599.0 (83.3)	36.5 (17.3)	80.1 (46.1)
Defined-Benefit Plans			
1975	103.3	33.0	24.2
1976	114.0	34.2	28.5
1977	121.7	35.0	31.2
1978	128.4	36.1	27.6
1979	139.5	36.8	40.6
1980	148.1	38.0	42.6
1981	167.3	38.9	47.0
1982	175.0	38.6	48.4
1983	175.1	40.0	46.3
1984	168.0	41.0	47.2
1985	170.2	39.7	42.0
1986	172.6	40.0	33.2
1987	163.1	40.0	29.8
1988	146.0	40.7	26.3
1989	132.5	40.0	24.9

Source: Data are drawn from U.S. Department of Labor (1993).

ues to be, an important attraction of these plans. Second, 401(k)s are more flexible than many other pension arrangements. Since each eligible employee can determine the amount of saving he or she does through the 401(k) plan, these plans are likely to be more attractive at firms with heterogeneous workforces. Finally, from the firm's perspective, 401(k) plans may cost less for a given level of employer contribution to the median employee.[2] With other DC

2. The median employee may be critical in determining how the firm's wage payments adjust to the level of employer contribution. Provided there is some trade-off between wages and pension benefits from the worker's perspective, the net cost of an employer pension contribution is smaller than the amount of this contribution.

plans, the employer must contribute on behalf of all eligible workers. Even though participation in 401(k) plans is high, however, not all eligible employees participate in these plans. For a given level of employer contribution per participating employee, therefore, the firm's total cost will be lower with a 401(k) than with other DC plans.

7.2 Sample Survey Design

It is not possible to study the substitution between 401(k) plans, DB pension plans, and other DC pension plans using the household-level data sets that underlie prior research on 401(k)s and household saving. Household data sets such as the Survey of Income and Program Participation and the Current Population Survey (CPS) do not collect sufficiently detailed information on the respondent's pension arrangements. In addition, neither of these data sets contains any information on the pension arrangements at the respondent's firm *before* the 401(k) option became available.[3]

To remedy these data deficiencies, we prepared a new survey instrument and mailed it to a subset of U.S. corporations. Our questionnaire draws heavily on a General Accounting Office survey in 1987 (see U.S. GAO 1988a, 1988b), but includes additional questions on the origins of the 401(k) plan at the survey firm, whether it had replaced a previous DB or DC plan, and the degree of overlap between 401(k) and other pension coverage for the firm's employees. We also queried firms about both the *current* structure of their 401(k) plan and historical attributes of their plan. This enables us to chart patterns in 401(k) participation and contributions *conditioning* on a firm effect.

We obtained addresses for 401(k) plan administrators from IRS form 5500 data filings for 1987, the most recent year for which public use data were available when we mailed our questionnaires. Given the skewed size distribution of 401(k) plans, the characteristics of the average plan may be quite different from the plan that is available to the average worker. To achieve some representativeness with respect to workers, we adopted a sampling scheme that assigned a higher sampling probability to larger plans.

Table 7.2 shows the number of 401(k) plans in the form 5500 database. We disaggregate plans by their number of participants, and show the selection probability we used to identify survey recipients as well as our response rate to date. We mailed 786 questionnaires. After a dismal first-round response of only 33 surveys, we designed a shorter follow-up survey, which we mailed to 100 nonrespondents. This was followed with a telephone call to explore the status of the survey and, if necessary, provide an opportunity for the 401(k) administrator to report information by telephone. This second-stage survey

---

3. The Health and Retirement Survey, which will become available for public use in the near future, includes more detailed data on pension arrangements. It will therefore be possible to study some of these substitution issues using that data set.

Table 7.2   **Sample Survey Design**

Plan Size (participants)	Plans on 1987 Form 5500 Tape	Surveys Distributed	Usable Responses
0–500	7,380	275 (4%)	6
500–5,000	2,660	266 (10%)	13
>5,000	405	245 (60%)	24
Total	10,445	786	43

Source: Authors' tabulations from survey responses.

yielded another 10 usable responses. Much of our analysis is therefore based on data from 43 firms.[4]

Our survey response rate is disappointing, and raises important questions about the representativeness of the firms in our sample and the generality of our results. Our response rate is apparently similar, however, to typical response rates to mail surveys conducted by the Department of Labor. In light of the small sample size, the results below should be viewed with caution.

Table 7.3 reports summary characteristics for the 401(k) plans that responded to our survey. The overwhelming majority of these plans involve both a salary-reduction component and a company matching rate. This arrangement characterizes more than two-thirds of the plans and participants in our sample.

Table 7.3 also provides information on the distribution of company matching rates for 401(k)s. While 10% of the responding plans do not match employee contributions, these plans are smaller than average, and account for only 2% of the *participants* in our survey. Ten percent of the responding plans, representing nearly one-third of the participants, match employee contributions *dollar for dollar.* Nearly 90% of the participants in the responding 401(k) plans face matching rates of at least 25 cents per dollar contributed.

These results on matching rates are comparable to those in other surveys of 401(k) plans. The General Accounting Office (1988a) found that 51% of firms with 401(k) plans match employee contributions and that, conditional on matching, more than two-thirds provided at least a 25% matching contribution. A separate survey by the Massachusetts Mutual Life Insurance Company (1991) found that 20% of plans had matching rates of 100% or more, while 29% had no employer matching. Hewitt Associates' (1991) survey found that 84% of 401(k) plans provide some level of employer matching funds.

7.3 401(k) Plans and Other Pension Arrangements

One battery of questions on our survey inquired about how and why the 401(k) plan was established. We asked if the 401(k) plan was a new plan, or if

---

4. Four surveys were returned because the 401(k) plan no longer existed, for example, because the parent firm had ceased operations. We also received six responses indicating that the firms did not participate in surveys.

Table 7.3   **Summary Statistics and 401(k) Plan Characteristics (%)**

	Simple Average	Participant-Weighted Average
Features of 401(k) plan		
Salary-reduction plan	84	83
Thrift plan	79	75
Profit-sharing plan	14	39
Section 125 flexible spending account	7	2
Contribution structure		
Employer contributions only	0	0
Salary reduction only	9	1
Salary reduction and company matching	70	69
Salary reduction and company discretionary	2	0[a]
Salary reduction, company matching, and		
company discretionary	19	30
Company matching rate (1990)		
0	10	2
0.01–0.25	10	9
0.26–0.50	41	37
0.51–0.75	23	19
0.76–0.99	0	0
1.00	10	30
>1.0	5	4

Source: Authors' tabulation of survey results.

[a]Actual value was 0.46, which was rounded to 0.

it replaced another pension plan. Table 7.4 summarizes the survey responses. Forty-five percent of the responding firms, representing 37% of the 401(k) participants in our survey, indicated that another pension plan was *converted* to the 401(k).[5]

Two percent of the responding firms (one firm) reported that DB pension plans were terminated and replaced with a 401(k). Many more firms reported that they converted previous thrift plans or profit-sharing plans to 401(k)s. Our findings also suggest that at least half of the 401(k) plans did *not* replace previous plans. These results do not support the view that 401(k) contributions are simply a relabeling of contributions that were previously directed to other pension plans.

The motivation for converting thrift and profit-sharing plans to 401(k)s, as noted above, was that contributions to the former were made on an after-tax basis, while 401(k) contributions were made before employee taxes. In addition, until TRA86 tightened the limits on both 401(k) contributions and with-

5. This estimate is based on the thirty-three responses to our initial "long form" questionnaire. We have confirmed the survey responses for most of our sample firms by examining their 5500 filings. We find clear evidence for some firms that one or several DC plans were either terminated or ceased receiving contributions when the 401(k) plan was established.

Table 7.4   401(k) Plan Initiation Decisions (%)

	Simple Average	Participant-Weighted Average
Date when 401(k) plan started		
Before 1981	14	19
1981–83	16	30
1984–86	51	42
Since 1986	19	15
New plans[a]	55	63
Type of plan converted[a]		
Thrift/saving	53	49
Profit-sharing	40	50
Other	7	1
Why was plan started?		
Supplement primary defined-contribution plan	19	14
Supplement primary defined-benefit plan	63	66
Replace primary defined-contribution plan	9	6
Replace primary defined-benefit plan	2	17
Optional tax-deferred saving plan	58	59
Is the 401(k) the primary retirement plan? (% yes)	26	6
Percentage of 401(k) eligibles also covered by		
Defined-benefit plan		
1986	85	88
1990	73	82
Defined-contribution plan		
1986	37	32
1990	36	30
Percentage of 401(k) eligibles for whom the		
401(k) is the *only* retirement plan		
1986	5	4
1990	19	10

Source: Authors' tabulations from survey responses.

[a]Questions that were not asked on the second-round survey; tabulations are based on thirty-three rather than forty-three responses.

drawals, 401(k)s offered a highly liquid and tax-favored means to accumulate assets. The limit on 401(k) contributions was $30,000 per year until 1986, and with federal marginal tax rates of 50% on high-income individuals, the incentive to defer income and accumulate savings at the pretax rate of return was substantial.

The survey responses indicate that 401(k)s are typically supplemental plans, added to preexisting DB (63%) or DC (19%) plans. A direct test of whether 401(k) plans have replaced *all* other pension coverage is provided by our question on the fraction of 401(k) eligible workers who are also covered by other pension arrangements at the firm. In 1990, 82% of the participants in 401(k) plans were also covered by another DB plan at the same firm, and 30% were also covered by another DC plan. These responses are not exclusive: 401(k) eligibles could be covered by both. The 401(k) was the *only* retirement plan for covered workers at 19% of the plans, representing 10% of the participants.

The survey findings on the extent of sole pension coverage by 401(k) plans can be compared with information based on published tabulations from the IRS form 5500 filings. For 1989, the most recent year for which data are available, the Department of Labor (1993) reports that 14% of the assets of 401(k) plans with at least one hundred employees were held in plans that were the only employer-sponsored pension plan for employees.[6] This suggests that, at most, a small fraction of current 401(k) plans could possibly have displaced all other pension arrangements at providing firms.

There is some indication that the pattern of pension plan coverage for 401(k) participants has been changing. Between 1986 and 1990, the share of 401(k) participants covered by another DB plan fell from 88% to 82%, and the share covered by another DC plan fell from 32% to 30%.[7] The fraction of 401(k) *plans* that represented the only pension coverage for participants rose during this period, but this increase was concentrated among smaller plans.

The disparity between the results in the first and second columns of table 7.4 suggests important differences between the roles played by 401(k) plans at large and small firms. Small firms are more likely to rely on 401(k)s as their primary retirement vehicle. The diffusion of 401(k)s across firms during the 1980s began with large firms; recent adopters are, on average, smaller than those with established plans.

The differences between large and small firms are apparent even in our small sample. The 401(k) was the only retirement plan for 14% of the workers at firms that started their 401(k) plans in 1986 or later, compared with only 7% of the workers at firms with plans that started before 1986. While 18% of the plans that began before 1986 are primary retirement plans, 40% of the post-1986 plans are primary plans.

The foregoing results suggest that only a small minority of firms replaced DB pension plans with 401(k) plans. Only one of our sample respondents, but a relatively large firm, indicated that this was the origin of the 401(k) plan. There is more evidence, although it applies at less than half of the firms with 401(k)s, that these plans replaced previous DC thrift plans. Estimating the size of the thrift-plan contribution flow that was redirected to 401(k)s requires more detailed information on these plans than our survey collected.

7.4   401(k) Plan Characteristics and Participation Rates

One of the central questions about 401(k) plans, as well as other types of tax-deferred retirement saving programs, is the sensitivity of plan contributions

---

6. The 401(k) plans with at least one hundred participants accounted for $41.5 billion of the $46.1 billion of 401(k) contributions in 1989.

7. With our current sample size, we cannot reject the null hypothesis that the percentage of 401(k) eligibles covered by other plans was the same in 1986 and 1990.

to tax and other incentives. One strategy for analyzing this question is to compare the participation rates in 401(k)s with different employer matching rates. While the matching rate may be endogenous, it is not clear why one would expect a high matching rate as opposed to a high employer contribution at firms where large pools of workers want to participate in a 401(k).[8] In this case, the correlation between matching rates and participation rates may reflect firm decisions rather than employee decisions regarding the amount to save through the 401(k).

One unique feature of our data set is the presence of repeated observations on employee participation rates, as well as some aspects of the 401(k) plan such as the matching rate. This permits us to study the persistence of participation and contribution rates, as well as the intertemporal stability of employer matching rates.

Table 7.5 summarizes the joint distribution of the employer matching rate in 1986 and 1990. We present these data in a transition matrix, showing the pattern of matching rates in both 1986 and 1990. The table shows that there is very strong persistence in the matching rates that firms apply to employee contributions. Eighty-six percent of the firms responding to our survey applied the same matching rate in 1986 and 1990, and the relatively small number that did not changed relatively little. With one exception, the set of firms with zero matching rates in both years, this fraction is relatively insensitive to the choice between plan and participant weighting, as the similarity between the upper and lower panels of the table suggests.

Table 7.6 uses a format similar to table 7.5 to report information on employee participation rates in 401(k) plans in both 1986 and 1990. This table again suggests important stability. We divide firms into four participation-rate groups, and 78% of the plans are in the same group in 1986 and 1990. Larger plans are more likely than smaller firms to exhibit *high* participation rates, but they exhibit the same degree of stability as smaller firms. The panel B of table 7.6, which weights participation rates by plan size, shows that 90% of the 401(k) participants in 1990 were in plans with participation rates of 75% or more. In contrast, only 65% of the plans have participation rates this high. The distribution of participation rates provides a check on the representativeness of our sample. Weighting firms by their number of participants, the average participation rate is approximately 76%. Tabulations from the 1991 CPS reported in Poterba, Venti, and Wise (1995) suggest an average participation rate of 71%. Papke (1995) also finds similar participation rates in tabulations of the 1989 IRS form 5500 filings.

The strong persistence of participation rates across firms suggests, but does not prove, that employees do not alter their 401(k) status with any frequency.

---

8. Further analysis of participation decisions, recognizing the potential endogeneity of the matching rate, would require a more extensive data set with information on firm and worker characteristics, possibly from a time period before the growth of 401(k)s.

Table 7.5   **Distribution of Employer Matching Rates, 1986 and 1990 (%)**

A. Distribution of Plans

1986 Matching Rate	1990 Matching Rate					
	0	0.01–0.25	0.26–0.50	0.51–0.75	0.76–0.99	>0.99
0	12	0	0	0	0	0
0.01–0.25	0	9	0	0	0	0
0.26–0.50	0	0	38	15	0	0
0.51–0.75	0	0	0	12	0	0
0.76–0.99	0	0	0	0	0	0
>0.99	0	0	0	0	0	15

B. Distribution of Plan Participants

1986 Matching Rate	1990 Matching Rate					
	0	0.01–0.25	0.26–0.50	0.51–0.75	0.76–0.99	>0.99
0	2	0	0	0	0	0
0.01–0.25	0	4	0	0	0	0
0.26–0.50	0	0	36	13	0	0
0.51–0.75	0	0	0	8	0	0
0.76–0.99	0	0	0	0	0	0
>0.99	0	0	0	0	0	37

Source: Authors' tabulations from survey responses.

Table 7.6   **Distribution of Employee Participation Rates, 1986 and 1990 (%)**

A. Distribution of Plans

1986 Participation Rate	1990 Participation Rate			
	<.25	.26–.50	.51–.75	>.75
<.26	4	0	0	0
.26–.50	0	9	4	0
.51–.75	0	0	17	17
>.75	0	0	0	48

B. Distribution of Participants

1986 Participation Rate	1990 Participation Rate			
	<.25	.26–.50	.51–.75	>.75
<.26	0	0	0	0
.26–.50	0	2	0	0
.51–.75	0	0	8	39
>.75	0	0	0	51

Source: Authors' tabulations from survey responses.

Unfortunately, data on firm-level participation rates are not ideal for measuring the persistence of contributor behavior. One difficulty is that an individual can be a plan participant in a given year without making a contribution in that year. A second, and more difficult, problem, is that it is possible that *firm* participation rates are stable even though *individual* participation decisions are not. For example, a firm could display a 60% participation rate in two consecutive years if 40% of the workers participated in the first but not the second year, a separate 40% of the workers participated in the second year but not the first, and only 20% of workers participated in both years. Evidence against this possibility is presented in Kusko, Poterba, and Wilcox (1994). That study analyzes individual contribution data from one large 401(k) plan, and finds that contribution decisions are extremely persistent from one year to the next. This supports the view that deciding to contribute to a 401(k) plan is a form of self-control (see Shefrin and Thaler 1988) and that these contributions are effectively removed from the household's disposable income.

The information we have collected can be used to study how participation decisions are affected by employer matching rates. An ordinary least squares regression of plan participation rates in 1986 and 1990 on employer matching rates and an indicator variable for 1990 yields

$$\text{PART} = .602 + .187 \cdot \text{MATCH} - .008 \cdot \text{DUM90}.$$
$$\phantom{\text{PART} = }(.058) \quad (.070) \qquad\qquad (.055)$$

The R^2 for this equation is .124. A 10-percentage-point increase in the employer matching rate is predicted to raise the participation rate by almost 2 percentage points. The point estimate for the 1986 cross-section is somewhat smaller (1.6 percentage points, with a standard error of 1.3 points). We have also replaced the level of the matching rate with a sequence of indicator variables corresponding to matching rates of zero, 0.01–0.25, 0.26–0.50, and so forth. The estimates from such an equation show that moving from a matching rate of zero to one between 0.01 and 0.25 is associated with an increase in the participation rate of 15%. While higher matching-rate categories have higher participation rates still, we cannot reject the null hypothesis that participation rates at all matching rates above zero are the same.

Previous research on the association between matching rates and 401(k) participation and contribution decisions has generated mixed results. Papke (1995) analyzes plan-level data from IRS form 5500 filings, and finds that the effect of changes in the matching rate on the contribution rate is dependent on the level of the matching rate. At low levels of matching, increases in the matching rate appear to raise the share of salary contributed, although at high matching rates, there appears to be a negative effect. Andrews (1992) studies data from the May 1988 CPS, which includes information on whether an individual contributes to a 401(k), what fraction of salary is contributed, and whether or not the plan includes corporate matching. The CPS does not include information on the level of the matching rate. Andrews finds a positive relationship between participation and the presence of matching, but a negative relationship between the contribution rate and the matching rate.

Our survey data include two observations for most firms, so we can *difference* the matching rates and participation rates for the firms, allowing for unobserved plan effects. The resulting estimate is .139 (.116), suggesting that the effect of employer matching on the participation decision is not just the result of interplan heterogeneity.[9] This finding of a positive, but statistically weak, effect of changes in matching rates on changes in participation contrasts with the evidence for a single 401(k) plan in Kusko, Poterba, and Wilcox (1994). The study finds relatively little behavioral response to changes in employer matching rates.

Table 7.7 explores another aspect of 401(k) plan structure: where participants invest their assets. Most plans allow participants at least three investment options, including a stock fund, a bond fund, and a money-market fund. The table shows that 401(k) investors hold roughly half of their total assets in equities, with about 40% of the equity portfolio in *company* stock. The most common investment vehicles are guaranteed investment contracts (GICs), followed by common stock funds. The estimated portfolio shares are probably measured with some error, given our small sample size. They can be compared to VanDerhei's (1992) tabulations of aggregate 401(k) portfolio shares, based on 1989 form 5500 data. Those tabulations show that common stock accounts for 21% of the asset value in 401(k) accounts, while GICs account for 41% of asset holdings. Part of the difference between these results may be due to a shift away from GICs as the prospective returns on these investment vehicles has declined.

One of the central differences between 401(k) plans and traditional DB pension plans is that investment decisions are made by individual plan participants rather than by professional money managers. In more than half of the plans in our sample, participants have full control over the investment of both the employee and employer component of 401(k) contributions. In virtually all of the remaining plans, employees can self-direct their own contributions.

Table 7.8 provides information on another important aspect of 401(k) plan structure: the availability of hardship withdrawals and loans. A recent survey of 401(k) participants by John Hancock Financial Services (1993) suggest that many at least *consider* the possibility of using 401(k) assets for preretirement expenses. While 98% of their sample respondents indicated that they planned to use their 401(k) as a retirement saving vehicle, 27% suggested that they might use the funds for educational expenses, 27% for medical expenses, and 12% for home purchase. Table 7.8 shows that 87% of the 401(k) participants in our survey participate in 401(k)s that allow loans, and that 91% of the plans

---

9. Our data set includes information on the employer matching rate as well as the maximum percentage of salary that is eligible for matching. The cross-section data show that firms that match at a higher rate cap the share of salary they will match at a lower level.

Table 7.7   Financial Assets in 401(k) Plans, 1990 (%)

	Simple Average	Participant-Weighted Average
Equity mutual funds	19	30
Company stock	24	22
Guaranteed investment contracts	36	29
Money market funds	7	4
Bonds (government and other)	7	7
Other	7	8

Source: Authors' tabulation of results from initial "long form" survey, based on a total of thirty-three responses.

Table 7.8   Loans and Hardship Withdrawal Provisions

	Simple Average	Participant-Weighted Average
Plans with loan provisions (%)	70	87
Hardship withdrawal provisions (%)		
Employee contributions	92	91
Employer contributions	61	69
Definitions of hardship withdrawal (%)		
Major medical expenses	93	95
Family education	93	100
House purchase/renovation	97	100
Layoff	14	3
Divorce	10	2
Immediate unplanned financial need	34	29
Number of outstanding loans/participant	0.32	0.14
Hardship withdrawal claims/participant	0.11	0.04

Source: Authors' tabulation of results from initial "long form" survey, based on a total of thirty-three responses.

allow hardship withdrawal of employee contributions. A smaller share of the plans, 61%, allow employees to make hardship withdrawals of *employer* contributions.

Table 7.8 also reports information on the types of hardship that qualify for withdrawals at various plans. Virtually all of the plans consider medical expenses, home purchase, and family education as acceptable justifications for withdrawal. Many fewer plans consider divorce and layoff in this category. There is some evidence that smaller plans are more generous in their definition of hardship withdrawals. One question about 401(k)s that may become increasingly important in the future is whether the current 401(k) contributors will withdraw their funds before retirement, or instead allow the funds to build and to support them in old age. Since the buildup of assets in these plans is a recent phenomenon, resolving this issue must await further experience with 401(k)s.

7.5   Antidiscrimination Rules and 401(k) Plans

One of the important advantages of 401(k) plans over traditional DC pension plans is that they permit different employees to contribute different amounts to the plan. To avoid the possibility that tax-deferred saving plans with employer matching could be used to channel additional compensation to selected groups of employees, with tax subsidy, Congress has enacted a set of *nondiscrimination tests* that 401(k) plans must satisfy. These regulations restrict the share of each year's contributions to 401(k) plans that can be made by "highly compensated employees." Analogous rules apply to DB plans and other types of retirement and benefit programs.

Until 1986, the average percentage of salary deferred by the highest-paid one-third of the participant group could not exceed the greater of (1) 150% of the average deferral percentage (ADP) for other eligible employees, or (2) the lesser of 250% of ADP for other employees, and the other-employee ADP plus 3%. This was known as the "1/3, 2/3 test." TRA86 limited the tax deferral benefits that highly compensated employees could receive. First, it reduced the maximum elective pretax contribution limit from $30,000 to $7,000. Second, TRA86 changed the changed the structure of antidiscrimination provisions and added specific 401(k) nondiscrimination tests to the general rules prohibiting discrimination in contributions and benefits.

TRA86 also introduced what became known as "the ADP test." The test required that the ADP deferred by highly compensated employees could not be more than (1) 125% of the ADP for all other eligible employees, or (2) the lesser of twice the ADP for all other employees, or the ADP for all other employees plus two percentage points.[10] For example, if the ADP of the highly compensated group is 6%, and the ADP for the non–highly compensated group is 4%, the plan would pass the test because it satisfies the second set of criteria. If the ADP for the highly compensated group were 6.5%, the plan would fail. Even though under criteria 2 6.5% is less than twice 4%, it is more than two percentage points higher than the ADP for non–highly compensated workers. TRA86 also added a second test, the actual contribution percentage (ACP) test, which applies a similar set of restrictions to the combined employee after-tax and employer contributions to the plan.

If a 401(k) plan fails to satisfy either or both of the ADP and ACP tests, the firm can either make additional contributions on behalf of lower-paid employees, so-called helper contributions, or restrict contributions by highly compensated employees. Helper contributions include qualified, nonelective employer contributions and qualified matching contributions. As a result of these contributions, the stated matching rate in some 401(k) plans is a lower bound on

---

10. TRA86 defined highly compensated employees as those who were more than 5% owners, officers who earn more than $45,000 per year, employees who earn more than $75,000, and employees who earn more than $50,000 and are in the top 20% of paid employees.

the *effective* matching rate for participants outside the highly compensated group.

Table 7.9 provides information on how the antidiscrimination rules affect 401(k) plans in our sample. The first question we asked was whether the plan was forced to limit or return contributions by high-wage employees. Only 15% of the plans responded affirmatively, and only 3% of the participants were at these firms. Three percent of the plans reported making additional contributions for low-wage employees.

Parallel evidence on the importance of ADP testing is found in the Massachusetts Mutual Life Insurance (1991) survey of 401(k) plans. This survey found that 81% of plans passed the ADP test without any correction such as helper contributions. The most important difference between plans that passed and those that did not initially pass the ADP test was the participation rate of non–highly compensated employees: 70% at firms that passed, 57% at firms that required correction. The evidence from the current study, and that from the Massachusetts Mutual (1991) survey, contrasts with the findings of an earlier Buck Consultants (1989) survey, and the Hewitt Associates (1991) survey. The former found that, for the 1988 plan year, only 60% of the surveyed plans

Table 7.9   Antidiscrimination Rules and 401(k) Plans

	Percentage of Plans Sample	Percentage of Participants Sample
Plans that returned high-wage employee contributions in 1990	15	3
Plans that made additional contributions for low-wage workers in 1990	3	0
Plan average employees in low-wage group		
1986	76	51
1990	76	55
Plan average of employees in high-wage group		
1986	24	49
1990	21	45
Actual deferral percentages		
Low-wage group, 1986	4.0	4.1
Low-wage group, 1990	5.0[a]	5.8[a]
High-wage group, 1986	5.1	5.6
High-wage group, 1990	6.0[a]	6.8[a]
All workers, 1986	4.5	4.5
All workers, 1990	5.6[a]	7.4[a]
Salary breakpoint for 1/3, 2/3 test	$38,800	$47,100

Source: Authors' tabulation of survey results.

[a]Results are based on a total of forty-three responses to both the first- and second-round surveys; others are based on thirty-three responses to the first-round survey only.

passed the ADP test without corrective action, and the Hewitt (1991) survey found that 60% of plans needed some adjustment to pass the nondiscrimination test. While the difference between surveys could reflect changes in the overall difficulty of complying with ADP rules through time, this does not appear to be a sufficient explanation for the differences. This issue requires further investigation.

The relative infrequency with which these constraints bind does not imply that high- and low-wage employees are contributing equal shares of their compensation. Table 7.9 shows the actual deferral percentages for workers categorized in the high- and low-wage groups. The participant weighted-average ADP for the high-wage group is 6.8% in 1990, compared with 5.8% for the low-wage group. The ratio of these ADPs is very close to the 125% constraint value described above. One important issue that our results raise is whether the positive "externalities" received by highly compensated employees when their lower-income counterparts contribute to a 401(k) plan are a key factor in the drive by employers to encourage widespread participation in 401(k) plans.

7.6   Conclusion

This paper reports the preliminary findings from a new survey of firms that provide 401(k) plans for their employees. Our results do not support the view that 401(k) plans replaced preexisting DB pension plans at firms that adopted 401(k)s in the mid-1980s. None of the firms in our data sample reported substituting a 401(k) plan for a DB plan. Several firms, however, reported replacing previous thrift or profit-sharing plans with the 401(k) plan, presumably because 401(k)s provided more attractive opportunities for employees to defer taxable income.

Our survey results also provide new evidence on patterns of 401(k) participation. We collected data on 401(k) participation rates in 1986 and 1990, and found very little variation in these rates across this four-year period. This pattern of stability confirms other findings, based on data for individual contributors to 401(k) plans, that suggest that 401(k) participants are not making marginal decisions of whether to contribute to the plan in a given month, or even year, but rather make long-term commitments. We explore the link between corporate matching rates and 401(k) participation rates, and find evidence of a statistically significant, but substantively small, positive relationship. The predicted effect of a 50% employer matching rate is only a 10% increase in participation, which suggests that other factors, such as employer encouragement or a desire to take advantage of tax-deferral schemes, must explain the high overall participation rate in 401(k) plans.

References

Andrews, Emily S. 1992. The Growth and Distribution of 401(k) Plans. In *Trends in Pensions, 1992,* ed. John A. Turner and Daniel J. Beller. Washington, DC: Government Printing Office.

Beller, Daniel J., and Helen H. Lawrence. 1992. Trends in Private Pension Plan Coverage. In *Trends in Pensions, 1992,* ed. John A. Turner and Daniel J. Beller. Washington, DC: Government Printing Office.

Bernheim, B. Douglas, and John B. Shoven. 1988. Pension Funding and Saving. In *Pensions in the U.S. Economy,* ed. Zvi Bodie, John B. Shoven, and David A. Wise. Chicago: University of Chicago Press.

Buck Consultants. 1989. *Current 401(k) Plan Practices: A Survey Report.* Secaucus, NJ: Buck Consultants.

Chang, Angela. 1991. Explanations for the Trend Away from Defined Benefit Pension Plans. Congressional Research Service Report 91-647 EPW. Washington, DC.

———. 1993. Sensitivity of Pension Contributions to Taxes. Economics Department, Massachusetts Institute of Technology. Mimeo.

Clark, Robert L. 1987. Increased Use of Defined Contribution Plans. Report to the U.S. Department of Labor.

Hewitt Associates. 1991. *401(k) Plan Design and Administration, 1991.* Lincolnshire, IL: Hewitt Associates.

John Hancock Financial Services. 1993. *Insights into Participant Behavior: Defined Contribution Plan Survey.* Boston: John Hancock.

Kruse, Douglas L. 1995. Pension Substitution in the 1980s: Why the Shift toward Defined-Contribution? *Industrial Relations* 34 (2): 218–41.

Kusko, Andrea L., James M. Poterba, and David W. Wilcox. 1994. Employee Decisions with Respect to 401(k) Plans: Evidence from Individual-Level Data. NBER Working Paper no. 4635. Cambridge, MA: National Bureau of Economic Research.

Massachusetts Mutual Life Insurance Company. 1991. *401(k) Survey Report.* Springfield: Massachusetts Mutual Life Insurance.

Papke, Leslie. 1995. Participation in and Contributions to 401(k) Plans: Evidence from Plan Data. *Journal of Human Resources* 30(2): 311–25.

Poterba, James M., Steven F. Venti, and David A. Wise. 1994. 401(k) Plans and Tax-Deferred Saving. In *Studies in the Economics of Aging,* ed. David A. Wise. Chicago: University of Chicago Press.

———. 1995. Do 401(k) Contributions Crowd Out Other Private Saving? *Journal of Public Economics* 58 (September): 1–32.

Shefrin, Hersh M., and Richard H. Thaler. 1988. The Behavioral Life-Cycle Hypothesis. *Economic Inquiry* 26:609–43.

Silverman, Celia. 1993. Pension Evolution in a Changing Economy. EBRI Issue Brief 141. Washington, DC: Employee Benefit Research Institute.

U.S. Department of Labor. 1993. *Private Pension Plan Bulletin.* Washington, DC: U.S. Department of Labor, Office of Research and Economic Analysis.

U.S. General Accounting Office (GAO). 1988a. *401(k) Plans: Incidence, Provisions, and Benefits.* Washington, DC: General Accounting Office.

———. 1988b. *401(k) Plans: Participation and Deferral Rates by Plan Features and Other Information.* Washington, DC: General Accounting Office.

VanDerhei, Jack. 1992. New Evidence That Employees Choose Conservative Investments for Their Retirement Funds. *Employee Benefit Notes* 13 (February): 1–3.

Comment   Richard Thaler

There is a lot for a behavioral economist to like about this paper. First of all, it provides new data, always welcome. Second, it highlights a little-discussed feature of 401(k) saving plans, namely, that once people get started they tend to keep contributing. I have two sorts of comments: the first concerning the survey methods used, the other regarding the best conceptual framework for thinking about the role of 401(k)s.

Economists are generally reluctant to collect their own data through surveys, as the authors of this paper have done. There seem to be two reasons for this. First there is what we might call the *machine-readable illusion of validity*. Most economists seem to feel that numbers are not real unless they are on computer tape and someone else has taken care of putting them there. So the Panel Survey of Income Dynamics (PSID) and the census data are "hard," but surveys collected personally are "soft." People who have looked carefully at the PSID are likely to conclude that both data sources are a mixed bag, but it is time we all agreed that some data is better than none. The second reason why economists don't like to collect their own data is well illustrated by this paper—it is a pain in the neck! These authors exerted a lot of effort to survey firms about their pension plans, only to be frustrated by a very low response rate. Those economists who might have been tempted to collect their own data will hardly find this team's experience comforting. However, before we give up on surveys again, I think it is important to think about why the response rate was so low. In this case my main guess is that the survey instrument was simply too long. With the benefit of hindsight, I think that more would have been learned from the combination of a shorter instrument and a higher response rate. Other potential surveyors should take note.

My other comments are about the general question of evaluating programs such as 401(k)s as a vehicle for increasing the rate of private saving. Elsewhere (Thaler 1990, 1994) I have stressed that when evaluating a savings program we need to take a long-term perspective. It seems ironic to have to make this point, since saving is, per se, about the future. However, many authors have continued to stress essentially short-run factors when discussing IRAs, 401(k)s, and the like. The short-run questions are, where did the money come from? and do these programs represent "new" saving? The question I think we need to address is, over the next few decades, will the existence of such programs increase the rate of capital accumulation by U.S. households? The magnitude of the long-run increase in saving is determined by several behavioral factors. In the case of 401(k)s I would like to emphasize three phenomena: initiation (how

Richard Thaler is professor of behavioral science and economics at the Graduate School of Business, University of Chicago, and a research associate of the National Bureau of Economic Research.

people get started), leakage (does the money stay put), and persistence (do people keep putting more money in).

What determines whether an employee will start contributing to a 401(k) plan? Two economic factors are important, and are correctly stressed in this paper: taxes and matching. Contributions and accumulations are tax free, creating an obvious incentive to participate, and many firms actually match employees' contributions in whole or in part. As Papke, Petersen, and Poterba show, employees seem to be sensitive to this matching provision. The higher the matching rate, the higher the participation rate. While these factors are important, there are also behavioral factors that determine how many employees contribute. (1) Peer pressure: if contributing to the 401(k) is considered the "smart thing to do," more employees will do so. A high matching rate undoubtedly helps produce this peer pressure. (2) Salience: firms may engage in drives to encourage employees to participate (in part because of the antidiscrimination rules). Just as advertising may have helped sell IRAs, a push within the firm may also help, especially for lower-income workers who have many pressing demands on their paychecks. (3) Ease of joining: economists think of saving as a rational calculation, but we all know that inertia matters in our own daily lives. If contributing to a saving plan is made easy, more people will do it. Of course this is just reducing a transactions cost, but my point is that eliminating a seemingly trivial one-time cost, such as going to a bank and setting up an IRA account (trivial in comparison to the costs of an underfunded retirement), may play an important role. (4) Payroll deductions: from a psychological perspective, the least painful way of saving money is to have it deducted from your paycheck. What you don't see doesn't hurt to give up.

Getting the money into a savings vehicle is just the first step. For people to successfully save for retirement, as opposed to next month's splurge, the money has to stay invested. In the life-cycle framework it makes no difference where wealth sits. Households simply consume the annuity value of the wealth in every period. However, the evidence suggests that the marginal propensity to consume differs across various mental accounts (Shefrin and Thaler 1988). In particular, people are much more likely to spend from liquid assets such as savings accounts than they are from money coded as retirement savings, for example, IRAs and 401(k)s. (For clear evidence of this, see Gale and Scholz 1994.) In this sense, 401(k)s are savings repositories that exhibit low *leakage*.

The third factor in determining long-term saving is what might be termed persistence. Contributing to a pension plan for a year is good, but contributing for many years is much better. What we would like to know is something like a transition probability: if a worker contributes to a 401(k) in year t, what is the chance that he or she will contribute again in year $t + 1$? To answer this question properly, one needs panel microdata (another survey!). However, the data presented here give a strong suggestion that for 401(k)s the persistence rate is quite high because the percentage of employees who contribute is remarkably stable over time. IRA contributors also appear to display remarkable persistence, although this has not been studied carefully either. I believe that the issue of persistence of contributions deserves more study.

References

Gale, William G., and John Karl Scholz. 1994. IRAs and Household Savings. *American Economic Review* 84 (December): 1233–60.
Shefrin, Hersh M., and Richard H. Thaler. 1988. The Behavioral Life-Cycle Hypothesis. *Economic Inquiry* 26 (October): 609–43.
Thaler, Richard H. 1990. Saving, Fungibility, and Mental Accounts. *Journal of Economic Perspectives* 4 (winter): 193–205.
———. 1994. Psychology and Savings Policies. *American Economic Review: Papers and Proceedings* 84 (May): 186–92.

8   Is Housing Wealth a Sideshow?

Jonathan S. Skinner

8.1   Introduction

Housing prices rose by 18% in real terms during the 1970s, delivering a $700 billion windfall to homeowners. Housing prices are projected to decline by as much as 47% during the next few decades (Mankiw and Weil 1989), delivering a potential loss of $3 trillion to the next generation of homeowners. These changes certainly affect the accounting wealth of households, but do they really affect the welfare of households? More to the point, will the prospect of future housing-price downturns tarnish the golden years of retirement for the aging baby-boom generation?

In the conventional life-cycle model, a large decline in housing prices should have a strong impact on life-cycle wealth and hence on retirement consumption and welfare. But there is growing empirical evidence that housing wealth changes don't influence consumption and saving behavior. First, Venti and Wise (1991) showed that the annuitized value of housing wealth for the median homeowner is small compared with Social Security and pension wealth, so that a 47% decline in housing wealth would have only minor effects on living standards of the median homeowning retiree. Second, only rarely do the elderly spend down their housing equity at retirement. Merrill (1984) and Venti and Wise (1990) found that, when the elderly move, they are as likely to move into a larger house as a smaller house. Given the scarcity of reverse mortgages, this evidence suggests that the elderly either could not, or did not, tap into the housing windfalls from the boom years of the 1970s. Finally, Skin-

Jonathan S. Skinner is professor of economics at Dartmouth College and a research associate of the National Bureau of Economic Research.

The author is indebted to Don Fullerton, John Sabelhaus, John Shoven, David Weil, Stephen Zeldes, and seminar participants at the NBER conference on aging for very helpful comments, and to Haralabos Gakidis for outstanding research assistance. Funding from the National Institute on Aging is gratefully acknowledged.

ner (1989) and Levin (1992) found little evidence that changes in housing wealth among homeowners generated offsetting saving responses. Housing prices may decline by 47%, but if younger homeowners don't save more in response to the price decline, and if retired homeowners don't touch their housing equity, then the price change will have little impact on overall welfare. In short, trends and fluctuations in house prices and housing equity would be just a sideshow.[1]

This paper reconsiders the question of whether housing wealth is a sideshow. I address this question in three general models. The first is the orthodox certainty life-cycle model with the possibility of moving costs and the lack of well-functioning reverse mortgages. That is, one explanation for why housing wealth appears to be a sideshow is simply the presence of moving costs and the inability to tap into housing equity. The second model generalizes the life-cycle model to include a simple bequest motive or the existence of mental-accounting saving behavior (Shefrin and Thaler 1988). In the mental-accounting behavioral approach to saving, for example, housing wealth is "nonfungible" (Levin 1992); therefore changes in housing wealth in this model could have little impact on saving or lifetime welfare.

Finally, the third model considers how uncertainty about retirement income or out-of-pocket health expenses determines the effect of housing wealth on consumption and saving. In the precautionary approach, owner-occupied housing is used as a form of insurance; should the "bad" income or medical draw occur at retirement, housing equity is cashed out, both because of the need for additional cash and because the demand for housing services has declined.

Each of these three models holds different predictions for two key behavioral parameters: (1) What is the marginal propensity to consume housing windfalls for existing (younger) homeowners? and (2) What is the propensity to consume out of housing wealth at retirement for older homeowners? I test each of these hypotheses, as well as the importance of potential housing wealth changes in consumption decisions, using data on saving and housing wealth from the 1989 wave of the Panel Study of Income Dynamics (PSID) and aggregate time-series evidence.

The first behavioral parameter, whether people consume housing windfalls while they are young, is tested using two approaches: the Euler equation approach using aggregate time-series data, and quantile saving regressions using panel microeconomics data. For the aggregate data, the estimated effects are large and quantitatively important, swamping any wealth effects from the stock market. The panel data suggests a more modest effect, with a reduction in median younger homeowner saving of 1–2 cents for every $1 increase in housing wealth, an amount consistent with precautionary saving and life-cycle models.

1. With apologies to Morck, Shleifer, and Vishny (1990).

In the life-cycle model, the housing windfall is used in part to finance retirement consumption. However, the PSID suggests that few retirees actually draw down their housing wealth in any given year (also see Sheiner and Weil 1992; Ai et al. 1990). For those who do "cash out," it is often the consequence of changes in family composition such as widowhood, or because of adverse events such as health declines. Using saving data constructed from the 1984 and 1989 PSID wealth data, I estimate that for those who tap into housing equity, roughly 73% of the proceeds have been spent within four years.

Neither the standard life-cycle model with moving costs and financial constraints, nor the mental-accounting model or bequest model can adequately explain both empirical phenomena. In the life-cycle model, if housing windfalls are reflected in higher consumption while young, there is less nonhousing wealth to finance consumption at retirement. Hence there must be some way to tap into housing equity while retired, to supplement the depleted nonhousing wealth. In the mental-accounting model, housing wealth is nonfungible (i.e., a sideshow) that is consciously set aside, so that windfalls are unlikely to be spent while the homeowner is young. In the bequest model, the housing windfall is spent while young: households simply use the money that had been set aside for their inheritance. In turn, these households would bequeath at death their now more valuable house. The problem with this explanation is that few younger households have enough liquid wealth to provide for their own retirement, much less hold additional wealth available for bequests.

The precautionary saving model, however, can potentially reconcile both of the empirical findings that homeowners spend down housing windfalls while young, yet do not typically tap into housing windfalls while old. Housing wealth is a form of self-insurance that can be drawn upon in the bad state of the world in which liquid cash is needed and housing demand is low. Housing windfalls therefore reduce the need for other types of precautionary saving, and increase consumption among middle-aged homeowners. Because housing wealth is held as a contingency against future risk, many homeowners will not experience the adverse risk. Therefore in the population of elderly, only a small fraction will be observed to tap into their housing equity. In short, housing wealth is *not* a sideshow, but a key component in insuring against retirement contingencies.

8.2 The Life-Cycle Model with Financial or Moving Constraints

I first consider a very simple two-period life-cycle model. Because the major focus of this paper is on the saving behavior of middle-aged homeowners, and the dissaving behavior of the elderly, I assume that the first period corresponds to "middle age," say between 40 and 60, while the second period corresponds to retirement, between age 60 and 80. The choice of initial housing is ignored; each individual has already purchased a house. Households may change their housing consumption at retirement in the second period, although doing so will entail a psychic moving cost.[2] In considering these results, it should be kept in mind that these results focus on the roughly 75% of households who are homeowners before retirement, and ignores the behavior of renters who may purchase houses once they retire (e.g., Venti and Wise 1989; see also Sheiner 1989).

Let expected utility be written

$$(1) \qquad EU = U(C_1, h_1) + \frac{1}{1 + \delta} E[U(C_2, h_2) + \lambda m],$$

where C_i is consumption and h_i housing in period i; δ the time preference rate; and E the expectations operator. The endogenous indicator variable λ is equal to one if the individual moves, and zero otherwise. The variable m is the psychic cost of moving. Venti and Wise (1990), for example, estimate that such moving costs are sufficiently high to prevent most elderly families from moving, even when their housing equity diverges from their "desired" amount. To evaluate the magnitude, as well as the direction, of changes in consumption, I assume an isoelastic strongly separable utility function

$$(2) \qquad U(C_i, h_i) = \frac{C_i^{1-\gamma}}{1-\gamma} + \mu \frac{h_i^{1-\gamma}}{1-\gamma}.$$

The budget constraint is written

$$(3) \quad C_1 + \rho_1 h_1 + \frac{C_2 + \rho_2 h_2}{1 + r} = Y_1 + \rho_1 h_1^*$$

$$+ \frac{Y_2 + [\lambda(h_1^* - h_2^*) P + \rho_2 h_2^*]}{1 + r} + \frac{v h_2^* P}{(1 + r)^2},$$

where r is the net rate of return, Y_i are labor earnings in period 1 and retirement income in period 2, ρ_i is the user cost of housing (and the implicit return on housing as an investment, given that taxes are ignored), and P is the price of a unit of housing in the second and subsequent periods; families are assumed to own the house in full at the beginning of period 1. Since everyone is initially a homeowner, consumed housing services, h_1, is equal to owned housing assets h_1^*. In the second period, households may either move to a smaller house but remain owner-occupiers ($h_1^* > h_2^* = h_2$), or simply sell their house and become renters ($h_2 > 0$, $h_2^* = 0$). The house is sold at the end of the second period.

There are two potential restrictions that prevent the individual from attaining the unconstrained optimum. The first is that moving costs m are sufficiently high that the household does not move. That is, maximum lifetime utility corresponds to the (discrete) choice between $EU^*(\lambda = 0)$, in which no move takes

2. To simplify the model, I ignore the monetary costs of moving.

place but $h_2 = h_2^* = h_1^*$, and $EU^{**}(\lambda = 1)$, in which the move occurs, the cost m is incurred, but the household is then free to choose a new level of housing services. Rather than focus on the explicit solution for whether the household moves or not, I will consider two cases in the analysis below. One is the case where few households move, because moving costs are high, or because neither housing prices P nor second-period income Y_2 have unexpectedly changed by enough to make a move necessary. The second general case is one in which housing prices or second-period income have fluctuated by so much that most households are willing to undergo the moving costs m to choose a new level of housing services.

Moving costs may restrict the ability of the elderly to get access to their home equity. The absence of reverse mortgages is another potential constraint. In a reverse mortgage, the bank supplements income of the "housing-rich" elderly, in return for title to the house at death. A 100% reverse annuity implies $v = 1$, while the absence of a reverse annuity implies $v = 0$ (if v is 0.8, for example, only 80% of the housing equity would be eligible for a reverse mortgage). To the extent that perfect reverse mortgages do not exist, perhaps because of self-selection problems (so that $v < 1$) or because $h_2^* > 0$, there will always be "accidental" bequests of housing equity that yield no utility in this model.

The budget constraint is simplified by subtracting ρh_1^* from both sides of equation 3; when $\lambda = 0$, $\rho_2 h_2^*$ can also be subtracted from both sides. When the housing asset yields a normal return r, $P = \rho_2(1 + r)/r$, and equation 3 is rewritten

$$(4) \qquad C_1 + \frac{C_2 + \lambda \rho_2 h_2}{1 + r} = Y_1 + \frac{Y_2}{1 + r} + \frac{P}{(1 + r)^2}[\lambda(1 + r)\, h_1^*$$

$$+ \, h_2^*(v - \lambda)].$$

Maximization of equation 1 subject to 4 yields the solution

$$(5) \qquad C_1 = \frac{L(v, \lambda)}{K(\lambda)},$$

where the value of lifetime resources L and the denominator K are written

$$(6) \qquad L(v, \lambda) = Y_1 + \frac{Y_2}{1 + r} + \frac{P}{(1 + r)^2}[\lambda(1 + r)h_1^* + h_2^*(v - \lambda)]$$

and

$$(7) \qquad K(\lambda) = 1 + \left[\frac{1 + r}{1 + \delta}\right]^{1/\gamma}\left[1 + \lambda\left(\frac{\rho_2}{\mu}\right)^{-1/\gamma}\rho_2\right](1 + r)^{-1}.$$

To analyze how a change in the price of housing P affects consumption and saving, one must first make some assumptions about *why* the price of housing has risen. The simplest approach is to assume that ρ_2 has increased, perhaps because of demographic effects of population growth on a fixed supply of land. Then

$$
(8) \quad \frac{dC_1}{dP} = \frac{\dfrac{dC_1}{d\rho_2}}{\dfrac{dP}{d\rho_2}} = \frac{\lambda h_1^*(1 + r)\ (v - \lambda)\ h_2^*}{(1 + r)^2\ K(\lambda)} - \frac{C_1}{K(\lambda)}\frac{dK(\lambda)}{dP}.
$$

To develop the intuition of the model, consider the case in which utility is log-linear ($\gamma = 1$), in which case ρ_2 will not affect the denominator K, so that the second term on the right-hand side of equation 8 can be ignored. Then the change in C_1 is just the present value of the discounted change in housing prices, depending on whether the individual moves, or whether reverse mortgages exist. This derivative holds only when the change in ρ_2, and hence in P, does not precipitate a move (i.e., the change in P induces a switch from $\lambda = 0$ to $\lambda = 1$), and conversely.

Table 8.1 presents numerical calculations for a combination of hypothetical cases depending on the value of λ and v, under the more empirically relevant case in which γ is equal to three. A number of other assumptions were also made about the magnitude of the coefficients. For example, I assume that each period lasts for twenty years, first-period income is $40,000, and second period income $20,000. The share of housing services is assumed to be 25% of income in the first period, so that normalizing $\rho = 1$ yields housing services $h_1 = 10,000$. The annual interest rate r and time preference rate δ were assumed to be 3%, which corresponds to 0.806 accumulated over twenty years. Below, I consider each of the hypothetical cases.

Table 8.1   The Marginal Propensity to Consume from Housing Wealth and Housing Equity Reductions: Four Cases in the Life-Cycle Model

Moving Costs	Reverse Annuities	MPC from Housing Wealth[a]	Reduction in Housing Equity (annualized)[b]
No moving costs ($m = 0, \lambda = 1$)	Perfect markets ($v = 1$)	0.025	−0.05
No moving costs ($m = 0, \lambda = 1$)	Nonexistent markets ($v = 0$)	0.025	−0.05
Large moving costs ($m > 0, \lambda = 0$)	Perfect markets ($v = 1$)	0.014	−0.05
Large moving costs ($m > 0, \lambda = 0$)	Nonexistent markets ($v = 0$)	0	0

[a]The annual marginal propensity to consume (MPC) in the first period from a $1 change in the value of housing wealth.

[b]The average implied fractional change in housing windfalls during the second retirement period. In other words, a value of −0.05 means that, for every dollar in housing windfalls, the life-cycle household will reduce equity at the rate of 5 cents per year, so that by the end of the twenty-year period, there is no equity remaining.

No Moving Costs, Perfect Reverse Mortgages

Consider first the standard life-cycle model with perfect reverse annuity markets and with small or nonexistent moving costs, so that homeowners can both tap into home equity at retirement and costlessly adjust the size of their house. Then as table 8.1 indicates, the marginal propensity to consume out of a $1 windfall in housing wealth is only 2.5 cents.[3] The results are not particularly sensitive to the Arrow-Pratt measure of risk aversion, the interest rate, or the time preference rate; it is essentially a wealth effect that depends on the ratio of housing wealth to overall lifetime wealth. There are two reasons why the impact is so small. The first is that the shift in the value of the asset is spread over a large number of years, so the change in the flow of consumption in any given year will be relatively small. More importantly, though, the housing capital gains are discounted back from the time when the homeowner actually *sells* the house. Table 8.1 also reports the annual (percentage) reduction in housing equity during the second period. The conventional life-cycle model implies an active reduction of housing equity at retirement, either by moving to a rental unit or by reverse mortgage arrangements. That is, if housing prices rise while people are young, life-cycle homeowners save less for retirement in other forms. To finance retirement consumption, they cash out the now increased housing wealth. No rational life-cycle homeowner dies with any housing equity remaining. Table 8.1 reports an annual decline of 5% in housing equity; this is the yearly deaccumulation of housing stock that insures housing equity is exhausted at the end of the twenty-year second period.

No Moving Costs, Absence of Reverse Mortgages

The life-cycle estimates above assume very well functioning markets for reverse mortgages. Will the assumption that reverse mortgages do not exist make housing wealth a sideshow? The answer is no. If moving costs are sufficiently low so that every homeowner can move, changes in housing prices will exert an effect both on consumption while young and dissaving while old that is equivalent to the life-cycle model with perfect reverse mortgage markets. The reason is that the ability to move, and the ability to obtain reverse mortgages, are substitute methods for obtaining housing equity. As shown in table 8.1, households also reduce their housing equity at an annual rate of 5% to insure that equity is exhausted by the end of the twenty-year period.

Large Moving Costs, Perfect Reverse Mortgages

Suppose next that the costs of moving are recognized, so that few elderly choose to change their housing wealth. Suppose also that reverse mortgage markets function very efficiently, so that $v = 1$. Once again, housing wealth is not a sideshow. While individuals do not move during the second period, they can extract all of the housing equity through reverse mortgages, so they do not

---

3. This is the annuitized annual flow of consumption over the twenty-year period.

die with any remaining housing equity. Because they cannot adjust the level of housing consumption in the second period, they cannot spend down their housing wealth to the same extent, so the marginal propensity to consume from housing wealth in the first period is somewhat less, 1.4 cents, relative to the two cases considered above. There is still complete deaccumulation of housing windfalls during the second period through the use of reverse mortgages.

Large Moving Costs, Absence of Reverse Mortgages

When both moving costs are large and financial barriers exist, housing wealth *is* a sideshow, in that the price of housing has no effect on saving or consumption decisions. Homeowners find it difficult to extract housing wealth in the second period, either because reverse mortgages are not available, or because moving costs are excessively high. If they cannot extract housing equity while old, they will not spend housing windfalls while young. Because housing equity is held until death, it becomes an unintended bequest yielding no value to the (life-cycle) consumer. Table 8.1 reports that the marginal propensity to consume from housing wealth while young is zero, and net deaccumulation of housing wealth while old is zero.

In sum, the prediction of the life-cycle model is that household wealth is treated in one of two ways: either households spend housing windfalls while young and draw down housing equity to tap into housing windfalls while retired, or they spend windfalls neither while young nor while old.

8.3   Mental Accounting and Bequest Motives

More general models of saving can also imply that housing wealth is a sideshow. If families maintain "mental accounts" in the sense of Shefrin and Thaler (1988) and Thaler (1990), individuals control their spending impulses by creating "nonfungible" types of assets that are either not spent or, if spent, are saved for emergencies. Levin (1992), for example, suggests that the marginal propensity to consume out of housing wealth is low for those families near retirement. Hence an increase in housing wealth is not predicted to cause households to increase consumption. There are two predictions of the mental-accounting model. The first is that windfall housing gains will not be reflected in higher consumption levels while young; in other words, the marginal propensity to consume from housing wealth is predicted to be zero for those who are not yet retired. The second prediction is that housing windfalls will be spent when the retired households are in financial distress, and only after other, more liquid assets are spent (Levin 1992).[4]

Another approach is to consider how the presence of a bequest motive might

---

4. This scenario is also consistent with a standard life-cycle model in which tax-preferred assets with the ability to step up the basis at death—that is, housing—are held longest, since they are most valuable as bequests.

affect predictions for how housing windfalls will affect consumption and saving. There are two types of bequest models; one in which bequests simply yield utility or value, and the other in which the utility of one's descendants enters one's own utility function. In the former case, housing windfalls would be consumed while young, with nonhousing assets previously earmarked for bequests devoted instead to financing retirement consumption, and the extra housing equity used for the bequest. In this scenario, one might observe a positive marginal propensity to consume housing wealth while young, with little drawdown of housing equity while old. Such a model presumes that there is enough nonhousing wealth, previously targeted for bequests, to provide liquidity for the younger homeowner with housing windfalls. Empirical data suggest that median households near retirement hold only $6,600 in liquid wealth (Venti and Wise 1991). If one presumes that most of this wealth will be devoted to maintaining consumption during retirement, there would be little remaining for bequests.[5] In other words, few families have the financial resources (and bequests) to make this story plausible.

The latter approach to bequests, that parents account for their children's utility functions, could imply that housing wealth would be a sideshow. If housing prices rise, parents may choose to pass along the windfall to their children so the next generation might afford the now more expensive housing. In other words, the dynastic bequest motive could neutralize the impact of housing wealth changes on consumption and saving.

8.4   The Precautionary Saving Model

To this point, the life-cycle model made the strong assumption of perfect certainty: households know future disposable income levels, and plan accordingly. The risk of shocks to income, health status, or widowhood during retirement could affect family saving and consumption decisions prior to and during retirement.[6] To capture the inherent uncertainty associated with retirement, consider a simple model in which there is a second-period good state, in which health and income remain favorable, and a bad state, in which a spouse dies, out-of-pocket medical expenses jump, or inflation erodes nominal pension payments. In the good state, the family does not sell the house, and the moving cost m is not incurred. In the bad state, the change in circumstances is sufficiently large that it is optimal to sell the house and incur the psychic moving cost m. Once the house is sold, the proceeds can be used to finance consumption or medical costs. Note that in this model, the possibility of a future bad

---

5. Of course, the possibility remains that the $6,600 represents liquid wealth after families have already spent largely from the housing windfalls of the 1970s. There is little evidence that the amount of liquid wealth has fallen dramatically since the 1960s (Hubbard, Skinner, and Zeldes 1995).

6. See Deaton (1992), Carroll (1991), Carroll and Samwick (1992), Caballero (1991), Skinner (1988), and Zeldes (1989) for a fuller discussion of the precautionary saving approach.

state of the world can strongly affect consumption and saving plans while young, even if in fact the bad state does not occur.

The original utility function in equation 1 is rewritten

$$(9) \qquad EU = U(C_1, h_1) + \frac{[\pi U(C_2^g, h_2^g) + (1 - \pi) U(C_2^b, h_2^b)]}{1 + \delta},$$

where π is the probability of the good state, denoted by superscript g, and $(1 - \pi)$ the probability of the bad state, denoted by b. It is convenient, but not crucial, to assume that reverse mortgage markets are nonexistent. As noted above, in the good state the homeowner does not move, so that consumed (and owned) housing in the second period is simply h_1^*. In the bad state, the homeowner moves, say because second-period disposable income Y_2 has declined. In this bad state, the individual has the opportunity to reoptimize with respect to housing consumed (and owned) in the second period.[7]

Consumption in each state is

$$(10) \qquad C_2^g = S(1 + r) + Y_2^g,$$

and

$$(11) \qquad C_2^b = S(1 + r) + Y_2^b + h_1^*P - \rho_2 h_2^b,$$

where S is saving from the first period. That is, the family supplements the low disposable income in the bad state ($Y_2^b < Y_2^g$) by selling the house and using the proceeds either for rent or for nonhousing consumption.

This model can be solved easily for the parameters used in the certainty model above, but with the assumption that in the good state, which occurs 75% of the time, disposable income net of medical expenses Y_2 equals $25,833, while in the bad state, occurring 25% of the time, Y_2 equals $2,500 (on average, Y_2 is $20,000, as in the certainty model above). Given this assumption, the marginal propensity to consume from housing wealth is calculated to be 1.0 cents per dollar. The reason why the marginal propensity is relatively large is that a decline in housing wealth of $1 would imply a $1 fall in consumption during the bad state of the world. And while this bad state occurs only 25% of the time, its impact on saving is magnified by the relatively high marginal utility of consumption in that state.

While the precautionary saving model may resemble the life-cycle model in its implications for the marginal propensity to consume out of housing wealth in period 1, it differs in its prediction for the spending down of housing equity in period 2. Only in the bad state (25% of the time in the example above) does the household sell the house; otherwise there is no downscaling of housing wealth.

Before one can really test whether housing wealth affects saving and con-

7. If the homeowner moves, he or she would be wise to set $h_2^* = 0$, given that reverse mortgages are assumed unavailable. I assume that homeowners do in the simulations below.

sumption, one must first establish that housing wealth is an important component of financial resources at retirement inclusive of Social Security and pension wealth. Results from the PSID suggest that, while the annuity flow of housing is relatively unimportant for the median homeowner in the sample, it is quantitatively large—as much as 50% of money income—for a sizable fraction of lower-income and older retirees. In the sections that follow, I consider three empirical questions. The first is whether the magnitude of housing price changes on consumption and saving are large enough to matter. The second and third are, as noted above, whether families spend housing windfalls, and whether they dip into housing equity at retirement. A negative answer to question one, or to both two and three, would suggest that housing wealth is unimportant in determining the financial status of households at retirement.

8.5   Is Housing Wealth Important in the Financial Security of the Elderly?

Is the magnitude of housing equity large enough to make a difference in retirement consumption? Venti and Wise (1991) suggest that the reverse mortgage could supplement income for the median retired families by only 4–10% of their existing income. That is, even a complete loss in (annuitized) housing equity would have little impact on consumption. These hypothetical cases, however, are for household members aged 65 who expect to remain in the same house until death. As is shown below (and as Venti and Wise also mention), housing equity matters much more for a sizable fraction of the population: those with low income and above age 75.

The 1989 PSID wealth data are used to sample households with heads over age 65 and with reported money income in excess of $2,000. All values are weighted by the 1989 population weights. I calculate the annuity-equivalent value of housing wealth and contrast that with money income of the household.[8] One can therefore infer the potential impact on retirement consumption of a change in housing wealth (holding constant the price of housing services). For example, if a household's housing equity could be annuitized so that it yields 30% of money income, then a 47% slide in housing prices would reduce potential retirement consumption by nearly fifteen percentage points.

The annuitized value of housing is straightforward to calculate for single male or single female homeowners over age 65 by appropriate use of life tables and assuming a real interest rate of 3%. For couples, I assume that the annuity contract corresponds to a payment until the last member of the couple dies.[9]

---

8. This measure is different from the Venti and Wise (1991) calculation. It corresponds to the value of cashing out the house today and placing the money in a (perfect) annuity. By contrast, the Venti and Wise annuity measure corresponds to the present value of the remaining housing equity at death. In their case, the homeowner is allowed to remain in the house until death.

9. I am grateful to Michael Palumbo for letting me use his life tables for these three groups; see Palumbo (1993).

Table 8.2 presents the distribution of annuitized housing wealth (net of mortgage balances), as a percentage of income, by both age and household money income.[10] For example, table 8.2 indicates that 23.86% of families aged 65–74, and with income less than $15,000, hold annuitized values of housing that exceed their money income by 50%. Forty percent of households aged 74 and above, and with money income less than $20,000, hold housing equity that exceeds 50% of money income. Even a 25% decline in housing wealth could potentially reduce the annuitized income stream by at least 12.5% (50 × .25) for a nontrivial fraction of the elderly population.[11]

A somewhat different calculation is to suppose that an individual sells his or her house and moves to smaller rental quarters; how much money is left over from the housing sale to finance current consumption at an annuitized rate? Assume that housing rental return is 6% of the house value, and that the homeowner(s) move into rental property that is worth three-fourths of the original house. So after the house is sold, I set aside the present value of the annuitized rental stream, which in each year is assumed to be 4.5% of the original house value. The importance of the annuitized value of housing wealth that remains is shown in table 8.2 in italics. A substantial fraction of homeowners could still increase their income flow by downsizing their housing wealth. Nearly one-third of households who are over age 74, and whose income is less than $10,000, could increment their money income more than 50% by moving to smaller rental units.

In sum, a change in housing prices may have relatively little effect on the annuitized income flow for the median household, especially among younger groups. However, it could have a large impact among a smaller group of poorer, older households. Furthermore, selling one's house and moving to rental units can—at least potentially—increase money income for a nontrivial percentage of elderly. If housing wealth is at least plausibly important in economic decisions at retirement, then does housing wealth affect saving and consumption behavior? I address this question in the next two sections.

8.6   Do Younger Households Consume Housing Windfalls?

One explanation for the saving slowdown of the 1980s is that housing wealth windfalls stimulated consumption. Capital gains from housing and land are not included in national income and product accounts, so a rise in the price of housing would have had no impact on measured income, but could cause consumption to rise. Thus the declining saving rate (as conventionally measured)

10. Income brackets differ between the two age groups to adjust for lower average income levels among the "old-old." The household's age bracket is determined by the age of the household head.
11. Recall that these numbers establish only the potential for housing wealth to be important. Annuity markets are not sufficiently developed to allow homeowners to extract their wealth at "fair" rates. Also, the presented numbers assume that the price of housing services has not changed as well.

Table 8.2   **The Annuity Value of Housing Wealth Relative to Income, 1989**

	Percentage of Sample	Ratio of Annuitized Housing Wealth to Income			
		Not Homeowner	<20%	20–50%	>50%
Age 65–74, income < $15,000	38.70	36.70	17.27	22.17	23.86
			27.47	*21.06*	*14.77*
Age 65–74, income $15–25,000	24.87	19.50	22.40	41.37	16.73
			42.33	*32.46*	*5.71*
Age 65–74, income > $25,000	36.43	6.62	46.45	38.41	8.52
			73.64	*17.61*	*2.82*
Age 65–74, total	100.0	21.46	29.18	32.86	16.50
			47.74	*22.64*	*8.16*
Age > 74, income < $10,000	46.03	44.58	6.67	10.38	38.37
			8.03	*15.72*	*31.67*
Age > 74, income $10–20,000	26.05	35.89	5.31	18.19	40.61
			8.37	*30.62*	*25.12*
Age > 74, income > $20,000	27.91	17.87	18.10	46.85	17.18
			28.10	*44.30*	*9.72*
Age > 74, total	100.00	34.86	9.51	22.59	33.04
			13.72	*27.58*	*23.83*

Source: Panel Study of Income Dynamics.

Notes: The numbers in roman typeface are the percentage of each age and income group for whom the annuity value of their house is within the given percentage of 1989 household money income. The numbers in italics are the percentage of each age and income group for whom the annuity value of their house minus the annuity value of the assumed cost of the rental housing is within the given percentage of 1989 household money income.

could have been the consequence of increased consumption by homeowners flush with windfall housing gains (Skinner 1994; Munnell and Cook 1991).

There have been two general approaches to testing this hypothesis.[12] First, aggregate linear time-series consumption functions have been estimated, using housing wealth as an independent variable. Bhatia (1987) used housing wealth, and Hendershott and Peek (1989) used tangible assets, to estimate that consumption rose between 4 and 5 cents per dollar of housing equity.

The second approach is to use microeconomic panel data. An important study by Bosworth, Burtless, and Sabelhaus (1991) documented the dramatic decline in household saving during the 1980s using both the Survey of Consumer Finance (SCF) and the Consumer Expenditure Survey (CES). They found that much of the observed decline in saving rates between 1963 and the 1980s (in the case of the SCF) and between 1972–73 and the 1980s (in the case of the CES) occurred among homeowners. For example, using the SCF, the saving rate declined by 6.4% for homeowners between 1963 and 1983–85,

12. See Skinner (1994) for a review of the literature on housing and saving.

but declined by only 0.5% for renters.[13] One problem with their comparisons is that owner-occupied housing is prevalent among older and higher-income families, so that the implicit control group—older families who do not own a house—may not provide a valid comparison, given how little they save.

Skinner (1989) followed a different microeconomic approach by using the panel aspect of the PSID to construct changes in family specific consumption (a weighted sum of consumption components in the PSID), and to regress these changes on income changes and housing price changes, using the Euler approach. Those results suggested that housing price shifts had no effect on consumption.[14]

8.6.1 New Tests Using Aggregate Time-Series Data

Consider first the conventional Euler approach (e.g., Hall 1988; see Deaton 1992) expressing consumption changes as a random walk;

$$\ln C_t - \ln C_{t-1} = \beta x + \varepsilon,$$

where x comprises both factors that should matter (e.g., ex ante interest rates) and factors that, by the logic of intertemporal optimization, should not matter (e.g., lagged income and stock market changes). The variable ε is typically unspecified, but it reflects the change in consumption that reflects new information revealed between time $t - 1$ and time t. The approach below is to measure whether changes in housing wealth between t and $t - 1$ affect ε, and hence consumption choices, conditional on lagged consumption. One cannot place strong structural interpretations on these contemporaneous shocks, but they do allow one to ask whether the magnitude of the partial correlation between housing wealth and consumption is consistent with simulated marginal propensities of consumption.[15]

The change in housing wealth is defined to be the real change in the value of owner-occupied housing structure plus land, less real net investment in owner-occupied housing (Federal Reserve System 1993a, 1993b). Stock market wealth changes are the revaluation of household-owned corporate equity, based on Federal Reserve System (1993a), after adjusting for inflation. This definition of stock wealth therefore excludes pension wealth. Percentage changes in real housing wealth and real stock wealth are used as independent variables, along with the real change in disposable personal income (results are similar when real earnings are used).

13. Surprisingly, the same pattern was not repeated in Canada. Bosworth, Burtless, and Sabelhaus calculated that, in Canada between 1978 and 1986, saving rates fell by 1.3% for homeowners and by 3.1% for renters.

14. A study by Levin (1992) finds similar results for families in the panel Retirement History Survey. His sample consists of those nearing retirement or already retired, so they are not, strictly speaking, "young" homeowners.

15. The estimated regression result may also reflect anticipated changes in housing prices if, for example, wealth gains are serially correlated, although there is little evidence of serial correlation in housing windfall gains.

Figure 8.1 displays a graph of changes in housing wealth and changes in the log of total consumption (less durables) for each year 1950–92. The graph shows a strong positive correlation between housing wealth shifts and consumption growth, although the correlation is dominated by 1990, in which there was both a substantial drop in housing wealth and slow consumption growth. (It is shown below that excluding the anomalous years 1990 and 1991 yields similar results.)

Regressions that control for changes in disposable personal income (DPI) and changes in the stock market are presented in table 8.3. While changes in DPI exert a strong influence on consumption changes, the stock market variable has little effect.[16] The regression implies that a 1% increase in housing wealth raises consumption by 0.10% (with a t-statistic of 2.5). Converting this to a marginal propensity to consume from housing wealth (multiplying by the ratio of consumption to housing wealth) yields roughly 6 cents per dollar of housing wealth, which is larger than would be suggested by the life-cycle model.

Figure 8.2 shows the residuals of consumption and housing wealth changes conditional on changes in stock markets and DPI with the years 1990 and 1991 excluded; the estimated coefficient, shown in the figure, is 0.131, with a t-statistic of 2.5.[17] Splitting the sample into two parts, 1950–70 and 1971–92, had little effect on the housing wealth coefficients, 0.184 (t-statistic of 2.3) for the earlier period and 0.114 (t-statistic of 2.0) for the later period. In short, the large and significant marginal propensity to consume out of housing wealth seems robust to different selections of sample years.

Including the after-tax interest rate (columns 2 and 3 in table 8.3) affects the coefficient on housing wealth only when the model is run using two-stage least squares with consumption growth lagged two years and DPI growth lagged both one and two years as instruments. In column 3, the coefficient on housing wealth is reduced to 0.071, insignificant but still implying a large marginal propensity to consume out of housing wealth.

Housing wealth appreciation may be a leading indicator of future income gains, rather than exerting an independent effect on consumption. To control for this more fully, both lagged and lead changes in DPI are included in the consumption regression. The lead change in DPI is significant and reduces the coefficient on housing wealth to 0.052, which is roughly consistent with the life-cycle model (although the coefficient is no longer significant). Finally, column 5 in table 8.3 presents coefficient estimates for just nondurables. This controls for any spurious correlation between imputed housing values in consumption services and housing wealth. The coefficient on housing wealth is

16. Blinder and Deaton (1985) use much the same framework to find that shocks in unanticipated wealth affect consumption growth, although they do not distinguish among different types of wealth.

17. That is, the horizontal axis is the residual of housing wealth, and the vertical axis the residual of consumption, after controlling for the change in DPI and stock market wealth.

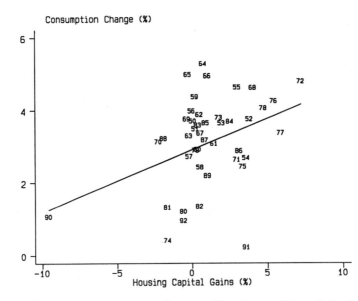

Fig. 8.1   Percentage consumption change and housing wealth capital gains, 1950–92

Note: Data from the year 1979 is superimposed on 1960.

Table 8.3   Euler Equation Consumption Regressions (%)

Dependent Variable	Nondurables and Services	Nondurables and Services	Nondurables and Services	Nondurables and Services	Nondurables
Change in housing wealth	0.108 (2.50)	0.110 (2.53)	0.071 (1.34)	0.052 (1.44)	0.143 (2.50)
Change in stock market wealth	0.002 (0.33)	0.001 (0.12)	0.012 (1.17)	0.052 (1.43)	0.009 (1.01)
Change in real disposable personal income	0.511 (8.15)	0.503 (7.87)	0.629 (6.81)	0.528 (9.63)	0.644 (7.73)
Real after-tax interest rate		0.030 (0.68)	−0.154 (1.44)		
Lagged change in disposable personal income				0.059 (1.09)	
Lead change in disposable personal income				0.187 (3.06)	
R^2	0.660	0.655	0.575	0.781	0.645
Instrumental variables?	No	No	Yes	No	No

Sources: Data on stock market and housing wealth changes from Federal Reserve System (1993a, 1993b). Consumption and income data from Survey of Current Business.

Notes: Dependent variable is the log change in consumption, 1950–92. Numbers in parentheses are *t*-statistics.

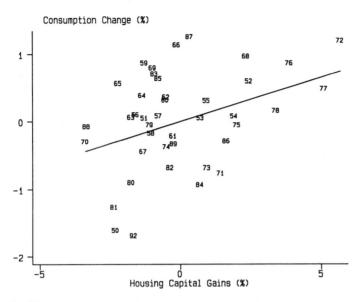

Fig. 8.2   **Percentage consumption change and housing wealth capital gains, 1950–92: conditional on income, stock market changes**

0.143, with a t-statistic of 2.5. In sum, the evidence suggests a strong partial correlation between housing wealth and consumption.

8.6.2   New Tests Using Microeconomic Data

The next step is to consider microeconomic tests of whether housing windfalls affect saving behavior. To do this, I use the 1989 wave of the PSID that includes detailed information on wealth in both 1984 and 1989. The 1989 wave contains a key variable, "active" saving, that attempts to net out capital gains (inactive gains) from the overall change in wealth between 1984 and 1989. Active saving is well suited to addressing the question of how housing windfalls affect saving choices. However, the definition of active saving makes it difficult to correct for inflation, and presupposes that households do not offset active saving in response to "inactive" saving through capital gains in stock, pension, and business assets.

Despite the attempt to remove inactive saving from this measure, the five-year saving rates are highly skewed. In the sample of households considered below, the mean of active saving is $10,918, with a standard deviation of $324,980. The problem of handling the very large outliers without ad hoc procedures for excluding observations suggests the use of quantile (median) regressions. The disadvantage of quantile regressions is that the estimated coefficients are for median savers, not average savers.

The household was included in the sample if total family money income was at least $1,000 in each year (in 1989 dollars), if the households were less than age 61, did not move, had a house worth at least $2,000, and did not experience a major change in family composition during the 1984–89 period. A total of 1,970 families remained. Quantile regressions, weighted by the 1989 family weights, are presented in table 8.4. Note that the Income 1984 variable, for example, is income reported in the 1984 wave of the PSID, but it is asked about the previous calendar year.

The first column describes the quantile regression for the entire sample. The (dollar) change in real housing capital gains (less home-improvement costs) is shown in the first row. The coefficient on housing wealth is −2.5 cents (with a *t*-statistic of 2.28). How might this be converted to annual changes in saving, since the active saving measure reflects a five-year shift in wealth? Assume the housing price change occurs in the midpoint of the five-year period, then the coefficient should be divided by 2.5. Hence the coefficient in column 1 of table 8.4 implies a 1-cent reduction in saving for every dollar increase in housing wealth, a number somewhat less than the life-cycle model with either moving constraints or the absence of reverse mortgages, but equal to that implied by the precautionary saving model.[18]

Bosworth, Burtless, and Sabelhaus (1991) suggest that much of the decline in saving was the consequence of older rather than younger households. Columns 2 and 3 in table 8.4 therefore separate families headed by someone aged 45 or older from those less than 45. The results show that the estimated marginal effect is much larger for younger households, equal to a reduction of 5.4 cents in saving per dollar increase in housing wealth (or 2.1 cents after converting to annualized saving rates). This result casts doubt on the proposition that older households' saving behavior is more sensitive to a given dollar change in housing values. However, the overall impact of a given percentage increase in housing values may still fall more heavily on older households, since they tend to own more expensive houses. Quantile regression estimates that controlled for the presence of second mortgages, a possible indicator of households eager to spend down their wealth (Manchester and Poterba 1989), yielded similar results but are not reported here.

Finally, consider the same regression with positive and negative housing wealth gains separated (columns 4 and 5, table 8.4). The coefficients suggest that housing wealth gains are treated much differently than housing wealth declines. For those younger than 45, the results imply an increase in saving of 10 cents per dollar decline in housing wealth (after converting to annualized saving rates); by contrast, the effect on saving of increasing housing capital gains is only 0.4 cents, and insignificant. How should these results be interpreted? One possibility is that most homeowners in 1984 anticipated housing wealth gains during the next five years. For those who did experience a gain,

---

18. The model estimates also provide an estimate of the long-term marginal propensity to save from income. Summing up the income coefficients and dividing by five yields an estimate of the marginal propensity to save equal to 8 cents per dollar of permanent income.

Table 8.4   **Quantile Regressions for Active Saving: Homeowners Who Did Not Move, Age ≤ 60**

| | Full Sample (1) | Housing Capital Gains | | Asymmetric Housing Capital Gains | |
		Age ≥ 45 (2)	Age < 45 (3)	Age ≥ 45 (4)	Age < 45 (5)
Housing capital gains	−0.025	−0.028	−0.054		
	(2.28)	(2.86)	(2.28)		
Housing capital gains (positive)				−0.021	−0.010
				(1.51)	(0.32)
Housing capital gains (negative)				−0.097	−0.253
				(6.17)	(4.29)
Age	467	1,172	3,399	1,389	2,984
	(1.47)	(2.12)	(0.90)	(2.41)	(0.76)
Age²	−3.14	−8.53	−51.03	−10.27	−45.83
	(1.12)	(2.02)	(0.99)	(2.32)	(0.85)
Sex	−3,883	−4,336	−4,469	−4,783	−4,927
	(2.11)	(2.72)	(0.89)	(2.93)	(0.96)
Family size	−2,216	−3,910	−247	−4,041	−715
	(3.86)	(6.42)	(0.23)	(6.47)	(0.65)
Change in family size, 1984–89	−940	−2,843	−1,624	−2,930	−2,077
	(1.16)	(3.31)	(1.18)	(3.36)	(1.57)
Income in 1984	−0.098	−0.102	−0.105	−0.099	−0.160
	(3.03)	(3.68)	(1.04)	(3.44)	(1.49)
Income in 1985	−0.209	−0.187	−0.076	−0.207	−0.010
	(5.90)	(5.90)	(0.79)	(6.26)	(0.10)
Income in 1986	0.261	0.007	0.539	0.004	0.462
	(5.99)	(0.17)	(5.47)	(0.09)	(4.52)
Income in 1987	−0.128	0.043	−0.319	0.049	−0.355
	(3.64)	(1.38)	(3.71)	(1.53)	(3.99)
Income in 1988	0.106	−0.018	0.185	−0.020	0.243
	(3.52)	(0.68)	(2.29)	(0.72)	(2.93)
Income in 1989	0.491	0.748	0.214	0.737	0.186
	(15.57)	(26.94)	(3.23)	(25.00)	(2.72)
Constant	−13,563	32,512	−60,132	−39,724	−50,302
	(1.52)	(1.85)	(0.89)	(2.10)	(0.71)
Sample size	1,970	1,264	706	1,264	706

Note: Absolute value of *t*-statistics in parentheses. Dependent variable is the level of active saving during 1984–89.

the increased wealth was anticipated, and hence had no impact on consumption. But for those who experienced a loss, the loss was unanticipated, and hence engendered a real change in consumption and saving behavior.

In sum, the macrodata have suggested large effects, and the microdata more modest effects, of housing wealth on saving. The results taken together with Bosworth, Burtless, and Sabelhaus (1991) suggest that the empirical rate at which housing wealth is spent down by younger households is not inconsistent with the life-cycle models that allow for households to tap into housing equity, and the precautionary saving model. It is inconsistent with the view of housing wealth as a sideshow.

8.7   Do Households Consume Housing Equity at Retirement?

The next empirical question is whether retired households spend housing windfalls by downsizing their houses. In practice, this question is difficult to answer because of the difficulty in matching all housing windfalls from past years with current retirees. So I address a more general question—do households, most of whom experienced housing windfalls during the 1970s, downsize housing to spend accumulated housing wealth during retirement? Presumably, a negative answer to the second question implies a negative answer to the first.

A number of recent studies have found little evidence of the gradual downsizing of home equity implied by the life-cycle model (Merrill 1984; Venti and Wise 1989, 1990; Feinstein and McFadden 1989). In fact, these studies have found that retired households on average are as likely to increase their housing equity as to decrease it. Merrill (1984) reports that more retired households switch from *renters* to *owners,* than from owners to renters, not a transition normally associated with life-cycle "downscaling." Additional evidence comes from Feinstein and McFadden (1989), who suggest that more than one-third of elderly households reside in dwellings with at least three more rooms than the number of inhabitants, and are hence "overconsuming" housing services.

Sheiner and Weil (1992) present persuasive evidence that elderly households do reduce their housing services, although it generally occurs later in the life cycle and is often precipitated by widowhood.[19] For example, the homeownership rates of all women aged 65–69 is 77%; by ages 80–85 the percentage drops to 59, with less than half owning their house after age 85. They also report that, for widows, homeownership falls by twelve percentage points, and median home equity by roughly 30%, in the four years after the husband's death. Based on comparisons of homeownership for high- and low-income households, they suggest that these changes in housing tenure are a consequence of taste changes rather than of financial necessity.[20]

The results below use data from the 1989 wave of the PSID to shed light on this question. I first consider differences in income patterns between those who moved and those who did not, and focus in particular on those who both moved and extracted housing equity. I then use quantile regressions to consider at

19. Venti and Wise (1989) and Feinstein and McFadden (1989) earlier noted the strong impact of events such as widowhood, children moving, or divorce on mobility decisions, but did not directly test the impact of such changes on ownership patterns. Also see Hurd (1989) and Hurd and Shoven (1989) for documentation of financial changes precipitated by widowhood.

20. Feinstein and McFadden (1989) suggest that families with both low incomes and low levels of liquid wealth are more likely to switch from owner-occupied to rental property conditional on moving.

what rate the equity removed (or put into) housing was reflected in changing consumption patterns.

To examine the pattern of housing wealth change among the elderly, I consider all those who were both homeowners and over the age of 54 in 1989. Consider three groups: those who did not move during the period 1984–89 (85.9%), those who moved and increased the market value of their house (5.8%), and those who moved and reduced the market value of their house (8.3%). Their weighted median and average family money income levels are presented in table 8.5 by year. Observations are not excluded because of family composition changes, since such changes are often causes of income declines (or increases in the case of remarriage). On average, those who moved into smaller houses were 1.5 years older than those who moved into larger houses.

For the group that did not move, median income declined by 19%, and mean income by 12% during the period. This is the likely consequence of a decline in labor income during retirement. Among those increasing housing equity, median and mean income declined by 14 and 6%, a smaller amount than the benchmark for nonmovers. Finally, for those moving into smaller houses, median income dropped by 25%, and mean income fell by 32%, substantially more than the reference group. Note that the mean and median income for this latter group was nearly identical in 1982 to that for the group who did not move at all. Figure 8.3 shows these patterns, with 1982 income normalized at one hundred. After adjusting for the general downward trend in income, the pattern suggests that, even at retirement, changes in family income exert a strong influence on housing demand.

A different view of this pattern is to normalize the level of income by its amount relative to the year in which the family moved. Figure 8.4 shows these calculations. If individuals moved in 1986, for example, their $T - 1$ income

Table 8.5		Mean and Median Income of Homeowners, by Moving Status, 1984				
	Did Not Move		Moved into Larger House		Moved into Smaller House (or Rented)	
Year	Median	Mean	Median	Mean	Median	Mean
1982	22,650	32,437	25,000	34,380	21,287	29,993
1983	22,022	32,151	25,688	34,590	18,507	30,358
1984	21,797	30,264	28,120	34,160	19,021	27,746
1985	21,209	30,976	25,047	35,723	18,435	26,356
1986	20,287	30,151	26,026	32,733	16,817	24,214
1987	18,922	28,726	23,175	33,559	15,893	22,603
1988	18,250	28,974	21,580	30,378	14,829	20,581
1989	18,400	28,497	21,428	32,234	15,939	20,506
Percentage change, 1984–89	−18.8	−12.1	−14.3	−6.2	−25.1	−31.6

Notes: All medians and means weighted by PSID population weights. Age of head in 1984 is 55 or above.

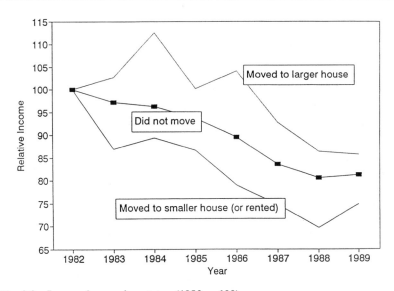

Fig. 8.3   Income by moving status (1982 = 100)

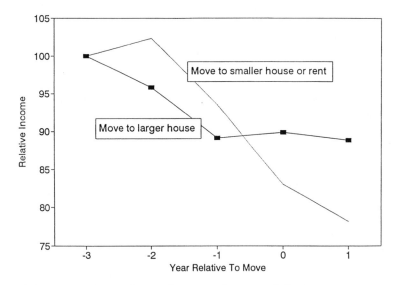

Fig. 8.4   Average income by moving status, by year relative to move (1982 = 100)

level is from the 1986 wave (applicable for 1985), and their $T + 1$ income level is from the 1988 wave. Both samples show a decline in family income in years $T - 3$ and $T - 2$. The difference becomes apparent in the year of the move, where income of those who increased housing wealth flattens out (or rises relative to trend), while income of those who downsized continues to fall.

In sum, families who experience an income downturn appear to be more likely to cash out their housing wealth than those who do not, a result that is consistent with much of the previous literature. Partly this is because of a change in family composition; of those who reduced housing equity, 19% had become widows or widowers during 1984–89, compared to 10% for those who did not move. However, it is not just family composition that matters; 18% of those who *increased* housing equity were widows.[21]

A better predictor of housing wealth reductions is unexpected shocks, such as health reasons and widowhood. For those who moved, 35% responded that they did so because of outside events such as health reasons, divorce, retirement because of health, or eviction. Of those who replied that their move was precipitated by an unexpected shock, 79% reduced their net housing equity.[22] In sum, widowhood is not the only initiating reason for downsizing. A decline in income or an unexpected health problem also initiates households to tap into housing equity.

Is the housing equity spent? Past studies have had difficulty finding the proceeds of housing sales in subsequent asset reporting (Sheiner and Weil 1992), suggesting that the entire housing proceeds are spent in a few years. I now consider how housing equity extracted from the sale of housing affects active saving. Note that, when the house is sold, for say $50,000, active saving is decreased by $50,000 unless the money is returned through the purchase of other assets. A coefficient of 1.0 corresponds to housing wealth being entirely spent by 1989. The null hypothesis corresponds to housing wealth being entirely saved. Table 8.6 reports quantile regressions of the type discussed in section 8.6, with the sample restricted to homeowners aged 55 and above in 1984. Net proceeds from the house sale are defined to be negative for those who move to smaller houses, zero for nonmovers, and positive for those buying a larger house.

The coefficient on the net proceeds from the house sale is 69 cents per dollar of housing wealth change (column 1 of table 8.6), and is highly significant. This result implies that, by 1989, 69 cents of every dollar withdrawn from housing sales has been consumed, and 31 cents saved, from the typical housing sale.

It is likely that the coefficient of housing wealth on saving differs depending on whether the household increased or decreased its housing equity, and when during the sample period the house was sold. To test this, consider four categories of housing wealth change, shown in column 2 of table 8.6. For those who sold their house in 1985–86 and reduced housing equity, 73 cents of every

---

21. An alternative explanation for the increase in housing equity among some widows is that they moved from a large house with a mortgage to a smaller house bought with cash, although few people over age 65 hold mortgages.

22. By contrast, 21% who moved did so because of "purposive consumption reasons," conventional anticipated life-cycle reasons involving reduced space or lower rent. See question V16651 in the 1989 PSID.

Table 8.6   **Quantile Regressions for Active Saving, Homeowners Aged > 55**

	Equation 1 Coefficient	Equation 2 Coefficient
Net housing wealth	0.688	
	(25.87)	
Net housing wealth: sale in 1985–86, moved to less costly house (or rented)		0.734
		(17.92)
Net housing wealth: sale in 1987–89, moved to less costly house (or rented)		0.590
		(26.65)
Net housing wealth: sale in 1985–86, moved to more costly house		1.144
		(21.63)
Net housing wealth: sale in 1987–89, moved to more costly house		1.055
		(23.83)
Age	220.81	1,718.80
	(0.14)	(1.49)
Age^2	−1.94	−11.81
	(0.18)	(1.49)
Income in 1984	−0.109	−0.101
	(3.03)	(3.92)
Income in 1985	−0.708	−0.561
	(13.60)	(14.96)
Income in 1986	0.627	0.435
	(9.98)	(9.64)
Income in 1987	0.321	0.302
	(7.79)	(10.20)
Income in 1988	0.103	0.175
	(3.36)	(7.88)
Income in 1989	0.148	0.141
	(3.18)	(4.19)
Constant	−6,669.68	−63,447.97
	(0.11)	(1.52)
Sample size	922	922

Note: Absolute value of *t*-statistics in parentheses.

dollar was spent by 1989. In contrast, those who sold their house later in the sample period, 1987–89, spent only 59 cents on each dollar. These coefficients taken together imply that roughly half of housing wealth is spent near the time of the housing sale, with an additional 5 cents per initial dollar of housing capital (net of interest) spent in subsequent years.

People who "upsized" by moving into more expensive housing did not appear to do so by spending down reported assets; the coefficient exceeds 1.0 regardless of when the housing transaction occurred. Perhaps realized capital gains or other sources of wealth not measured by active saving were used to finance the housing expansion. In sum, each year a small group of individuals downsize their housing stock in response to an adverse shock to disposable family income. For this group, housing wealth appears to be used in financing extraordinary consumption in the year of the sale, and in financing subsequent consumption at an approximate actuarial rate.

8.8 Conclusion

Recent fluctuations in housing prices have led to some concern that the windfall gains enjoyed by many of those currently retired could be matched in the future by windfall losses when the baby-boom generation retires. This paper has considered whether housing price fluctuations play an important or unimportant role in the economic security of retirees—that is, whether housing wealth is just a sideshow to the determination of consumption and saving.

The empirical results in this and other papers present a somewhat paradoxical view of housing wealth. On the one hand, housing wealth does appear to affect the saving behavior of homeowners prior to retirement. The microestimates in this paper suggest that, for younger homeowners, a $1 increase in housing wealth reduces saving by 1–2 cents, a magnitude consistent with the certainty life-cycle and the precautionary saving model. The macroestimates are substantially larger, corresponding to a roughly 6-cent increase in consumption when housing wealth rises by $1.

According to the life-cycle model, if households respond to housing windfalls while young by saving less for retirement, they should be using those housing windfalls while old to help finance retirement consumption. However, the results suggest that housing wealth windfalls affect consumption for the elderly only for a small group of people buffeted by adverse economic events.

One way to reconcile these two empirical regularities is to view housing wealth as a precautionary "buffer" that can be cashed out in the event of an income or a health downturn, or widowhood, when the demand for housing services is likely to decline as well. This precautionary saving view of the household can potentially explain the puzzle of why housing wealth affects saving while young but is rarely used by the elderly to finance consumption. If housing wealth declines, households hold less insurance against future contingencies and will respond by saving more to build up (nonhousing) wealth for future contingencies during retirement. Since not every elderly household encounters a bad outcome requiring the liquidation of housing equity, one can also explain why the median elderly family doesn't spend down its housing wealth.

Viewing housing wealth as a buffer against contingencies during retirement can also explain why the demand for reverse mortgages has not been strong. Retired households do not wish to draw down their housing equity in the good states of the world because it is a contingency against the bad state of the world. And if the bad state of the world occurs—poor health or a serious financial setback—households desiring to economize on housing services would want to sell their house in any case. At that point, equity in the house can be cashed out and used for subsequent consumption or medical bills.

A somewhat different issue is whether housing prices will decline by as much as Mankiw and Weil (1989) suggest. In a general equilibrium model of housing demand and supply, McFadden (1992) predicts a gradual flattening of housing prices in the future, rather than the sharp decline forecast by Mankiw and Weil (1989).[23] And while baby-boom homeowners are clearly worse off than early generations that shared in the dramatic upswing in housing prices, McFadden finds that the impact of these differences on consumer welfare are quite small. He predicts that feasible lifetime consumption for generations born around 1950 will be lower by only 0.7% because they lost out on the housing capital gains of the earlier generations.

Suppose that the McFadden projections are correct, and aggregate housing prices remain stable for the next forty years. Then wouldn't the logic of this model suggest that housing prices should be unimportant? The answer is no, for two reasons. First, I use as a benchmark housing equity of a generation that has profited from the large housing price increases of the 1970. Current households may expect more housing wealth appreciation than actually occurs, a result given support by the empirical findings that housing wealth downturns exert a much larger impact on saving than housing wealth upswings. If households make saving plans based on expected housing wealth appreciation, their retirement plans may be inadequate if housing prices remain constant.

Second, and more important, there are wide regional variations in housing wealth and housing prices even when aggregate price indices are flat. Households in the Northeast during the late 1980s, for example, experienced wide fluctuations (both positive and negative) in housing prices during a period when aggregate prices were relatively constant. Both of these considerations suggest that the economic well-being of future and current generations will be affected by whether they made money, or lost money, on their house. That is, housing wealth is not a sideshow.

References

Ai, Chunrong, Jonathan Feinstein, Daniel McFadden, and Henry Pollakowski. 1990. The Dynamics of Housing Demand by the Elderly: User Cost Effects. In *Issues in the Economics of Aging,* ed. David A. Wise. Chicago: University of Chicago Press.

Bhatia, Kul B. 1987. Real Estate Assets and Consumer Spending. *Quarterly Journal of Economics* 102 (May): 437–43.

Blinder, Alan, and Angus Deaton. 1985. The Time-Series Consumption Function Revisited. *Brookings Papers on Economic Activity,* 465–521.

Bosworth, Barry, Gary Burtless, and John Sabelhaus. 1991. The Decline in Saving:

23. The Mankiw and Weil predictions have also been criticized by others; see Hendershott (1991) and other articles in the December 1991 issue of *Regional Science and Urban Economics.*

Evidence from Household Surveys. *Brookings Papers on Economic Activity,* 183–256.

Caballero, Ricardo J. 1991. Earnings Uncertainty and Aggregate Wealth Accumulation. *American Economic Review* 81 (September): 859–71.

Carroll, Christopher D. 1991. Buffer Stock Saving and the Permanent Income Hypothesis. Board of Governors of the Federal Reserve System, November. Mimeo.

Carroll, Christopher D., and Andrew Samwick. 1992. The Nature and Magnitude of Precautionary Wealth. Board of Governors of the Federal Reserve System. Mimeo.

Deaton, Angus. 1992. *Understanding Consumption.* Oxford: Clarendon Press.

Federal Reserve System, Board of Governors. 1993a. *Balance Sheets for the U.S. Economy, 1945–92.* Publication C-9. Washington, DC: Federal Reserve System.

———. 1993b. *Flow of Funds Accounts.* Publication Z.1 (June 8). Washington, DC: Federal Reserve System.

Feinstein, Jonathan S., and Daniel McFadden. 1989. The Dynamics of Housing Demand by the Elderly: Wealth, Cash Flow, and Demographic Effects. In *The Economics of Aging,* ed. David A. Wise. Chicago: University of Chicago Press.

Hall, Robert. 1988. Intertemporal Substitution in Consumption. *Journal of Political Economy* 96 (April): 339–57.

Hendershott, Patric H. 1991. Are Real Prices Likely to Decline by 47 Percent? *Regional Science and Urban Economics* 21 (4): 553–63.

Hendershott, Patric H., and Joe Peek. 1989. Aggregate U.S. Private Saving: Conceptual Measures and Empirical Tests. In *The Measurement of Saving, Investment, and Wealth,* ed. Robert E. Lipsey and Helen Stone Tice. Chicago: University of Chicago Press.

Hubbard, R. Glenn, Jonathan Skinner, and Stephen P. Zeldes. 1995. Social Insurance and Precautionary Saving. *Journal of Political Economy* 103 (2): 360–99.

Hurd, Michael D. 1989. The Poverty of Widows: Future Prospects. In *The Economics of Aging,* ed. David A. Wise. Chicago: University of Chicago Press.

Hurd, Michael D., and John B. Shoven. 1989. The Wealth and Poverty of Widows: Assets before and after the Husband's Death. In *The Economics of Aging,* ed. David A. Wise. Chicago: University of Chicago Press.

Levin, Laurence. 1992. Are Assets Fungible? Testing Alternative Theories of Life-Cycle Saving. Santa Clara University, Santa Clara, CA. Mimeo.

McFadden, Daniel. 1992. Demographics, the Housing Market, and the Welfare of the Elderly. Berkeley, CA. Mimeo.

Manchester, Joyce M., and James M. Poterba. 1989. Second Mortgages and Household Saving. *Regional Science and Urban Economics* 19 (May): 325–46.

Mankiw, N. Gregory, and David N. Weil. 1989. The Baby Boom, the Baby Bust, and the Housing Market. *Regional Science and Urban Economics* 19 (May): 235–58.

Merrill, Sally R. 1984. Home Equity and the Elderly. In *Retirement and Economic Behavior,* ed. Henry J. Aaron and Gary Burtless. Washington, DC: Brookings Institution.

Morck, Randall, Andrei Shleifer, and Robert W. Vishny. 1990. The Stock Market and Investment: Is the Market a Sideshow? *Brookings Papers on Economic Activity* 2:157–216.

Munnell, Alicia H., and Leah M. Cook. 1991. Explaining the Postwar Pattern of Personal Saving. *New England Economic Review, Federal Reserve Bank of Boston* (November–December): 17–27.

Palumbo, Michael G. 1993. Health Uncertainty and Precautionary Saving near the End of the Life Cycle. University of Houston. Mimeo.

Shefrin, Hersh M., and Richard H. Thaler. 1988. The Behavioral Life-Cycle Hypothesis. *Economic Inquiry* 26:609–43.

Sheiner, Louise M. 1989. Housing Prices and the Savings of Renters. Joint Committee on Taxation, Washington, DC, November. Mimeo.

Sheiner, Louise M., and David N. Weil. 1992. The Housing Wealth of the Aged. NBER Working Paper no. 4115. Cambridge, MA: National Bureau of Economic Research, July.

Skinner, Jonathan. 1988. Risky Income, Life Cycle Consumption, and Precautionary Savings. *Journal of Monetary Economics* 22:237–55.

———. 1989. Housing Wealth and Aggregate Saving. *Regional Science and Urban Economics* 19 (May): 305–24.

———. 1994. Housing and Saving in the United States. In *Housing Markets in the United States and Japan,* ed. Yukio Noguchi and James M. Poterba. Chicago: University of Chicago Press.

Thaler, Richard H. 1990. Anomalies: Saving, Fungibility, and Mental Accounts. *Journal of Economic Perspectives* 4 (winter): 193–206.

Venti, Steven F., and David A. Wise. 1989. Aging, Moving, and Housing Wealth. In *The Economics of Aging,* ed. David A. Wise. Chicago: University of Chicago Press.

———. 1990. But They Don't Want to Reduce Housing Equity. In *Issues in the Economics of Aging,* ed. David A. Wise. Chicago: University of Chicago Press.

———. 1991. Aging and the Income Value of Housing Wealth. *Journal of Public Economics* 44:371–97.

Zeldes, Stephen P. 1989. Optimal Consumption with Stochastic Income: Deviations from Certainty Equivalence. *Quarterly Journal of Economics* 104 (May): 275–98.

Comment   John B. Shoven

This paper is about a very important topic, and it exhibits much of the usual clarity of thought that one associates with the author. We know that housing wealth represents a large fraction of total household wealth for many Americans, particularly the elderly. The question that Skinner addresses is what would be the consequences if the same demographic forces that drove up housing prices so dramatically in the 1970s were to drive them sharply lower over the next few decades. The author uses the 1989 projection of Mankiw and Weil of a 47% decline in real housing prices over the next thirty years or so as a backdrop for his evaluation of whether changes in housing prices affect aggregate consumption, saving, and individual economic welfare.

The Mankiw and Weil prediction comes about because they forecast a sharp decline in the growth in housing demand as the baby-boom generation ages and as the baby-bust generation enters into its home-buying years. A couple of things should be noted about the Mankiw and Weil prediction and its impact on Skinner's study. First, if the slowdown in the growth of housing demand is predictable and well understood, it would be anticipated and would affect housing prices today as well as in the future. To the extent that declines in

John B. Shoven is the Charles R. Schwab Professor of Economics and dean of the School of Humanities and Sciences, Stanford University, and a research associate of the National Bureau of Economic Research.

housing prices were not surprises, but rather anticipated, they would not be expected to affect consumption and saving decisions significantly as the expected decline indeed occurs. The point of this is that, in an empirical investigation of the effect of changes in housing prices on consumption and saving, it would be desirable to be able to separate surprising price changes from those that were anticipated. This would be difficult and is not attempted in Skinner's paper. Second, the very uneven demographic structure of the U.S. population can be expected to affect asset prices more generally, not just housing prices. For example, pension funds have been accumulating assets and contributing massively toward national saving in the past ten to fifteen years. However, when the baby-boom generation retires, one can anticipate that pension funds will cease being net accumulators of assets and may in fact attempt net sales of the stocks and bonds that the baby-boom generation has set aside for retirement. This change on the part of pension funds could affect real interest rates, stock prices, and housing prices, for that matter. If the pattern of pension fund demands for assets is anticipated, the effects on saving and consumption may already be operative and the uneven demographic structure may already be affecting intertemporal asset prices.

Housing assets are different in important ways from other assets. First, owner-occupants both own an asset and consume the services generated from that asset. In one sense, owning a house is a bit like having a lifetime subscription to a magazine or a lifetime membership in a golf club. If you own one of these lifetime claims and do not intend to sell it, then changes in the price of lifetime memberships does not affect your welfare. This phenomenon is one of the reasons that Skinner is writing this paper; it opens up the possibility that changes in housing prices are just a sideshow and do not have major welfare implications. Presumably assets such as stocks, bonds, and bank accounts do not directly provide consumable services in the same way as a house does, and therefore the welfare consequences of changes in their value is less ambiguous. Second, one needs to keep in mind the significant difference between the effects of price levels and the effects of anticipated price changes. Expected price declines would cause an increase in the rental cost of housing while a low level of housing prices would translate into a low imputed rent for owning a home. Ideally one would separately include in one's investigation of the effect of housing prices on saving, consumption, and welfare both price-level effects and price-change effects.

One of the reasons that this is an important paper is that, as is often the case, economists have a surplus of theories regarding the effect of changes in housing prices on behavior. Skinner examines four widely used models regarding lifetime consumption and asset allocation and finds their predictions quite distinct. This raises one's hopes that maybe the facts can sort out the theories for us. There are several reasons why house prices could be simply a sideshow. First, people might behave as if they lived forever, perhaps because of a bequest motive such that they treat their heirs as a continuation of their own life.

If people lived forever (and if houses provided an infinite stream of housing services), then changes in housing prices would not affect those who were never going to sell. Second, institutional constraints such as high moving costs and capital market imperfections (such as an absence of reverse annuity mortgages) and a lack of a bequest motive might combine so as to make a homeowner indifferent to the price of her or his home. Finally, people might treat housing assets separately from other financial assets (in a separate "mental account") and not think of them as marketable, liquid assets.

There are other economic models that tell us that house prices should matter for consumption and saving decisions. First, the traditional life-cycle model predicts dissaving during retirement, including the downsizing of one's house. Second, a precautionary saving model would suggest that housing equity can serve as a valuable contingent asset in the event that the household experiences bad financial luck. These models would place houses as one of the assets in a "self-insurance" system for the household. Higher equity in a house would improve the condition of the self-insurance fund. Finally, if you have a general bequest motive and not one defined only in terms of housing, then higher house values implies larger bequests, and this will affect one's complete lifetime consumption/saving plan.

I think that Skinner's investigation into which of these models most closely conforms to observations is interesting. I also must admit to some pleasure in my reading of his conclusion that the precautionary motive for saving is most consistent with the facts. The simple life-cycle model fails because the elderly as a whole do not reduce their housing demand as much as that model would predict. The infinite-horizon model fails because changes in housing prices do affect behavior, a great deal for a minority of the population. I find the institutional-rigidities model fairly unconvincing because I think that capital markets are pretty well developed. For instance, even if there are not widely available reverse annuity mortgages, the elderly can still consume a good fraction of their home equity while remaining in their house. They could do this by using traditional mortgages or home equity loans. The fact may be that most of them do not consume their equity, but this does not support the model that constrains them for doing so. In fact, in the precautionary savings model only those who experience economic setbacks would be expected to avail themselves of the equity in their home (either by borrowing or by selling).

I found Skinner's investigation into whether the "middle-aged" change their saving and spending habits depending on house appreciation interesting, but to be honest I don't think that he added much to the Bosworth, Burtless, and Sabelhaus study that he references. They found that the much-documented decline in savings rates between the 1960s and 1980s was much more dramatic for homeowners than for nonhomeowners. In fact, almost all of the decline in personal saving was accounted for by homeowners. This is pretty solid evidence that homeowners were increasing consumption and spending some of their accrued housing capital gains. Skinner looks at this issue with both a macro- and a microanalysis. The microstudy uses new data and finds qualitatively the same result as Bosworth, Burtless, and Sabelhaus, so it can be interpreted as verifying and supporting their conclusion. The macroanalysis is also broadly consistent.

Skinner provides ample evidence that, for a large subset of the elderly, housing wealth is important enough to make the investigation worthwhile. He finds that those who suffer income declines are much more likely to tap their home equity. He finds that, while for most people their ex post behavior will not be that different with dramatically lower housing prices than it would have been in the absence of such a decline, for the minority who are forced to use the self-insurance value of having considerable housing equity, the decline makes them significantly worse off. To answer the question posed in the title of the paper, housing prices are not a complete sideshow. While the consequences of a 47% decline in prices would not be devastating for many, it would be harmful to most and seriously harmful to those who are at least fortunate.

It is my feeling that Skinner's findings are one more nail in the coffin for the simple life-cycle model and one more bit of evidence in support of the precautionary model of saving.

V   Stylized Models and Simulations

9 Elderly Health, Housing, and Mobility

Jonathan S. Feinstein

9.1 Introduction

The growing population of elderly persons in the United States poses many challenges for American society and policymakers; some of the most important challenges involve providing appropriate housing for the elderly who suffer from health-related disabilities.

Elderly persons are vulnerable to a wide spectrum of disabilities, of differing degrees of severity, creating a need for many different kinds of elderly housing and home services, extending from the demand for homes with particular architectural features, like wheelchair access, through the need for home health care and basic community services, to requirements of severely disabled individuals for intensive nursing home care. During the past few decades the need for these many kinds of housing has been widely recognized, and the growth in alternative elderly housing arrangements holds out the promise of a world in which each elderly person is matched to his or her "ideal" kind of housing, and, when the person's health status changes, he or she moves into a new preferred housing state.

Although this vision is appealing, it ignores a number of important issues, especially the role of mobility costs and economic factors in elderly housing decisions. Previous research supports the view that most elderly persons who have lived in their dwelling for an extended period of time prefer not to move, if possible; see for example Feinstein and McFadden (1989), Venti and Wise (1989), and Sheiner and Weil (1992), all of whom document the fact that mobility rates are very low among the elderly. In part the unwillingness of elderly persons to move derives from the emotional attachment they feel to their

Jonathan S. Feinstein is associate professor of economics at the Yale School of Management and a research associate of the National Bureau of Economic Research.

The author thanks the John M. Olin Foundation for financial support.

homes (see Danigelis and Fengler 1991), and in part it derives from the very high costs that moving imposes on the elderly, including psychological, health-related, and financial costs (see Golant 1984). The elderly often seem more willing to endure the daily hardships and inconveniences caused by the mismatch between their impaired functional skills and those demanded by their living environment, than to bear the high cost of moving. The fact that an elderly person may not wish to move as her health deteriorates significantly complicates the simple vision that imagines perfectly matching housing to health status, and suggests that attachment behavior and mobility costs must be included in any policy analysis that seeks to evaluate the attractiveness and likely utilization of alternative housing options.

In addition, housing of almost any kind is expensive to own or to rent, and many kinds of home-related health services, notably nursing care, are also extremely costly. Hence elderly housing decisions invariably depend upon the prices of the various housing options, expected changes in those prices, and household wealth, and we are linked to decisions about consumption and desired bequests, themselves complex topics that have been widely investigated (see the survey by Hurd [1990]). Again, comprehensive analyses of elderly housing must consider the effect of prices, and the link between housing decisions and other economic decisions made by elderly households.

My purpose in this paper is to investigate the relationship between elderly health and elderly housing decisions, and, in particular, to examine the effect of mobility costs and economic factors on this relationship. To explore these issues, I construct a conventional dynamic economic model, draw upon published sources to parameterize the model, and then present the results of computer simulations that I have used to characterize the model's implications. I actually construct two models, the first simpler and designed to illustrate the main ways in which health and housing interact, and the second extending the first to incorporate economic factors.

The two models share a number of features that are central to my investigation. Both follow an elderly person from age 65 through age 90, determining the individual's mobility decision and housing choice at each age, as a function of sex, health status, and previous year's housing state. Both also employ particular parameterizations of morbidity and mortality transition probabilities, based on published sources, which specify an individual's future health status, as a function of age, sex, and current health. Finally, in modeling health and housing states, both models consider a world in which an elderly person can fall into one of three health states, good health, moderate disability, or poor health, and must choose to live in one of three housing states: conventional (nonelderly specific) housing; transitional housing, which is meant to include a variety of housing options, including retirement communities, life care (see Feinstein and Keating 1992 for a discussion), and shared living; or institutional housing, including nursing homes and hospices.

Within this general context the first model focuses on two issues. First, it introduces a simple utility function that assumes that an individual's utility is highest when his residence type "matches" his health status, and lower when the two are mismatched; according to this specification a moderately disabled individual is happiest living in transitional housing, and earns lower utility in either conventional housing or an institution, while a person in good health prefers conventional housing, and a person in poor health does best in an institution. Second, this first model considers several kinds of mobility costs, including a separation or attachment cost, a direct but temporary utility cost, and a health cost.

The analysis of the first model confirms that when there are no mobility costs an individual will always move in response to changes in his health status (into his new preferred housing state), and that moving costs reduce mobility, with higher costs reducing mobility to a greater extent. More interestingly, the analysis highlights the importance of transitional housing. I find that for most parameterizations individuals who fall into moderate disability choose to move into transitional housing. In contrast, individuals who fall into poor health often choose not to move into an institution, even in versions of the model with relatively low mobility costs, and especially at younger ages. When combined, as they are in many of the simulations, these two patterns result in transitional housing playing the role of an "absorbing state," so that once an elderly person moves into such housing she stays there for the rest of her life. As a related finding, a mobility pattern rarely observed is one in which an elderly person skips over transitional housing, choosing not to move from conventional housing into transitional housing when first becoming moderately disabled, and then moving directly into an institution when she falls into poor health.

The second model extends the first to place greater emphasis on household wealth and bequest, to incorporate housing prices, and, most importantly, to model the individual's consumption decision each period jointly with his housing decision. The simulation results for this model generally confirm the findings for the first model, particularly the importance of transitional housing. The results also illustrate the link between consumption, savings, spend down of assets, and housing choices; for example, elderly with very low wealth are predicted to follow a "bankruptcy" strategy in which they consume their remaining wealth, then move into an institution where they become a ward of the state. Generally, both the first and second model seem able to predict realistic mobility patterns, offering support for the augmented economic model of elderly decision making that I develop.

The remainder of the paper is organized as follows. The section 9.2 describes the first model, including the parameterizations of the health transition matrices and other key variables. Section 9.3 presents the simulation results for the first model. Section 9.4 describes the second model, and section 9.5 presents the simulation results for this model. Finally, section 9.6 offers some concluding comments, and an appendix discusses the procedure used to construct the transition matrices.

9.2   Initial Model: Specification and Parameterization

In this section I present an initial, relatively simple model of elderly health and mobility. This first model assumes that an elderly person's utility in any year depends only on the match between housing type and health in that year, and on whether the person has moved in the current or previous year. Lifetime utility is assumed to be equal to the sum of discounted annual utilities, plus a bequest. Since it is focused almost entirely on the relationship between health and housing, the model is well suited to an investigation of the relationship between changes in health status and both housing mobility and housing characteristics, as I hope to show in section 9.3, where I review the results of simulating the model. However, the model cannot address how elderly health status and mobility costs affect and are affected by financial incentives and economic decisions, because it includes only a very limited role for household wealth (restricting its impact to the bequest), and does not incorporate any role for annuity income, housing prices, or consumption decisions. The second model, presented in section 9.4, extends the model of this section to include these various factors.

In presenting the model, I first define the various health states, health transition probabilities, and housing states used in the analysis. Next I describe utility, and two kinds of mobility costs, direct utility costs of moving and indirect health costs. Finally I consider the elderly person's decision-making process in more detail, outlining the dynamic programming method of analysis I have used to determine the mobility patterns implied by the model. Since I analyze the model via computer simulations, I must parameterize several different functions and distributions that appear in the model, including health transition probabilities, mortality profiles, and utility. The parameterizations I have chosen are described together with the model, and presented in several tables, with the appendix providing greater details about the sources and methods used to construct these tables. For completeness and to provide greater understanding of how sensitive the model's solution is to changes in parameterization, separate parameterizations are specified for men and women.

I end this brief introduction to the model with two notes. First, most aspects of the model, including the parameterizations, are carried over to the model presented in section 9.4. Second, throughout the paper the analysis is couched in terms of a single elderly person (a one-person household), either male or female; the extension to an elderly couple, possibly living with or as dependents, is important but is left to future work.

9.2.1   Health and Housing States

Consider a 65-year-old man or woman, who lives alone but is assumed to have heirs who will inherit any remaining wealth, including housing wealth, when he or she dies. The man or woman is assumed to be in good health, and to own his or her home.

Beginning at age 66, and for each year thereafter, the individual faces a risk of deteriorating health or death. To formalize this risk and the different levels of ill health associated with it, I assume that in each year for which she remains alive the individual finds herself in one of three health states: "good health," "moderately disabled health," or "poor health." I define good, moderately disabled, and poor health in terms of limitations of activities of daily living (ADLs) and instrumental activities of daily living (IADLs), so as to conform with standard gerontologic terminology. Thus "good health" means that the individual has essentially no limitations of daily life, that is, zero ADLs and zero to two IADLs. A person in "moderately disabled health" suffers from several IADLs and perhaps one or two ADLs. Such an individual is likely to endure minor or moderate inconveniences in a traditional family home, particularly if there are stairs or other encumbrances, and may benefit from living in an environment of congregate or shared housing, a suitable retirement community, or simply a well-designed apartment with ready access to transportation, shopping, and other activities (see Altman, Lawton, and Wohlwill 1984 for a fuller discussion). Someone in "poor health" possesses significant limitations, including several ADL limitations and numerous IADL limitations. Thus "poor health" is, as defined, approximately equivalent to the condition of patients who would benefit from consideration for, are resident in, or are about to be admitted to a long-term care facility such as a nursing home. The fact that these definitions mesh with standard gerontologic terminology is critical for my analysis, because the published data I have relied upon to parameterize the model describes health status almost exclusively in terms of ADL and IADL limitations.

An individual of given health status at age t will, at age $t + 1$, either be in one of the three health states described above or be dead. Further, as will become clear later in this section, the elderly person's decision whether to move at age t, and where to move, depends on his expectation of what his health is likely to be like at age $t + 1$ and subsequent ages. Thus a central feature of the model is the parameterization of the transition probabilities that describe the movement from health states at age t to states at age $t + 1$. Tables 9.1 and 9.2 depict these transition probabilities. Table 9.1 lists, for each age t and separately for men and women, the nine numbers contained in the three-by-three transition matrix that governs transitions from each health state at age t to each of the three living states at age $t + 1$; as the table makes clear, these probabilities are different at each age. Table 9.2 describes the mortality risk at age $t + 1$, as a function of health at age t, again separately for men and women.

The health transition probabilities depicted in tables 9.1 and 9.2 apply only to the case in which the individual does not move at age t, or moves but suffers no increased risk of ill health or death as a consequence. Later in this section I will describe how the numbers in tables 9.1 and 9.2 are altered, in models in which mobility is assumed to increase the risk of ill health and death, if an elderly man or woman chooses to move at age t.

The appendix provides details about the construction of tables 9.1 and 9.2.

Table 9.1   **Probability of a Transition from One Health State to Another, by Age and Sex, Base Case**

	From Good Health to			From Moderately Disabled to			From Poor Health to		
Age	Good	Moderate	Poor	Good	Moderate	Poor	Good	Moderate	Poor
				A. Men					
65	.9180	.0510	.0158	.0730	.8500	.0395	.0000	.4600	.0500
66	.9110	.0550	.0158	.0700	.8465	.0395	.0000	.4600	.0500
67	.9032	.0600	.0158	.0680	.8425	.0395	.0000	.4600	.0500
68	.8952	.0650	.0158	.0650	.8375	.0395	.0000	.4600	.0500
69	.8855	.0700	.0175	.0630	.8270	.0450	.0000	.4600	.0500
70	.8780	.0750	.0190	.0610	.8240	.0480	.0000	.4500	.0500
71	.8698	.0800	.0202	.0590	.8185	.0505	.0000	.4500	.0500
72	.8618	.0840	.0202	.0570	.8105	.0505	.0000	.4500	.0500
73	.8538	.0880	.0202	.0550	.8035	.0505	.0000	.4500	.0500
74	.8465	.0900	.0215	.0540	.7940	.0520	.0000	.4500	.0500
75	.8400	.0950	.0230	.0530	.7895	.0575	.0000	.4000	.0500
76	.8332	.1000	.0248	.0500	.7860	.0620	.0000	.4000	.0500
77	.8191	.1100	.0269	.0450	.7838	.0672	.0000	.4000	.0500
78	.8048	.1200	.0292	.0400	.7810	.0730	.0000	.4000	.0500
79	.7884	.1300	.0316	.0350	.7810	.0758	.0000	.4000	.0500
80	.7725	.1400	.0345	.0300	.7789	.0811	.0000	.4000	.0500
81	.7561	.1500	.0379	.0250	.7758	.0872	.0000	.4000	.0500
82	.7380	.1600	.0420	.0200	.7676	.0924	.0000	.3900	.0500
83	.7198	.1700	.0472	.0160	.7636	.0944	.0000	.3700	.0500
84	.7025	.1800	.0525	.0120	.7630	.0950	.0000	.3600	.0400
85	.6798	.1900	.0602	.0110	.7570	.1020	.0000	.3600	.0400
86	.6518	.2000	.0682	.0100	.7510	.1090	.0000	.3400	.0400
87	.6285	.2050	.0765	.0100	.7350	.1150	.0000	.3400	.0400
88	.6095	.2100	.0855	.0100	.7170	.1280	.0000	.3300	.0400
89	.5875	.2150	.0975	.0100	.6940	.1460	.0000	.3000	.0400
90	.5635	.2200	.1125	.0100	.6730	.1570	.0000	.2800	.0400
				B. Women					
65	.9224	.0600	.0158	.1000	.8535	.0395	.0000	.4750	.0550
66	.9159	.0650	.0158	.0900	.8575	.0395	.0000	.4750	.0550
67	.9092	.0700	.0158	.0800	.8605	.0395	.0000	.4750	.0550
68	.9074	.0700	.0158	.0800	.8533	.0395	.0000	.4750	.0550
69	.8967	.0770	.0175	.0750	.8462	.0438	.0000	.4600	.0500
70	.8880	.0830	.0202	.0700	.8445	.0505	.0000	.4500	.0460
71	.8808	.0900	.0202	.0650	.8485	.0505	.0000	.4340	.0460
72	.8728	.0970	.0202	.0580	.8515	.0505	.0000	.4340	.0460
73	.8628	.1050	.0202	.0500	.8575	.0505	.0000	.4340	.0460
74	.8505	.1130	.0215	.0420	.8592	.0538	.0000	.4340	.0460
75	.8385	.1220	.0230	.0350	.8595	.0575	.0000	.4250	.0450
76	.8272	.1300	.0248	.0300	.8580	.0620	.0000	.4150	.0450
77	.8161	.1380	.0269	.0260	.8584	.0646	.0000	.4150	.0450
78	.8028	.1460	.0292	.0220	.8544	.0686	.0000	.4150	.0450
79	.7894	.1540	.0316	.0190	.8483	.0727	.0000	.4150	.0450
80	.7735	.1620	.0345	.0160	.8431	.0759	.0000	.4080	.0420
81	.7591	.1700	.0379	.0130	.8415	.0795	.0000	.3990	.0410
82	.7430	.1780	.0420	.0100	.8390	.0840	.0000	.3900	.0400

Table 9.1 (continued)

	From Good Health to			From Moderately Disabled to			From Poor Health to		
Age	Good	Moderate	Poor	Good	Moderate	Poor	Good	Moderate	Poor
83	.7258	.1860	.0472	.0070	.8343	.0897	.0000	.3810	.0390
84	.7085	.1940	.0525	.0050	.8305	.0945	.0000	.3720	.0380
85	.6918	.2020	.0602	.0030	.8247	.1023	.0000	.3630	.0370
86	.6718	.2120	.0682	.0010	.8179	.1091	.0000	.3540	.0360
87	.6505	.2220	.0765	.0000	.8112	.1148	.0000	.3440	.0360
88	.6305	.2320	.0855	.0000	.7977	.1283	.0000	.3440	.0360
89	.6085	.2420	.0975	.0000	.7787	.1463	.0000	.3340	.0360
90	.5805	.2520	.1125	.0000	.7655	.1575	.0000	.3240	.0360

Table 9.2   **Probability of Death in the Next Year as a Function of Current Health State, by Age and Sex, Base Case**

	Men				Women		
Age	Good Health	Moderately Disabled	Poor Health	Age	Good Health	Moderately Disabled	Poor Health
65	.0150	.0370	.4900	65	.0018	.0070	.4700
66	.0180	.0440	.4900	66	.0033	.0130	.4700
67	.0210	.0500	.4900	67	.0050	.0200	4700
68	.0240	.0580	.4900	68	.0068	.0272	.4700
69	.0270	.0650	.4900	69	.0088	.0350	.4850
70	.0280	.0670	.5000	70	.0088	.0350	.5040
71	.0300	.0720	.5000	71	.0090	.0360	.5200
72	.0340	.0820	.5000	72	.0100	.0400	.5200
73	.0380	.0910	.5000	73	.0120	.0420	.5200
74	.0420	.1000	.5000	74	.0150	.0450	.5200
75	.0420	.1000	.5500	75	.0165	.0480	.5300
76	.0420	.1020	.5500	76	.0180	.0500	.5400
77	.0440	.1040	.5500	77	.0190	.0510	.5400
78	.0460	.1060	.5500	78	.0220	.0550	.5400
79	.0500	.1080	.5500	79	.0250	.0600	.5400
80	.0530	.1100	.5500	80	.0300	.0650	.5500
81	.0560	.1120	.5500	81	.0330	.0660	.5600
82	.0600	.1200	.5600	82	.0370	.0670	.5700
83	.0630	.1260	.5800	83	.0410	.0690	.5800
84	.0650	.1300	.6000	84	.0450	.0700	.5900
85	.0700	.1300	.6000	85	.0460	.0700	.6000
86	.0800	.1300	.6200	86	.0480	.0720	.6100
87	.0900	.1400	.6200	87	.0510	.0740	.6200
88	.0950	.1450	.6300	88	.0520	.0740	.6200
89	.1000	.1500	.6600	89	.0520	.0750	.6300
90	.1040	.1600	.6800	90	.0550	.0770	.6400

Here I restrict myself to several brief comments about the tables. I have relied primarily on two sets of sources in constructing the tables. One source is the series of papers published by Manton and his coauthors, which present data from the National Long-Term Care Survey (see especially Manton 1988; see also Liu, Manton, and Liu 1990); these papers provide considerable information on the transitions between good health, moderate disability, and death. The other source is the tables presented in Feinstein and Keating (1992), which are derived from the National Nursing Home Survey and several econometric analyses of nursing home admissions and discharge data; these tables provide information about the transition into and out of what I have called poor health. The numbers in these two sources do not always agree; when they do not, the numbers in tables 9.1 and 9.2 generally represent a compromise between them. In addition, the probabilities in the tables reflect smoothing, which was used to guarantee certain monotonicity properties over time, for example, that the probability a man in good health at age t remains in good health at age $t + 1$ falls smoothly as t rises. One limitation of the tables is that the numbers contained in them refer to a representative or "base case" elderly man or woman; in reality, of course, elderly men, and elderly women, differ substantially from one another in their actual morbidity and mortality experiences, and these individual differences are not captured by the tables.

Just as a person finds herself in one of three health states in each year, she also occupies one of three kinds of housing. One kind of housing is denoted "conventional"; this housing, of which a good example is a detached single-family dwelling, is best suited to individuals in good health, and poses modest difficulties for individuals in moderately disabled health, and severe difficulties for individuals in poor health. The second kind of housing is denoted "transitional," and may be thought of as catering to the moderately disabled elderly person; included in this group are congregate and other kinds of shared housing, retirement communities in which services are provided by management or are otherwise readily accessible, and other kinds of independent housing— generally apartments and flats—located near transportation, shops, and other services. Finally, the third kind of housing is "institutional care," including nursing homes, hospices, and other kinds of intensive-care facilities.

In introducing three housing states I am positing a slightly richer housing state space than has been used in most previous studies in the economics of aging, which have either focused exclusively on what I have called conventional housing, or have considered the dichotomous choice between conventional housing and institutional care. I am thus taking one step toward the direction of incorporating into analytic model building the vast swath of "transitional housing" available to the elderly. In fact, I am greatly simplifying the actual diversity of housing types available to elderly persons, since I have consolidated many different kinds of housing into the single category "transitional"; nonetheless, as the analysis to follow will demonstrate, even this simple extension of the standard approach yields considerable insight into elderly mobility patterns.

In each period the elderly person chooses whether to remain in the previous housing state, or to move to a new housing state. I discuss this decision-making process further below.

9.2.2   Utility and Bequest

The health and housing states described above are linked by a utility function that specifies that utility in a given year depends upon the match between health and housing. The idea behind this formulation is that each health state has associated with it an ideal housing situation that provides the optimal mixture of support and amenities. Thus good health is most enjoyable if an elderly person lives in conventional housing, with the many amenities that conventional homes afford, including privacy, space, and aesthetic value. In contrast, moderately disabled health is most successfully accommodated in transitional housing, in which an elderly person finds support that makes daily living easier and simpler, while maintaining a reasonable amount of freedom and independence. Finally, poor health is tolerated best if the elderly person resides in a long-term care facility.

The utility function formalizes the idea of an optimal match between health and housing by letting utility in a given year depend upon both health and housing state. For a given health state, utility is highest if a person resides in the home that matches that health state, as described above, and is reduced if the person resides in some other kind of home. Table 9.3 depicts the utility values used as benchmarks for most of the simulations reported later in the paper. Utility is set to 1.0 if a person is healthy and resides in a conventional home. Utility falls to 0.9 if the person is healthy but lives in transitional housing, and falls to 0.5 if the person is healthy but lives in an institution or equivalent. Similarly, if a person is in moderately disabled health, utility attains its highest level, 0.7, if he lives in transitional housing, and falls to 0.4 if he lives in conventional housing or institutional housing. Finally, utility is 0.4 if a person in poor health lives in an institution, and falls to 0.1 and 0.2, respectively, if that person lives in conventional or transitional housing. Note that utility is assessed at the end of the period, so that, if a person moves, his utility in the year in question corresponds to the match between his health and his final housing state.

The diagonal entries of the utility matrix correspond to the highest utility that can be achieved in each health state. The first diagonal element, 1.0, is a normalization, but the remaining two diagonal entries reflect the degree to which utility falls as health deteriorates, even when a person resides in an optimal living environment. The value 0.7 was chosen to reflect evidence on health-dependent utilities presented by Torrance (1986) and Viscusi and Evans (1990) and the collection of articles in Walker and Rosser (1993). Torrance

Table 9.3   **Utility as a Function of Health and Housing, Base Case Parameterization**

| | | Housing | |
		Conventional	Transitional	Institutional
Health	Good	1.0	0.9	0.5
	Moderately disabled	0.4	0.7	0.4
	Poor	0.1	0.2	0.4

discusses in some detail the methodologic underpinnings of using a quality adjusted life year (QALY) index to measure the disutility of ill health, and provides estimates suggesting that a year spent in moderate ill health has a QALY-equivalent of about .7 of that of a year spent in good health. Viscusi and Evans estimate health-dependent utility functions, and find that the marginal utility of a given level of income is approximately .7 or .8 as large in states of moderate ill health as in states of good health; assuming a simple multiplicative form for utility (as I do in the model specified in section 9.4) and that other forms of consumption remain constant, generates the implication that a year spent in moderate ill health is worth .7 or .8 of a year spent in good health. The edited edition by Walker and Rosser contains descriptions of several of the most well-known indices used to measure quality of life.

The value 0.4 was chosen based on consideration of various sources that describe the reductions in quality of life that accompany various kinds of disabilities; see the collection of papers in Walker and Rosser (1993) and Birren et al. (1991) for further discussion of the various indices used to assess the impact of disability.

The off-diagonal elements in the utility matrix indicate the reduction in utility an elderly person experiences when she does not reside in the housing state that matches her health status. Since there is little direct evidence available that might help determine these values, I have tried to pick reasonable values. I have also explored the sensitivity of my results to variations in the most important of these off-diagonal elements, which turns out to be element (2, 1), which describes the utility accruing to a moderately disabled person who lives in a conventional home. This particular element is important for several reasons. First, it describes the most common nonoptimal match: when an elderly person enters the model at age 65 in good health and living in conventional housing, the health transition that he is most likely to experience in subsequent years is to moderate disability, in which case, if he chooses not to move, his utility is given by element (2, 1). Second, the model allows considerable discretion in the choice of this value, particularly as compared with the range of feasible values for the off-diagonal elements corresponding to the case of poor health. Thus utility for an individual whose health status is moderately disabled can rise as high as 0.7 if he chooses to live in transitional housing, leaving considerable latitude in the choice of how far utility falls if the individual instead lives in a different kind of housing; in contrast, for an individual in poor health, the highest utility he can achieve is 0.4 (realized if the individual resides in an institution), a rather small number that leaves less latitude in the choice of how far utility falls in nonoptimal housing states.

Element (2, 1) of utility is set at 0.4 in the base case, a reduction of approximately 43% from the peak utility of 0.7 attainable in the health state of moderate disability. One can argue that this is too steep a reduction; hence in the simulations I have explored alternative values of this parameter, specifically 0.5 (28% reduction), 0.6 (15% reduction), and 0.63 (10% reduction).

Lifetime utility is the discounted sum of annual utilities, discounted at a rate of either .9 or .95 in the simulations.[1]

In addition to accruing utility in each year of life, an elderly person gains utility upon death in the form of a bequest left to her heirs. Following Feinstein and Keating (1992), I assume that total lifetime utility is an additively separable function of the sum of discounted annual utilities and a bequest function that takes the form

$$B(W) = [\beta(W - ec)]^{\alpha},$$

---

1. This is in fact a rather large discount rate, meaning that in this model the elderly place a high value on the future. Note, however, that mortality risk is explicitly included in the model, so this reflects true discounting, with no correction for the risk of death.

where W is end-of-life wealth, *ec* are end-of-life health costs, and β and α are parameters; the bequest is discounted at the same rate as annual utility. I assume that the elderly person possesses wealth W_0 at age 65; for the simulations I report in section 9.3, W_0 is set at \$500,000, while in the later simulations of the model presented in section 9.4, W_0 is chosen to be \$250,000. In the model of this section, in which wealth plays only a small role, I assume that wealth then shrinks by a fixed proportion θ each year the individual remains alive, an assumption that is meant to represent a very crude form of asset spend down, and I set θ to 0.9. Following Scitovsky (1988), *HC* is set equal to \$20,000, independent of age or sex.[2] Finally, β is set equal to .00002 and α is set equal to 0.5; at these values, a bequest of \$1,000,000 is worth approximately 4.5 years of healthy life lived in conventional housing, and a bequest of \$100,000 is worth approximately 1.5 years of healthy life.

9.2.3   Mobility Costs

For the model developed in this section, I consider three kinds of mobility costs. The first kind is a temporary utility cost, whereby an individual's utility in a particular year is lowered by a fixed amount if he has moved during the year or, in some specifications, if he has moved during either the current or previous year. The second kind is a health cost, which increases the probability that an individual will either suffer a deterioration in health status or death in the year(s) following a move. Finally, the third kind of mobility cost is a separation cost, meant to capture the emotional loss experienced when a person moves away from a home in which she has lived for a prolonged period. I apply the concept of separation cost by assuming that at age 65 an individual occupies a dwelling she has lived in for a long time, and that, upon her first move away from this home, she suffers a fixed utility loss that continues for all the remaining years of her life.

Most of the evidence about these three kinds of mobility costs is anecdotal, and cannot be used to determine the specific magnitude of each cost.[3] In the case of the temporary utility and separation costs, I have avoided choosing a single numerical value for the costs, preferring instead to simulate the model

---

2. Scitovsky shows that end-of-life health costs vary only slightly with age and sex of the deceased.

3. Some interesting quantitative evidence on the direct, transient utility costs of moving has been assembled by Venti and Wise (1990), in the context of estimates of mobility based on the Retirement History Survey. They assume that the transaction costs of moving are proportionate to utility (they assume a multiplicative, or log-linear, form for utility), and allow the magnitude of these costs to depend on initial health status. Venti and Wise then infer the magnitude of these costs by estimating a model of mobility; as mobility is very low in their data, they infer a quite large value for transaction costs, as much as 50% of one-year utility; they also find that costs (as a proportion of utility) are larger when an individual is in worse health. However, Venti and Wise do not specify any sort of morbidity or mortality tables, and do not allow for the possibility that a move may affect morbidity or mortality. In addition, they do not explicitly posit a utility function that depends on both housing and health, and do not fit an optimizing dynamic model of the kind I develop in this paper.

over a relatively wide range of alternative values. The specification of health costs is more complex, however, and is less amenable to alternative parameterizations; to capture some of the potential variability in these costs I have considered both the case in which they last one year and the case in which they last two years. Below I describe my parameterization of each of the three kinds of costs in greater detail.

Consider first temporary utility costs of moving. I consider two distinct patterns for these costs. The flat cost pattern assumes that the utility cost is the same across all health states. For this pattern I simulate the model under the alternative cost values 0, 0.1, 0.2, 0.3, and 0.4. Note that these five values cover a wide range; in particular, when the disutility of moving costs 0.4 units, the magnitude of the transaction cost is at lest 40%—its value when an individual in poor health moves to conventional housing—and as much as 100%—when an individual in poor health moves to institutional housing.[4] The other pattern assumes costs that are proportional to the utility of the best housing state available to a person of given health status. These cost structures are 0.1 0.08 0.04, 0.2 0.16 0.08, 0.3 0.24 0.12, and 0.4 0.32 0.16, where, for each triplet, the first number refers to the disutility suffered by a person in good health, the second to the disutility suffered by a moderately disabled person, and the third to the disutility suffered by someone in poor health. For both kinds of cost patterns, I consider separately and simulate separately models in which these direct utility costs last for one year (the year in which the move is made) or two years.

The health costs associated with mobility possess a more complex structure than the corresponding temporary utility and separation costs. In particular, the impact of a move on an individual's risk of falling into worsened health or death is likely to depend upon the individual's age, sex, and initial health status. To formalize the relationship between mobility and health, I define a set of multipliers that multiply the baseline morbidity and mortality transition probabilities set forth in tables 9.1 and 9.2, leading to a new pair of tables, 9.4 and 9.5, which apply to individuals who have moved. As the numbers in tables 9.4 and 9.5 indicate, the effect of the multipliers is to raise the probability of a transition into worsened health and death, and to lower the probability of a transition to improved health. The multipliers vary in size; in general they are smaller the larger is the baseline probability they multiply, and are somewhat larger for persons whose initial health status is moderately disabled or poor, since the available evidence suggests that mobility is more deleterious for such persons. I determined the multipliers by first choosing values for ages 65 and 90, and then using a linear interpolation scheme and a small amount of smoothing to determine the value of the multipliers that apply between these ages.[5]

4. When the transaction cost is this high, the results never exhibit a mobility pattern in which a person in poor health moves to transitional housing, in which case total utility would have been negative.
5. Subject to a monotonicity constraint that says that, for example, the probability of death is nondecreasing with age.

Table 9.4   **Probability of Transition from One Health State to Another, by Age and Sex, Effect of Mobility—Modified Case**

	From Good Health to			From Moderately Disabled to			From Poor Health to		
Age	Good	Moderate	Poor	Good	Moderate	Poor	Good	Moderate	Poor
					A. Men				
65	.8056	.1020	.0474	.0365	.7722	.0988	.0000	.2150	.0500
66	.7911	.1089	.0468	.0364	.7582	.0972	.0000	.2150	.0500
67	.7749	.1176	.0461	.0364	.7470	.0956	.0000	.2150	.0500
68	.7593	.1261	.0455	.0364	.7315	.0940	.0000	.2150	.0500
69	.7392	.1344	.0497	.0364	.7062	.1053	.0000	.2150	.0500
70	.7259	.1425	.0532	.0364	.6991	.1104	.0000	.2150	.0500
71	.7110	.1504	.0558	.0364	.6867	.1141	.0000	.2150	.0500
72	.6963	.1562	.0549	.0364	.6694	.1121	.0000	.2150	.0500
73	.6821	.1619	.0541	.0363	.6552	.1101	.0000	.2150	.0500
74	.6686	.1638	.0568	.0363	.6384	.1113	.0000	.2150	.0500
75	.6583	.1710	.0598	.0363	.6289	.1208	.0000	.1910	.0500
76	.6476	.1780	.0635	.0360	.6223	.1277	.0000	.1910	.0500
77	.6277	.1936	.0678	.0333	.6170	.1357	.0000	.1910	.0500
78	.6047	.2088	.0724	.0304	.6111	.1445	.0000	.1910	.0500
79	.5773	.2236	.0771	.0273	.6116	.1471	.0000	.1910	.0500
80	.5520	.2380	.0828	.0240	.6079	.1541	.0000	.1910	.0500
81	.5264	.2520	.0894	.0205	.6033	.1622	.0000	.1910	.0500
82	.4978	.2656	.0974	.0168	.5966	.1682	.0000	.1910	.0500
83	.4699	.2788	.1076	.0138	.5939	.1680	.0000	.1910	.0500
84	.4452	.2916	.1176	.0106	.5979	.1653	.0000	.1968	.0400
85	.4096	.3040	.1324	.0099	.5905	.1734	.0000	.1968	.0400
86	.3639	.3160	.1473	.0092	.5837	.1809	.0000	.1862	.0400
87	.3272	.3198	.1622	.0092	.5777	.1863	.0000	.1862	.0400
88	.3012	.3234	.1778	.0092	.5595	.2022	.0000	.1862	.0400
89	.2703	.3268	.1989	.0092	.5350	.2248	.0000	.1601	.0400
90	.2370	.3300	.2250	.0092	.5153	.2355	.0000	.1440	.0400
					B. Women				
65	.8254	.1200	.0474	.0500	.8303	.0988	.0000	.2400	.0550
66	.8116	.1287	.0468	.0468	.8176	.0972	.0000	.2400	.0550
67	.7975	.1372	.0461	.0432	.8028	.0956	.0000	.2400	.0550
68	.7931	.1358	.0455	.0432	.7845	.0940	.0000	.2400	.0550
69	.7701	.1478	.0497	.0432	.7549	.1025	.0000	.2450	.0500
70	.7534	.1577	.0566	.0420	.7424	.1162	.0000	.2282	.0460
71	.7427	.1692	.0558	.0403	.7462	.1141	.0000	.2114	.0460
72	.7302	.1804	.0549	.0371	.7420	.1121	.0000	.2114	.0460
73	.7123	.1932	.0541	.0330	.7444	.1101	.0000	.2114	.0460
74	.6884	.2057	.0568	.0286	.7375	.1151	.0000	.2114	.0460
75	.6678	.2196	.0598	.0245	.7300	.1208	.0000	.2124	.0450
76	.6490	.2314	.0635	.0216	.7227	.1277	.0000	.2124	.0450
77	.6316	.2429	.0678	.0192	.7217	.1305	.0000	.2124	.0450
78	.6084	.2540	.0724	.0167	.7111	.1358	.0000	.2124	.0450
79	.5860	.2649	.0771	.0148	.6977	.1410	.0000	.2124	.0450
80	.5578	.2754	.0828	.0128	.6870	.1442	.0000	.2154	.0420
81	.5352	.2856	.0894	.0107	.6855	.1479	.0000	.2164	.0410
82	.5094	.2955	.0974	.0084	.6827	.1529	.0000	.2174	.0400

Table 9.4   (continued)

	From Good Health to			From Moderately Disabled to			From Poor Health to		
Age	Good	Moderate	Poor	Good	Moderate	Poor	Good	Moderate	Poor
83	.4824	.3050	.1076	.0060	.6770	.1597	.0000	.2163	.0390
84	.4565	.3143	.1176	.0044	.6738	.1644	.0000	.2115	.0380
85	.4328	.3232	.1324	.0027	.6661	.1739	.0000	.2070	.0370
86	.4061	.3350	.1473	.0009	.6607	.1811	.0000	.2027	.0360
87	.3773	.3463	.1622	.0000	.6567	.1860	.0000	.1977	.0360
88	.3506	.3573	.1778	.0000	.6400	.2027	.0000	.1977	.0360
89	.3190	.3678	.1989	.0000	.6174	.2253	.0000	.1977	.0360
90	.2828	.3780	.2250	.0000	.6064	.2362	.0000	.1960	.0360

Table 9.5   **Probability of Death in the Next Year as a Function of Current Health State, by Age and Sex, Effect of Mobility—Modified Case**

	Men				Women		
Age	Good Health	Moderately Disabled	Poor Health	Age	Good Health	Moderately Disabled	Poor Health
65	.0450	.0925	.7350	65	.0072	.0210	.7050
66	.0533	.1082	.7350	66	.0129	.0385	.7050
67	.0613	.1210	.7350	67	.0192	.0584	7050
68	.0691	.1380	.7350	68	.0256	.0783	.7050
69	.0767	.1521	.7350	69	.0324	.0994	.7050
70	.0784	.1541	.7350	70	.0324	.0994	.7258
71	.0828	.1627	.7350	71	.0324	.0994	.7426
72	.0925	.1820	.7350	72	.0344	.1088	.7426
73	.1018	.1984	.7350	73	.0403	.1126	.7426
74	.1109	.2140	.7350	74	.0492	.1188	.7426
75	.1109	.2140	.7590	75	.0528	.1248	.7426
76	.1109	.2140	.7590	76	.0562	.1280	.7426
77	.1109	.2140	.7590	77	.0578	.1285	.7426
78	.1141	.2140	.7590	78	.0651	.1364	.7426
79	.1220	.2140	.7590	79	.0720	.1464	.7426
80	.1272	.2140	.7590	80	.0840	.1560	.7426
81	.1322	.2140	.7590	81	.0898	.1560	.7426
82	.1392	.2184	.7590	82	.0977	.1560	.7426
83	.1436	.2243	.7590	83	.1050	.1573	.7447
84	.1456	.2262	.7632	84	.1116	.1573	.7505
85	.1540	.2262	.7632	85	.1116	.1573	.7560
86	.1728	.2262	.7738	86	.1116	.1573	.7613
87	.1908	.2268	.7738	87	.1142	.1573	.7663
88	.1976	.2291	.7738	88	.1142	.1573	.7663
89	.2040	.2310	.7999	89	.1142	.1573	7663
90	.2080	.2400	.8160	90	.1142	.1573	.7680

As an example of how the multipliers were determined, consider males in good health. The multipliers chosen for age 65 multiply the probability of a transition to moderate disability by 2.0 (raising it from .051 to .102), the probability of a transition to poor health by 3.0 (raised from .0158 to .0474), and the probability of death by 3.0 (raised from .015 to .045); the probability of remaining in good health in the transition from age 65 to 66 is then set to be the residual probability, one minus the sum of the other three revised transition probabilities. At age 90, the three multipliers fall in value to 1.5, 2.0, and 2.0, so that the probability of a transition to moderate disability rises from .22 to .33, that for a transition to poor health rises from .1125 to .225, and that for death rises from .104 to .208. Between ages 65 and 90, a linear interpolation scheme smoothly adjusts each multiplier from its value at age 65 to its value at age 90, subject to the monotonicity requirement that each probability (other than that of remaining in good health) be nondecreasing with age. In the simulation, I consider both the case in which the mortality and morbidity costs of moving last only a single year, and the case in which these costs last two years.

Finally, consider separation costs. This cost refers to the psychic disutility that an elderly person experiences when she is uprooted from a home she has lived in for an extended period. The tremendous pain that accompanies such a move is widely recognized in the gerontologic literature. For example, in *No Place Like Home* (1991), Danigelis and Fengler write: "Home has many attractions for the elderly homeowner. The sense of history and family tradition as expressed through memories and possessions; the feeling of familiarity and resulting security from a long tenancy in this residence; privacy, and above all the sense of mastery and control over environment all combine to make home an attractive place to live out one's life" (9). They go on to cite a number of studies that have used surveys and interviews to verify the importance of attachment to home among the elderly.

The separation cost can be modeled as follows. First, assume that at age 65 the elderly person lives in the "family home." If the elderly person leaves the home, he or she suffers a fixed disutility, *which persists for an extended period,* as much as the rest of his or her life, in sharp contrast to the relatively brief costs associated with leaving more temporary abodes. Further, once the elderly person leaves the family home, this fixed cost begins, and it continues, regardless of later mobility patterns. I specify the alternative values 0, 0.1, 0.2, and 0.3 for this cost.

9.2.4   Decisions and Method of Analysis

In the model developed above, in each period the elderly person chooses whether to remain in his current residence, or to move to one of the two alternative housing states available to him; if he does choose to move, he incurs any mobility costs included in the model. The individual's decision-making process must take into account not only the positive utility earned and possible mobility costs incurred in the current period, but the impact of his decision on his future expected utility. To model this decision-making procedure and determine the elderly person's optimal choice, I employ standard dynamic programming techniques.

Let i denote the individual's current housing state, let j denote his current health state, let k_1 and k_2 denote the two alternative housing states, and let h_1, h_2, and h_3 denote the three health states in the model. Further, define $U(r, s)$ to be current utility when an individual of health status r occupies housing state s, let $x(r)$ denote the utility or separation costs of moving (which may or may not depend on health status r), let $q_0(r, z; t)$ denote the baseline probability of a transition from health state r in period t to health state z in period $t + 1$, and let $q_m(r, z; t)$ denote the probability of a transition from r to z when the individual is experiencing a health cost related to moving. Finally, let $V(r, z; t)$ denote the value function, defined below.

Consider now the case in which the utility and health costs of moving last only one year, and there are no separation costs of moving. An individual who finds himself in health state j and housing state i at the start of period t has the following total expected utility if he chooses not to move:

$$U(j, i) + \delta \sum_{z=1,2,3} q_0(j, z; t)V(z, i; t + 1) \, \delta\left[1 - \sum_{z=1,2,3} q_0(j, z; t)\right]B(W_t - ec_t),$$

where δ is the discount factor, $B()$ is the bequest function, defined earlier, and W_t and ec_t are wealth and end-of-life costs in year t, also both defined earlier. If the individual moves to housing state k_l, his total expected utility is

$$U(j, k_l) - x(j) + \delta \sum_{z=1,2,3} q_m(j, z; t)V(z, k_l; t + 1)$$

$$+ \delta\left[1 - \sum_{z=1,2,3} q_m(j, z; t)\right]B(W_t - ec_t).$$

The individual compares these expressions across his three options, choosing that option with highest total expected utility; this maximal expected utility is then denoted $V(j, i; t)$.

To solve for the elderly person's optimal decision each period, I have followed conventional methods and worked backward, beginning at age 90. For each year I have analyzed each possible combination of health and housing states that an individual might possess at the beginning of the period—nine total states in this model—and, for each initial combination, have determined the optimal decision.

For the most part, the procedure I have just outlined is quite straightforward. There is one subtlety, however, that arises whenever mobility costs last for two years. In that case one must distinguish two different value functions for each health and housing combination i and j: one value function, denoted $V_1(i, j; t)$ refers to the value of being in states i and j in t when one has moved in the previous period and must incur further mobility costs this period, regardless of whether or not one moves again; while the other, denoted $V_0(i, j; t)$, refers to the value of being in states i and j in t and not having moved in the previous period. The above expressions for total expected utility then become

$$U(j, i) + \delta \sum_{z=1,2,3} q_0(j, z; t)V_0(z, i; t + 1)$$
$$+ \delta \left[1 - \sum_{z=1,2,3} q_0(j, z; t) \right] B(W_t - ec_t)$$

and

$$U(j, k_l) - x(j) + \delta \sum_{z=1,2,3} q_m(j, z; t)V_1(z, k_l; t + 1)$$
$$+ \delta \left[1 - \sum_{z=1,2,3} q_m(j, z; t) \right] B(W_t - ec_t)$$

in the case in which the elderly person did not move last period, with the optimal expected utility generating $V_0(j, i; t)$; when the elderly person did move last period, the second expression remains the same, but the first becomes

$$U(j, i) - x(j) + \delta \sum_{z=1,2,3} q_m(j, z; t)V_0(z, i; t + 1)$$
$$+ \delta \left[1 - \sum_{z=1,2,3} q_m(j, z; t) \right] B(W_t - ec_t),$$

and the optimal expected utility is denoted $V_1(j, i; t)$.

The expressions for total expected utility are slightly different for the separation cost model. Consider this model for the case in which there are both separation costs and a one-year health cost of moving. If the individual has never left his age-65 home, his utility from remaining there is

$$U(j, i) + \delta \sum_{z=1,2,3} q_0(j, z; t)V_0(z, i; t + 1)$$
$$+ \delta \left[1 - \sum_{z=1,2,3} q_0(j, z; t) \right] B(W_t - ec_t),$$

where V_0 refers to the value function when he resides in his age-65 home and has never moved in the past. If has never left his age-65 home but contemplates moving, his utility is

$$U(j, k_l) - x + \delta \sum_{z=1,2,3} q_m(j, z; t)V_1(z, k_l; t + 1)$$
$$+ \delta \left[1 - \sum_{z=1,2,3} q_m(j, z; t) \right] B(W_t - ec_t),$$

where x is the separation cost and V_1 refers to the value function if he has moved. Finally, if he lives elsewhere than in his age-65 home, his utility is

$$U(j, i) - x + \delta \sum_{z=1,2,3} q_0(j, z; t)V_1(z, i; t + 1)$$
$$+ \delta \left[1 - \sum_{z=1,2,3} q_0(j, z; t) \right] B(W_t - ec_t)$$

if he chooses not to move, and

$$U(j, k_l) - x + \delta \sum_{z=1,2,3} q_m(j, z; t)V_1(z, k_l; t + 1)$$
$$+ \delta \left[1 - \sum_{z=1,2,3} q_m(j, z; t) \right] B(W_t - ec_t)$$

if he chooses to move.

9.3   Simulation Results for the First Model

In this section I summarize the results of an extensive set of simulations of the model presented in section 9.2. The most interesting aspect of this model is its predictions of how mobility patterns and housing choices are likely to vary in response to variations in the magnitude of mobility costs. In order to properly gauge this response pattern, I have considered a wide range of mobility cost parameters in the simulations. Further, since these mobility patterns and housing choices are my main interest, I focus most of my discussion on these issues, and say very little about either the calculation of utility or the predicted value functions.

In interpreting the simulation results, it is useful to define a benchmark against which to measure the extent of mobility predicted by any particular parameterization of the model. For this purpose note that, according to the model, when all mobility costs are zero an elderly person will move each time she experiences a change in health status, generating what may conveniently be called the complete mobility pattern. In much of the discussion below, I will present results in terms of the ways in which a particular mobility pattern deviates from the complete mobility pattern.

Figure 9.1 presents some descriptive results from simulating the model with no mobility costs. This figure, and all subsequent figures, forecasts the life history of an elderly person who enters the model at age 65 in good health and living in conventional housing. Figure 9.1a depicts the probability of a move, as a function of age; specifically, the panel shows, for both men and women, the conditional probability, given that the individual is alive in a particular year, that the individual will move, with the probability assessed based on a population that is in good health and conventional housing at age 65, and that experiences health transitions according to the probabilities in tables 9.1 and 9.2. Note that the probability of a move increases sharply with age. This increase is due to two factors: first, as individuals age, those in good health are more likely to experience a deterioration in health status; and second, at older ages a larger fraction of the population is likely to suffer from some degree of disability, and therefore be relatively more likely than those in good health to experience a change in health status. In interpreting this and subsequent figures, note that an individual may well move more than once; thus the predicted probability of a move in later years is an average of three terms, each term representing the product of the probability of residing in one of the three possible housing states at the beginning of the year multiplied by the probability of a move, conditional on beginning the period in that housing state. The average annual mobility rate implied by the figure is 14%, well above the true mobility rate among the elderly, which is closer to 7%, according to figures presented in Feinstein and McFadden (1989).

Figure 9.1b illustrates the probability that the elderly person will live in conventional, transitional, or institutional housing, again as a function of age

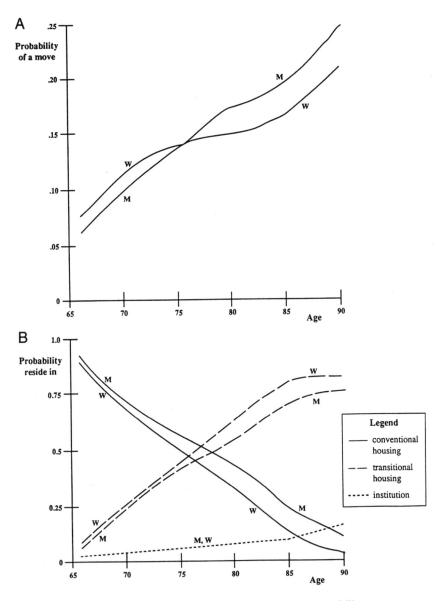

Fig. 9.1 Simulation results, first model, no mobility costs. *a,* mobility; *b,* residence.

and separately for men and women. Notice that the probability of living in transitional housing rises sharply with age, reflecting the fact that most of those alive at later ages belong to the moderately disabled health category; the probability of residing in an institution rises more slowly, increasing from approximately 1% at younger ages to approximately 15% by age 90.

I first discuss the results of simulating models in which there is both a temporary utility cost of moving and a health cost, then go on to discuss results from models in which there is both a separation cost and a health cost, and conclude by examining the sensitivity of some of my results to variations in the off-diagonal utility element (2, 1), a particularly crucial parameter that was mentioned earlier and that measures the extent to which utility falls when a moderately disabled person lives in conventional housing.

Consider first the class of models in which there is both a temporary utility cost and a health cost of moving. Figure 9.2 provides some descriptive results for a particular model in this class, the one for which the utility cost of moving is set at 0.4 and lasts for two years, and the health cost also lasts for two years; this particular model contains the highest level of mobility costs of any I have examined in this class, and hence offers a particularly striking and informative comparison with the zero-mobility-cost model discussed above, for which comparable results are depicted in figure 9.1.

Figure 9.2a reveals that mobility is substantially lower in this case than in the zero-mobility-cost case. In particular, for both men and women mobility is comparable to the zero-cost case at young ages, but does not rise smoothly with age; instead, for women mobility gradually falls, only to rise sharply during the last few years of life, while for men, after increasing for a few years, mobility plummets to zero (at age 72), then rapidly increases from zero at age 77, only to fall thereafter. Figure 9.2b depicts, for each age, the fraction of the population living in conventional, transitional, and institutional housing. As in figure 9.1b, the proportion of individuals living in conventional housing falls with age, while the proportion living in transitional housing rises. The most significant difference between this graph and the corresponding graph in figure 9.1 is that in this case the proportion of individuals residing in institutional housing is zero at all ages.

A detailed examination of the simulation results produces the following explanations for these patterns. At younger ages, for both men and women, individuals who fall into moderate disability always choose to move immediately into transitional housing. However, beginning at age 74, continuing until age 78, and then beginning again at age 87, men who fall into moderate disability and live in conventional housing choose not to move; this fact explains both the deep trough in the male mobility pattern between ages 74 and 77 and the sharp spike at age 78 (due to a queue), as well as the decline in male mobility at later ages. At all ages individuals who fall into poor health choose not to move into an institution, and individuals who live in transitional housing and recover to good health choose not to move back into conventional housing; these facts explain why mobility is lower overall in this case than in the zero-cost case, and contributes toward an understanding of why mobility rates do not increase with age. Finally, for women mobility decreases between ages 85 and 87 as those in moderate disability choose not to move into conventional housing, only to rise sharply during the last few years of life when moves into transitional housing resume.

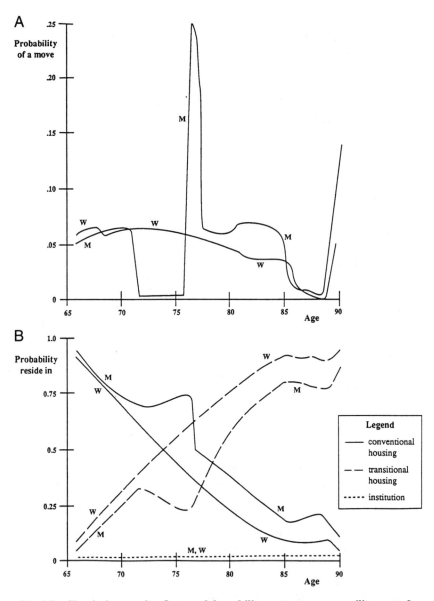

Fig. 9.2   Simulation results, first model, mobility costs: two-year utility cost of
0.4 plus two-year health cost. *a,* mobility; *b,* residence.

Although results from models in which the utility cost and health costs of
moving last only one year, or in which the utility cost if less than 0.4, differ in
some respects from the model discussed above, the results from all models in
this class share certain qualitative features. Overall, the simulation results for
this class indicate that mobility is less common as mobility costs increase, as

expected. Nonetheless, the results also show that mobility costs must be quite substantial in order to significantly reduce mobility. To see this, consider again the model discussed at length above. In this model mobility is in fact considerably lower than in the zero-mobility-cost model depicted in figure 9.1; in particular, average mobility has fallen from approximately 14% a year to approximately 5%, a value that is reasonably consistent with empirical evidence. However, this model incorporates very substantial mobility costs: the direct utility costs are 40% of the highest attainable one-year utility, are considerably more than 40% for those in worse health, and last over two years, while the indirect health costs last over two years and are, by any measure, steep. Apparently, mobility costs must be this high in order to produce realistic mobility patterns.

Beyond the simple finding that mobility falls with increasing costs, the simulation results suggest several other conclusions. One conclusion is that individuals who fall into poor health often are unwilling to bear the relatively high transaction costs of moving (relative to utility) to an institution, and often choose to remain in current housing. Interestingly, the results suggest that individuals who fall into poor health are most likely to move at more advanced ages, presumably in part because they are then less likely to experience an improvement in health in the future, and therefore can expect to benefit less from staying where they are. A second conclusion is that persons whose health improves from moderately disabled or poor to good are often unwilling to move back into conventional housing, especially at advanced ages, presumably because they are likely to lapse back into poor health in the near future. Thus reverse flows are discouraged by mobility costs. A third result is that, for many sets of simulations, transaction costs affect mobility more at older ages than at younger ages, in the sense that mobility patterns vary more with variations in transaction costs at these ages (this result is well illustrated by a comparison of figures 9.1a and 9.2a).

Perhaps the most striking mobility pattern concerns individuals who fall into the health category *moderately disabled.* Throughout nearly all of the simulation results such individuals, whether they were previously in good or poor health, choose to move (immediately) into transitional housing upon falling into moderate disability. In contrast, in models for which the transaction costs of moving are high, individuals do not always move into institutional housing if they fall into poor health, and do not always move back into conventional housing if their health improves from poor or moderately disabled to good. The combination of these two patterns results, in many circumstances, in transitional housing being a predeath absorbing state: once an individual moves into this kind of housing, he or she may never leave, even when his or her health status changes.

The fact that individuals move into transitional housing so often has several important implications. First, this finding highlights the importance of including such a housing state in empirical models of aging and housing choice— reducing housing to the two states "conventional" and "institutional" precludes exactly those mobility patterns that economic theory, as developed in this paper, predicts will occur most frequently in an elderly population. Second, from the viewpoint of elderly housing policy, this finding suggests that transitional housing could play an important role in improving elderly well-being, particularly in a world in which mobility is costly.

On examination, the finding that individuals choose to move into transitional housing so readily can be explained as due in part to the fact that in this intermediate housing state the elderly can choose not to move again should their health either deteriorate further or improve, without suffering a huge disutility as a consequence (support for this hypothesis comes from the fact that the elderly do not always move when they fall into poor health or when their health improves from moderately disabled to good). This rationale would not be uncovered by static or nonoptimizing models, but is highlighted by the dynamic programming approach taken in this paper.

It is interesting to note that, according to the simulation results, the movement into an institution tends to be reduced relatively more by mobility costs than does the movement into transitional housing. Specifically, the results suggest that it is often the case that an individual will move into transitional housing upon a deterioration from good to moderately disabled health, and then choose not to move into an institution when his health deteriorates further to poor; whereas the opposite mobility pattern, in which the individual chooses not to move from conventional into transitional housing when his health first deteriorates from good to moderately disabled, but then moves directly from conventional housing into an institution when his health deteriorates further to poor, *is never observed*.

With one exception, it is never the case that an individual who chooses to move decides not to move into the housing state that matches his current health status. This one exception occurs when a person who was previously in poor health recovers to good health (this transition has probability zero in the simulations and therefore is not directly relevant; but the mobility pattern described still has inherent interest). In this situation, and for certain parameter values, the person moves into transitional housing, a result that again highlights the importance of the dynamic programming approach (since this would never occur in a one-period static model).

Now consider the class of models in which there is both a permanent separation cost incurred when an individual leaves his "family home" (his home as of age 65), as well as a one-year health cost incurred following all moves. Figure 9.3 describes the model in this class for which the separation cost is 0.2. Figure 9.3a shows that for both men and women there is no mobility until age 71, at which age there is a very large mobility spike, followed by an initially steep and progressively more gradual decline in mobility at later ages. This mobility pattern is not difficult to understand, in the light of the nature of the mobility costs individuals face. Young elderly are unwilling to leave their age-65 home, since doing so results in a permanent cost. Eventually, in this case at age 71, the benefits of moving outweigh the costs for those in moderate

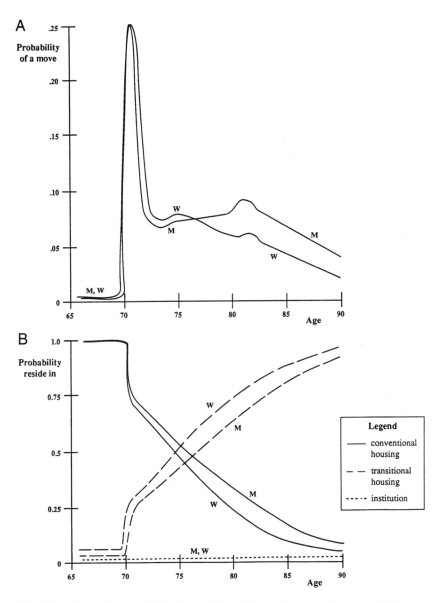

Fig. 9.3   Simulation results, first model, mobility costs: sepration cost of 0.2 plus one-year health cost. *a,* mobility; *b,* residence.

disability or poor health, and the large number in these health states do move—hence the spike at this age. In subsequent years the elderly continue to move from conventional housing into transitional housing when their health deteriorates from good to moderately disabled; but since fewer and fewer persons live in conventional housing and possess good health, this flow contributes less to overall mobility. Meanwhile, at all ages individuals who fall into poor health choose not to move into an institution. Together, these two phenomena explain the gradual decline in mobility at older ages. Figure 9.3b depicts the fraction of residents in each of the three housing states, at each age, and is fully consistent with the discussion above.

The fact that the separation-cost model predicts a somewhat different mobility pattern than the temporary-utility-cost model suggests that the relative importance empirically of these two kinds of mobility-cost models could perhaps be determined with appropriate data.

One striking qualitative feature shared by nearly all the results reviewed above is the finding that individuals who fall into moderately disabled health often move into transitional housing. While this result holds true both for individuals previously in poor health and institutionalized as well as for individuals previously in good health and living in conventional housing, it is far more common for an elderly person to deteriorate from good health to moderate disability than to recover from poor health to moderate disability. Since the sequence of events in which an elderly person deteriorates from good to moderately disabled health is so common, and the simulation results predict that the move into transitional housing that accompanies this health transition is relatively likely, this particular mobility decision seems worthy of further investigation; in particular, we may ask how variations in the utility benefits of occupying transitional housing (as opposed to conventional housing) affect the willingness of elderly people to move in this situation.

Recall that the utility parameterization sets the utility associated with moderate disability and transitional housing to 0.7, and the utility associated with moderate disability and conventional housing to 0.4. I have explored how an increase in this second parameter affects the willingness of elderly persons to move when they fall into moderate disability. I note that, whenever this parameter is small enough that a moderately disabled person living in conventional housing always wishes to move, the parameter has no impact (that is, within this range varying this parameter has no effect on the model's solution). I have found that when the parameter is raised to 0.5, the elderly continue to move in this health state.

When the parameter is raised to 0.6, at which point the disutility associated with remaining in conventional housing is approximately 15% (from the level of 0.7 achieved when the elderly person moves to transitional housing), whether or not the elderly move depends on the transaction costs of moving. In particular, when the health cost of moving lasts one year and the utility cost is at or below 0.1 and lasts for one year, individuals always move; when the utility cost is between 0.1 and 0.2, individuals sometimes do and sometimes do not move, depending on their age and sex; and when the cost is 0.25 and above, no one moves.

Now consider what happens when the off-diagonal utility element is raised from 0.6 to 0.63, so that the disutility associated with not moving into transitional housing is only 10%. Again, assume health costs of moving that last one year. When the utility cost of moving is zero, mobility is still not assured: among men, a move takes place only for those 81 or older; among women, a move is made for those aged 65 to 69, and 71 on. When the utility cost is raised to 0.07 for one year, itself 10% of the maximal utility in the moderately disabled health state, mobility falls further: men never move; women move beginning at age 74. When the utility cost is raised to 0.1, women move only between ages 78 and 83 (men never move); finally, when the cost is 0.15 and above, no one ever moves in this situation.

I conclude that, if the disutility of "mismatched" housing is 15% or more, then even when there are substantial costs associated with moving (one-year health costs plus moderate utility costs), the elderly will, according to the model, move into transitional housing.

9.4   Second Model

In this section I extend the model developed in section 9.2 to include a role for housing prices, a financial transaction cost on the sale of a home, interest rates, mortgage rates, annuity income, and an explicit consumption decision made each period jointly with the housing decision already described.

The most important extension of the first model modifies the definition of utility to include consumption, and computes the elderly individual's optimal consumption choice each period jointly with her housing decision. Recall that in the first model utility depends primarily on the quality of the match between housing and health, according to the function $U(j, i)$, where j is the individual's health state and i her housing state. The new utility function specifies utility to be equal to $\log[c(t)]U(j, i)$, where $c(t)$ is consumption in period t, measured in dollars spent. When the individual moves and incurs utility or separation costs x, utility is defined to be $\log[c(t)][U(j, i) - x]$. Note that according to this specification the marginal utility of consumption depends on both health status and the match between housing and health. Thus the marginal utility is highest for an individual in good health residing in conventional housing, and lower for individuals in worse health, or living in ill-suited housing. When there are utility costs of moving, the marginal utility of consumption also falls following a move. In contrast to the logarithmic form for consumption, I have also explored the implications of using an alternative linear specification, in which utility is equal to $c(t)[U(j, i)]$; in section 9.5 I briefly discuss the results of simulating models based on this alternative specification.

I modify the bequest function so as to preserve the value of the bequest relative to the utility associated with a year of healthy life. In particular, I multiply the earlier function by seven, so that the bequest is now defined to be

$$B(W) = 7.0[\beta(W - ec)]^\alpha.$$

Comparing the modified bequest function to the modified utility function reveals that a $1 million bequest is now worth approximately three years of good health to an individual living in a conventional home and spending approximately $20,000 annually on consumption.

Total utility continues to be equal to the expected value of the sum of the discounted annual utilities plus the discounted value of the bequest.

Consider now the modifications introduced by including housing prices in the model. Denote these prices as $p_1(t)$, $p_2(t)$, and $p_3(t)$, where $p_1(t)$ and $p_2(t)$ refer to the price of, respectively, a conventional and a transitional home in year t, and $p_3(t)$ refers to the cost charged for spending year t in an institution. For the simulations I set $p_1(65)$ equal to $200,000, somewhat above the median price for a detached single-family dwelling in the United States, $p_2(65)$ equal to $150,000, on the supposition that transitional housing, of which prime examples are retirement condominiums and townhomes, will typically be somewhat smaller and less expensive than conventional housing, and $p_3(65)$ equal to $25,000, which is approximately the average cost of one year in a private nursing home facility in the United States at the present time. Then I define $p_i(t) = p_i(65)(1 + \pi_i)^{t-65}$, where the π_i are rates of appreciation (or depreciation) for the three kinds of housing.

To determine explicit values for the π_i, I turn to several recent publications. Mankiw and Weil (1989) and Poterba (1991) discuss possible rates of real appreciation (or depreciation) for conventional homes over the next several decades, and argue that homes will either appreciate a small amount or depreciate. Based on their discussion, I set π_1 equal to .01, reflecting a 1% annual real appreciation. Elderly housing prices are likely to fare at least as well as conventional housing prices in the decades ahead, as the number of elderly grows; hence I also set π_2 equal to .01. To explore the sensitivity of my results to alternative rates of appreciation and depreciation, I have run a number of additional simulations, discussed in the next section, in which I experiment with smaller values for π_1 and larger values for π_2. Based on evidence presented by Maple, Donham, and Cowan (1992), I assume that the price of one year in an institution will rise at a real rate of 2% per year, so that $\pi_3 = .02$. In a number of additional simulations I assume, as an alternative, that $\pi_3 = .04$, reflecting a 4% annual rate of increase in the price of institutional care. I have not incorporated price uncertainty into the model, for reasons of computational complexity.

The calculation of household wealth is considerably more complicated in the new, extended model than in the original model. I will therefore describe this calculation in some detail, first defining a number of key variables, and then outlining the steps required to compute wealth in each period, for each possible housing state.

Define r to be the real rate of interest earned on savings, and define r_m to be the real interest rate assessed on mortgages when individuals purchase a home whose value exceeds their current wealth;[6] in the simulations I assume that r equals .02 and r_m equals .04. Next define $A(t)$ to be the amount of real annuity income an individual earns at the start of each period in which he is alive; I assume that $A(t) = A_0(1 + r)^{t-65}$, where A_0 is the value of the annuity at age 65, set to $18,000 in the simulations. In keeping with the earlier model, define W_0 to be total wealth as of age 65, and define W_t to be total wealth in year t. For the simulations I assume that W_0 equals $250,000, of which $200,000 is equity in the elderly person's home (which is assumed to be a conventional home on which no debt is owed), and the remainder is savings; these numbers are consistent with the findings of Feinstein and McFadden (1989), Venti and Wise (1990), and Ai et al. (1990) that the vast majority of all elderly wealth resides in homeownership. Finally, I assume that there is a financial transaction cost incurred whenever an elderly person sells a home of either the conventional or transitional type, assessed at 6% of the value of the home at the time of the sale.

Suppose now that household wealth is W_t at the beginning of year t. To calculate W_{t+1}, household wealth at the beginning of the following year, it is useful to distinguish the case in which the elderly person lives in conventional or transitional housing from the case in which she lives in an institution. Suppose first that the household lives in either conventional or transitional housing at the start of year t, denoted in what follows as housing state i. Two cases then arise: either total wealth exceeds the value of the home, in which case the household has additional savings; or total wealth falls short of the value of the home, in which case the household has a mortgage. If the household does not move in year t, then, in the first case, its wealth at the start of year $t + 1$ is equal to

$$p_i(t + 1) + (W_t - p_i(t) + A(t) - c(t))(1 + r),$$

where it is implicitly assumed that $c(t)$ is chosen to be less than $W_t + A(t) - p_i(t)$, disposable income.[7] In the second case, defining $y = (p_i(t) - W(t))/(p_i(t))$ to be the fraction of the home not owned by the household (so that $1 - y$ is the fraction that is owned), household wealth is

$$(1 - y)p_i(t + 1) - yp_i(t)r_m + (A(t) - c(t))(1 + r)$$

if the household consumes less than its annuity income, and

$$(1 - y)p_i(t + 1) - yp_i(t)r_m - (c(t) - A(t))(1 + r_m)$$

6. In the simulations I impose the restriction that a household is not allowed to move into a house if its total wealth falls below 25% of the house's price, an assumption that serves to eliminate the possibility of a household increasing its debt to very high levels, and is consistent with most mortgage-lending rules.

7. This and the other implicit assumptions made in the following few paragraphs are all part of all the optimal solutions found via the computer simulations.

if the household consumes more than its annuity income, where the first term refers to the percentage of capital gains captured by the household, the second to the mortgage payment, and the third to either the net savings or net debt created by the difference between annuity income and consumption.[8] If the household does move in year t, the calculation is similar, but slightly more complex. If the household moves to either conventional or transitional housing, denoted housing state k in what follows, it pays a transaction cost d equal to the value of the home being sold, so that $d = .06p_i(t)$. Thus total proceeds for the sale of the home are $S = (1 - y)p_i(t) - d$, where $y = 0$ if there is no mortgage on the initial home (it is implicitly assumed that S is positive). Now let $\hat{W}$ denote the household's total wealth immediately following sale of the home; $\hat{W}$ is equal to $S + A(t) + W_t - p_i(t)$ if the household's initial wealth exceeded $p_i(t)$, and $S + A(t)$ if not. Again, we must distinguish the case in which the household's total wealth $\hat{W}$ exceeds the price $p_k(t)$ of the new home from the case in which it does not. When $\hat{W}$ does exceed the purchase price, the household's wealth in year $t + 1$, W_{t+1}, is given by

$$p_k(t + 1) + (\hat{W} - p_k(t) - c(t))(1 + r),$$

while, when $\hat{W}$ falls short of the purchase price, W_{t+1} is given by

$$\frac{\hat{W}}{p_k(t)} p_k(t + 1) - (p_k(t) - \hat{W} - c(t))(1 + r_m).$$

If the elderly person moves into an institution, the calculation of $\hat{W}$ above is identical. If $\hat{W}$ exceeds $p_3(t)$, the price of institutional care, household wealth in year $t + 1$ is simply calculated to be

$$(\hat{W} - p_3(t) - c(t))(1 + r),$$

where $c(t)$ is constrained to be no more than $\hat{W} - p_3(t)$. If $\hat{W}$ falls short of $p_3(t)$, then $c(t)$ is set equal to zero (in the simulations, set to a very small finite value) and W_{t+1} is also set equal to zero.

Finally, let us consider the case in which the elderly person lives in an institution at the start of year t. I assume that an individual, for whom the sum of his wealth plus annuity income falls short of the price of institutional care, remains in the institution as a ward of the state, an assumption that is consistent with spend-down rules prevalent in most states. In this situation $c(t)$ is set to zero, wealth in year $t + 1$ is also zero, and the individual is not allowed to move. If the individual's wealth exceeds the cost of institutional care, then, if she chooses not to move, her wealth at the start of year $t + 1$ is given by the maximum of zero and

$$(W_t - p_3(t) + A(t) - c(t))(1 + r),$$

8. I am assuming that the household cannot refinance its mortgage, and that it simply pays the interest due on its loan, based on the home's current price, $r_m y p_i(t)$, each period.

where $c(t)$ is constrained to be no larger than $W_t - p_3(t) + A(t)$. If she moves to housing state k, then, if her total wealth, $W_t + A(t)$, exceeds the cost of the home, her wealth in $t + 1$ is given by

$$p_k(t + 1) + (W_t + A(t) - p_k(t) - c(t))(1 + r),$$

if $c(t) < W_t + A(t) - p_k(t)$, and

$$p_k(t + 1) - (c(t) - W_t - A(t) + p_k(t))(1 + r_m),$$

if $c(t) > W_t + A(t) - p_k(t)$, while if her wealth is less than the cost of the new home her wealth is given by

$$\frac{W_t + A(t)}{p_k(t)} p_k(t + 1) - (c(t) + p_k(t) - W_t)(1 + r_m).$$

To conclude my discussion of the model of this section, I will outline how the method used to analyze the earlier model must be extended to compute individuals' optimal consumption and housing decisions in the revised model.

As for the earlier model, let i denote the individual's current housing state, let j denote his current health state, let k_1 and k_2 denote the two alternative housing states, and let h_1, h_2, and h_3 denote the three health states in the model. In the revised model the value function V depends not only on health and housing, but also on wealth, and is denoted $V(W, r, z; t)$, where W is the household's wealth at the start of period t.

In the extended model the individual chooses both where to live and the level of consumption in each period. To determine the optimal housing choice and level of consumption, it is convenient to break the problem into two steps. In the first step each housing alternative is considered in turn, and for each alternative the optimal level of consumption is computed, assuming that alternative were to be chosen. Thus we define three interim value functions, one for each housing alternative, as follows:

$$R_i = \max_{c(t)} \log[c(t)]U(j, i) + \delta \sum_{z=1,2,3} q_0(j, z; t)V(W_{t+1}, z, i; t + 1)$$
$$+ \delta \left[1 - \sum_{z=1,2,3} q_0(j, z; t)\right] B(W_{t+1} - ec_t)$$

$$R_{k_l} = \max_{c(t)} \log[c(t)][U(j, k_l) - x] + \delta \sum_{z=1,2,3} q_m(j, z; t)V(W_{t+1}, z, k_l; t + 1)$$
$$+ \delta \left[1 - \sum_{z=1,2,3} q_m(j, z; t)\right] B(W_{t+1} - ec_t),$$

where $l = 1, 2$; W_{t+1} is wealth at the start of period $t + 1$, which depends upon $c(t)$ and must be computed separately (and in general will be different) for each of the three housing states according to the procedure described above; and x is the utility cost of moving, as before. In the second step a comparison is made among the three values R_i, R_{k_1}, and R_{k_2}, and the largest of these three is chosen; consumption is then equal to the value that was found to maximize the above expression for the appropriate R function.

The extension of this calculation to the case in which mobility costs last more than one year, and to the case in which there is a separation cost, is straightforward and is not presented here.

9.5   Simulation Results for the Second Model

In this section I present results obtained from simulating several different versions of the extended model of elderly housing and consumption. I first present results for a version of the model in which there are no mobility costs apart from a financial transaction cost. Then I turn to results for specifications of the model in which there are mobility costs, beginning with a model in which there are both temporary utility costs and health costs, and then discussing a specification in which there are both permanent separation costs and health costs. Finally, I explore the sensitivity of my findings to modifications in my parameterizations of the bequest function, the utility function, and the rate of appreciation of future housing prices. Throughout, I contrast the results for the extended model to the comparable results for the simpler model of elderly housing decisions analyzed in section 9.3.

As my detailed review of the results will show, the results for the extended model tend to corroborate the earlier findings for the first, simpler model of mobility. In particular, mobility is significantly affected by mobility costs, the pattern of mobility (with age) is different depending on whether there are temporary utility costs or a permanent separation cost of moving, and transitional housing emerges as an important modeling construct, housing a large proportion of the population, especially at older ages, and, in some versions of the model, serving as a predeath absorbing state.

Figure 9.4 presents a set of simulation results for the version of the extended model in which the only mobility cost is the 6% financial charge on the sale of a conventional or transitional home. In this figure, and figures 9.5 and 9.6, the graphs refer to the projected experience of an elderly person, who as of age 65 is in good health, lives in a conventional home that he or she owns and that is worth $200,000, and possesses an additional $50,000 in liquid assets. Figure 9.4a depicts the average probability of a move, at each age, separately for men and women. For both sexes mobility is approximately 6% at age 65, rises steadily to its peak in the early 80s, at which point it is 15% for women and 17% for men, and then falls sharply. Figure 9.4b depicts the fraction of individuals living in conventional, transitional, and institutional housing, again as a function of age. As expected, the fraction living in conventional housing falls steadily over time, from near 100% to near 0%, the fraction living in transitional housing rises steadily, from near 0% to near 100%, and the fraction living in institutions rises slowly, from near 0% at age 65 to slightly less than 10% in the late 80s (before falling at age 90). Finally, figure 9.4c depicts the

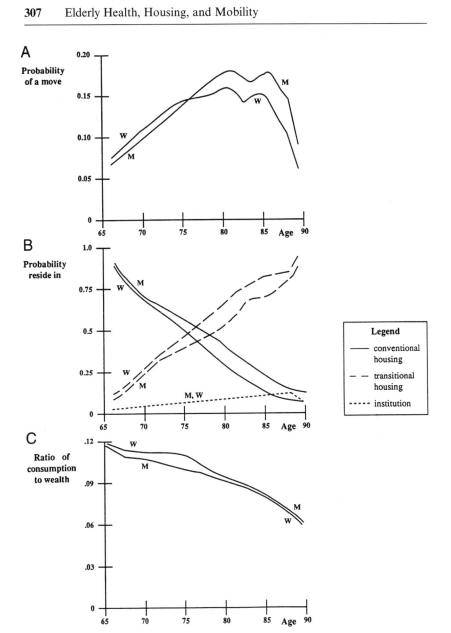

Fig. 9.4   Simulation results, second model, only mobility cost: financial transaction cost. *a,* mobility; *b,* residence; *c,* ratio of consumption to wealth.

average ratio of consumption to wealth among those living at each age, again separately for men and women. According to the graph, for both men and women the proportion of wealth consumed is near 12% at age 65, and falls slowly with age, to approximately 6% at age 90; women exhibit slightly larger consumption ratios than men at younger ages, and ratios essentially identical to those of men at older ages.

Figures 9.4a and b are directly comparable to figures 9.1a and b, which depict the corresponding graphs for the zero-mobility-cost specification of the first model of elderly housing, considered in sections 9.2 and 9.3. The only substantial difference between the two models is that in the earlier model mobility rises monotonically with age, whereas in the model of this section mobility first rises, but then falls at very old ages.

To gain greater insight into the shapes of the graphs depicted in figure 9.4, consider several facts that emerge from a detailed examination of the simulation results for the model. First, as in the earlier zero-mobility-cost model, the elderly nearly always move into their optimal housing state immediately following a change in health status. Thus the financial transaction cost does not by itself discourage mobility; further, the elderly do not choose to move out of conventional housing in order to invest more of their assets in savings, so as to earn a higher rate of return (2% versus 1% on housing) on their wealth. The one situation in which the elderly do not always choose to move into their preferred housing state is when they possess very low wealth; in this case they often choose not to move and, when they do move, at times follow what may be called a "bankruptcy" strategy in which they intentionally move to an institution, exhaust all of their wealth, and become a ward of the state.

A second set of facts concerns the consumption decisions of the elderly. At most ages and for most housing and health states, consumption is only slightly more than annuity income. The primary reason consumption is maintained at this modest level is to protect the size of the bequest, which exerts a substantial impact on total utility. In fact, the importance of the bequest helps explain why the ratio of consumption to wealth falls at very old ages: at these ages death is imminent (recall that in the model all individuals die by age 91), and individuals would rather hoard their wealth for the bequest than spend it on consumption. A contributing factor in this explanation is that many individuals suffer from either moderate disabilities or poor health at these older ages, and therefore benefit less from consumption (recall that utility is the log of consumption multiplied by a function that depends on health and housing). A last reason why consumption is maintained at modest levels is to hoard resources that may be needed either to pay the financial transaction cost associated with selling a conventional or transitional home, or to pay the cost of institutional care.

The simulation results also provide information about the relationship between wealth, mobility, and housing. Consider the results for men. At age 68, average wealth among the living is $229,000, $21,000 below wealth at age 65. At this age, among those who move average wealth is $227,000, among those living in conventional housing average wealth is $229,000, and among those living in transitional housing average wealth is $234,000. At age 80, average wealth has fallen slightly to $213,000. At age 80, average wealth is $209,000 among those who move, $207,000 among those living in conventional housing, and $217,000 among those living in transitional housing. Note that average wealth is highest for those living in transitional housing; at least in part this result is due to the fact that for these individuals the marginal utility of consumption is lower than for those in (good health and living in) conventional housing. Results are similar for women and are not reported here.

Now consider a version of the extended model in which there are both two-year temporary utility costs of moving and two-year health costs, in addition to the financial transaction costs. I assess the health costs at the same level as in the earlier models. When the utility costs are set at a value of 0.4, comparable to those used to generate the results presented in figure 9.2 and discussed at length in section 9.3, the simulation results indicate that there is *no mobility*. Apparently, the combination of substantial health, financial, and utility costs is sufficient to discourage all mobility. When the utility costs are reduced to 0.2, there is mobility, and it is this specification that I will discuss in detail.

Figure 9.5 presents results from the simulation of the model with two-year utility costs of moving set at the value 0.2 (plus two-year health costs and financial costs of moving). Interestingly, the mobility pattern predicted by this model, shown in figure 9.5a, is very close to that predicted by the corresponding earlier model with utility costs of 0.4, depicted in figure 9.2a. In both models the mobility of men is approximately 6% from age 65 to early 70s, then plunges to zero, soars to a height of 25% for a single year, then falls sharply back to under 10% the next year, followed by a gradual descent, and then a sharp increase at age 90. Clearly, this complex pattern is not an artifact induced by a peculiarity of specification, but is robust to alternative modeling structures. For women, mobility is much smoother over time, remaining at approximately 6% from age 65 to age 80, and then falling smoothly, rising sharply at age 90. Figure 9.5b illustrates the fraction of individuals residing in conventional, transitional, and institutional housing, as a function of age, and is again very similar to figure 9.2b. Finally, figure 9.5c depicts the average ratio of consumption to wealth, separately for men and women, as a function of age. As in figure 9.4c the ratio falls with age, and the ratio is somewhat higher for women, especially at younger ages.

A detailed examination of the simulation shows that the only move that the elderly consistently make is from conventional housing to transitional housing, undertaken when their health deteriorates from good to moderately disabled. They *never* move into an institution, except occasionally at very low wealth levels when they adopt the bankruptcy strategy alluded to earlier. Further, they never move back from transitional housing to conventional housing when their health improves. Thus, as in the earlier models with mobility costs, transitional housing turns out to be a predeath absorbing state. The conclusion is that the

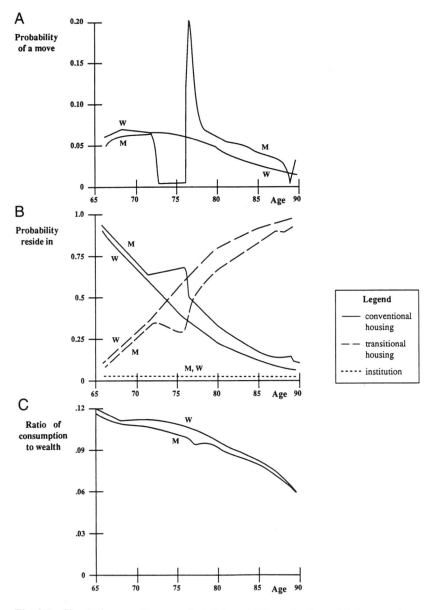

Fig. 9.5   Simulation results, second model, mobility costs: financial, two-year utility cost of 0.2, and two-year health cost. *a*, mobility; *b*, residence; *c*, ratio of consumption to wealth.

basic importance of transitional housing is preserved when the original model is extended to include a far richer specification of economic variables and decisions.

The finding that the ratio of consumption to wealth is slightly higher for women than for men, true in both of the two models just considered, seems to be due to the fact that men are relatively more likely to die, and therefore more likely to leave a bequest in the near future. Since the value of the bequest is quite high and, in particular, the marginal value of additional dollars preserved for the bequest is high relative to the marginal value of extra dollars of consumption (evaluated at the relevant baseline values indicated by the simulations), men have greater incentive to hoard their wealth.[9]

The extended model with separation and health costs of moving is depicted in figure 9.6; for this figure, the model was simulated with a separation cost of 0.2 and a one-year health cost of moving, the same specification used to generate the comparable results for the earlier model for which results are depicted in figure 9.3. As figure 9.6a shows, men do not move at all until past age 80; they then experience a sharp spike in mobility, which lasts for several years and is due to the unleashing of mobility among those in mismatched housing, followed by a decline to modest mobility levels in the last years of life. For women, mobility first begins at age 77, is followed by a very sharp one-year spike in mobility, and then gradually declines to modest levels. These mobility patterns are quite similar to those depicted in figure 9.3a, except that mobility begins at later ages in the model depicted in figure 9.6. Figure 9.6b depicts the fraction of individuals living in the various housing states, and is again quite similar to figure 9.3b. Finally, figure 9.6c denotes the average ratio of consumption to wealth; as with the earlier graphs of this ratio in figures 9.4 and 9.5, the ratio falls smoothly with age, in this case beginning just above 12% and falling to approximately 6%, with the ratio higher for women than for men at all ages.

9.6   Concluding Comments

The analysis of elderly mobility presented in this paper has generated a number of interesting insights. Most importantly, I have found that the economic model of mobility can predict realistic levels of mobility, when enriched to include a variety of mobility costs. In addition, my analysis indicates the importance of transitional housing, which is predicted to become an absorbing state for the elderly in many situations.

I believe the analysis could be fruitfully extended in several directions.

---

9. A simple calculation shows that the marginal utility associated with an additional $1,000 invested in the bequest, when its baseline value is $200,000, is nearly ten times higher than the marginal utility associated with consuming the extra $1,000, when the baseline level of consumption is $20,000. In part this difference is due to the absolute worth of the bequest; but it is also due to the fact that the bequest is a square-root function, whereas consumption is logarithmic, and hence relatively flatter at high dollar values.

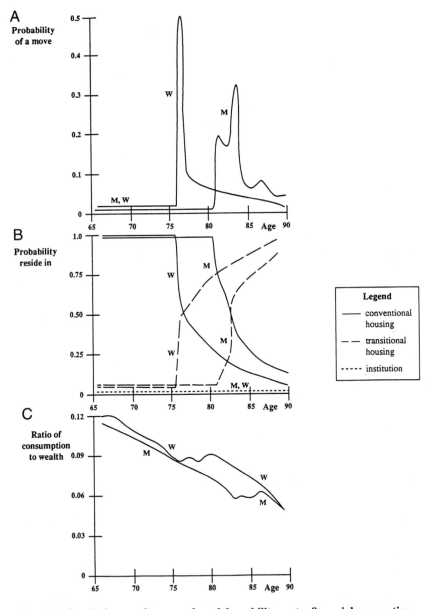

Fig. 9.6   Simulation results, second model, mobility costs: financial, separation cost of 0.2, and one-year health cost. *a*, mobility; *b*, residence; *c*, ratio of consumption to wealth.

Rather than specifying only three housing states, it would be more realistic to consider a larger number. One way to do this would be to define a bundle of housing attributes, including architectural design variables, location variables, and health services variables. Then each particular bundle of attributes might be considered to be a viable housing alternative. If prices were attached to each attribute (or small bundle of attributes), such a model would fit naturally into the framework developed in section 9.4.

A second important extension would incorporate uncertainty over future housing prices. Finally, a third extension would refine the definition of health states, perhaps by considering several "representative" patterns of aging. For each such pattern, a specific health transition matrix could be specified. In addition, each pattern could be associated with its own health-housing matching utility function, based on the relationship between the health scenario and specific housing attributes.

Appendix

In this appendix I describe the sources used and steps taken to construct tables 9.1 and 9.2. The two primary sources for these tables are Manton (1988) and Feinstein and Keating (1992). In table 4 of his 1988 paper Manton presents estimates of two-year transition probabilities based on data from the 1982 and 1984 National Long-Term Care Survey. Manton considers the following 1982 groups: no disability; IADL only; 1 to 2 ADLs, 3 to 4 ADLs; 5 to 6 ADLs; and institutionalized (there are also nonrespondents). Since I am specifying a model with only three health states, I have combined certain of Manton's categories; in particular, I have considered Manton's first group, "not disabled," to be equivalent to my category "good health"; his categories "IADLs," "1 to 2 ADLs," "3 to 4 ADLs," and "5 to 6 ADLs," summed, to be equivalent to my category "moderately disabled health"; and his "institutionalized" category to be equivalent to my category of the same name. For the 1984 data Manton forms the same categories, plus one additional category, "deceased" (again, there is a small problem with nonrespondents).

I have needed to make two main modifications to Manton's data. First, his data refers to transitions over a two-year period, whereas I require one-year transition probabilities. Second, his numbers clearly sharply understate the probability that an individual will be admitted to an institution at some point between 1982 and 1984, since it records institutionalization only at a single 1984 date; related to this is the fact that his numbers greatly overstate the probability of death when in "good" or "moderately disabled" health, since they do not capture a common sequence in which an elderly person enters an institution for a short stay before dying. To resolve these two issues I have drawn on tables in Feinstein and Keating.

I use Manton's numbers, unmodified, to compute

> Probability(good health in $t + 1$ | moderately disabled in t)

and

> Probability(moderately disabled health in $t + 1$ | good health in t)

separately for men and women, for each of the five-year age averages Manton reports (65–69, 70–74, 75–79, 80–84, 85–). I also impose the assumption that

> Probability(good health in $t + 1$ | poor health in t) $= 0$

for all ages for both men and women. I use Feinstein and Keating, table 1, directly for

> Probability(poor health in $t + 1$ | good health in t)

(this probability is assumed to be equivalent to the probability of nursing home entry as reported in that table; in that sense, it is probably something of an underestimate). I also rely on certain multipliers reported in Feinstein and Keating to set

> Probability(poor health in $t + 1$ | moderately disabled health in t).

For younger ages I set this value to 2.5 times the probability assessed for those in good health in year t; at older ages I reduce this figure to 1.5 times the probability assessed for those in good health in year t.

I use table 4 of Feinstein and Keating (based on data from the National Nursing Home Survey), which reports detailed statistics on nursing home duration and discharge status, to determine

> Probability(moderately disabled health in $t + 1$ | poor health in t).

Note that, whereas Feinstein and Keating present a discrete hazard model in which length of stay varies from as little as fourteen days to as much as seven years, for the purposes of this paper I have simplified their numbers to a simple one-year probability; the probability that a person continues in poor health in $t + 1$, denoted

> Probability(poor health in $t + 1$ | poor health in t),

is taken from their numbers. But in the construction I am using in this paper, nursing home duration is assumed to follow a Markov process; empirical results reported by Garber and MaCurdy (1989) suggest that this is incorrect, and that there is some duration dependence. I also use the Feinstein and Keating numbers to assess

> Probability(death in year $t + 1$ | poor health in t).

The most complex calculation I have performed in constructing tables 9.1 and 9.2 involves determining

Probability(death in year $t + 1$ | good health in t)

and

Probability(death in year $t + 1$ | moderately disabled health in t),

neither of which can be drawn directly from Manton's work, for reasons I discussed above. To estimate these probabilities, I have modified Manton's numbers by subtracting from each of the death probabilities he reports for these two health groups an estimate of the probability that an individual of that health level first entered an institution (poor health in my model) and then died. The probability of death, given institutionalization, is set as follows: .5, men aged 65 to 74; .46, men aged 75 to 84; .48, men aged 85 to 90; .5, women aged 65 to 74; .54, women aged 75 to 84; and .62, women aged 85 to 90. Since Manton's sample shrinks with age, I have deduced this rate of shrinkage and, assuming constant proportionate reduction in sample size each year, determined age weights. This step is necessary because, as shown in Feinstein and Keating's table 1, the probability of nursing home entry varies with age. The shrinkage numbers are .88 per year for men aged 65 to 74 (no shrinkage); .88 per year, men aged 75 to 90; .94 per year, women aged 65 to 74; .91 per year, women aged 75 to 84; .85 per year, women aged 85 to 90. For a shrinkage parameter μ, for initial state i (good or moderately disabled), and for probability of death conditional on institutionalization of δ, I then computed

$$P(\text{death} \mid i) = \text{Manton\#} - \delta \, \frac{\sum\limits_{i=\text{ages}} P(\text{poor health in } t + 1 \text{ or } t + 2 \mid i)\mu^{(i-1)}}{\sum\limits_{i=\text{ages}} \mu^{(i-1)}}.$$

For future reference, I will refer to this computed probability as λ_i.

Ultimately I wished to compare my estimate of these death probabilities based on Manton's table with the corresponding numbers in Feinstein and Keating. However, Feinstein and Keating, using data from National Life Tables, do not divide the population into good health and moderately disabled health (they simply use noninstitutionalized versus institutionalized—a division that is commonplace since separate death statistics are generally commonly available only for nursing home patients, who are assumed, in my model, to be in poor health). I have formed a weighted (by population) average of my modified Manton probabilities for the two health classes, good and moderately disabled, for each age and sex class, and compared these to the Feinstein and Keating numbers. For the most part the two different estimates are close, though not identical. I have generally chosen a number midway between the two, and used that as my estimate of

Probability(death in $t + 1$ | good or moderately disabled in t).

This gives me a scaling factor for the Feinstein and Keating numbers, which are 1.17, men aged 65 to 74; 1.08, men aged 75 to 84; 1.06, men aged 85 to

90; 1.7, women aged 65 to 74; 1.1, women aged 75 to 90. For reference below, I will denote the scaled Feinstein and Keating values as *FKMOD*. The number for women age 65 to 74 is so high because the probability of death, when in good or moderately disabled health, is very low for this group, so that small errors in either set of numbers generate large proportionate differences.

Having determined an estimate of

Probability(death in $t + 1$ | good or moderately disabled in t),

I then decompose this into separate estimates of the probabilities for those in good health as opposed to those who are moderately disabled. I do this in several steps. First, since Manton's figures suggest that the relative size of these two classes varies with age, I have determined weights that reflect these relative percentages; the weights, denoted w_1 and w_2 (they sum to one) are chosen to vary with age so as to smoothly interpolate between the average ratios within each age group. Second, I use my original modified estimates from Manton's numbers of Probability(death | good health) (λ_1) and Probability(death | moderately disabled) (λ_2) to assess the relative chances of death in each class,

$$\frac{\lambda_1}{\lambda_2} = \alpha,$$

and solve the following equation for λ_1:

$$w_1\lambda_1 + w_2\alpha\lambda_2 = FKMOD$$

for each age and sex class. I then have values for each of λ_1 and λ_2. As a final step I smooth these probabilities over ages, so that they are nondecreasing.

References

Ai, Chunrong, Jonathan Feinstein, Daniel McFadden, and Henry Pollakowski. 1990. The Dynamics of Housing Demand by the Elderly: User Cost Effects. In *Issues in the Economics of Aging*, ed. David Wise, 33–82. Chicago: University of Chicago Press.

Altman, Irwin, M. Powell Lawton, and Joachim Wohlwill. 1984. *Elderly People and the Environment*. New York: Plenum Press.

Birren, James E., et al., eds. 1991. *The Concept and Measurement of Quality of Life in the Frail Elderly*. San Diego: Academic Press.

Danigelis, Nicholas, and Alfred Fengler. 1991. *No Place Like Home*. New York: Columbia University Press.

Feinstein, Jonathan S., and Edward G. Keating. 1992. An Economic Analysis of Life Care. NBER Working Paper no. 4155. Cambridge, MA: National Bureau of Economic Research.

Feinstein, Jonathan S., and Daniel McFadden. 1989. The Dynamics of Housing Demand by the Elderly: Wealth, Cash Flow, and Demographic Effects. In *The Economics of Aging*, ed. David Wise, 55–86. Chicago: University of Chicago Press.

Garber, Alan, and Thomas MaCurdy. 1989. Predicting Nursing Home Utilization among the High-Risk Elderly. NBER Working Paper no. 2843. Cambridge, MA: National Bureau of Economic Research.

Golant, Stephen M. 1984. *A Place to Grow Old*. New York: Columbia University Press.

Hurd, Michael D. 1990. Research on the Elderly: Economic Status, Retirement, and Consumption and Saving. *Journal of Economic Literature* 28:565–637.

Liu, Korbin, Kenneth Manton, and Barbara Marzetta Liu. 1990. Morbidity, Disability, and Long-Term Care of the Elderly: Implications for Insurance Financing. *Milbank Quarterly* 68 (3): 445–92.

Mankiw, Gregory N., and David N. Weil. 1989. The Baby Boom, the Baby Bust, and the Housing Market. *Regional Science and Urban Economics* 19:235–58.

Manton, Kenneth. 1988. A Longitudinal Study of Functional Change and Mortality in the United States. *Journal of Gerontology* 43 (5): S153–61.

Maple, Brenda T., Carolyn S. Donham, and Cathy A. Cowan. 1992. Health Care Indicators. *Health Care Financing Review* 13 (3): 173–99.

Poterba, James M. 1991. House Price Dynamics: The Role of Tax Policy and Demography. *Brookings Papers on Economic Activity* 143–203.

Scitovsky, Anne. 1988. Medical Care in the Last Twelve Months of Life: The Relation between Age, Functional Status, and Medical Care Expenditures. *Milbank Quarterly* 66 (4): 640–60.

Sheiner, Louise M., and David N. Weil. 1992. The Housing Wealth of the Aged. NBER Working Paper no. 4115. Cambridge, MA: National Bureau of Economic Research, July.

Torrance, George W. 1986. Measurement of Health State Utilities for Economic Appraisal. *Journal of Health Economics* 5 (1): 1–30.

Venti, Steve, and David Wise. 1989. Aging, Moving, and Housing Wealth. In *The Economics of Aging*, ed. David Wise, 9–48. Chicago: University of Chicago Press.

———. 1990. But They Don't Want to Reduce Housing Equity. In *Issues in the Economics of Aging*, ed. David Wise, 13–29. Chicago: University of Chicago Press.

Viscusi, W. Kip, and William Evans. 1990. Utility Functions That Depend on Health Status: Estimates and Economic Implications. *American Economic Review* 80 (3): 353–74.

Walker, Stuart R., and Rachel M. Rosser, eds. 1993. *Quality of Life Assessment: Key Issues in the 1990s*. Dordrecht, the Netherlands: Kluwer.

Comment   Daniel L. McFadden

In an ideal world without transactions costs, a household would adjust living arrangements instantaneously to provide the best possible environment, given the health status of its members. In the real world with substantial out-of-pocket and psychic costs of moving, there are substantive questions about the optimality of behavior, and the efficacy of policies that promote arrangements such as conjugate living and life care. Questions of particular interest are whether households are rational in anticipating future declines in health status

Daniel L. McFadden is professor of economics at the University of California at Berkeley and a research associate of the National Bureau of Economic Research.

or onset of disabilities, and how they handle the risk associated with fluctuations in health status.

Jonathan Feinstein has undertaken a thought experiment that examines the mobility of decision makers confronted with probability distributions of future health status, and facing transactions costs for movement between living arrangements. For a simplified choice problem, he sets up a dynamic stochastic program that can be solved numerically by backward recursion. Using a careful synthesis of knowledge on transition probabilities between health states, and a stylized characterization of living arrangements and payoffs to various health and living combinations, he describes lifetime mobility patterns as a function of transactions costs. If health distributions are measured accurately, then tastes can be estimated, formally or informally, by matching simulations from the dynamic stochastic program to observed mobility patterns. Transactions costs can also be estimated, provided there is enough variation in exogenous variables to permit identification. The fidelity of a fitted model to observed mobility patterns allows testing of the hypothesis of life-cycle rationality.

Feinstein's paper is a useful first step in this research program, but it should be emphasized that it is only a first step. The paper does not systematically fit the model to observed mobility patterns, or develop an econometric framework for doing so. There are several critical limitations that need to be addressed before the model can be applied seriously for empirical analysis.

The model uses a stylized description of living arrangements, with categories of independent, assisted, and institutionalized housing. Feinstein contrasts the dominant role of assisted living in his simulations with the dominant role of independent living in real data, and suggests that this may arise because individuals in truth fail to make appropriate strategic responses to declining health. However, it is premature to draw this conclusion before making a careful empirical definition of living arrangement categories that can be matched to data on elderly households. For example, a disabled individual living independently with a nondisabled spouse may be in at least as satisfactory an arrangement as a similar individual living in conjugate housing. The distinction between assisted living and institutionalization is also blurred by the increasingly important "life care" category. For econometric and policy analysis, it would probably be more useful to define living arrangements using classifications corresponding to census or other data set definitions, or to medical insurance categories.

The Feinstein model deals only with individual decision makers, and does not address the problem of multiple-person households that share living arrangements, but may have different health levels. A number of complexities arise in this case. First, the adequacy of a living arrangement for an individual with a given level of disability depends not only on the physical facility, but also on the level of care that can be provided by other household members, and this in turn depends on their presence (e.g., working or at home) and health status. Second, the payoff to a given housing facility is a possibly complicated combination of the utilities of each household member. Third, strategic evaluation of housing alternatives must take into account the joint probabilities of health state and survival of all household members. Fourth, the possibility of household dissolution via divorce, or separation via institutionalization of one member, must be taken into account.

The model does not contain any explicit costs of housing, or characterization of the impact of these costs on (indirect) atemporal utility. Thus, it cannot answer questions of how the adequacy of living arrangements varies with income or wealth, or how mobility would change if, say, the effective cost of institutionalization fell. In fact, the distribution of living arrangements is strongly correlated with wealth, and in surveys living expense is often cited as a leading factor in choice of living arrangements.

The Feinstein model makes the assumption that living costs are entirely financed from an exogenous level of current consumption expenditures. The model allows no discretionary intertemporal substitution, and there is no intertemporal budget constraint that influences choice of living arrangements. Thus, the model cannot account for effects like precautionary savings motives that lead households to preserve wealth by postponing moves to more expensive living arrangements, or retention of owner-occupied housing that is protected from Medicaid spend-down provisions.

The model assumes that utility levels for each combination of health status and living arrangement are invariant with age. This implies that the effects of age on tastes operate solely through health status. While this is not implausible, it is a substantive hypothesis that needs to be checked.

The model considers several interesting alternative forms for transactions costs, including the possibility that they have transitory or permanent impacts on utility, or that they operate by modifying the (possibly subjective) probabilities of change in health status. However, it does not consider exogenous variables, such as age or location of family members, that may be related to transactions costs and may be used to identify its effects, and it does not parameterize or characterize transactions costs in dollar equivalents that would aid their economic interpretation.

The classification of health in the model (as good, moderate, poor, or dead) is relatively crude. One could, alternatively, seek one or more indices of health that weight ADLs and IADLs to isolate disabilities that require adjustments in living arrangements, or that by some criterion maximize the correlation of health status and housing choice. From the standpoint of simulating solutions to the dynamic stochastic program, it should make little difference whether health status is characterized as a discrete or continuous variable.

The model assumes that health status transitions follow a first-order Markov process. There is in fact considerable evidence for unobserved heterogeneity in the population, with "frail" individuals having permanently higher probabilities of transition to poor health states than "robust" ones. Either inherited genetic propensities or unmeasured cumulative exposure to environmental risks, be they exogenous or the result of behavior, will induce heterogeneity. One consequence of heterogeneity is that the Markov model will predict more "churning" among health states than actually occurs. A numerical example makes the point: Suppose a stationary population with half "frail" and half "robust" individuals, and "good" and "bad" health states. Assume the transition probabilities satisfy $P(G \mid G,R) = 0.9$, $P(G \mid B,R) = 0.5$, $P(G \mid G,F) = 0.5$, $P(G \mid B,F) = 0.1$. The Markov transition probabilities that would be inferred from one-period rates are $P(G \mid G) = P(B \mid B) = 0.7$. Then, the Markov model predicts that 9% of the population will switch health states twice in two periods, whereas in fact this will happen for only 5%. As a result, the Markov model will lead to a prediction of higher mobility rates, or higher transactions costs in order to match observed mobility rates, than a model that correctly accounts for heterogeneity. If individuals know whether they are "frail," then this heterogeneity will also induce heterogeneity in behavior, with individuals less willing to switch housing to match an excursion from their "normal" health state.

In conclusion, the Feinstein paper carries out a thought experiment that identifies anomalies in patterns of health and housing mobility, and concentrates on the role of transactions costs in explaining these anomalies. This is a useful approach to explaining housing decisions of the elderly. Further development of the model, along some of the lines suggested in this comment, are needed to make it sufficiently realistic to be a serious policy tool.

10   Intergenerational Transfers, Aging, and Uncertainty

David N. Weil

The large wealth of the elderly, and the prospect for its transfer to a younger generation, is a subject that has attracted much attention from both economists and the popular press.[1] This interest has been spurred by two factors: the increased wealth of the elderly, and changes in the ratio of the number of the elderly to their children that have been part of population aging. For example, the ratio of the average net worth of households with heads aged 66–75 to the average net worth of households with heads aged 36–45 rose from 1.55 in 1962 to 2.10 in 1983.[2] Similarly, the lifetime fertility rate fell from 3.14 for women born 1886–90 (those who would be leaving bequests in the 1960s) to 2.29 for those born 1906–10 (those leaving bequests in the 1980s).[3]

Economists differ in their views on the importance of intergenerational flows in general, and bequests in particular, for the levels of saving and capital accumulation. Kotlikoff and Summers (1981) calculate that at least 80% of the wealth of those currently alive is the result of transfers (both bequests and inter vivos transfers) from previous generations. Arguing against the importance of bequests, Modigliani's (1988) rough estimate is that they constitute an annual flow of approximately 1% of wealth. But even this low estimate of the importance of bequests leaves them a significant role: assuming a wealth/income

David N. Weil is associate professor of economics at Brown University and a faculty research fellow of the National Bureau of Economic Research.

The author is grateful to Angus Deaton, Rachel Friedberg, Laurence Kotlikoff, Andrew Samwick, and Jonathan Skinner for helpful comments. Support for this project was provided by grant 5-T32-AG00186 from the National Institute on Aging.

1. "Baby-boomers will hit an $8 trillion inheritance jackpot, a staggering transfer of wealth that will change the nation" (New Way to Get Rich 1990).

2. Author's calculations based on the 1962 and 1983 Survey of Consumer Finance. Net worth includes housing equity.

3. Ryder (1986). Following 1906–10 cohort, lifetime fertility increases gradually to a peak of 3.20 for the 1931–35 cohort, and then falls dramatically to an estimated 1.92 for the 1951–55 cohort.

ratio of three, the size of the bequest flow is significant in comparison to the personal saving rate, which hovers around 5%.

Such a large flow of wealth should have a large effect on the behavior of those who receive it. Evaluating how changes in the size of these flows—due, for example, to demographic change or to fiscal policy—will affect other aspects of the economy requires proper modeling of the role of these transfers in the decisions of their recipients. A number of papers have considered how the size of these flows is affected by changes in institutions or population age structure.[4] In this paper, I examine the effects of the *uncertainty* that surrounds bequest receipt.

Uncertainty has already been incorporated into the literature on intergenerational wealth flows in several ways. Barsky, Mankiw, and Zeldes (1986) and Feldstein (1988) consider intergenerational transfers in a world in which there is uncertainty about future wage income, either one's own or one's children's. Similarly, Davies (1981) and Hurd (1989), among others, consider the role of life-span uncertainty in generating bequests. Uncertainty about possible medical expenses at the end of life has also been cited as a motivation for the elderly to hold onto substantial resources as they age, and thus as a source of accidental bequests (Palumbo 1991).

In this paper, I examine the importance of uncertainty on the part of the *recipients* of the inheritances. Uncertainty about receipt of inheritances is in large part the flip side of the uncertainty that generates bequests. The same end-of-life and medical-expense uncertainties that can generate bequests will be reflected in the expectations of those who may receive an inheritance. Indeed, one would expect that the uncertainty surrounding bequest receipt (in the case of accidental bequests) could only be larger than the uncertainty that generated the bequest: in many cases, children may not really know how wealthy their parents are or the exact nature of their parents' wills.

Recent literature on consumption has stressed the role of individual uncertainty as a factor affecting decision making (see Deaton 1992 for a discussion). Individual uncertainty about future wages, for example, is large in comparison to aggregate uncertainty about future wages. Similarly, individual uncertainty about future bequest receipts may be large in comparison to uncertainty about the aggregate flow of bequests. The uncertain nature of bequest flows, combined with their large size, means that modeling consumption out of expected bequests as if there were certainty about bequest receipt will tend to overstate the effects of such expected bequests. If consumers are risk averse, then the expected utility of an uncertain bequest flow will be lower than in the case of certainty. Similarly, if consumers are "prudent" (Kimball 1990), then the path of consumption in the case of uncertainty will differ from what would be observed in a world with certainty. Skinner (1988) shows that uncertainty about future income flows effectively increases the discount rate that is applied to

4. For example, Hubbard and Judd (1987) or Lee (1992).

their expected values. The fact that people "underconsume" (from the perspective of certainty equivalence) out of expected bequests also means that consumption will, on average, rise rapidly as uncertainty about bequest receipt is resolved. Thus the expected lifetime path of consumption will slope upward more steeply than would be the case under certainty.

In this paper, I examine the difference between the certainty and uncertainty models for a widely studied application: the effect of population aging on saving. Population aging, by changing the relative sizes of the bequeathing generation and those receiving bequests, has the potential to affect the average size of bequests received, and the saving of bequest-receiving generation. In a world with certainty equivalence, these anticipated changes in bequest flows would have immediate effects on the consumption decisions of those who expect to receive them. If uncertainty is important, by contrast, bequest flows will have their impact on consumption—and a larger impact than under certainty—only at the time that they are received. Since the difference between when a person can form expectations about receiving bequests and when the uncertainty about their receipt is resolved can be a full generation, allowing for uncertainty can dramatically change the timing of the effects of changes in the bequest flow.

Uncertainty also matters in evaluating the effects of changes in the annuitization of the elderly, as discussed in Auerbach, Kotlikoff, and Weil (1992). Providing annuities to the elderly reduces expected bequests—how this affects consumption and saving of the young depends on how much the young were consuming out of these expected bequests. The immediate impact of annuitization on saving will be larger (that is, more negative) in a world where the uncertainty of bequests is taken into account than in a world of certainty equivalence. In both cases, the consumption of the elderly who receive annuities will rise. In a world of certainty, saving of the young will rise to partially offset the loss of the bequests, while in a world with uncertainty, the young would not initially be consuming out of expected bequests, and so would not alter their consumption much in response to a decline in expected bequests.[5]

The rest of this paper is organized as follows. In section 10.1, I examine an overlapping-generations model in which bequests are generated by uncertainty about one's own date of death, and in which this uncertainty is reflected in the consumption decisions of potential inheritors. I show how allowing for bequest-receipt uncertainty affects the lifetime path of consumption in both partial and general equilibrium. In section 10.2, I extend the model to allow for a second uncertainty: the possibility of large end-of-life medical expenditures. Section 10.3 uses the model to examine the effects of population aging on

---

5. Similarly, accounting for uncertainty in bequest receipt will change the analysis of the welfare implications of introducing annuities, as in Hubbard and Judd (1987). Uncertainty makes expected bequests less valuable, and so reduces one welfare loss from annuities that would eliminate accidental bequests.

saving and the level of wealth. I show that accounting for uncertainty leads to a larger adjustment of the wealth/income ratio in response to changes in population age structure than would otherwise be observed, and thus delays the effects of aging on the saving rate. Section 10.4 discusses the generality of the effects highlighted in this paper.

10.1   Modeling Uncertainty in Bequest Receipt

10.1.1   Previous Work

Hubbard and Judd (1987) consider an overlapping-generations model in which bequests are generated by end-of-life uncertainty in the absence of annuities. In their model, however, the uncertainty that generates bequests is not passed on to the next generation: all the members of a cohort receive the same bequest, which is equal to the average bequest left each year by their parents' cohort. The fact that individuals' inheritance receipt is invariant to their own family's mortality history means that all members of a birth cohort are ex ante identical. In the models of Abel (1985) and Eckstein, Eichenbaum, and Peled (1985), by contrast, individuals receive as a bequest the actual wealth held by their parent, rather than the average wealth of the previous generation. But in these models, individuals receive bequests at birth (if they receive them at all), and so face no uncertainty about bequest receipt. Thus bequest receipt affects the level, but not the shape, of the lifetime consumption profile. Kotlikoff, Shoven, and Spivak (1989) use a four-period model in which life-span uncertainty generates bequests to analyze the effects of different intergenerational bargaining outcomes on the distribution of wealth. Potential heirs face uncertainty about their inheritances at the beginning of life. The model I present below has a similar structure, but extends the model to sixty periods, allowing for a much more realistic simulation of the lifetime paths of uncertainty, bequest receipt, consumption, and wealth.

The analysis of the effects of demographic change in an overlapping-generations model with bequests that is presented in this paper is similar to that of Auerbach et al. (1989). In that paper, there is no life-span uncertainty, and bequests are generated directly by a "joy of giving" on the part of parents. Children receive their bequests upon their parents' deaths, but know with certainty the size of their inheritances from the beginning of life. Below I show that allowing for uncertainty in bequest receipt changes the timing of a demographic change's effect on saving.

10.1.2   The Basic Model

This section describes the basic model that will be used in the analysis. Individuals live for a maximum of 60 years. For the first 30 years of life there is no probability of dying. For the next 30 years, there is some known hazard, $p(i)$, of dying at age i, conditional on having reached age $i - 1$. Corresponding to the set of hazards are a set of probabilities of being alive at each age i, $P(i)$. Individuals who reach age 60 know with certainty that they will die in the next period.

Families consist of a single parent and N children. Children are exactly 30 years younger than their parents; thus there is no chance that an individual will die before his parent. There is no altruism or annuity market in the model, and so all bequests are accidental.[6] There are two uncertainties that face individuals in the model. First, individuals are uncertain about their own date of death. As is standard in many models, this uncertainty leads individuals to leave accidental bequests with some probability. Second, bequest recipients are uncertain as to when they will receive a bequest, if at all, and how large it will be.

The model is structured so that these two uncertainties face the individual sequentially: by the end of his 30th year of life, an individual has completely resolved uncertainty about bequest receipt, but has not yet resolved any uncertainty about his own date of death. As in Abel's (1985) model, the wealth that an individual inherits will be a function of not only his parent's date of death, but also of the dates of death of all of his ancestors. However, a sufficient statistic summarizing all of a family's history is the wealth of an individual at the end of his 30th year of life. This is all that a person's child needs to know in order to form an expectation of bequest receipt.

Throughout this paper I take the interest rate and the path of wages as exogenous, and focus on how changes in uncertainty affect the paths of consumption, saving, and bequests.

The Individual's Problem

The individual takes as exogenous (and known from the beginning of life), a vector $\pi(i)$, corresponding to the probability of receiving a bequest at age i, given that a bequest has not yet been received, and a second vector, $b(i)$, corresponding to the size of the bequest that will be received at age i, given that one is received in that period. The individual is assumed to maximize the expected value of a utility function that is time-separable and has constant relative risk aversion:

$$(1) \qquad U = \sum_{i=1}^{60} \frac{c^{(1-\rho)}}{1 - \rho} \left(\frac{1}{1 + \delta} \right)^i P_i,$$

where δ is the pure rate of time discount, P_i is the probability of being alive in period i, c is consumption, and ρ is the coefficient of relative risk aversion.

The individual's wealth (measured at the beginning of each period) evolves according to

---

6. There is also no risk sharing between generations. Such an outcome will hold in the model of Kotlikoff, Shoven, and Spivak (1989) if parents cannot credibly threaten not to leave any wealth left over at the end of their lives to their children.

(2) $w_i = (1 + r)*(w_{i-1} + y_{i-1} - c_{i-1}) + D_i b_i,$

where y_i is labor income in period i, r is the real interest rate, and D_i is a dummy variable taking the value of one if a bequest is received in period i. Individuals are born with no assets and are subject to the constraint that they cannot die in debt.

Given that an individual has already resolved his uncertainty about receiving a bequest, it is easy to solve for the lifetime paths of wealth and consumption. The first-order condition for the individual's optimization problem gives the growth rate of consumption as

(3) $c_{i+1} = c_i \times \left[\dfrac{(1 + r)(1 - p_{i+1})}{1 + \delta} \right]^{1/\rho},$

and so consumption at age i is just a function of age, wealth, and the present discounted value of future wages:

(4) $c_i = \dfrac{w_i + \sum\limits_{j=i}^{30} \dfrac{y_j}{(1 + r)^{j-i}}}{\sum\limits_{j=i}^{60} \left(\left(\dfrac{1 + r}{1 + \delta} \right)^{j-i} \dfrac{P_j}{P_i} \right)^{1/\rho} \dfrac{1}{(1 + r)^{j-i}}}.$

Given certainty about bequest receipt, it is also easy to calculate an individual's wealth path, and the path of his conditional bequest—that is, the bequest that he will leave at age i if he dies at that age.

Solving for the individual's path of consumption when facing uncertainty about the date and size of bequest receipt is more complicated. However, because of the nature of the uncertainty, solution is not nearly as complex as many other problems involving consumption under uncertainty. Define $c^{nb}(i)$ as the consumption at age i of an individual who has not received a bequest (because his parent is still alive), and $c^b(i)$ as consumption of an individual who has just received a bequest in period i. Similarly, define $w^{nb}(i)$ as the wealth of an individual who has not received a bequest, and $w^b(i)$ as the wealth of an individual who has just received a bequest in period i.[7]

The wealth of an individual who receives a bequest in period $i + 1$ is simply

(5) $w^b_{i+1} = (w^{nb}_i + y_i - c^{nb}_i) \times (1 + r) + b_{i+1}.$

This individual faces no future uncertainty except about his own life span: his consumption is the simple function of wealth and future wages derived above. Thus, given wealth and consumption in period i, it is easy to calculate wealth and consumption in period $i + 1$ for an individual who does receive a bequest.

---

7. Note that c^b_i and w^b_i refer only to individuals who receive their bequests in period i itself. Thus c^b_{i+1} is the consumption in period $i + 1$ of a person who received a bequest in period $i + 1$, and not the consumption in period $i + 1$ of a person who received a bequest in period i.

It is trickier to calculate the path of consumption in the case where a bequest has not yet been received, c^{nb}. I take advantage of the first-order condition:

$$(6) \qquad u'(c_i^{nb}) = E_i[u'(c_{i+1})]\left(\frac{1+\delta}{1+r}\right)$$
$$= \left[(1 - \pi_{i+1})u'(c_{i+1}^{nb}) + \pi_{i+1}u'(c_{i+1}^{b})\right]\left(\frac{1+\delta}{1+r}\right).$$

Given values of c_i^{nb} and c_{i+1}^{b}, one can use this equation to calculate the value of c_{i+1}^{nb}. Thus, given an initial value of c_1^{nb}, one can use the first-order condition to calculate the full path of c^{nb}. And given the paths of c^{nb} and w^{nb} up through any age i, it is easy to calculate the paths of wealth and consumption from date $i + 1$ onward, given that a bequest is received. The final step in calculating the path c^{nb} is to find the correct value for c_1^{nb}. To do this, I take advantage of the fact that c_{31}^{nb}, that is, consumption at age 31 given that no bequest has been received, can be calculated two different ways. First, since there is no uncertainty about future bequests in this period, it can be calculated from the level of wealth that the individual carries into this period. Second, it can be calculated from the first-order condition relating the marginal utility of consumption in adjacent periods. Only if these two values of consumption in the thirty-first period match was the initial guess at c_1^{nb} correct. Finding the correct value of c_1^{nb} is accomplished through a simple bracketing procedure.[8]

Given an individual's bequest expectations, one can calculate all of the possible consumption paths that the individual may follow. Figure 10.1 illustrates some of the possible paths of individual wealth and consumption, depending on the date of bequest receipt. Wages are constant over the first 30 years of the individual's life, and zero thereafter. The wage is set so that the present value of lifetime wages is equal to one hundred. The interest rate is set at 5%, and there is no time discounting. The coefficient of relative risk aversion is four.[9] The conditional mortality probabilities are those for women aged 65–95 in the United States in 1980, from Faber (1982). The paths of bequest probabilities and conditional bequest sizes are taken from the steady state of the model in the case where there is no uncertainty about bequest receipt, which is described more fully below.

Figure 10.1 shows how consumption jumps in response to the realization of bequest receipt. Those who inherit early in life receive the most, since their parents have not run down their assets. Consumption growth for individuals who have already received bequests is constant until age 31, after which rising

---

8. An alternative way of describing the final step in the solution procedure is as follows: Given an initial value of c^{nb}, one can use equations 4 and 6 to calculate the lifetime path of consumption for a person who never receives a bequest (noting that, after age 30, the value of π is simply zero). This path of consumption can then be checked against the lifetime budget constraint to see whether wealth at the end of the last possible period of life is zero. Only one initial value of c^{nb} will satisfy this condition.

9. Note 13 below discusses the effects of deviating from this baseline set of parameters.

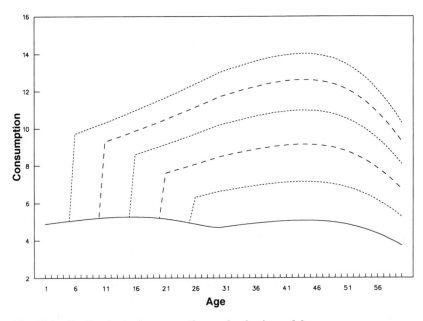

Fig. 10.1   Realizations of consumption paths: basic model

mortality hazard reduces it and eventually leads to falling consumption. The path of consumption during the first 30 years of life for those individuals who have not received a bequest is relatively flat and may even slope downward, despite the fact that the interest rate is greater than the discount rate and there is no possibility of death over this period. The reason for this phenomenon is that people who do not receive bequests receive a negative shock in each period to their expected bequests. Both positive and negative shocks are smaller as individuals approach age 30 and the amount of wealth that their parents have available to bequeath to them falls. At the same time, however, not receiving a bequest becomes more of a surprise as individuals age and their parent's mortality hazard increases.

Partial Equilibrium Effects of Uncertainty

I begin by examining the paths of consumption and wealth for individuals with given expected bequest paths. I compare the case of certain bequest receipt with uncertainty, holding the size of the bequest flow constant. This partial equilibrium case is relevant if one wants to know how to evaluate a given level of expected bequest flow. In general equilibrium, of course, the size of the expected bequest flow received by a given generation will be dependent on the uncertainty faced by their parents. Thus, in the next section, I examine the general equilibrium patterns of wealth and consumption in the certainty and uncertainty cases.

I compare consumption paths with and without uncertainty about bequest receipt, holding the expected path of bequests constant. More concretely, I compare the average consumption of a cohort of individuals each of whom faces a vector of inheritance receipt probabilities $\pi(i)$ and conditional inheritance sizes $b(i)$, with the consumption path of a cohort in which each individual receives his ex ante expected inheritance at each age.[10] When bequest receipt is uncertain, the average path of consumption is just the average across different realizations of bequest receipt of the paths shown in figure 10.1.

The two consumption paths, labeled "no uncertainty" and "partial equilibrium effect of uncertainty," are shown in figure 10.2.[11] Note that in both these cases there is still uncertainty about the date of one's own death; the cases differ only in whether there is uncertainty about bequest receipt. The average level of consumption within the group that receives uncertain bequests rises more rapidly than consumption for the group with certain bequests, as individuals in the group get the news that they have received an inheritance. Put another way, uncertainty at the individual level depresses the initial level of consumption for members of this group. Members of the group that receives uncertain bequests also hold more wealth in old age as a result of their depressed initial consumption—and thus will leave larger bequests. The next section discusses the general equilibrium effects of this difference in estates left as a function of expected inheritances received.

General Equilibrium Effects of Uncertainty

By the time an individual completes his 30th year, his uncertainty regarding the age of death of his parent has been resolved. As in standard models of accidental bequests, the individual chooses consumption over the rest of his life, facing only life-span uncertainty. In choosing this path for consumption and wealth, the individual also determines a path of contingent estates, $B(i) = W(i)$. From the point of view of that individual's children, these contingent estates are a stream of contingent inheritance receipts. Given that children are exactly 30 years younger than their parents, and that each parent has N children, the conditional inheritance receipt at age i for an individual in family j is $b_{i,j} = B_{i+30,j}/N$. Similarly, the probability of bequest receipt in each period of the child's life conditional on not having yet received a bequest is given by his parent's mortality hazard: $\pi_i = p_{i+30}$.

---

10. There are two ways to model the case where there is no uncertainty: first, one can give to each member of a birth cohort in each year of his life his share of the total bequest left in that year by his parent's cohort. This is equivalent to giving each member of the cohort in each year his expected bequest receipt for that year, and is the technique that I use here. Second, one can simply imagine that each individual knows the date of death (and thus the bequest) of his own parent. In terms of the cohort-average paths of consumption, saving, and wealth, these two approaches give the same results, since the propensities to consume out of a dollar of expected bequest (in the case of certainty) are invariant to the size of the bequest. Of course, the two approaches have different implications for the within-cohort distribution of wealth.

11. The bequest paths, $b(i)$ and $\pi(i)$, are those produced as steady states in the case of certain bequest receipt examined below.

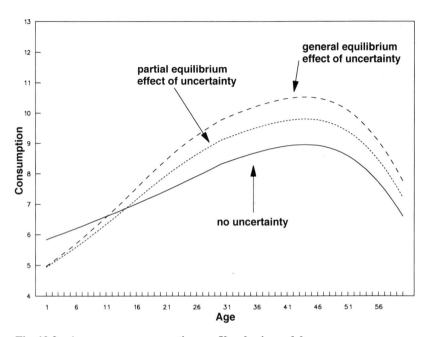

Fig. 10.2   Average age-consumption profiles: basic model

At birth, individuals in a cohort differ only in the path of conditional bequests that they face. The wealth of an individual at the end of his 30th year of life, and thus the conditional bequest receipt path faced by that individual's children, is a function of the conditional bequest receipt path faced by the individual and of the actual date of death of the individual's parent. Thus any individual's wealth is a function of the full history of his family. The individual's wealth at the beginning of his 31st year, W_{31}, serves as a sufficient statistic to summarize all of a family's history. Considering a large population, there will be a steady-state distribution of W_{31}.[12]

The line in figure 10.2 labeled "general equilibrium effect of uncertainty" shows the average path of consumption in the steady state. Because uncertainty

12. To solve for the steady-state distributions of consumption and wealth, I discretized the range of possible values of W_{31}. I then calculated a transition matrix between parent's value of W_{31} and child's value of W_{31}; each element in the matrix corresponds to the probability that the child will have a given level of wealth for the particular level of the parent's wealth. A single row of the matrix is constructed by considering a single level of parental wealth and calculating the child's wealth for all possible dates of death of the parent. Taking this transition matrix to a high power yields a matrix in which each row is the steady-state distribution of W_{31}. Average life-cycle paths of consumption and wealth in the steady state are then calculated by combining the distribution of W_{31} with all possible dates of death of the parent. This approach to finding the properties of the stochastic steady state turns out to be far more computationally efficient (and precise) than the approach of actually drawing random dates of death and then simulating over a large number of generations, as is done in Kotlikoff, Shoven, and Spivak (1989).

about bequest receipt leads to a shifting of consumption to later in life, bequests are larger under uncertain bequest receipt than when bequests are certain. Thus the general equilibrium effect of uncertainty about bequest receipt is larger than the effect in partial equilibrium. The increase in expected bequests has only a minor effect on consumption early in life—once again, as a result of prudence—and so the average lifetime consumption profile is more steeply sloped than in the partial equilibrium case. Average wealth per capita (assuming a constant population) is 22% higher in general equilibrium when there is uncertainty about bequest receipt than when there is no such uncertainty. By contrast, the partial equilibrium effect of allowing for uncertainty about bequest receipt is to raise wealth per capita by 12%.[13]

10.2   Adding Uncertainty about Medical Expenditures

In the basic model presented above, the only uncertainty facing an elderly person (who has already resolved his bequest receipt uncertainty) is about the date of his death. Among the undesirable properties of this model is that on the last possible day of life, wealth of the elderly goes down to zero.[14] The slow speed with which the elderly do run down their assets has raised the question of whether such a pattern would be observed in a world where there were a last possible day of life—that is, whether the elderly have motivations other than their own future consumption for holding on to assets.

In this section, I extend the model by having the elderly carry wealth until death. There are several interpretations that can be put on this wealth. First, it may represent money saved for end-of-life medical expenses. More generally, the household may have some chance of entering a state in which the marginal utility of a given level of consumption rises dramatically, and may save for such an eventuality. Second, as has been well documented, the elderly hold a large fraction of their wealth in the form of houses, which are often held until death (Venti and Wise 1990; Sheiner and Weil 1992).[15] Whether this housing wealth is held out of a desire to consume a specific bundle of housing itself,

---

13. The values of the key parameters that produced this result were $r = 5\%$, $\rho = 4$, and $\delta = 0$. Changing a single parameter (holding the other two at their base case values) had the following effects on the ratio of wealth per capita under uncertainty to wealth per capita under certainty (which is 1.22 in the base case): lowering ρ to 2 lowers the ratio to 1.15; lowering r to 0.03 lowers the ratio to 1.09; raising δ to 0.03 lowers the ratio to 1.17.

14. In the model, parents run down their wealth to zero at death, and thus children face uncertainty about the size of bequests received. But note that, even if parents keep the real value of wealth constant until death, there is uncertainty for the child about the present discounted value of bequest receipts. It is only when parents allow wealth to grow at the real interest rate that there is no uncertainty about the present discounted value of inheritances on the part of the children.

15. Price variability in real estate is presumably less risky from the point of view of an elderly person than from the point of view of a potential heir. Homeowners are to a large extent insulated from risk from the price of their own home, since their housing cost falls in the state of the world where the asset value falls. But variation in the price of a parent's home, which may constitute most of an expected bequest, is not similarly insured.

out of a desire to provide for end-of-life medical expenses, or as an asset shielded from Medicaid's tax is not clear.

To be concrete, I focus on the possibility of end-of-life medical expenditures as an additional source of uncertainty facing the elderly. This modification affects the certainty of bequest receipt in two ways: first, because of health uncertainty, the elderly will carry higher assets, thus potentially leaving higher bequests. Second, the lottery over end-of-life health adds more uncertainty to bequest receipt. It also moves this uncertainty later into the child's life, and thus reduces the number of years over which shocks can be spread.

Uncertainty about medical expenditures is introduced into the basic model as follows: I assume that individuals face a constant probability, q, of facing extra consumption needs in the last period of life. For simplicity, I hold this level of these needs constant at ten years' worth of wages. Thus individuals who have a possibility of dying will always have assets greater than this level. When individuals do die, their estate is equal to their total wealth with probability $(1 - q)$, and to their total wealth less this emergency fund with probability q.

The basic model presented above can be straightforwardly extended to the case of end-of-life uncertainty modeled here. Once again, consumption for an individual who has resolved his uncertainty about receiving an inheritance, and who faces uncertainty only about his own date of death and his own end-of-life expenditures, can be written as a function of wealth, age, and future wages. The first-order condition used to determine the path on consumption in the case where the parent has not yet died is

(7)
$$u'(c_i^{nb}) = \left[(1 - \pi_{i+1})u'(c_{i+1}^{nb}) + q\pi_{i+1}u'(c_{i+1}^{m})\right.$$
$$\left. + (1 - q)\pi_{i+1}u'(c_{i+1}^{nm})\right]\left(\frac{1 + \delta}{1 + r}\right),$$

where c_i^m is consumption in period i if the individual's parent died and had end-of-life medical expenses and c_i^{nm} is consumption in period i if the individual's parent died and did not have such expenses.

Figure 10.3 shows some potential realizations of the path of consumption in the model with uncertainty about end-of-life expenditures. There are now two uncertainties facing a potential heir: when his parent will die, and whether the parent will consume his emergency fund. The probability that a parent will face end-of-life expenditures (q) is set at 10%. For heirs who are young when their parents die, there is a positive shock whether or not the parent has end-of-life expenses. For heirs who are old when their parents die, on the other hand, having a parent who faces large end-of-life expenditures constitutes a negative shock, and consumption falls.

Figure 10.4 shows the partial and general equilibrium effects of uncertainty about bequest receipt in this model. Uncertainty about one's own end-of-life needs motivates people to leave larger expected bequests in this model, and

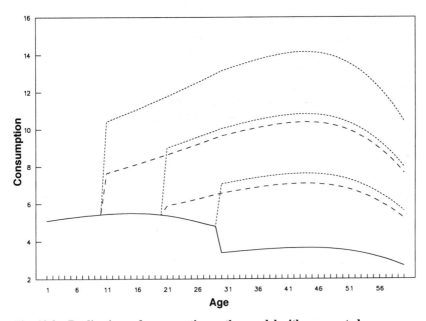

Fig. 10.3   Realizations of consumption paths: model with augmented uncertainty

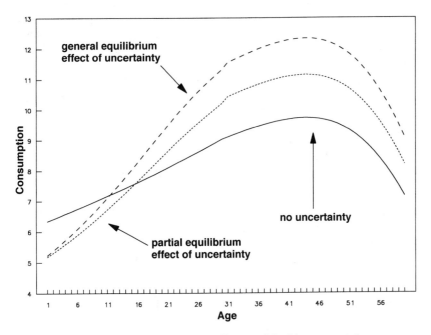

Fig. 10.4   Average age-consumption profiles: model with augmented uncertainty

these larger bequests drive a bigger wedge between the behavior of consumption when bequest receipt is modeled as being certain and its behavior when bequest receipt is uncertain. The partial equilibrium effect is to raise consumption in the second half of life (after uncertainty about bequest receipt has been resolved) 15% above the level with certainty, as opposed to 9% in the basic model. In general equilibrium, consumption in the second half of life is 27% above its level with certainty, as opposed to 18% in the basic model.

10.3   The Effects of Population Aging

Over the next decades, the ratio of old people to working-age population will be growing dramatically. Although this population aging is the product of decreases in both mortality and fertility rates, it is the latter that is by far the dominant force (Keyfitz 1985; Weil 1993). In changing the ratio of the elderly to their children, population aging affects either the size of bequests left, the size of bequests received, or both. In this section, I consider how the effects of population aging depend on the level of uncertainty surrounding bequest receipt.[16]

10.3.1   Steady States

I begin by comparing steady-state levels of consumption and wealth (both aggregate and age profiles) for different levels of population growth and for different treatments of bequest uncertainty. Figure 10.5 considers the four cases: with or without uncertainty about bequest receipt, and with or without uncertainty about end-of-life medical expenditures. For each case, the steady-state profile of consumption is plotted for the case where each individual has 1.5 children and the case where each individual has 1 child (this is meant to correspond to a movement from 3 children per couple to 2 children per couple). The effect of having fewer children is to increase the size of bequests. Raising the level of bequests in turn raises the importance of uncertainty surrounding their arrival.

Increasing end-of-life uncertainty or bequest receipt uncertainty increases the impact of changing the population growth rate. Steady-state consumption at age 31 is 13% higher due to a drop in population growth when neither uncertainty is present (fig. 10.5a); 25% higher when uncertainty about bequest receipt alone is present (b); 18% higher when uncertainty about end-of-life expenses alone is present (c); and 37% higher when both uncertainties are present (d). In the cases where bequest receipt is uncertain, reducing the rate of population growth has only a small effect on initial levels of average consumption, and so induces a rapid growth rate of consumption over the course of life (as uncertainty is resolved). By contrast, when there is no uncertainty about be-

16. The discussion here intentionally ignores the many other factors, such as changes in the youth and old-age dependency burdens, that will affect the saving rate as the population ages.

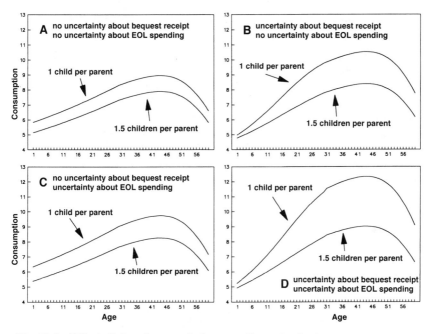

Fig. 10.5   Effect of changing population growth on steady-state age-consumption profiles. EOL = end of life.

quest receipt, reducing the rate of population growth leads only to a parallel shift upward in the lifetime consumption profile.

These same effects can be seen in changes in assets. Reducing the rate of population growth raises the steady-state level of wealth per capita by 25% when neither uncertainty is present (a); by 40% when only uncertainty about bequest receipt is present (b); by 28% when only uncertainty about end-of-life expenditures is present (c); and by 49% when both uncertainties are present (d). The fact that wealth per capita rises by more in the case of uncertainty than in the case of certainty means that, as will be shown below, there is a force offsetting the negative effect of a slowdown in population growth on saving.

10.3.2   Dynamic Effects of Aging

I now turn to the effects of population aging on the aggregate saving rate. My goal is to show how allowing for uncertainty in bequest receipt alters a model's predictions for the response of saving to demographic change. I consider the following experiment: the economy is taken to be in a steady state in which each parent has 1.5 children and in which each birth cohort is 1.36% ($= 1.5^{1/30} - 1$) larger than the one that preceded it. Starting in year t, the number of births is taken to remain constant. The decline in the birthrate is taken, in turn, to be a product of some of parents in the cohort of 31-year-olds having birthrate of 1 (one child per parent), while the rest have a birthrate of 1.5. Over time, the fraction of 31-year-olds who have only one child rises until, after thirty years, all parents have a birthrate of 1. Thus, following the demographic transition, each birth cohort is made up of some fraction of people who have sibship of 1, and some who have sibship of 1.5.[17] After thirty years, all people born will have sibship of 1, but people within a birth cohort will differ in the number of generations in their family since the birthrate changed: for example, of the children born forty years after the demographic transition begins, 38% will be the second generation born with sibship of 1 (that is, their parents will also have had sibship of 1) and 62% will be the first generation born with sibship of 1 (that is, their parents will have sibship of 1.5).[18]

Figure 10.6 shows the paths of the saving rate, relative to its level in the initial steady state, for four cases considered above: with or without uncertainty about bequest receipt, and with or without uncertainty about end-of-life medical expenditures. With or without medical expenditures, allowing for uncertainty about bequest receipt delays the onset of lower saving in response to a decline in population growth. This is because, when bequest receipt is uncertain, individuals in the cohorts that will be receiving larger bequests do not immediately raise consumption in response to their larger expected bequests, but rather wait until these bequests have been received. In the forty-fifth year of the demographic transition, the saving rate is equal to 30% of its initial level when there is no uncertainty about bequest receipt or end-of-life medical expenditures; 42% of its initial level when there is uncertainty about bequest receipt but not medical expenditures; 35% of its initial level when there is uncertainty about medical expenditures but not bequest receipt; and 50% of its initial level when both uncertainties are present.

10.4   Extensions and Modifications

Although the model presented above takes an important step in showing how uncertainty about bequest receipt can be incorporated into a life-cycle simulation, it is still very stylized. In this section, I discuss some of the ways in which the real world differs from the model, and I examine how these changes would affect the importance of the effects that are present in the model.

A first point to be noted is the low level of financial wealth held by most households. Other than a house, pension plans, and Social Security, most households in the United States have few assets. Given the large annuity provided by Social Security, this may be optimal behavior for households with life-cycle preferences. Alternatively, it may be evidence that something like a

17. A person's "sibship" is equal to one plus the number of his siblings.
18. This somewhat complicated scheme is chosen to avoid the "cycling" of age-group sizes that would normally be observed if the birthrate for all families jumped simultaneously, and at the same time to allow for feasible computations in which only two possible levels of sibship are considered.

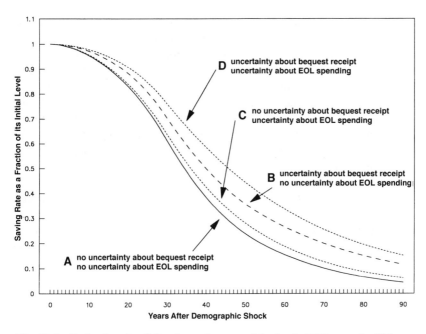

Fig. 10.6   Path of saving following a demographic shock. EOL = end of life.

buffer stock model of saving (Deaton 1991; Carroll 1992) is applicable to most households. To the extent that the degree of saving in annuitized assets is not fully under the control of the household (which is certainly true for Social Security), households with low saving will be even less prone to consume out of expected bequests than the households facing uncertainty modeled above. Households will not be able to consume out of bequests until they are received, because they have no wealth to run down, and because uncollateralized borrowing is fairly limited.

A second important consideration is the degree of uncertainty surrounding bequest. It seems clear that, among the very wealthy, although the timing of bequests is not known, the size (or more accurately, the present discounted value) of bequest receipts is not particularly uncertain. The very wealthy pass on assets at death for tax or personal reasons, not because the parents may need the money for their own consumption. Taken together these two points—the low level of life-cycle saving of most people, and unimportance of uncertainty for the wealthy—mean that uncertainty about bequest receipt is probably more important for the median household, but less important for total saving and wealth accumulation, than is implied by the model presented here.

In terms of analyzing the effects of demographic change, the model presented here has addressed some important phenomena. The model holds constant both the average age difference between parents and children and the average age of heirs at the time that their parent dies. While the former of these is not a terrible assumption for the United States, the latter is clearly false. In the United States, women's life expectancy at the birth of the last child rose from 40.4 for women born 1900–1909 to 47.5 for women born 1940–49. This means that the average age of resolution of the uncertainty surrounding receipt of inheritances will have similarly risen, amplifying the effects analyzed here. Individuals who might fund their retirements with inheritances received from their parents may now have to wait until the time of their own retirements to see whether such inheritances are forthcoming. Prudent children faced with such a prospect will save for retirement on their own and, on average, see their postretirement consumption rise dramatically.

Finally, a key question is how different uncertainties interact. Hubbard, Skinner, and Zeldes (1994) focus on the interaction of three sources of uncertainty that face individuals: wages, health, and date of death. In this paper I have highlighted a fourth uncertainty: the date and size of bequest receipt. If one believes that bequests are an important factor in wealth accumulation, and that a significant fraction of bequests are accidental, then uncertainty about bequest receipt should be added to the list of the "usual suspects."

References

Abel, Andrew B. 1985. Precautionary Saving and Accidental Bequests. *American Economic Review* 75 (4): 771–91.

Auerbach, Alan J., Laurence J. Kotlikoff, Robert P. Hagemann, and Giuseppe Nicoletti. 1989. The Economic Dynamics of an Aging Population: The Case of Four OECD Countries. *OECD Economic Studies* 12 (spring): 97–130.

Auerbach, Alan J., Laurence J. Kotlikoff, and David N. Weil. 1992. The Increasing Annuitization of the Elderly: Estimates and Implications for Intergenerational Transfers, Inequality, and National Saving. Brown University. Mimeo.

Barsky, Robert B., N. Gregory Mankiw, and Stephen P. Zeldes. 1986. Ricardian Consumers with Keynesian Propensities. *American Economic Review* 76 (4): 676–91.

Carroll, Christopher D. 1992. The Buffer-Stock Theory of Saving: Some Macroeconomic Evidence. *Brookings Papers on Economic Activity* 2:61–156.

Davies, James. 1981. Uncertain Lifetime, Consumption, and Dissaving in Retirement. *Journal of Political Economy* 89:561–77.

Deaton, Angus. 1991. Saving and Liquidity Constraints. *Econometrica* 59 (5): 1221–48.

———. 1992. *Understanding Consumption.* Oxford: Clarendon Press.

Eckstein, Zvi, Martin S. Eichenbaum, and Dan Peled. 1985. The Distribution of Wealth and Welfare in the Presence of Incomplete Annuity Markets. *Quarterly Journal of Economics* 100 (3): 789–806.

Faber, Joseph F. 1982. *Life Tables for the United States, 1900–2050.* Actuarial Study no. 87. Social Security Administration, September.

Feldstein, Martin. 1988. The Effects of Fiscal Policies When Incomes Are Uncertain: A Contradiction to Ricardian Equivalence. *American Economic Review* 78 (1): 14–23.

Hubbard, R. Glenn, and Kenneth L. Judd. 1987. Social Security and Individual Welfare: Precautionary Saving, Borrowing Constraints, and the Payroll Tax. *American Eco-*

nomic Review 77 (4): 630–46.

Hubbard, R. Glenn, Jonathan Skinner, and Stephen P. Zeldes. 1994. The Importance of Precautionary Motives in Explaining Individual and Aggregate Saving. *Carnegie-Rochester Conference Series in Public Policy* 40:59–125.

Hurd, Michael D. 1989. Mortality Risk and Bequests. *Econometrica* 57 (4): 779–813.

Keyfitz, Nathan. 1985. *Applied Mathematical Demography.* New York: Springer-Verlag.

Kimball, Miles S. 1990. Precautionary Saving in the Small and in the Large. *Econometrica* 58 (1): 53–73.

Kotlikoff, Laurence J., John Shoven, and Avia Spivak. 1989. Annuity Insurance, Savings, and Inequality. In Laurence J. Kotlikoff, *What Determines Savings?* Cambridge: MIT Press.

Kotlikoff, Laurence J., and Lawrence H. Summers. 1981. The Role of Intergenerational Transfers in Capital Accumulation. *Journal of Political Economy* 89 (August): 706–32.

Lee, Ronald D. 1992. The Formal Demography of Population Aging, Transfers, and the Economic Life Cycle. University of California, Berkeley. Mimeo.

Modigliani, Franco. 1988. The Role of Intergenerational Transfers and Life Cycle Savings in the Accumulation of Wealth. *Journal of Economic Perspectives* 2 (2): 15–40.

The New Way to Get Rich. 1990. *U.S. News and World Report,* 7 May.

Palumbo, Michael G. 1991. Health Uncertainty and Optimal Consumption near the End of the Life Cycle. Ph.D. dissertation, University of Virginia.

Ryder, Norman B. 1986. Observations on the History of Cohort Fertility in the United States. *Population and Development Review* 12 (4): 617–43.

Sheiner, Louise M., and David N. Weil. 1992. The Housing Wealth of the Aged. NBER Working Paper no. 4115. Cambridge, MA: National Bureau of Economic Research, July.

Skinner, Jonathan. 1988. Risky Income, Life Cycle Consumption, and Precautionary Savings. *Journal of Monetary Economics* 22 (2): 237–55.

Venti, Steven F., and David A. Wise. 1990. But They Don't Want to Reduce Housing Equity. In *Issues in the Economics of Aging,* ed. David A. Wise. Chicago: University of Chicago Press.

Weil, David N. 1993. The Economics of Population Aging. Brown University. Mimeo.

Comment   James M. Poterba

This paper addresses a substantively important but under-studied question about the relationship between intergenerational transfers and the consumption behavior of potential transfer recipients. Much previous research has focused on the possibility that retired households have bequest motives, and that this affects their rate of asset decumulation. Yet there has been little previous work on the link between expected bequests and accumulation behavior of the groups that may receive such transfers.

    This question is particularly important today, because the current older generation is wealthier than its predecessors. One estimate suggests that more than

James M. Poterba is professor of economics at the Massachusetts Institute of Technology and director of the Public Economics Research Program at the National Bureau of Economic Research.

$6 trillion in net worth is held by elderly households, those aged 60+ in 1989. The combined effects of rising real estate values and unexpected Social Security benefit increases in the 1970s, and a strong stock market in the 1980s, have left some current retirees quite wealthy. The expected transfers from this generation to their children are therefore substantial. One could ask whether these expected transfers explain the low saving rate of the U.S. economy in the 1980s. This paper does not perform this applied exercise, but rather tackles a prior question by developing a model for the consumption behavior of those who can expect to receive bequests.

The centerpiece of this model is a set of stochastic assumptions about the timing and amount of bequests that recipients can expect. Conditional on a donor's wealth at a given age, the only uncertainty about the bequest received stems from the donor's uncertain mortality. In practice, this assumption is likely to substantially *understate* the actual uncertainty facing potential recipients.

There are at least five additional sources of bequest "noise." First, many children are uncertain about their parents' wealth holdings. Articles in the popular press describing how recipients respond to the news of their inheritances stress that many have significantly misestimated the bequest they were eligible to receive. There are obvious reasons why this information is difficult to obtain: few families like discussing issues surrounding the parents' death. Second, there is uncertainty about bequest division. While most children receive equal shares, there can be transfers to caregivers, churches, universities, or other groups that can substantially change the asset base available for children. Third, estate tax rules are subject to flux and, given their high marginal rates, can have an important effect on the after-tax bequest received by children of those with large estates. Fourth, there can be significant uncertainty about the parents' consumption behavior, even excluding their needs for medical care. Will they move to Florida and buy a new home? How many vacations will they take? Finally, potential recipients may be uncertain about the asset returns that their parents will earn. Expected bequests can be sensitive to the expected trajectory of real house prices, a subject about which there is significant controversy. For recipients of larger bequests, they can also depend on the path of stock market returns. All of these factors *reinforce* the central finding of this paper, which is that uncertainty about bequest receipt makes the consumption effects of these transfers relatively small.

There is another dimension along which the model could also be extended: to recognize endogenous earnings by bequest recipients. There is some evidence that bequest recipients are more likely to start their own businesses, and more likely to retire, than are those who do not receive such transfers. The retirement option is particularly important for the current analysis, since the model assumes a fixed stream of labor income for the recipient generation. If recipients can vary their labor supply and consume more leisure in the event of a significant inheritance, then they will not modify their prebequest consumption behavior as much as they will when labor supply is fixed. Once again, incorporating this behavioral reality is likely to strengthen the central findings in this paper.

My final comment about this paper concerns the analysis in the closing sections of how a demographic shock, a decline in fertility, will affect an economy's aggregate saving rate. The paper presents a partial equilibrium calculation, and it is important to recognize that there are important countervailing effects that make the net saving effect of a fertility decline ambiguous. These effects are particularly evident when society chooses to transfer resources to those at the beginning and end of the life cycle, and to finance those transfers with taxes on those of middle age. This transfer pattern, which characterizes most industrialized nations, creates a tension between two effects. In the short run, a decline in fertility reduces the transfer burden on working individuals because there are fewer young dependents to care for. This operates to raise current consumption and reduce the national saving rate. As the generation that had fewer children ages, however, the economy's dependency burden rises, and in the new steady state with a lower fertility rate, there will be more elderly households for each working-age person. This long-run increase in the dependency burden is a factor that encourages current saving. How individuals and society respond to a fertility shock depends critically on the rate of time preference, and whether the near-term benefits of reduced dependency burdens are more or less important than the persistent long-term costs of higher dependency. The present paper refines our understanding of the consumption response to expected bequests, but (by design) it does relatively little to resolve the uncertainty concerning the effects of fertility changes on saving.

Contributors

John Ausink
1200 Crystal Drive, #1114
Arlington, VA 22203

Axel Börsch-Supan
Department of Economics
University of Mannheim
D-68131 Mannheim 1
Germany

Angus S. Deaton
211 Bendheim Hall
Princeton University
Princeton, NJ 08544

Jonathan S. Feinstein
Yale School of Management
Yale University
Box 20-8200
New Haven, CT 06520

Jonathan Gruber
Department of Economics
E52-274C
Massachusetts Institute of Technology
Cambridge, MA 02139

Michael D. Hurd
Department of Economics
State University of New York at Stony
  Brook
Stony Brook, NY 11974

Robin L. Lumsdaine
Department of Economics
Princeton University
Princeton, NJ 08544

Mark B. McClellan
Department of Economics
Stanford University
Stanford, CA 94305

Thomas E. MaCurdy
Department of Economics
Stanford University
Stanford, CA 94305

Daniel L. McFadden
Department of Economics
University of California
655 Evans Hall, #3880
Berkeley, CA 94720

Brigitte C. Madrian
Graduate School of Business
University of Chicago
1101 East 58th Street
Chicago, IL 60637

Leslie E. Papke
Department of Economics
101 Marshall Hall
Michigan State University
East Lansing, MI 48824

Mitchell Petersen
Finance Department
Kellogg School
Northwestern University
2001 Sheridan Road
Evanston, IL 60208

James M. Poterba
Department of Economics
E52-350
Massachusetts Institute of Technology
Cambridge, MA 02139

Reinhold Schnabel
Department of Economics
University of Mannheim
D-68131 Mannheim
Germany

John B. Shoven
Dean's Office of Humanities and
    Sciences
Building One
Stanford University
Stanford, CA 94305

Jonathan S. Skinner
Department of Economics
Dartmouth College
Hanover, NH 03755

James H. Stock
Kennedy School of Government
Harvard University
79 JFK Street
Cambridge, MA 02138

Richard Thaler
Graduate School of Business
University of Chicago
1101 East 58th Street
Chicago, IL 60637

Steven F. Venti
Department of Economics
6106 Rockefeller
Dartmouth College
Hanover, NH 03755

David N. Weil
Department of Economics
Brown University
Box B
Providence, RI 02912

Robert J. Willis
Department of Economics
Institute of Social Research
University of Michigan
Box 1248
Ann Arbor, MI 48106

David A. Wise
National Bureau of Economic Research
1050 Massachusetts Avenue
Cambridge, MA 02138

Richard J. Zeckhauser
Kennedy School of Government
Harvard University
79 JFK Street
Cambridge, MA 02138

Author Index

Abel, Andrew B., 324, 325
Advisory Council on Social Security, 26n13
Ai, Chunrong, 243, 303
Akerlof, George A., 80
Allen, Steven, 35n23
Altman, Irwin, 279
Anderson, Joseph, 52
Andrews, Emily S., 230
Argüden, Yilmaz R., 101
Auerbach, Alan J., 323, 324
Ausink, John A., 90n1

Baldwin, Robert H., 83–84
Barsky, Robert B., 322
Barth, Michael C., 21, 49n33
Bartholomew, Herbert A., 84, 86
Bazzoli, Gloria J., 115, 117
Beller, Daniel J., 43, 220n1
Ben-Akiva, M., 202
Berkovec, James, 16, 73
Bernheim, B. Douglas, 220
Bhatia, Kul B., 253
Birren, James E., 285
Blau, David, 17, 18, 44, 63
Blinder, Alan S., 43, 255n16
Börsch-Supan, Axel, 194, 196, 198, 211, 213
Boskin, Michael J., 44
Bosworth, Barry, 253, 258, 259
Bound, John, 115
Bowman, Charlie T., 86
Brechling, Frank, 17t, 26
Brook, Robert H., 151
Buck Consultants, 234

Burkhauser, Richard, 16, 19t, 23n10, 34, 39t, 41, 45
Burtless, Gary, 31, 44, 46, 115, 126, 129, 131, 253, 258, 259
Byrne, Daniel J., 165

Caballero, Ricardo J., 249n6
Carroll, Christopher D., 249n6, 337
Chang, Angela, 220, 221
Clark, Robert L., 29, 35n23, 220n1
Cogan, John, 28
Congressional Budget Office (CBO), 90
Congressional Research Service, 121
Cook, Leah M., 253
Cowan, Cathy A., 302
Crawford, Vincent, 44

Danigelis, Nicholas, 276, 290
Danziger, S., 194, 213, 214
Daula, Thomas V., 73, 83–84, 92
Davies, James, 322
Deaton, Angus, 249n6, 254, 255n16, 322, 337
Diamond, Peter A., 115, 128, 129, 130, 131
Donham, Carolyn S., 302
Dutka, Anna B., 38, 39

Eckstein, Zvi, 324
Eichenbaum, Martin S., 324
Ellis, Randall, 153n1
Ellwood, D. T., 194
Employee Benefits Research Institute, 117
Evans, William, 283

Subject Index

Activities of daily living (ADLs): definitions of health status, 279; as indicator of health, 194, 196, 199. *See also* Instrumental activities of daily living (IADLs)

Actual contribution percentage (ACP) test, 233

Acute myocardial infarction (AMI), 151, 167–73, 181

ADLs. *See* Activities of daily living (ADLs)

ADP. *See* Average deferral percentage (ADP) test

Age: discrimination because of, 47–50; effect of population aging, 334–38; health insurance coverage by, 120–22; relation to employer costs, 26–28; relation of health care costs to, 26–27

Age Discrimination in Employment Act (1986), 41

Age of retirement: differences in, 2–3; effect of discrimination on, 47–50; liquidity effect on, 41–42, 44. *See also* Retirement, early; Retirement hazard rates; Retirement rates, age 65

AMI. *See* Acute myocardial infarction (AMI)

Annual Housing Survey (AHS), 194

Annualized cost of leaving model, 4, 90–91, 93–101, 104

Average deferral percentage (ADP) test, 233–35

Aviation Career Incentive Pay (ACIP) Act (1974), 85

Aviator Continuation Pay (ACP), 86

Aviator Retention Study (1988), Department of Defense, 85, 90, 101

Benefits: fringe benefits for older job changers, 38–40; Social Security earnings test, 30–34. *See also* Continuation coverage

Bequest function: mental-accounting model of life-cycle, 248–49; in model of elderly health and mobility, 285–86

Bequests: intergenerational transfers of wealth, 321–22; modeling uncertainty in expected receipt of, 323–34; uncertainty in generation and receipt of, 322–23

Bonuses: for military pilots, 86, 90, 101–3

Bribery hypothesis, 214

CABG. *See* Coronary artery bypass graft (CABG)

Career Compensation Act (1949), 84

CCU/ICU. *See* Coronary- or intensive-care-unit bed (CCU/ICU)

COBRA. *See* Consolidated Omnibus Budget Reconciliation Act (COBRA), 1985

Compensation, military: Compensation Model of, 90; for pilots, 85–86; Special Separation Benefit (SSB), 104–6; Voluntary Separation Incentive (VSI), 104–6

Consolidated Omnibus Budget Reconciliation Act (COBRA), 1985: continuation coverage provisions, 5, 116, 123–25, 135–37, 145–46; health insurance coverage before and after, 125–26

349